D0812410

Through the
Year with
Jimmy Carter

Also by Jimmy Carter

The NIV Lessons from Life Bible:
Personal Reflections from Jimmy Carter

Through the
Year with

366 DAILY
MEDITATIONS
from the
39TH PRESIDENT

Jimmy Carter *with* Steve Halliday

▌ZONDERVAN®

ZONDERVAN.com/
AUTHORTRACKER
follow your favorite authors

ZONDERVAN

Through the Year with Jimmy Carter
Copyright © 2011 by Jimmy Carter

This title is also available as a Zondervan ebook.
Visit www.zondervan.com/ebooks.

This title is also available in a Zondervan audio edition.
Visit www.zondervan.fm.

Requests for information should be addressed to:

Zondervan, *Grand Rapids, Michigan 49530*

Library of Congress Cataloging-in-Publication Data

Carter, Jimmy.
    Through the year with Jimmy Carter / by Jimmy Carter.
        p. cm.
    Includes bibliographical references
    ISBN 978-0-310-33048-6 (hardcover)
    1. Devotional calendars – Baptists. 2. Baptists – Prayers and devotions. I. Title.
    BV4811.C364 2011
    242'.2 – dc23   2011034169

Cover design: John Hamilton Design
Cover photography: © William 1 Coupon / Corbis®
Interior design: Sarah Johnson
Interior image: iStockphoto®
Editorial team: Sandra Vander Zicht, Bob Hudson, Leigh Clouse, Britta Eastburg

Printed in the United States of America

11 12 13 14 15 16 17 /DCI/ 22 21 20 19 18 17 16 15 14 13 12 11 10 9 8 7 6 5 4 3 2 1

CONTENTS

PART 4: MATURING

INTRODUCTION

Many centuries ago a wise author warned, "Of making many books there is no end" (Ecclesiastes 12:12). While I'm not sure how many books *he* wrote, I'm pretty sure that, unless I've lost count, *Through the Year with Jimmy Carter* is my twenty-sixth. That's a lot of books!

But this one is special.

For one thing, it's a devotional. I hope it encourages you to grow deeper in your Christian faith and to experience more of what Christ has for you, regardless of where you might be on life's journey. I'm just a few months shy of my eighty-seventh birthday, and I have to admit that the Lord has brought me on a very different kind of journey than the one I thought was beginning on a farm near Plains, Georgia, during the Great Depression. None of us can know where our journeys with God will take us even tomorrow—let alone a decade from now—so it's a good idea to spend a few moments each day to connect with God and ask, "Well, where do you want to take me today?"

The Bible tells us that a man named Enoch "walked faithfully with God" for three hundred *years*, until one day God simply "took him away" (Genesis 5:24). It's nice to assume that the pair got to know each other so well that when one walk went a little long one evening, God said, "Hey, it's late. Why don't you just come over to my place?" Daily walks are good for creating that kind of close friendship, and I hope that this devotional might help you to draw nearer to God in a similar way.

Each page is based on a different Sunday school lesson I've taught, either while president or at Maranatha Baptist Church in Plains. The earliest entry comes from a class in 1977, and the most recent from one in June 2011 (the dates are noted at the top of each page). Sometimes the entries mention historic events, such as the Camp David Accords of 1978; at other times I refer to some personal incident from my boyhood or family life; and in still other entries I simply focus on a Bible verse or passage and try to suggest how it might apply to our lives today. But in every case my goal is to interact faithfully with the wisdom in God's Word in order to encourage and promote fresh thinking that moves both our hearts and minds closer to the Savior.

Since the book covers a lot of historical, biblical, and personal territory,

I've divided it into four sections. In the first, "Launching," we'll take a look at some of the foundations of our Christian faith, because we need to have a solid grasp of the essentials if we want to launch successfully into the great adventure God has waiting for us. In the second, "Growing," we'll consider how to build on the foundation to grow into the kind of Christians who both enjoy life and bless others. In the third, "Serving," we'll explore how the Spirit of Christ inevitably draws us into a life of service, not to constrict our lives, but to expand and liberate our hearts and enlarge the kingdom of God. In the fourth, "Maturing," we'll ponder the radical influence for good that mature followers of Christ can have on our families, friends, neighborhoods, and world—for the glory of God and the benefit of the people God has made.

If there is one theme that keeps reappearing in these devotions, it's that God calls us to live out our faith. I don't know what that might mean to you, but I do know that Jesus asks us to listen to his words and then to act on them. Rosalynn and I read the Bible together every night. I teach Sunday school, write books about my religious faith, listen to sermons, debate with theologians, and teach classes in the Departments of Theology and Religion at Emory University. I would put all those things under the category of "hearing." They are just words—spoken words, written words, words listened to and, perhaps, nothing else.

It is good if we hear Jesus' words, but we must not take pride and become complacent in that achievement. We must also *live* by his words, which may mean taking a hard look at ourselves and asking, "What keeps me from being a devoted doer of his words?"

We can do so every day, as we follow a path to peace, harmony, gratification, and real success in the eyes of God.

PART I

❧LAUNCHING❧

As the only president who served in submarines, I was especially honored in 2004 when the USS *Jimmy Carter* was launched. We prayed that this unique naval vessel would be an instrument for peace and harmony among nations.

Launching a ship and launching a Christian life have many things in common. The transformation of a ship from resting in a building dock to immersion in the sea is perhaps the most significant moment in her life; but every other step is crucial, including design, creation, and testing in action.

In a similar way, to enjoy a successful Christian life and effectively launch out into the grand adventure to which God calls us, we need to lay a proper foundation, build with the right materials, and have a good idea of our ultimate mission. In this first section, we'll focus on many key building blocks of a thriving Christian experience. We'll ponder a God-centered life, rejoice in God's love, meditate on grace and faith, consider the ongoing need for confession and repentance, discuss the fundamental role of Jesus Christ and his death and resurrection, and look forward to eternity with him.

When we prepare and build well, we set ourselves up for a thrilling launch into a successful Christian life. Who knows what wonderful opportunities and awesome challenges await us on our life's journey with God? When properly built, we can be ready for anything that comes our way. God urges you and me to build our whole lives on his Son, Jesus Christ, whom the Bible calls our foundation.

"For no one can lay any foundation other than the one already laid, which is Jesus Christ" (1 Corinthians 3:11).

1

Whom Do You Trust?

Blessed are those whose help is the God of Jacob, whose hope is in the
LORD their God.
PSALM 146:5

Even our dearest loved ones and most trusted friends can't provide for us a firm foundation throughout our lives, because unpredictable circumstances can always intervene. That is why this psalm urges us to put our hope in God, who is a permanent and all-knowing partner and whose plans never perish. If we're looking for a repository of confidence—someone in whom to put our faith—then we must look to God, the Creator of the universe and the one who gave us life.

Too often, unfortunately, we don't turn to God. Instead, we put our trust in politicians or bankers or business partners or family members. Or we turn to money and say, "If I could just hit the lottery and win five million bucks, then all my troubles would be over." But those are false hopes.

Some of the richest people in America, who make several million dollars a year acting in movies or recording songs or playing sports, often wind up in jail or land on skid row after becoming addicted to drugs or alcohol. Some lose their families or reputation because of misconduct. This should be very sobering to us. We tend to think that money and fame and the adulation of others will make us happy—but we come to realize that those things are not foundations for real success. Material things can always let us down, even (maybe especially) the things that make lavish promises. But God never will.

The Holy Word urges us to turn to God first and place our trust in Christ. For good reason the Bible says, "He remains faithful forever" (Psalm 146:6). Who else can make that staggering claim? Or more to the point, who else has made good on that promise?

O God, help me see more clearly that you truly are my only foundation
for hope. When life drags me down and I feel abandoned, give me the
firm conviction that you are with me, both now and always. And, Lord,
enable me to share this good news with others, that they too may place
their hope in you. In Jesus' name I pray. Amen. ❧

God Keeps His Promises

I will not violate my covenant
or alter what my lips have uttered.
PSALM 89:34

Even the most powerful people on earth don't always keep their promises. Unfortunately, United States presidents are no exception. Woodrow Wilson, for example, promised that he would not go to war and was elected because of that promise. But later on, several changes prompted Wilson to violate his promise and enter World War I.

President Eisenhower made a public statement to Soviet leaders in 1960 that we did not have surveillance planes flying over Russian missile sites. Shortly after this, one of our U-2 spy planes had been shot down and the pilot, Francis Gary Powers, was captured. The Soviets provided firm proof that Eisenhower had lied, which deeply embarrassed our nation.

High government officials told many lies to the American people during the Vietnam War. More recently, President George H. W. Bush made a public promise that he would not introduce any new taxes. He boldly stated, "Read my lips: No new taxes." But he ended up approving new taxes, and so lost his reelection bid.

Good and honest people sometimes have to break promises because of changing circumstances or after acquiring new information.

I made every effort to keep the pledge I had made to the American people that I would not lie or make a misleading statement. I also promised that I would try to stay at peace, and even though we had a lot of serious challenges while I was president, we never dropped a bomb, fired a missile, or shot a bullet in combat. Still, I was not able to keep 100 percent of my campaign promises.

God Almighty, our Creator, *always* keeps his promises. God never lies and always remains in control. The Scripture says, "I will not violate my covenant or alter what my lips have uttered." Those lips, we can believe. Always.

Dear God, it gives me a deep sense of assurance to know that you always stand by your Word, never recant anything you say, and never forget promises you have made. Help me be a person of my word, so that others can depend on me because I belong to you. Make me a blessing to those around me. In Jesus' name I pray. Amen. ❧

An Unchanging Promise

*Then Caleb silenced the people before Moses and said, "We should go
up and take possession of the land, for we can certainly do it."*
NUMBERS 13:30

As an American who has been president of the United States, I would like to say that the values of our country don't change. But they do.

The Supreme Court interprets basic issues in various ways at different times. Authorization for the death penalty comes and goes, and now it is permitted in thirty-five states. The United States has a higher portion of citizens in jail than any other nation, a result of severe prison sentences. (Civil liberties have been restricted since 9/11.) Our rapidly changing times make me glad for the never-changing promises of God, in which Caleb believed.

Out of more than a million Israelites who had fled Egypt and were waiting at the edge of Canaan to inherit their new land, Caleb was one of only two who actually would go in and dwell there. Ten of the spies whom Moses sent into Canaan to survey the land said, "We can't take it because it's inhabited by giants. There's no hope!" But Caleb told the truth. With courage and faith he replied, "With God's support, we can indeed take the promised land." Because Caleb believed God, Moses said to him, "The land on which your feet have walked will be your inheritance and that of your children forever, because you have followed the LORD my God wholeheartedly" (Joshua 14:9). That land ended up being Hebron, where Abraham and Sarah, Isaac and Jacob lived and are buried. Caleb believed God's promise, and so inherited the Promised Land.

While all else may change, God's promises remain firm. The most important was that Jesus would come as the Messiah. And when we build our lives on this bedrock promise, it gives stability and confidence to all our days.

*O Lord, laws and customs change so often that sometimes it seems that
I wake up to a different country every morning. I am thankful for your
Word and for the unchanging promises it contains. Teach me how to
build my life on your Word so I can successfully navigate my way through
this world, for your glory. I pray this in Jesus' name. Amen.* ❧

4

At the Core

"Do not think that I have come to abolish the Law or the Prophets; I
have not come to abolish them but to fulfill them."
MATTHEW 5:17

What would you identify as the core of your existence? On what foundation
do you build your life?

Christ says that he came to fulfill Moses' laws and the words of the prophets, not to change them. Jesus had just shaken up the crowd (and deeply
disturbed his own disciples) by speaking what we know as the Beatitudes.
But he insisted, "I am not a new Moses." He had not descended from Mount
Sinai with a new set of commandments. His life on earth, as the promised
Messiah, was a fulfillment of ancient Scriptures—an explanation of their
meaning and of the character of God.

The Bible is unchanging and eternally valid, as the apostle Paul recognized. In his far-flung missionary journeys, Paul always tried to convince
people that his message fully agreed with the Hebrew Scriptures. Trends and
human customs may come and go, but the Word of God endures forever.
Until the kingdom of God arrives in its fullness, nothing in Scripture will be
changed or forgotten. There's a permanence about it. How important this is
as we search out the core meaning of our lives!

We don't want that core to change constantly, but to remain stable, pre-
dictable, and secure. We want an unshakable foundation for our existence.
And here Christ tells us that we have such a solid foundation—Holy Scripture—on which to build our lives. Nothing can ruin it. War can't alter it.
The loss of our loved ones can't devastate it. Failure in business can't demolish
it. Bankruptcy can't wipe it out. Not even death can destroy it.

If we want a solid core, a firm foundation, around which to build our
lives, then we must choose the Word of God. When everything else falls to
the ground, it alone will remain standing.

O Lord, when changing times and shifting circumstances threaten to
undo me, help me remember that you have given us your Holy Word to
serve as an anchor and an unchanging foundation for my life. Give me
the wisdom to search its depths and the courage to act on what it says—
as did both Jesus and Paul. In Christ's name I pray. Amen. ❧

5

Awestruck by the Glory of God

When he heard this, Jesus said, "This sickness will not end in death.
No, it is for God's glory so that God's Son may be glorified through it."

JOHN 11:4

It's hard to believe that God let Lazarus die just so Jesus could perform a miracle of resuscitation, or that the Lord made a man blind just so Jesus could heal him (see John 9). But it is certain that these sad cases provided special opportunities for Jesus to demonstrate the power and love of God, the Creator of the universe.

A man had died, and Jesus raised him. A man couldn't see, and Jesus gave him sight. Through these curing miracles, God's glory shone forth, giving us the opportunity to recognize that glory and to accept Jesus as Savior. John explains why he recorded these miracles: "that you may believe that Jesus is the Messiah, the Son of God, and that by believing you may have life in his name" (John 20:31). We don't have to know *how* the miracles were done or explain all that happens in Scripture. We simply must recognize the truths about God and his Son, Jesus Christ.

When Jewish religious leaders questioned the formerly blind man and accused Jesus of being a sinner, the man replied, "Whether he is a sinner or not, I don't know. One thing I do know. I was blind but now I see!" (John 9:25). In effect, he was saying, "Hey, I'm no theologian. I don't know how to analyze Scriptures or interpret the prophets. All I know is that a miracle has happened to me."

We too can have faith in Jesus Christ, based on the Bible's simple accounts of his life and ministry. When we read of these miracles, we too can witness the power and glory of God—and respond to the Lord in awe and wonder.

O Lord, despite the familiarity of these stories, help me feel their impact
and revel in your glory, as revealed by these amazing miracles. Bring
to my heart the unshakable conviction that the same Jesus who raised
the dead and gave sight to the blind wants to be present in my heart,
bringing full and joyful lives to those around me. I pray in Jesus' glorious
name. Amen. ❧

An Encounter with God

He had a dream in which he saw a stairway resting on the earth,
with its top reaching to heaven, and the angels of God were
ascending and descending on it.
GENESIS 28:12

Whenever I got sick as a child, I knew that in addition to my aches and pains, I also would be afflicted with a nightmare. A rabid dog, foaming at the mouth, always chased me. I tried to run, but my feet could hardly move. The dog drew closer and closer, and just as he started to bite, I'd wake up in a cold sweat.

Later, when I became prominent and began making speeches, I had a different bad dream. In this one, I couldn't find anything to wear. I searched high and low, but my clothes were all in rags or covered with oil. Sometimes I could find no clothes at all.

Jacob also had a dream, but it was no nightmare; it was a confrontation with God. In a place called Beersheba, he dreamed about a ladder reaching to heaven, with angels climbing up and down on it. The Lord suddenly appeared to him and said, "I am the LORD, the God of your father Abraham and the God of Isaac" (Genesis 28:13).

Before this, Jacob had been interested only in himself. But now, in this strange dream, God reaffirmed the covenant made with Abraham. Although Jacob didn't deserve it—after a lifetime of lies and deceit—God reached out to him, loved him, and said, in effect, "I will protect you for the rest of your life."

We all share something of Jacob's position. We all are sinful and looking out for ourselves. Even so, God has reached out to us and told us that if we believe in Christ, we will be saved, and nothing can separate us from God. *That* is protection. *That* is security. And that is all ours in Christ.

O God, thank you for including me, through Christ, in the blessing of the covenant made with Abraham and reaffirmed to Jacob. And thank you for reminding me that while I can do nothing to earn your forgiveness and blessing, I still have a responsibility to obey your commandments and to strive to model my life after that of your perfect Son, Jesus Christ, in whose name I pray. Amen. ❧

God's Covenant

"This is the covenant I will establish with the people of Israel after that time, declares the Lord. I will put my laws in their minds and write them on their hearts. I will be their God, and they will be my people."
HEBREWS 8:10

How would we distinguish between a modern-day contract and God's ancient covenant? For one thing, in a contract, two or more human beings come together looking for mutual advantage. They study a situation, negotiate, and finally say, "We've reached an agreement." Contracts usually concern money, property, or services.

I recently bought sixteen acres of land from a fellow church member. It was to her advantage to sell it because she wanted the money and didn't need the land. It was to my advantage to buy it because I wanted to expand my fish farm. Also, my father used to own that land, and I wanted some of it back. So Carol and I drew up a contract, now recorded in the courthouse. I have a deed to the land, while she has my money; a reasonable amount of cash for a reasonable amount of land.

When a dispute occurs or a contract gets violated, lawyers get involved and a court decides the matter. The law levies penalties against a person who breaks a contract.

All this differs markedly from God's covenant. Abraham didn't approach God and say, "Let's negotiate a covenant." No, God came to Abraham and said, "This is what I have to offer you. I see you are loyal and have faith in me, and now I will give you special status and privileges." The covenant depended on God's ability to keep his word, and on Abraham's faith.

With faith, we Christians inherited God's covenant with Abraham and also the final covenant, an intimate relationship with God through Jesus Christ. Through it, God has promised us eternal, abundant life. And God does not lie.

O God, I am thankful that through your grace and love you offered to Abraham — and to me — your covenant of forgiveness and reconciliation. Although it is free and I cannot earn this blessing, give me the will to serve you faithfully, with the help of the Holy Spirit. I pray in Jesus' name. Amen. ❧

Who's Lucky?

Then King David went in and sat before the LORD, and he said:
"Who am I, Sovereign LORD, and what is my family, that you have
brought me this far?"
2 SAMUEL 7:18

David felt stunned. Already God had done so much for him, and now the Lord promised to exalt both him and his family. The Messiah would come as David's descendant and rule forever.

David erupted in praise, awed and humbled by the grace of God. David recognized, as often we do not, that the great things he had accomplished—killing Goliath, defeating the Philistines, uniting Israel—were relatively insignificant in the overall plan of God. Although he was special and had won great honors, he recognized all these as relatively small things compared to this newest honor. David knew that he owed everything to God.

God also has blessed us, through Jesus Christ, in countless ways. Yet how often do we give God the credit? We don't see all our blessings—freedom, good health, security, and prosperity—as coming from the good hand of God. The fact is, no matter what we have done in the name of Christ to further God's kingdom, chances are that we have done nothing that tops the deeds of King David—and David looked upon his life's achievements as relatively insignificant in the big picture. So what does that mean for us?

God has chosen to use us. God gives us strength and judgment and opportunities to serve in our own way. God has done infinitely more for us than we have done for God, so self-congratulation and pride are, quite simply, stupid. If we think God is lucky to have us, then we are deceived. Even though everything we do in life is just a blip on the timeline of history, it can be important in God's kingdom. *All of it* is made possible by our Creator, who gives us the strength that those good deeds require.

Dear Lord, thank you for the countless benefits you send my way every day—sunshine, rain, and life itself. Teach me to ask myself, as the apostle did, "What do I have that I did not receive?" The answer, of course, is "nothing." Help me remember this and, like David, give you passionate thanks and praise. In Jesus' name I pray. Amen. ❧

Trust That God Is in Control

*Barak said to her, "If you go with me, I will go; but if you don't go
with me, I won't go."*
JUDGES 4:8

A remarkable woman named Deborah served as Israel's judge during the
time the nation languished under the harsh rule of Canaanite king Jabin,
whose military commander, Sisera, was both cruel and oppressive. He had a
powerful force of nine hundred iron chariots. When the Israelites asked God
for rescue, Deborah sent for a man named Barak and told him that God had
called him to muster troops and fight Sisera. God would bring Sisera into a
wadi and allow Barak to defeat him. But Barak said to Deborah, "If you don't
go with me, I'm not going." So Deborah agreed to go but predicted that the
fearful Barak would get no glory; instead, Sisera would die at the hands of
a woman.

A wadi is a draining area for a riverbed. It is normally dry but can become
a roaring torrent when it rains — a dangerous place to be. When Sisera heard
about Barak's troop movement, he got his army, including his iron chariots,
and rushed into the wadi. Barak attacked, and God brought down torrents
of rain, flooding the chariots and bogging them down in mud. Barak's army
overcame the enemy, but General Sisera escaped and fled to the home of a
friend named Heber. Heber's wife gave Sisera food and drink and a place to
sleep. But while he slept, she got a hammer and drove a spike through his
head — thus fulfilling Deborah's prediction.

Our lesson is this: We should never be afraid to step out in faith and
trust God's promise. That is what Deborah did and what Barak refused to
do without Deborah holding his hand. We can take risks and be bold in our
service to God when we trust that the Lord is in control.

*O God, may the story of Deborah and Barak encourage me and fill me
with faith in you. As a Christian, I know I am bound by your covenant,
through my faith in Jesus, as were Abraham, Moses, and Deborah. Give
me renewed inspiration and confidence as I honor my promises to you as a
follower of Jesus Christ, in whose name I pray. Amen.*

10

God's Plan

"I am your brother Joseph, the one you sold into Egypt! And now, do not be distressed and do not be angry with yourselves for selling me here, because it was to save lives that God sent me ahead of you."
GENESIS 45:4 – 5

Even when we think things have gone terribly wrong, God's plans remain in effect.

In 1920, about ten thousand foreign missionaries labored in China. But in 1949 the Chinese Revolution swept Mao Zedong into power, and instantly all religious worship was banned and all foreign missionaries expelled. That situation lasted for thirty years.

Then in 1978, Deng Xiaoping, vice premier of China, and I began months of intense secret negotiations. Finally, in December, we announced normalization of diplomatic relations between China and the United States. The next month, January 1979, I invited Deng Xiaoping to visit Washington. During his visit we had long hours of discussion on many subjects. Finally, he asked if I had any special favor to ask, not included in our official talks. I asked him to give people religious freedom and allow Bibles and missionaries to return to China. He pledged to do those things, except no foreign missionaries could return.

A couple of years later on a visit to China, I found churches overrun with worshipers. In Shanghai, they held four services a day to accommodate all the new believers. They had run out of special paper for printing Bibles and the government provided the paper.

Thirty years of intense persecution under the communist regime had forced Christians to consolidate, and their faith became more intense. When they finally received a breath of fresh air, the Christian faith exploded. And still today it continues to grow by leaps and bounds.

No matter how bad things may look, we must remember that God has a plan and remains in control—always.

O God, I admit that the divine control you exert over our world frequently doesn't look like what I expect. I appreciate stories like that of Joseph, where I see that despite bad mistakes and even disasters, you still bring about your holy will, for your glory and our benefit. Give me confidence to live boldly for you, knowing you always remain in control. In Jesus' name I pray. Amen. ❧

God at Work

*When he was twelve years old, they went up to the festival, according
to the custom. After the festival was over, while his parents were
returning home, the boy Jesus stayed behind in Jerusalem, but they
were unaware of it.*
LUKE 2:41 – 43

It is easy to lose a child. When I was in the Navy in California, we were watching a Rose Bowl parade with our three-year-old son and suddenly realized that he was missing! We searched frantically in the huge crowd, and finally some people told us they saw a little boy following the parading clowns. We gave fervent thanks to God when we found him.

How could Mary and Joseph go a whole day out of Jerusalem without noticing that their son was missing? Each parent probably assumed Jesus was with the other. They searched for him in their caravan and then returned to Jerusalem and looked there. Why did it take three days before they found him in the temple?

First, Jerusalem was a good-sized city, with as many as 100,000 residents. Second, they probably didn't expect him to be in the temple. If we had a twelve-year-old son who got lost in Macon, Georgia, the *last* place we'd look would be the church! But that's where Jesus was, talking with the teachers there. And "everyone who heard him was amazed" (Luke 2:47).

When his parents found him, his mother said, "Son, why have you treated us like this? Your father and I have been anxiously searching for you." Jesus replied, "Why were you searching for me? Didn't you know I had to be in my Father's house?" (Luke 2:48–49). His parents didn't understand his answer.

Sometimes we get so preoccupied with worldly, everyday questions we forget to consider spiritual answers. Sometimes we need to step back and consider how God might be at work even in a stressful situation.

*O Lord, help me do the same thing Jesus did when he was just twelve
years old: seek a better understanding of you through the Scriptures.
Remind me that you are never absent; in fact, you might be at work in
a very powerful way, if I just had eyes to see. Give me those eyes, Lord. I
pray in Jesus' name. Amen.* ❧

12

The Real Champion

*"It is not by sword or spear that the LORD saves; for the battle is the
LORD's, and he will give all of you into our hands."*
I SAMUEL 17:47

In the days of King Saul, the Philistines had grown so powerful they even
threatened the existence of God's chosen people. One day as the Philistine
and Israelite armies faced each other, the enemy's top warrior, a giant named
Goliath, bellowed a challenge: "Look, our armies don't have to kill each other.
Let me represent the Philistines and you get somebody to represent your side.
Whichever champion wins, gains the victory for his army." Of course, no
Israelite wanted to fight him.

At this time, David was tending his father's sheep. His older brothers
had been conscripted into Saul's army, like other Hebrews who could fight.
David's father said to him, "Why don't you take some food to your brothers?" So David set off to visit the front lines. When he arrived, he found all
the Hebrew soldiers cowering in fear of this huge giant. So David said, "I'll
take him on." He probably was just a teenager, and not very big, at least not
like King Saul, who was "head and shoulders taller than anyone else in the
country." When his own countrymen made fun of him, David said, "I have
absolute confidence, not in myself, but in God. By myself, I cannot prevail;
but God, through me, can prevail over any force that threatens his people."
So David ran to the battle line and slew Goliath with a single stone from his
slingshot.

We can have the same kind of confidence that energized David. So long
as we keep God as our top priority, make God's goals our own, and commit
to obey the Lord through the power of the Holy Spirit, we can rest easy. For
God alone is the real champion.

*Dear God, I marvel at the courage, daring, and faith of the boy David,
who as a teenager willingly took on a challenge that the most seasoned
veterans of Israel's army dared not accept. I recognize that his bravery
and prowess came from you, based in his ultimate confidence in your
faithfulness and love. Make me bold for you, Lord, as I face formidable
opponents in my own world. I pray in Jesus' name. Amen.* ❧

13

Power and Victory

The seventh angel sounded his trumpet, and there were loud voices in heaven, which said: "The kingdom of the world has become the kingdom of our Lord and of his Messiah, and he will reign for ever and ever."
REVELATION 11:15

What's the most extreme punishment that we can administer to others, or fear ourselves? Physical death. We can hardly imagine how a person, guilty of a horrible crime, feels when the death sentence is handed out.

Yet in the first century, Christians faced that verdict all the time. For their faith in Christ, thousands were condemned to torture and death.

But how did such a death apply to Christ? As a victory! While sometimes we weep when we sing the old hymns describing Christ's death on the cross — even his feeling of being abandoned by God — the New Testament presents the event as a great victory over death itself.

My favorite poet is Dylan Thomas. In "Refusal to Mourn the Death by Fire of a Child in London," his last line says, "After the first death, there is no other." I don't know what Dylan Thomas's religious faith was like, but I can't forget that line.

John was trying to remind his fellow first-century Christians that while human beings can suffer physical death, nothing can separate them from Christ and the triumph of living through eternity in the presence of God. Eternal life with Christ far transcends any suffering here, in our "first life."

We cannot remove ourselves from a world of suffering and fear. That's all a part of life on this earth. But John reminds us that no power can harm our relationship with God. No power here is strong enough to alter our place in God's kingdom.

The mightiest things on earth are subservient to Christ!

Thank you, God, for reminding me that Jesus Christ reigns over all, even over death. Although I may have to face many hardships and trials, yet through his death and resurrection Jesus can make me into a victor over everything, through faith in him. Give me the courage, Lord, to live for you, with the vision of Jesus ruling in righteousness, for all eternity — and by his grace, with me at his side. In Jesus' name I pray. Amen. ❧

14

Jesus Christ Is God

*The Son is the image of the invisible God, the firstborn over all
creation. For in him all things were created: things in heaven and on
earth, visible and invisible.*
COLOSSIANS 1:15 – 16

When we think about the identity of Jesus Christ, we tend to underestimate
the power and majesty that should surround our Savior—his glorious and
divine aura. I, at least, have that tendency. When I think about Jesus, I usually
dwell more on his earthly life and character than I do his heavenly attributes.
I think about him walking the dusty roads of the Holy Land, getting tired
and worn out from traveling and teaching, and sometimes discouraged and
frustrated from associating with "unsavory" people—the outcasts, Samaritans, lepers, tax collectors, and others who were ostracized and despised but
still sought him out because in him they recognized a friend.

I think about him calling disciples from their fishing boats and later crossing the Sea of Galilee to escape the clamoring crowds and get some rest.
I think about him being condemned by the powerful Jewish political and
religious leaders of his day and then being betrayed by one of his own. All
these things relate mostly to the human aspects of Christ's life. But there is
so much more!

Christ is supreme. Paul tells us he is "the image of the invisible God"
(Colossians 1:15). The word translated "image" in the original Greek is *eikon*,
which means an exact duplicate and not a painting or reflection in a mirror.
It's a personification. Christ is the very person of God.

It is not wrong to think of Christ as human. But he also is a heavenly
being, far above all others. He is God. Let us remember that staggering truth
and be in awe of him and worship him as our Savior.

*O Lord, grant me a fuller and deeper understanding of Jesus Christ.
When I study the Scriptures, give me new insight into your Son's glory,
and then use that insight to transform my life on earth. Lead me to a
greater appreciation for my Savior's divinity and help me transform my
worship, my service, and my very existence. In Jesus' holy name I pray.
Amen.* ❧

The Authority of Jesus

*When he saw Jesus from a distance, he ran and fell on his knees in
front of him. He shouted at the top of his voice, "What do you want
with me, Jesus, Son of the Most High God?"*
MARK 5:6 – 7

Where does authority originate? Sometimes it comes from elections. Every year in our church, we cast a secret ballot of eligible men and women, and those who get the most votes become deacons for the next term of service.

Another way to get authority is by appointment. I wasn't elected to be a Sunday school teacher; a church committee appointed me to teach an adult Sunday school class. The entire cabinet of the United States government is appointed, as is the cabinet of the British government.

But there's another way to get authority, and that is to have it innately. When I was a child, our school superintendent, Miss Julia Coleman, had that kind of authority. We obeyed her not just because she was the superintendent, but because we sensed a quality within her that earned our respect. When she gave a quiet suggestion, we eagerly carried out her request. She didn't even have to threaten punishment! She taught us that authority can come from within a person.

That's the kind of authority Jesus Christ had. An aura about Jesus flowed from his divine nature as the Son of God, and it gave him authority over the lives of those with whom he came into contact. As Mark reported, even demons submitted to him. That is why the unclean spirit afflicting the man living among the tombs called Jesus "Son of the Most High God" and begged for mercy.

The Bible does not call Jesus "Lord," "Master," and "Savior" for nothing. We should recognize his divine authority and submit ourselves to him with great joy.

God, as I acknowledge the authority of Jesus, help me willingly, eagerly, and joyfully submit to his guidance and direction. Whatever my ambitions, my unfulfilled desires, my troubles, or my challenges, let me remember that accepting Jesus into my heart and welcoming the presence of the Holy Spirit brings the assurance I need and the curative power I lack. I pray in the name of my Savior. Amen.

Power Enough

"Why are you so afraid? Do you still have no faith?"
MARK 4:40

On three separate occasions as a submarine officer, I thought I might die. Once I stood on the bridge of an old World War II submarine, with my feet only eight feet above water. As we sailed through a terrible storm, an enormous wave rose up under me and I found myself swimming in the open ocean. I've always thanked God that the ship was heading directly into the waves, because when it receded, the water carried me directly back over the submarine and I landed on top of our cannon on the main deck. I clung to it until the wave subsided, then dashed up to the bridge and lashed myself to the safety rail. If the wave had been traveling a little sideways, the submarine would have continued on without me and I would have drowned at sea.

It's horrible to sense impending death. I'm sure that's what the disciples felt during a ferocious storm on the Sea of Galilee. Jesus was sleeping, so they woke him up and asked, in effect, "Are you going to let us drown while you lie there dreaming?" Jesus got up, calmed the wind and waves, and then turned to his disciples and rebuked them for their fear prompted by a lack of faith.

Have we known such fear? Do we ever doubt God's ability to save us? God's all-encompassing power is available to us through Jesus Christ and is great enough to transcend anything that could make us afraid, powerful enough to assuage our sorrows, comprehensive enough to give us the wisdom to choose well, and generous enough to open up opportunities for Christlike action toward others.

Because the disciples had underestimated the power of Christ, they thought they were facing disaster. Let's not make the same mistake.

O Lord, help me realize that I am truly loved, and that at all times you offer me your help and power, through the saving grace of Jesus Christ. Help me recognize this power and tap into it, and so overcome my fears, failures, losses, and sorrows. Help me erase all these through faith in my Savior, as I pray in his name. Amen. ❧

A Shocking Revelation

Large crowds were traveling with Jesus, and turning to them he said:
"If anyone comes to me and does not hate father and mother, wife
and children, brothers and sisters—yes, even their own life—such a
person cannot be my disciple."
LUKE 14:25 – 26

I cannot "hate" my wife and four children, our twelve grandchildren, our six great-grandchildren, or the memory of my mother and father. So what can Jesus mean in this verse?

In the original Greek, the word translated "hate" is *miseo*, which could mean "to love less," or to put in a secondary position. Christ is saying that his followers must put their faith in him above family obligations or natural feelings of love for their closest kin. While this is easier to accept than "hate," it's still a difficult and even disturbing requirement. We must put *every* priority in life below our commitment to Christ. Our top priority must be to follow him, to keep his commandments, and to emulate his actions. That is a profound but greatly beneficial directive.

It gets even more profound and unsettling when Christ says his disciples must also choose to carry their cross and follow him. Ordinarily we think of carrying a cross as enduring some kind of trial. If we have a debilitating disease, we might say, "This disease is my cross to bear." Sometimes we treat it as a self-congratulatory thing: "I'm being courageous in the face of difficult setbacks." But that isn't what Jesus has in mind.

In those days, when Romans gave a sentence of crucifixion, they required the condemned to carry his cross to the place of execution, thus giving the impression that the condemned both acknowledged and accepted the justice of the sentence. Christ is saying, then, that we must associate with him and acknowledge the justness of his demands. We choose to follow him and identify with him—regardless of the cost.

God, I'm grateful that even disturbing lessons from your Word are
designed to make a permanent and positive impact on my life. Teach me,
in practical ways, what it means to put you first in everything I do, and
then give me strength to identify with you even in situations where doing
so might cost me dearly. I ask these things in Jesus' name. Amen.

18

A Shepherd Who Cares for Us

"I am the good shepherd.
The good shepherd lays down his life for the sheep."
JOHN 10:11

When Deng Xiaoping visited the White House in 1979, he described to me the big changes about to take place in China. At that time, the state owned everything and farmers worked the communal farms together. But Deng Xiaoping decided to give Chinese farmers a small amount of land (7 percent), and on that land they could farm for themselves.

In 1981, when Rosalynn and I next visited China, this amount of land had increased to 15 percent, and the state also let farmers develop a tiny industry. They could make clay pots, repair bicycles, raise several pigs, and so forth. It began a remarkable economic transformation that swept China.

Deng Xiaoping told me that Chinese farmers wouldn't stay up all night with a sick hog that belonged to the state. But if it were theirs, they would nurse it throughout the night to make sure it survived. Chinese officials found there was a big difference between owning land or farm animals and merely tending them for someone else.

That's what Jesus had in mind when he said, "The hired hand is not the shepherd and does not own the sheep. So when he sees the wolf coming, he abandons the sheep and runs away" (John 10:12). Much to the contrary, Jesus called himself "the good shepherd" who "lays down his life for the sheep."

We do not have to worry that when we get sick or lost or feeble or old, Jesus will abandon us for some better or more perfect person. There is no distinction among believers. We belong to him, and he has shown his eternal commitment to us by laying down his life for us on the cross. We are the sheep of his pasture, he is our Good Shepherd, and we will remain in his flock forever.

O Lord, thank you for our Good Shepherd, who laid down his life for
me. Help me bind myself to him more firmly, acknowledging my needs,
weakness, and sinfulness, but remembering my secure and everlasting
place in his flock. Let me work harmoniously with others, never
abandoning the weak among us, but realizing that you call me, like Jesus,
to serve others. In his name I pray. Amen. ❧

19

The Light of Life

When Jesus spoke again to the people, he said, "I am the light of the world. Whoever follows me will never walk in darkness, but will have the light of life."
JOHN 8:12

During my years in the Navy, light shaped my life. We had no satellites, so at sea we had to depend on the stars to ascertain our position. All officers had to be experts at using a sextant. We'd identify three stars, determine the altitude of each, and use the corresponding lines on a map to show us where we were. We could also use the sun and moon.

Lighthouses likewise are very important to sailors, because they're built on places of danger. When we saw the light from a lighthouse, we stayed clear to avoid running aground.

We also had to see clearly at night. Everything was kept very dark inside the ship. When I awoke at midnight to go on duty for four hours, before turning on a dim red light to find my clothes, I would put on dark goggles so my eyes would stay acclimated to the dark and I could see objects on the water's surface when I reached my post.

Since the beginning, God has used light symbolically. One of the first things he said at creation was, "Let there be light." He appeared to Moses in a bush that seemed to burn with fire. And later on, God led the Israelites out of Egypt with a pillar of fire by night.

This symbolism extends into the New Testament. When Jesus says he is the light of the world, he places himself in God's role as the source of all light. Those who believe in him will not stumble and lose their way in the darkness, but rather will be guided into new life through the light he provides. And we can live in that light, so long as we remain committed to following Christ.

Dear Lord, thank you for illuminating my path so I may keep safe as I find my way around this dark world. Help me live as a child of the light, who spreads your love and kindness and grace wherever I go, rather than plaguing others with the darkness of selfishness or unconcern. May the light you give me, through Christ, help others to find you. In Jesus' name I pray. Amen. ❧

20

Why Do You Call Me Good?

*As Jesus started on his way, a man ran up to him and fell on his
knees before him. "Good teacher," he asked, "what must I do to
inherit eternal life?"*
MARK 10:17

This encounter is not easy to understand. Something bothered this young
man so much that he ran up to Jesus and fell on his knees before him — and
devout Jews did not customarily kneel at the feet of a mere rabbi. The young
man then addressed Jesus in a very interesting way: "Good teacher."

Before answering, Jesus responded with a question, a common rabbini-
cal practice, both then and today. "Why do you call me good?" he asked.
"No one is good but God alone." In Hebrew, the word for "good" is *tov*, and
people used it to refer only to God. It carried the connotation of perfection.
So in effect, the young man had called Jesus "perfect teacher." Christ, who
was indeed both God and perfect, did not disavow the description; but he
wanted the young man to understand the implications of his own words. And
then Jesus immediately summarized the second half of the Ten Commandments, to which the young man replied, "Teacher, I have kept all these since
my youth." *Really?* The young man was essentially claiming never to have
violated any of God's commands; he was perfect, *tov*.

But Jesus knew better. He saw that the young man's great wealth had
become his god — a violation of the first commandment, to keep God first
in all things — and so he tested him with instructions to sell his possessions,
give the proceeds to the poor, and follow Jesus. With great sadness, the young
man walked away.

It's no good to revere the "good" Jesus and then turn away from this
perfect Savior in our daily life. Is our real treasure in heaven or among the
inferior things of earth? That's equally the question for us.

*God, it is sobering to put myself in the same position as the rich young
man who couldn't put Jesus first in all things. Help me look within my
own heart and identify the priorities that drive my life — and then
elevate loyalty to Jesus to top place. I ask this in his name. Amen.* ❧

A Wonderful Mystery

The mystery of Christ ... was not made known to people in other
generations as it has now been revealed by the Spirit to God's holy
apostles and prophets.
EPHESIANS 3:4 – 5

My father was a Mason. This organization features secret ceremonies and private handshakes and code words that members use to remain exclusive. College fraternities have very similar practices. Members hold their secrets close to the vest; they take an oath, in effect, not to reveal them to outsiders. Ceremonies and practices like this are a way of bonding together people who have made a mutual commitment, and there's nothing necessarily wrong with them.

But this is not the kind of "mystery" to which Paul referred. He did not have in mind a secret to be kept.

In Paul's theology, the "mystery" was something important and unexpected that for ages had remained undisclosed and not fully explained, but now had been revealed in its entirety. That the ministry of Christ could be used to unify people on a global basis—that all people, regardless of racial characteristics, would be treated equally in God's eyes—*that* was a surprising and transforming thing. How could this simple carpenter's son from Nazareth, who had only a three-year ministry on earth, have transformed the world in such a powerful way?

Jesus brought us a gift of love from God Almighty, so that no matter what we have done, if we repent, we can be totally forgiven and reconciled with God through faith in the risen Christ. How could God be so generous? How could God be so filled with love? It's hard to comprehend, and it still remains a mystery to many people, who find it too good to believe.

Yet that's exactly what Paul means when he talks about the mystery of Christ. God had planned this from the beginning—but revealed it through the ministry of Christ. It is a secret no longer, and we are to proclaim this good news to anyone who will listen.

Dear Lord, may I accept the wonderful revelation that through faith
in Christ I can be reconciled with you. Help me draw near to Jesus and
emulate his life and words. Most of all, let me be a success in your eyes
and a blessing to others, whom you love just as you love me. In Jesus'
name I pray. Amen. ❧

Building on the Foundation

By the grace God has given me, I laid a foundation as a wise builder,
and someone else is building on it. But each one should build with care.
I CORINTHIANS 3:10

Paul founded churches all over the Roman Empire, but everywhere he went, he laid exactly the same foundation: faith in Jesus Christ as the crucified and risen Son of God. Yet the churches he and others founded did not all look and act the same; they took on the characteristics, concerns, and peculiarities of the men and women of that church. And according to Paul, that's exactly how it should be—so long as they all worshiped in harmony.

When Paul wrote this letter, the congregation of the Corinthian believers had started to fracture, in part because they had turned to three different architects. In effect, one had designed the roof, another the walls, and a third had made plans for the doors and windows. When the people tried to implement the various proposals, their discussions broke down into arguments over which designer's plans to follow.

One faction liked Peter because he was a disciple; another liked Apollos and his eloquent preaching; and another preferred Paul and his wise interpretation of Scripture.

Paul said, "Wait a minute! You can't build a church by following me or Peter or Apollos. There's only one architect and builder, and that's Jesus Christ. All of us must follow him."

Christians come in many stripes: Baptists, Methodists, Catholics, Mennonites, Eastern Orthodox, and many others. Often divisions exist even within each group; but we should strive to live in harmony with one another as together we worship the Savior of us all, Jesus Christ.

O Lord, remind me what it means to build a worldwide, harmonious Christian church. Help me put aside merely human aspirations for power and self-exaltation. We differ from one another, and yet we are one in Christ, serving the same Master and obeying the same Lord. Thank you, God, for providing a way, through Christ, to unify this remarkable diversity. I pray in his name. Amen. ❧

A Perfect Mediator

For we do not have a high priest who is unable to empathize with
our weaknesses, but we have one who has been tempted in every way,
just as we are—yet he did not sin.
HEBREWS 4:15

Only the high priest of the Israelites could enter the Holy of Holies, the room in the inner temple that housed the ark of the covenant. And he could do so only once a year, when he offered sacrifices to propitiate God's wrath against the sins of the people.

How things changed with the coming of Jesus! He took on the role of Great High Priest and now remains with God Almighty, not for just one day of the year, but forever. And he makes atonement for the sins of the people, including us. He does so, not by offering animal sacrifices, but by having offered himself.

Not only is Jesus exalted above the angels; he is at the same time one of us, a human being. He suffered like we have and understands us personally and thoroughly, having faced the same things that confront us. In an important way, equality exists between Jesus Christ, the Son of God, and us.

And yet Jesus is unlike us, because he never sinned. He lived on earth as a human being—not with impunity, not in a protective cocoon, not isolated from hunger or thirst or weariness or hatred or suffering or abuse—and faced the same temptations that we face, yet always without sin. That is why he is qualified to be our perfect High Priest.

Therefore, we can approach God in prayer, not with timidity or reluctance, but with boldness. Through Christ, we can come directly to God with confidence and frankness, confessing our sins and repenting without hesitation and without fear—for we know Christ is there, as he promised, interceding for us.

Dear Lord, I'm not accustomed to thinking about Great High Priests
and approaching God with boldness; so it's good for me to be reminded of
this wonderful and exciting relationship I have with my Creator. Thank
you that I never need to feel hesitant to approach you with my problems,
needs, sorrows, or doubts, for I know that, through faith in Jesus Christ,
there is no separation between us. I pray these things in Jesus' name.
Amen. ❧

The Pain of Separation

*"And surely I am with you always,
to the very end of the age."*
MATTHEW 28:20

My parents, both sisters, and my only brother all succumbed to cancer in a relatively short period of time. While it was heartrending to lose all the members of my family, I realize that all of us experience that kind of sorrow. Such losses can bring times of crushing despair and sometimes even challenges to our faith. Separation is a difficult thing.

Those of us who have had young children know that many of them suffer nightmares involving the loss of a loved one. When this happens, the child wakes up screaming in the middle of the night or rushes to the parent's bedroom. When the parent tries to comfort the child, the little one says, "I thought you were gone! I thought you had left me!" And the parent says, "I'm right here with you. I'm not going anywhere."

Even for adults, a sense of abandonment or loneliness is a scary thing. It creates an empty space in our lives. Christ was trying to prepare his disciples for this when he explained to them, "My children, I will be with you only a little longer. You will look for me, and just as I told the Jews, so I tell you now: Where I am going, you cannot come" (John 13:33). But he also was trying to assure them that they would never be totally alone or abandoned, that the Holy Spirit would come to comfort them.

That same promise belongs to us. Jesus never abandons us. God loves us and has sent the Holy Spirit as our Comforter, which is why Jesus said, "Surely I am with you always, to the very end of the age." We can always turn to God for comfort whenever we feel the pain of separation.

O Lord, when I face troubles, doubts, fears, disappointments, or sorrows due to some painful separation, help me remember your promise to remain with me always. And as you comfort me, Lord, let me always be ready to comfort others. Help me reach out to the hurting, the sorrowing, and the lonely, to remind them of your never-dying love. I pray these things in the name of Jesus Christ, my Savior. Amen. ❧

Worthy of Worship

Jesus answered: "Don't you know me, Philip, even after I have been among you such a long time? Anyone who has seen me has seen the Father."
JOHN 14:9

A woman sleeping next to her husband heard the clock strike thirteen. She shook her husband awake and shouted, "Wake up, wake up! It's later than it's ever been before!"

A lot of people think that today, with all the conflicts erupting around the world and with all its dissension, uncertainty, and rapidly advancing technology, it's later than it has ever been. How do we approach modern-day life, with all its pressures and opportunities?

In my inaugural speech as president, I quoted my favorite teacher, Miss Julia Coleman: "We must accommodate changing times but cling to unchanging principles." This perspective has strongly affected my life.

It is important to identify the things that *never* change and imbed them in our hearts. We need to stop, pause from the frantic pace of our modern-day world, and ask, "What things really matter in life?"

One thing that never changes is the Easter story. Faced with it, we need to ask ourselves, "Do I believe in God? And if so, in what kind of God do I believe?"

The answer to that question is Jesus Christ. He is God. That is why Jesus replied to Philip, "Anyone who has seen me has seen the Father." In his earthly ministry, Jesus showed us the character of God — not only grace, love, and forgiveness, but also divine holiness that cannot compromise with or accept sin. Jesus died on the cross, innocent of any sin, in order to atone for ours, so that those who repent and believe in him can be forgiven and be reconciled with God.

These facts do not change. *This* is the God whom we worship, on whom we can always depend — an unchanging principle of life.

O Lord, thank you for the life-changing story of Easter. Help me immerse myself in the resurrection scene and absorb the deep meaning of this remarkable event. Help me strengthen my faith in Christ, to demonstrate to those who observe me, "this is what it means to be a Christian." Strengthen me in this determination and draw me closer to my Savior, in whose name I pray. Amen. ❧

The Most Important Moment in History

Jesus answered him,
"Truly I tell you, today you will be with me in paradise."
LUKE 23:43

Two criminals died on Roman crosses along with Jesus. During the execution, one of these felons turned to Christ and mocked him. "Aren't you the Messiah?" he sneered. "Save yourself and us!" But the other criminal replied, "Don't you fear God, since you are under the same sentence? We are punished justly, for we are getting what our deeds deserve. But this man has done nothing wrong." Then he turned to Jesus and said, "Jesus, remember me when you come into your kingdom" (Luke 23:39–42).

This man, in faith, asked for one simple favor. What he had seen that day convinced him that Christ was the promised Messiah and would come into his kingdom in heaven. In effect, in just a few words this man summarized a rich theology: "I know you're going to be in your kingdom, and I hope you'll remember me." Christ answered the man's short plea with the remarkable words, "Today you will be with me in paradise."

What happened when Jesus died? How did his death and resurrection make salvation possible? The answer is that by the voluntary sacrifice of his life, Christ willingly accepted the punishment for our sins, so that through our faith in him we could be reconciled with God — permanently. The resurrection was the single most important moment in the history of the world. Although he had never committed even a single sin, Christ accepted our punishment in order to save us — and then came to life again!

We do not find the most profound significance of Christ in his great teaching or in his perfect example. We find it instead in his role as our Savior. He died on the cross to save us and rose from the dead to conquer death! This is the essence of Christianity. All of history turns on this unique event.

God, as I remember what Jesus did for me, give me a deep humility and a searching, thankful heart. Help me rise above what's expected of me and be inspired to greatness in your sight by the memory of what Christ did. Thank you that I have the opportunity, through faith, to relate to you personally. I pray in the name of the Savior who died for me. Amen.

The Cost of Our Salvation

In him we have redemption through his blood, the forgiveness of sins,
in accordance with the riches of God's grace that he lavished on us.
EPHESIANS 1:7 – 8

In 1858, Frances Ridley Havergal visited Germany with her husband. The couple went to an art museum where she saw a painting of Christ on the cross that overwhelmed her with grief. She returned home and wrote a poem about it.

The next morning, she got up and read her poem but found it so emotional that it embarrassed her; she didn't want anyone to see it. When she heard her husband coming, she hurried to the fireplace and threw it in the flames. Somehow, the poem blew away from the fire and fell on the hearth. Her husband picked it up and read its first few words: "I gave my life for thee, my precious blood I shed, / that thou might ransomed be and quickened from the dead."

Do you recognize it? It's one of the world's favorite Easter hymns, expressing Mrs. Havergal's feelings about the crucifixion.

Crucifixion was terrible, and not only because of the pain of spikes driven through the hands and feet. As a condemned man hung there, he became unable to breathe and used his feet to push up and relieve the pressure on his lungs. As sundown approached, soldiers would break the prisoner's legs to hasten his death. The average length of this torture was twelve hours. Crucifixion is one of the most horrible ways ever devised to execute human beings.

Why did Jesus willingly die in this horrible way? He did so that "in him" we could have "redemption in his blood and forgiveness for our trespasses." Jesus purchased our forgiveness at the cost of the worst possible punishment a human can suffer. We must remember that Christ *chose* that death ... for our sake.

O Lord, when I ponder what Jesus went through to win my salvation, I am filled with praise and wonder. I remember that as your beloved Son took punishment upon himself for the sins that I committed, he cried out, "My God, my God, why have you forsaken me?" Yet you planned the crucifixion and Jesus submitted to it freely so that I could be reconciled with you. What a majestic and loving God you are! In Jesus' name I pray. Amen. ❧

28

The Horror of the Cross

About three in the afternoon Jesus cried out in a loud voice, "Eli, Eli,
lema sabachthani?" (which means "My God, my God, why have you
forsaken me?").
MATTHEW 27:46

We tend to obscure the horrible nature of Christ's passion: his back a gaping, bloody wound; him struggling down the street, barely able to stand; and then nailed, naked, to a crude cross. Most of us would rather not think about Christianity as a faith that requires suffering and sacrifice. We like, instead, to ponder the gentle Jesus, and forgiveness, mercy, kindness, grace, and love. Christ exhibited all those things, of course; but rarely do we deliberately ponder the true meaning of his crucifixion.

Jesus was a human being in all senses of the word. He walked on dusty roads, got tired and hungry, sweated, looked for a place to sleep, felt loneliness and betrayal, had friendships, and enjoyed good times. He was truly human; but unlike any of us, he remained perfect in everything he did. He abhorred sin, never lied, stole, hated, gossiped, or committed an injustice. He was entirely pure.

In the garden of Gethsemane, as Jesus looked ahead to the horror of Calvary—which would culminate in the resurrection, the most significant event in the history of the world—he agonized over what was to come. He sweated blood and asked God if there were any way to avoid it. He saw the dreadfulness of the cross, not only of the nails in his wrists and feet and the spear in his side, but far more, the taking upon himself of the world's sin, which would separate him (for however brief a time) from God the Creator.

We must never minimize Christ's sacrifice on the cross. When we thank God for what Jesus has done on our behalf, we should take special care to remember that every sin of ours added to his suffering.

> *O Lord, let me never forget the brutal nature of Christ's sacrifice on*
> *my behalf. May his obedience lead to my own transformation; as he*
> *consciously obeyed and served you by turning away from an easier, more*
> *comfortable life, may I do the same. In the name of Jesus Christ I pray.*
> *Amen.*

Chosen in Meekness

For the message of the cross is foolishness to those who are perishing,
but to us who are being saved it is the power of God.
I CORINTHIANS 1:18

A man was hanged this past week in Delaware. In Utah, a firing squad shot a condemned man. Georgia and many other states use the electric chair for executions.

Can you imagine using an electric chair or a gallows as a symbol for some religion? And yet we use a cross as the symbol of our Christian faith.

Usually we think of a cross as a beautiful thing, standing in front or on top of churches or hanging around the necks of priests or young women. But when we think about the historical meaning of the cross, it doesn't seem so beautiful. And yet Paul says that God saves those who believe through the "foolish" message of the cross.

In ancient days, like today, many people thought of themselves as self-sufficient. "I can comprehend signs," says one. "My mind can study various theologians and compare their theories," says another. Both mean, "I can take care of my own needs through logic and common sense; I don't need outsiders."

But to gain the power of God for our salvation, we must become receptive and humble enough to admit that *we need help*. And that requires courage and humility!

The Greeks couldn't imagine a god who could be punished, much less one susceptible to human execution. The Jews couldn't accept a messiah who didn't expel the Romans and establish a Jewish theocratic kingdom—much less someone hanged upon a tree!

It is through Christ's humiliation on the cross, however, that we can be reconciled to God. God cannot accept sin; it must be punished. Christ, in his perfection, was sacrificed for those who believe in him. That is the significance and the transforming nature of the cross.

O Lord, open my eyes that I might see where the cross of Christ shows
me what areas of my life need to change. Help me focus on the cross this
week, and reveal to me who might need to hear about it, through my own
words and testimony. I ask these things in Christ's name. Amen. ❧

Believe It!

"We are going up to Jerusalem," he said, "and the Son of Man will be delivered over to the chief priests and the teachers of the law. They will condemn him to death and will hand him over to the Gentiles, who will mock him and spit on him, flog him and kill him. Three days later he will rise."

MARK 10:33 – 34

The heart and soul of Christianity—its very foundation—is the resurrection of Jesus Christ. But if that's so, then why don't we hear more about it? I think it's because the reality is so difficult for us to understand. It's not that we don't believe; one recent poll reported that more than 80 percent of Americans say they believe in life after death. We just have a hard time conceiving of it.

The disciples were no exception. Jesus talked to them repeatedly about his coming arrest, trial, crucifixion, and resurrection. He said it so plainly that it shocks us. A lot of people say, "Jesus spoke in parables. He never plainly *told* the disciples what was going to happen; otherwise they would have expected it." But he *did* tell them, repeatedly and plainly. Still, they didn't understand; it just seemed too incredible.

So when Christ was crucified, the disciples felt overwhelmed with grief, despair, hopelessness, disillusionment, and embarrassment. And when Jesus rose from death and appeared to them, they were astonished.

We have to be careful that we do not fall into the same trap the disciples did. Even though we "believe" in the resurrection, we often live as though we don't. Even though we have faith that through Christ we will live after death, our doubts persist.

It is sometimes difficult to sustain a firm, unshakable belief that after we die we will enjoy eternal life with Jesus Christ. But since this is exactly what he has promised, we must labor to believe it with all our heart.

God, I am grateful that Jesus Christ died for my sins and rose again for my justification. Help me as I struggle to expand my mind, even as your disciples struggled to learn more and to be drawn closer to one another in the spirit of true love, humility, forgiveness, and service. Help me pattern my life as much as possible after that of my Savior, Jesus Christ, in whose name I pray. Amen. ❧

31

A Privilege to Profess

*For the wages of sin is death, but the gift of God is eternal life in
Christ Jesus our Lord.*
ROMANS 6:23

I ran for governor of Georgia in 1966 and lost to a prominent segregationist. Afterward I felt despondent and alienated from God. My sister Ruth Carter Stapleton, a world-famous evangelist, came to see me and advised me to volunteer for what we called a pioneer mission program.

I agreed and went to Pennsylvania, to Massachusetts, to Connecticut, and to the poor neighborhoods of Atlanta. In each place I spent a week going house to house, visiting people and explaining to them how to become a Christian. It was an eye-opener for me because I realized that my own fumbling explanations of the Scriptures were inadequate. I was not eloquent and felt timid and embarrassed.

When my traveling companion and I would walk up to a stranger's front porch, we would kneel down and pray in public for the Holy Spirit to be with us—with cars driving past and people laughing at us. Then we'd knock on the door; sometimes it got slammed in our faces, and sometimes we'd get invited in. In Lock Haven, Pennsylvania, we saw forty-eight people accept Christ in one week. Sometimes in what seemed to be the most miraculous way, people broke down in tears when we fumbled through our Bible verses. It was obvious that God had touched them directly, through the Holy Spirit.

The fact is that God loves us, even though as sinners we deserve condemnation. But God demonstrates his love for us in that Christ died for us (Romans 5:8); and through our faith, he takes the punishment our sins deserve. It is therefore our duty and privilege to profess these truths so that others will know them.

God, open my heart so that I can accept within myself the presence of the Holy Spirit. From this day forward, regardless of my age or status in life, empower me so that my life will be more closely attuned to that of my Savior, Jesus Christ. Help me represent you well and introduce others to you by the power of your Spirit. In Jesus' name I pray. Amen. ❧

Part of an Advancing Kingdom

The angel said to the women, "Do not be afraid, for I know that you
are looking for Jesus, who was crucified. He is not here; he has risen,
just as he said. Come and see the place where he lay."
MATTHEW 28:5 – 6

Every year I've lived in Plains since leaving the Navy in 1953, I've attended our church's Easter sunrise service. It's held outside, and only one year did it rain so hard that we had to move inside. We also lost power, so we held the service by candlelight and flashlight; a Lutheran preacher gave the morning's homily. It was one of the most memorable Easter sunrise services I've attended.

I also vividly remember the Easter services when I served as governor of Georgia. Rosalynn, our children, and I would walk to the top of Stone Mountain every Easter morning to see the sun rise, which for us commemorated Christ rising from the dead and the birth of the Christian church.

Easter Sunday morning is very special to me.

Roughly two thousand years ago, when Christ was thirty-three years old, he introduced God's kingdom to this earth. The impact of this truly remarkable event has been profound. It is fascinating to think about what has happened since that time.

Nowadays, of almost seven billion people on earth, about a third profess belief in Jesus Christ as Savior. This makes Christianity by far the largest faith in the world. About 80 percent of American citizens profess to be Christians, agreeing that Christ rose from the dead and that his suffering on the cross made it possible for our sins to be forgiven.

Each Easter, we would do well to keep these remarkable things in mind. Christ's kingdom is vibrant and alive and expanding! We are part of it, and should allow that tremendous fact to encourage us and strengthen us in his service.

Dear God, I am grateful for this reminder of how you are transforming millions of lives around the world through the resurrection of your Son and my Savior, Jesus Christ. Help me recognize the miraculous nature of Easter and what happened to the world because of it. But even more, let me realize that Christ's resurrection has the power to change every aspect of my life. In Jesus' name I pray. Amen.

No One's Perfect

I do not do the good I want to do,
but the evil I do not want to do—this I keep on doing.
ROMANS 7:19

Although it takes courage to confess it, all of us are prone to sin. Of course, it's easier and more comfortable to ignore it. That's why we tend to say, "Well, I'm not as bad as a lot of other folks. I'm certainly not as bad as some." But Paul, who was a very good man, confessed that his own inclination to sin separated him from God and filled him with anguish and despair.

Did Paul have a tendency toward selfishness? Did he take things for himself or try to get rich and exalt his name among other Christians? Although we don't know the exact nature of his sins, he does insinuate that one particular sin felt like a thorn in his flesh (2 Corinthians 12:7).

The point is, we need to put ourselves in the same boat with Paul. We must look at ourselves and recognize that while the "law of the Spirit" describes the kind of perfection every Christian should exhibit in daily life, the "law of sin and death" is what tends to prevail in us.

Let's imagine ourselves on trial, with God's law being read to us. The question finally comes: "Are you guilty under the law?" And we must confess, "Yes, I'm guilty. I'm guilty of not always promoting peace. I'm guilty of discriminating against others. I'm guilty of not sharing as much as I should. I'm guilty of gossip. I'm guilty."

We mustn't trick ourselves into thinking we're not sinful just because we're Christians. On this earth, sinfulness will always remain a struggle for us. Our best chance of fighting it is to acknowledge its presence. As John says, "If we claim to be without sin, we deceive ourselves and the truth is not in us" (1 John 1:8).

O God, help me be courageous enough for honest self-analysis. Help me look at myself—maybe in a few moments of solitude—and ask, "What am I? Who am I? What is the sum total of all the decisions I make?" Imbue me with the beautiful presence of the Holy Spirit, Lord, and help me humble myself in your sight. I ask in the name of my Savior. Amen. ❧

Vital Medicine

*Praise the LORD, my soul, and forget not all his benefits—who
forgives all your sins and heals all your diseases, who redeems your
life from the pit and crowns you with love and compassion.*
PSALM 103:2 – 4

Suppose you had an ear infection. To treat it, a doctor could give you an injection of antibiotics. The doctor is unlikely to stick a needle in your ear, however; rather, the injection will go in your arm.

If we didn't know any better, we might say, "How could the medicine possibly get from my arm to my ear?" The obvious answer is, "Because the ear and arm belong to the same body." The blood circulates from one place to the other and carries the medicine with it.

On the other hand, if I had an ear infection and my *wife* received an injection in her arm, it wouldn't help me at all. Her body is not connected to mine through the bloodstream. For the medicine to work, the intimacy of a single body is required; then the treatment given in one part gets carried to others.

Sin is like a spiritual infection, one that we cannot treat ourselves. Christ's sacrifice on the cross provides forgiveness for our fatal sin. When we put our faith in him, the Holy Spirit provides a healing process in us. He is the medicine for our spiritual infection.

The intimacy of living in Christ means that there is no space in us that can't be touched by God's healing power. We lack the strength to cure ourselves from the effects of our own sin, but God can heal us—*if* we are in Christ. That is why it is crucial to put our faith in Christ—each of us, individually—and so become a part of his spiritual body. His blood can cure only those with an intimate and inseparable connection to him, through faith.

O God, thank you for providing the remedy for my fatal disease of sin! I praise you for your grace and mercy in sending Jesus Christ to this world, to live as one of us and to give his life on the cross for my sake. Help me live for you and reach out to those who have yet to discover the salvation available in Jesus. I pray this in Christ's name. Amen. ❧

A Sin of the Heart

*"I tell you that anyone who looks at a woman lustfully has already
committed adultery with her in his heart."*
MATTHEW 5:28

On his deathbed, my brother called in one of his good buddies from Plains and said, "Everybody knows that I have only a few days to live. I don't want to die with something on my conscience. I have to tell you, in complete candor, that your wife and I have had an affair for the last three years."

His friend's face dropped. The man gulped a couple of times—and then Billy laughed and said, "No, I'm just joking." That was Billy.

In real life, of course, adultery is no laughing matter. In fact, I almost lost the presidential election because of it. As a Sunday school teacher, I felt qualified to explain what Christ had in mind when he spoke about adultery. I said he was setting an example that would force all of us to recognize our sinfulness. My mistake was that I explained this to magazine reporters, who published my edited remarks as an admission that I was constantly unfaithful to my wife by thinking sexually about other women. Once the magazine came out, it was too late for me to correct their misimpressions.

In fact, these verses prevent those of us who have remained loyal to our spouse from claiming that we've upheld the standards of Christ—which are nothing less than perfection. If we want to claim for ourselves a righteous moral standing, then Jesus insists that we meet his perfect standards. None of us can do so, of course. We all fall woefully short—and that is the point.

Jesus died on the cross because of our status as sinners in need of forgiveness. Only through faith in him, who led a perfect life, can we be reconciled with a holy God. That keeps us from bragging, even to ourselves.

*Dear Lord, thank you for the teaching of Jesus Christ, which shows me
that all people, myself included, fall short of your standard of perfection.
Remind me of this truth to prevent my becoming smug or self-satisfied in
my religion. Give me compassion for those who stumble and the grace to
treat them as equals in your sight. In Jesus' name I pray. Amen.* ❧

A Wicked Tradition

"You have let go of the commands of God and are holding on to human traditions."
MARK 7:8

The Pharisees had developed many religious traditions that they considered essential to winning God's favor. One of them concerned the ceremonial washing of hands and dishes, which made each meal a kind of religious ceremony.

Working-class people didn't comply; it was impractical out in the fields, boats, or workshops to go through a ceremonial washing before eating a piece of meat or bread. But for wealthy religious observers, this practice became very important, and eventually was considered necessary for earning God's acceptance.

When the Pharisees saw Jesus' disciples ignoring this tradition, therefore, they asked, "Why don't your disciples live according to the tradition of the elders instead of eating their food with defiled hands?" (Mark 7:5). They didn't attack Christ directly; they simply condemned his disciples. Jesus responded by calling them hypocrites and quoting Isaiah: "These people honor me with their lips, but their hearts are far from me. They worship me in vain; their teachings are merely human rules" (Mark 7:6–7).

Jesus then gave an example of how the Pharisees ignored God's law in favor of their traditions. The Scriptures required that a man use his wealth to take care of his elderly parents. But something called a *corban*, a special offering to God endorsed by the Pharisees, allowed a man to dedicate everything he owned to God. Once this had been done, none of those riches belonged to the man anymore; they were considered God's. The man retained control of them, but thus approved by the Pharisees, he didn't have to share them with his needy parents. The religious leaders had designed their tradition to benefit the rich—and themselves.

Jesus condemned all such twisted interpretations of God's Word. Ceremonies mean nothing apart from a redeemed heart—then or now.

Dear God, too often I find it easy to substitute outward ceremony or convenient use of Scripture for a genuine experience of faith with you. Forgive me for this sin, and help me commit myself to the things that Jesus saw as most important: peace, justice, generosity, forgiveness, and love. Help me renew my commitment to my Savior and walk in his footsteps. In his name I pray. Amen. ❧

37

A Bad Deal

*The devil led him up to a high place and showed him in an instant
all the kingdoms of the world. And he said to him, "I will give you
all their authority and splendor; it has been given to me, and I can
give it to anyone I want to. If you worship me, it will all be yours."*
LUKE 4:5 – 7

Satan offered Jesus the very thing that all the prophets predicted the Messiah
would have. Had he accepted the offer, no doubt he would have established
a benevolent administration to govern the world.

What a nice (but misleading) thought!

Can you imagine all nations on earth answering to Jesus as king? How
exemplary the justice! How perceptive the lawmaking! Jesus would have
cared perfectly for the needy and the diseased, providing them food and
health. Habitat for Humanity would have sprouted all over the world to
eliminate homelessness. The inarticulate and weak and scorned would have
been enfranchised. The proud and rich and powerful would have been unable
to dominate their fellow citizens. Had Jesus accepted the offer, he would have
reigned with absolute fairness, setting an example for all other rulers. We
could have looked back and said, "This is the way Jesus ruled the world, and
as a governor or president, I now have a perfect pattern for what government
should do."

But Jesus refused the offer. He told Satan, "It is written, worship the Lord
your God and serve him only." Jesus simply couldn't accept the offer, because
it came with a horrific, evil proviso: Worship Satan. The very thought is rep-
rehensible. Jesus would have had to abandon God for immediate earthly gain.

How easily we fall into this sin! We must take care never to place our
Christian faith in a secondary position to material gain. We must worship
God alone and not our jobs or possessions or relationships.

*O God, thank you for reminding me that good things done in evil ways
are evil and need to be rejected. Thank you for giving us the perfect
example of Jesus, who resisted all temptation to stray from the path you set
for him. Give me a like-minded determination to pursue justice, peace,
truth, humility, compassion, and unselfish love, in the way that most
honors you. I pray these things in Jesus' name. Amen.* ❧

38

Are You Free?

To the Jews who had believed him, Jesus said, "If you hold to my
teaching, you are really my disciples. Then you will know the truth,
and the truth will set you free."
JOHN 8:31 – 32

Since the United States of America was founded as a nation, beginning with the Declaration of Independence in 1776, we have considered ourselves a free people. So how could Jesus' statement about providing freedom have any relevance for us?

When Jesus spoke these words, he addressed them to his contemporaries, men and women of first-century Israel. His Jewish audience immediately asked the same question every American would ask: "We are Abraham's descendants and have never been slaves of anyone. How can you say that we shall be set free?" (John 8:33).

In fact, Abraham's descendants had been slaves for long periods of time. Ancient Israelites had spent centuries as slaves in Egypt, and both the northern and southern kingdoms of Israel had gone into slavery for their rebellion and wickedness against God. But Jesus' statement provoked his countrymen. They considered themselves very holy and considered themselves righteous persons of God, just because of their birthright through Abraham. That is why they considered it an insult to be called a slave.

Jesus responded, "Very truly I tell you, everyone who sins is a slave to sin. Now a slave has no permanent place in the family, but a son belongs to it forever. So if the Son sets you free, you will be free indeed" (John 8:34 – 36). Christ told them repeatedly that merely being a physical descendant of Abraham did nothing to guarantee freedom from the bondage of sin.

In the same way, just because we are free Americans doesn't mean we are free of the bondage of sin. To break away from the slavery of sin, we need to be set free by faith in God's Son, Jesus Christ.

O Lord, thank you for the freedom we enjoy in America; but I realize
that ultimate freedom, freedom of the spirit, comes only through uniting
myself with Jesus Christ, through faith in him. Help me become a more
effective ambassador of this freedom that only Christ provides, and
strengthen my faith as I thank you for this amazing opportunity. I ask
this in his name. Amen. ❦

39

The Problem of Intermarriage

"We promise not to give our daughters in marriage to the peoples around us or take their daughters for our sons."
NEHEMIAH 10:30

We have all seen people turn a legitimate enjoyment into a debilitating sin or a self-destructive habit. It's not a pretty scene to watch, and often it ends in tragedy.

In our day, this has become a very serious problem, particularly when it involves alcoholics or others with serious addictions, such as gambling or a promiscuous lifestyle. Almost every day in the news media we see sad reports of families unraveling, businesses imploding, and even governments falling because someone allowed a simple enjoyment to become a self-destructive habit.

In the days after the Babylonian captivity, intermarriage had become a serious problem for the Jews. Those who had stayed behind in Jerusalem during the time of the exile had intermarried with the nations around them, mingling with the Moabites and other pagan peoples of the region. In this they seriously transgressed the law of Moses.

Scholars say the Mosaic law was rooted in spiritual protection, not racial discrimination (witness the many non-Hebrew ancestors of Jesus), and that intermarriage with pagan nations led Israel to abandon God and worship Baal and other foreign gods. Bad company corrupts good morals, the Bible says.

It turned out to be quite a prescient prohibition, for we know what happened historically. Solomon, for example, married many heathen wives. As a result—and despite his God-given wisdom—he started visiting the pagan high places and there worshiped foreign gods, even as he continued to profess loyalty to the God of Israel. His family, kingdom, and heritage all suffered as a result.

While God does not call us to withdraw from the world (1 Corinthians 5:10), he does warn us against becoming intimate with it, experimenting with its wicked principles, and eventually becoming part of it. We are to let nothing compromise our life in Christ—and anything that does, we are to abandon, or "divorce."

O Lord, thank you for this reminder that I owe my ultimate allegiance to you and that anything that draws me away from you I am to banish from my life. May I encourage others in our mutual faith, and give us unity so that, through prayer and an attitude of humility and forgiveness, we might work together for your kingdom. I pray in Jesus' name. Amen.

Remain Faithful

The LORD said to him, "Go, marry a promiscuous woman and have
children with her, for like an adulterous wife this land is guilty of
unfaithfulness to the LORD."
HOSEA 1:2

God gave Hosea a strange command: "Marry a prostitute." He did so in order to create a living illustration of the broken relationship between God and the Israelites. Hosea brought Gomer out of prostitution, and she became bound to him in marriage; but she was unfaithful to him and kept prostituting herself.

In a similar way, God had brought the Israelites out of slavery in Egypt, and the people had entered into a covenant with God; but they kept prostituting themselves to false gods and other nations, lusting for wealth, power, and pleasure.

This became a regular cycle, repeated throughout the Old Testament. First, the chosen people would ignore their mutually binding covenant with God and continue the evil habits they had followed for years. Second, their sinful behavior got them in serious trouble. Third, a leader or prophet, ordained by God, came along to help them. Fourth, they were delivered when they repented and agreed to abide by God's covenant. And fifth, when good times came, they said, "We don't need God anymore. We can take care of ourselves, or we'll let the Syrians protect us. Let's get rich and enjoy ourselves!" Whenever this happened, God punished them again, and the cycle repeated itself. Like Gomer, they were unfaithful.

We too have entered a covenant relationship with Jesus Christ. And when we break his commandments or live in a way that dishonors him, we are being unfaithful, just as the Israelites were unfaithful to God and as Gomer was unfaithful to Hosea. That may sound like an exaggeration, but it's not. It's something that every serious Christian needs to consider.

O Lord, help me be a Christian in every sense of the word. Thank you
for your many blessings, and give me the determination to share your
blessings with others in the name of Christ. Let me never forget the firm
covenant that binds me in loyalty to Jesus, my Savior, in whose name I
pray. Amen. ❧

The Mystery of Grace

*... that is, the mystery made known to me by revelation, as I have
already written briefly.*
EPHESIANS 3:3

When Paul talks about a "mystery," what does he mean? It sounds strange to us, since we know that Christianity is not some secret organization. It's obviously important, since Paul repeatedly uses this word in Ephesians 3.

We should remember that at the time Paul wrote, the Gentiles were being incorporated into the church on an equal basis with Jews. No one saw this coming—a mysterious, revolutionary development. Who foresaw how the ministry of Christ would be used to unify people throughout the world? Who expected that *all* people, regardless of their ethnicity or background, would be treated equally in the eyes of God through their faith in Jesus Christ? Those were transforming things!

How could this carpenter's son, with only a three-year public ministry, transform global society and remove the stigma attached to Gentiles—the overwhelming portion of the earth's population? *That* is the "mystery" to which Paul refers.

God is filled with grace and is eager to forgive everyone who will come to Jesus through faith. And at what cost to us? What do we have to pay? Nothing. It's a free gift of love. God knows all of us, and if we repent of our sins and place our faith in Christ, we can be totally forgiven and reconciled with God. Jesus gave his perfect life so that God could bestow this enormous blessing upon us—a profound mystery to be understood.

How could God be so generous and filled with love? How could the brief life of Jesus transform the concept of life for everyone on earth? It's hard to understand, difficult to comprehend. For some people, it seems too good to believe. That's what Paul means when he talks about the mystery—not something secluded or hidden, but a truth now made open for everyone to grasp ... and enjoy.

*Father, help me accept this simple lesson from Paul, written to the
Ephesians but destined for me. Let me accept the mysterious message that
through my faith in Christ I can have a life filled with joy and peace.
And in this way I can please my Creator and bless those around me. I ask
these things in Jesus' name. Amen.* ❧

By Grace Alone

"Now then, why do you try to test God by putting on the necks of Gentiles a yoke that neither we nor our ancestors have been able to bear?"
ACTS 15:10

While Paul and Barnabas labored in Antioch, some Christians arrived from Judea who insisted, "Unless you are circumcised, according to the custom taught by Moses, you cannot be saved" (Acts 15:1). Paul and Barnabas disagreed strongly and went to Jerusalem to settle the issue with the other apostles and elders.

At the Jerusalem council, Peter stood up and declared how the conversion of the Gentile Cornelius—which God had blessed (Acts 10)—proved that salvation did not require circumcision. And he wondered aloud, "Why require the Gentiles to keep the law of Moses in order to be saved, which none of us Jews has *ever* been able to do? It's impossible." Salvation, he insisted, comes by faith, only "through the grace of our Lord Jesus" (Acts 15:11).

We must be careful never to fall into the error committed by the early Judean Christians, who tried to put extra conditions on salvation. Sometimes our Christian leaders can get so fervent about some special issue that they say, in effect, "Unless you believe this particular thing, you cannot be a Christian."

Rosalynn and I disagree on occasion about theological issues. Sometimes she reads my notes before I teach a Sunday school class, and we have quite a discussion at the breakfast table. At times I modify my notes; sometimes I don't. Take any small group of people from a congregation, and inevitably they will disagree on some issues. There's nothing wrong with that, but sometimes devout Christians get so entrenched in their beliefs that they want to include them almost as additional requirements for salvation.

We must *not* do this. Instead, let us remember the words of Peter: "It is through the grace of our Lord Jesus that we are saved."

Lord, may I carry in my heart the true message of reconciliation, emphasizing the crucial things like faith and grace, and relegating other things to secondary importance. Help me to proclaim the glorious message about our Savior and his grace, offered freely and in love, and to apply this vital message to my own day-to-day life. I ask this in the name of the Messiah, the Son of God, my Savior, Jesus Christ. Amen. ❧

43

The Greatest Truth

*No one can comprehend what goes on under the sun. Despite all
their efforts to search it out, no one can discover its meaning. Even if
the wise claim they know, they cannot really comprehend it.*
ECCLESIASTES 8:17

As a young man, I worked in the new and developing field of nuclear power.
When I began to study subatomic particles, I felt very eager and excited to
learn about this new aspect of God's world. I also became infatuated with the
depth and expanse of our universe and the geological history of our planet.
I've never found any incompatibility between my religious faith and the natural sciences.

It is healthy to remain curious about God's world and to gain a deeper
understanding about life, but it's also good to remember that we'll never
discover *all* the wonders of God's world. We learn a little more with every
generation, but God's creation is so vast and awe-inspiring that we will never
know it all.

As amazing as God's universe is, however, a far greater truth is found in
the most famous verse in the Bible: "For God so loved the world that he gave
his one and only Son, that whoever believes in him shall not perish but have
eternal life" (John 3:16). Indeed, "God did not send his Son into the world to
condemn the world, but to save the world through him" (John 3:17).

This is the greatest knowledge we could have. It is an adequate answer
to our questions about the meaning of life and our relationship to God
Almighty. It tells us that even though all of us have sinned, we can be free
of that sin and have a life secured by a never-changing faith in Jesus Christ.

We should take care that our search for more knowledge never leads us to
ignore the saving truth we already know.

*Lord, I marvel at your creation: the sun that keeps me warm, the moon
that creates the tides, the flora and fauna of a world blessed with teeming
life. It amazes me, Lord; but I ask that you keep the wonder of the cross
at the forefront of my mind. Help me remember Christ's sacrifice and to
pattern my own life after his perfect example as much as possible. I pray
in Jesus' name. Amen.* ❧

44

A Simple Gospel

*I am astonished that you are so quickly deserting the one who called
you to live in the grace of Christ and are turning to a different
gospel—which is really no gospel at all.*
GALATIANS 1:6 – 7

Suppose you were a brilliant philosopher in days gone by who wanted to create a believable religion. You wanted something that would be pure, honest, just, and fair, and would exemplify the finest aspects of human existence. It would be so perfect that no one in later days would question it. What would you put in this new religion?

As you sat down to write an outline, imagine that you knew all about ancient religions and theology and about what makes for good relationships between human beings. I'm guessing you would define a perfect religious person as one who believed in peace and justice and the alleviation of suffering, particularly for the poor; one who believed in telling the truth; a humble person; a servant to others; generous; forgiving those who hurt him; compassionate and self-sacrificing. And then you might say that people had to *be* that sort of person to enjoy a positive relationship with God.

What a wonderful religion you would have created! It would have been inspirational, positive, challenging. It would have inspired people to lead a better life. Does that sound like the Christian gospel?

Absolutely not.

Throughout his writings, Paul made sure we understood that this is *not* the gospel. There is no relationship between doing good works and gaining salvation. Our salvation comes from the grace of God, freely, because the Lord loves us. In fact, trying to be better than others does not inspire humility in us, but the opposite: pride, self-satisfaction, a smug sense of superiority, and a wholly egocentric life. It also makes us feel self-reliant, able to live without God. And yet the temptation always exists to make "trying to be good" our religion.

Stated simply, the gospel message is, "We are saved by the grace of God through our faith in Jesus Christ." What we have to contribute is faith, or trust. Our good works should come as an indication of our gratitude and a desire to emulate the perfect life of our Savior.

O God, thank you for reminding me that I can never earn your favor or work for my salvation. Teach me to lean into you for life and godliness and to depend on the power of your Spirit to help me grow in the faith so that I might truly be a compassionate, patient, kind, gentle, loving person. May others see Jesus in me as I walk with him. In Jesus' name I pray. Amen. ❧

Just Believe

Hearing this, Jesus said to Jairus,
"Don't be afraid; just believe, and she will be healed."
LUKE 8:50

Rosalynn and I recently toured the USS *Jimmy Carter*, a wonderful new ship that bears my name. It's a formidable submarine, the newest ship in the Navy and perhaps the most advanced ever built.

It's extremely quiet. At full speed, it makes less noise than do most submarines when docked with everything shut down. But it can also go fast and deep and maintain its depths very accurately. It's built to send out and retrieve robot vehicles to do top-secret missions. She's unique, and I'm very proud of her.

It's natural to feel proud of things, and that's why Jairus, a leader of the Capernaum synagogue, took pride in his eminent position. A synagogue leader often was the most respected and eloquent person in town; it was considered a great honor. As a Jewish religious leader himself, Jairus must have known that Jesus had become an outcast among other religious leaders — and that's what makes what he did so remarkable.

When Jairus's daughter became very ill, this proud man sought out Jesus and publicly begged him to come to his house. Just then, someone arrived to say it was too late; the girl had died. When Jesus heard this, he told Jairus, "Don't be afraid; just believe, and she will be healed." Jairus complied — and his daughter lived.

Pride in oneself can be very dangerous, but in some cases it can be acceptable. Pride must never exalt us above other people or distance us from God. As Jesus taught repeatedly, humility must grace the Christian. We must admit that we are powerless without God, as Jairus did, and then we can be blessed with saving power.

O Lord, thank you for giving me the ability, the strength, and the
resources to accomplish notable things; but thank you even more for your
grace and mercy that you bestow on me when I encounter challenges
that overwhelm me. Give me the humility that comes from an accurate
assessment of myself, along with a greater vision of your majesty. I pray in
Jesus' name. Amen. ❧

46

Ours for the Taking

The LORD said to me, "Go, show your love to your wife again, though she is loved by another man and is an adulteress. Love her as the LORD loves the Israelites, though they turn to other gods and love the sacred raisin cakes."
HOSEA 3:1

Sometimes we forget the simplicity of God's redemption, and then we become unwilling to acknowledge our shortcomings, weaknesses, and sins. But if we will remember that Christ promises his forgiveness under any circumstances, we will find it far easier to admit our failures, recognize our shortcomings, acknowledge our fears, confess our sins to Christ, and turn away from them.

In moments of solitude and prayer, we can talk to Jesus, knowing that he will forgive our sins completely, as though they had never occurred. That means we don't have to be afflicted with continuing guilt, or worry about alienation from God. Jesus invites us to be his true brothers and sisters.

Do you see how Gomer illustrates this principle? She is a direct mirror of the Israelites' betrayal of God. Hosea married Gomer, knowing of her profession as a prostitute. He took her into his house, but soon Gomer treated him unfaithfully; she sought out lovers while her husband sat at home wondering where she might be. When this happened, Hosea did not divorce his wife and throw her out of his house. Without condoning her wickedness, he reached out to her and forgave her.

In a similar way, God wants to forgive us. During his earthly ministry, Christ loved many people who never loved him back. Many of them simply were not lovable, by our standards. Yet he sacrificed himself for them — and for us — so that anyone who would receive his redemption could come to him freely.

No matter how many times we have been unfaithful, like Gomer, Christ still wants us to come home. It is with this assurance that we find it possible to confess our sins and turn away from them.

O Lord, let me never forget that Jesus offers to cleanse me from all my sins when I place my faith in him. Help me realize that this can give me the strength to face every circumstance of life. I thank you for these blessings through our Savior, Jesus Christ. In his name I pray. Amen. ❧

47

No "Worthier" Way

"If the prophet had told you to do some great thing,
would you not have done it? How much more, then,
when he tells you, 'Wash and be cleansed'!"
2 KINGS 5:13

Long ago Syrian forces kidnapped a little girl from Israel, and she became a servant in the household of Naaman, a powerful general. Naaman, however, had a terrible skin disease. One day the girl told him, "I know somebody back home who could cure you." When Naaman's boss heard this, he sent a message to Israel's king: "I understand somebody there can cure my suffering general. Please do so."

The message alarmed the king, but soon afterward, the prophet Elisha sent for Naaman. Naaman promptly loaded up donkeys with costly gifts; but when he arrived at Elisha's little shack, the prophet didn't even come out. He sent this word: "Go bathe yourself seven times in the Jordan River, and you will be healed." A furious Naaman told his servants, "Why should I bathe myself in such a dirty little river? We have bigger and better ones in Syria!" He mounted his horse to return home, but one wise servant said, "If you were told to do something heroic, wouldn't you do it?" Naaman, now humbled, agreed. So he followed Elisha's instructions ... and was cured.

We too receive an offer from God of the most wonderful blessing imaginable: forgiveness, strength, peace, and joy. All we must do is accept Jesus Christ as our Savior.

It seems too good to be true, and some of us react as Naaman did: "That's too easy! Let me perform a great task or pass some test to prove my worthiness." We must reject such arrogance. Forgiveness is a free gift from God—easy for us, unimaginably costly for Jesus, our Savior. We must be careful that we don't lose sight of this and wander off in search of a "worthier" way. There isn't one.

O Lord, you tell me that if I wish to be cleansed of my sin, I must wash
in the fountain of life offered to me through the death and resurrection of
Jesus Christ. Help me humble myself as Naaman did and submit to your
gracious instruction. And then, Lord, not only bless me with eternal life,
but send me out to tell others of your amazing gift. In Jesus' name I pray.
Amen. ❧

48

We Stand Innocent!

*Through Christ Jesus the law of the Spirit who gives life
has set you free from the law of sin and death.*
ROMANS 8:2

My father died from pancreatic cancer while I was training to serve on a nuclear submarine. His death shocked me, prompting me to leave the Navy. That was the first serious death in my family, and I didn't know how to react to it. Years later my mother and my two sisters and my brother died, all from pancreatic cancer. I have known sorrow, disappointment, and trepidation about the future, which has given me a profound realization of my sinfulness and shortcomings.

When Paul wrote the seventh chapter of Romans, he stripped his soul to reveal his own inner conflict. He gives us a torturous self-assessment, and at the end he cries out, "What a wretched man I am! Who will rescue me from this body that is subject to death?" No doubt Paul thought back over his life and felt anguished over his persecution of the first Christians. So with great sorrow he describes his former life outside of Christ.

And then comes one of the most remarkable passages in Scripture. An astonishing transformation takes place between the last verse of chapter 7 and the first verses in chapter 8. Paul describes a charged courtroom scene. He (and we) stands accused before God. The prosecutor is God's law, including the Ten Commandments. Our defense counsel is Jesus Christ. And what is the verdict, after all our sins are revealed?

Not guilty.

We stand rightly accused, because we cannot measure up to the law. But with Jesus as our defense attorney, spokesperson, and intercessor, the Lord finds us not guilty. We stand innocent before him, even in all his holiness! Why? Only because of what Jesus Christ has done for us on the cross. If we forget everything else, we must *never* forget that.

Lord, I stand amazed at your grace and mercy in giving me eternal life when I place my faith in your risen Son, Jesus Christ. I, like Paul, cry out, "How wretched I am! Who will deliver me?" And Jesus comes as my spokesman, defending me and paying my penalty through his own shed blood. Thank you, Lord, for such a staggering transformation! In Jesus' name. Amen. ❧

For All People

Then they cried out to the LORD, "Please, LORD, do not let us die
for taking this man's life. Do not hold us accountable for killing an
innocent man, for you, LORD, have done as you pleased." Then they
took Jonah and threw him overboard, and the raging sea grew calm.
JONAH 1:14 − 15

When the prophet Jonah decided to run away from God, he bought passage
on a ship headed in the opposite direction from where God told him to go.
After the ship reached open sea, a huge storm threatened to sink it. Immediately the sailors began to pray. I like this about these mariners (I'm prejudiced
toward sailors, since I was in the Navy for eleven years). Not being sure who
could help them, they remained open-minded theologically and willing to
seek help from any man's god.

When the sailors tried to learn who was responsible for the trouble, Jonah
admitted he was running from "the LORD, the God of heaven, who made the
sea and the dry land" (Jonah 1:9). The sailors grew afraid and asked what
they should do. Jonah told them to throw him overboard. Even then the
sailors showed good heart. Rather than following Jonah's instructions, they
tried to row back to shore—unsuccessfully. Finally, they cried out for God's
forgiveness and threw Jonah into the sea, which instantly grew calm. The
men "greatly feared the LORD," sacrificed to God, and vowed their allegiance.

The gospel of Christ is for all people. The grace of God is for all people.
The love of God is for all people. The forgiveness of God is for all people.
There is no place in God's kingdom for prejudice and no room for a "Jonah
attitude" that devalues those unlike us. We must align ourselves with the
truth: *anyone* who repents and calls on God for salvation, through Christ,
has a place in his kingdom.

God, may the story of Jonah draw me closer to my Savior and help me
root out all vestiges of self-exaltation and prejudice. Help me look upon
all people as equal in your eyes. I thank you for your grace, love, and
forgiveness, and I ask you to bind my heart together with others in Chris-
tian love. In the name of Jesus Christ I pray. Amen. ❧

Choose What's Important

"Again, the kingdom of heaven is like a merchant looking for fine
pearls. When he found one of great value, he went away and sold
everything he had and bought it."
MATTHEW 13:45 – 46

Anybody who grew up around railroads knows that they used to have white marble-sized pebbles to stabilize the roadbed. As most farm boys did, I always had a flip, or rubber slingshot, that I carried around in my hip pocket. It was just part of my clothes, like my pants and my shirt.

We used to go to the railroad and collect these little rocks, particularly the smooth round ones that would fly straight. We kept stashes of them around our yard to shoot at various targets. I remember one day I was coming from the railroad with my hands and pockets full of the best rocks I could find. My mother walked out on the front porch and called me: "Jimmy, come here. I've got something for you."

She was there with her eyes and heart full of love, holding a pan of freshly baked cookies. She held them out to me and said, "I baked some cookies for you." I will never forget standing there for a few seconds, trying to decide whether to drop those relatively worthless rocks and take my mother's cookies. It was a small event, but similar things on a much larger scale happen quite often.

As a farmer and as president, I sometimes had to decide whether to abandon some ideas I had been clinging to for the sake of something new and better. All of us tend to cling to old things instead of accepting the new life that Christ offers us. In our modern chaotic world, we sometimes fail to recognize the great opportunity for a simpler, more peaceful, and more gratifying life as we follow our Savior. But when we choose anything else, it's like clinging to dirty pebbles instead of fresh-baked cookies.

O God, help me recognize the dirty pebbles I'm holding in my hands.
Give me wisdom and strength to choose your best over anything else.
Let me come to you with open hands, asking you to fill them with good
things — not only to bless me, but that I might use those good things to
minister to others, in Jesus' name. Amen. ❧

51

Let God In

*You have searched me, LORD, and you know me. You know when I
sit and when I rise; you perceive my thoughts from afar. You discern
my going out and my lying down; you are familiar with all my ways.*

PSALM 139:1 – 3

A visiting pastor at our church in Plains once told a story about a priest from
New Orleans. Father Flanagan's parish lay in the central part of the city, close
to many taverns. One night he was walking down the street and saw a drunk
thrown out of a pub. The man landed in the gutter, and Father Flanagan
quickly recognized him as one of his parishioners, a fellow named Mike.

Father Flanagan shook the dazed man and said, "Mike!" Mike opened his
eyes and Father Flanagan said, "You're in trouble. If there is anything I can
do for you, please tell me what it is."

"Well, Father," Mike replied, "I hope you'll pray for me."

"Yes," the priest answered, "I'll pray for you right now."

He knelt down in the gutter and prayed, "Father, please have mercy on
this drunken man."

At this, a startled Mike woke up fully and said, "Father, please don't tell
God I'm drunk."

Sometimes we don't feel much of a personal relationship between God
and ourselves, as though we have a secret life full of failures and sins that
God knows nothing about. We want to involve God only when we plan to
give thanks or when we're in trouble and need help. But the rest of our lives,
we'd rather keep to ourselves.

We all have problems and failures, and God knows all about them
(whether we acknowledge them or not). If we continue to remain aware of
the presence of the Holy Spirit, however, we can have much more confident,
full, adventurous, and gratifying lives. So why not welcome a constant partner who wields all power and who already knows everything?

*Dear God, I often forget that you know all about me — my actions, my
unspoken plans, my secret desires, and my hidden habits. Remind me of
your comprehensive knowledge and that you still love me so much that
you sent your Son, Jesus Christ, to take the punishment for my sins. Help
me demonstrate your love to a needy world. In Christ's name I pray.
Amen.* ❧

52

Make a Choice

When Jesus entered Jerusalem, the whole city was stirred and asked,
"Who is this?"
MATTHEW 21:10

Passover had arrived, inundating Jerusalem with crowds. Large numbers of deeply religious Israelites had descended on the city and the temple for the enormous annual celebration—and Jesus picked this time for what we call the "Triumphal Entry."

Passover made it possible to resume friendships among individuals who hadn't seen each other for a year. The roads leading to Jerusalem, especially the one from the east, through Jericho and the Mount of Olives, were packed. And everyone, it seemed, had heard of Jesus.

I imagine that some in the crowd had actually seen Jesus heal people. Perhaps others had been present when he preached the Sermon on the Mount or fed a multitude. All of them probably had heard from their religious and political leaders that this Jesus was controversial. So when the Lord entered Jerusalem, we are told, everyone was eager to see and greet this famous man.

Jesus entered the city on a half-grown donkey. He did this, I think, to make a statement that he was indeed the Messiah. Israel had not been independent since the Maccabean revolt, two hundred years before. Since then, there had been no Jewish king. Yet the people who knew the Scriptures remembered Zechariah the prophet had said that the king, the Messiah, would enter Jerusalem on a colt. I think Jesus wanted to draw a line in the sand and say, "This is it. This is the culmination of my three years of ministry. What will you do with me? The time has come to choose."

That time comes for all of us. We too must choose what we will do with Jesus Christ. If we hail him as Lord and King, that choice has one set of implications. If we ignore him, that choice carries a different set of implications. But each of us must choose. What will we do with Jesus?

O God, although the crowds hailed Jesus on the day he entered Jerusalem,
I remember that just a few days later, many either ignored Christ or
turned against him. Today, all of us have a similar decision to make. Let
me remain loyal to him and help others to make the right choice. I pray
this in Jesus' name. Amen. ❧

53

Whoever Takes the Son

*Jesus answered, "I am the way and the truth and the life. No one
comes to the Father except through me."*
JOHN 14:6

In his early twenties, a man started collecting paintings, many of which later became famous: Picasso, Van Gogh, and others. Over the decades he amassed a wonderful collection.

Eventually, the man's beloved son was drafted into the military and sent to Vietnam, where he died while trying to save his friend. About a month after the war ended, a young man knocked on the devastated father's door. "Sir," he said, "I know that you like great art, and I have brought you something not very great." Inside the package, the father found a portrait of his son. With tears running down his cheeks, the father said, "I want to pay you for this."

"No," the young man replied, "he saved my life. You don't owe me anything."

The father cherished the painting and put it in the center of his collection. Whenever people came to visit, he made them look at it. When the man died, his art collection went up for sale. A large crowd of enthusiastic collectors gathered. First up for sale was the amateur portrait. A wave of displeasure rippled through the crowd. "Let's forget about that painting!" one said. "We want to bid on the valuable ones," said another. Despite many loud complaints, the auctioneer insisted on starting with the portrait. Finally, the deceased man's gardener said, "I'll bid ten dollars."

Hearing no further bids, the auctioneer called out, "Sold for ten dollars!" Everyone breathed a sigh of relief. But then the auctioneer said, "And that concludes the auction." Furious gasps shook the room. The auctioneer explained, "Let me read the stipulation in the will: "Sell the portrait of my son first, and whoever buys it gets the entire art collection. Whoever takes my son gets everything."

It's the same way with God Almighty. Whoever takes his Son gets everything.

*O Lord, help me grasp what it means to be called a fellow heir with
Christ. Give me a deeper appreciation for your loving kindness, and
allow it to shape how I live. Make me into a generous person who strives
to tell others about Jesus and who shares his love with the poor and the
suffering. In his name I pray. Amen.* ❧

54

A Perfect Day

You, however, are not in the realm of the flesh but are in the realm of the Spirit, if indeed the Spirit of God lives in you. And if anyone does not have the Spirit of Christ, they do not belong to Christ.
ROMANS 8:9

What makes for a perfect day? Maybe it's a promotion at work, making the final payment on a mortgage, a chance meeting with some longtime friends, or grandchildren coming for an unexpected visit. While there's nothing wrong with those things, something really is missing for any of them to rank as a "perfect day."

What is it?

The key is this: *Who's in charge of your control center?* From a Christian perspective, a perfect day is one in which the Spirit has complete control of your life, whether the sun shines or not. And how would anyone know whether God is in charge of us?

Paul gives us a clue when he distinguishes between "things of the flesh" and "things of the Spirit." Things of the flesh merely gratify natural tastes and desires, like holding a grandchild, something I'm sure Paul would approve of. The problem arises when these self-gratifying things, no matter how nice, become an obsession for us. In that case, they keep us from demonstrating our faith by doing the things that Christ did.

I must remind myself that I am a Christian, that Christ is at the core of my life. Unless we are careful, we can go from this moment all the way to the grave without ever adopting as a preeminent theme the presence of Christ in our lives. The real questions are: Do we exemplify the essence of Christianity? Are we pervaded with kindness, service, humility, forgiveness, and love?

We are blessed when we have Christ within us, regardless of our income or the weather or the number of grandchildren we have. Because Christ lives within us, we have the potential to enjoy a "perfect day" *every* day.

God, I pray that I might arrange my priorities so the Holy Spirit will take moment-by-moment control of my life. In that way, may the presence of Jesus Christ transform me from within, so that I might make a difference in the world outside. In Jesus' name I pray. Amen. ❧

Turn to God without Fear

"Speak to us yourself and we will listen. But do not have God speak
to us or we will die."
EXODUS 20:19

On May 18, 1980, Mount Saint Helens erupted in one of the most violent volcanic explosions in modern history. The top 1,300 feet of the mountain blew away, and every tree for a great distance got blasted flat to the ground. The day after the disaster, I visited the site, because as president I wanted to make sure that those who had lost homes, farms, and loved ones received proper services. We flew over the still-active volcano and saw huge icebergs floating in hot ash, smoking like dry ice. The horrendous sight put such fear into both my helicopter pilot and me that we decided to get out of there before the mountain erupted again.

That awesome scene can give some idea of what the Israelites felt as they stood at the base of Mount Sinai and saw lightning and smoke and heard the thunderous voice of God delivering the Ten Commandments. The Israelites had witnessed a supreme manifestation of the Lord's presence, and they reacted with fear instead of with thanksgiving, praise, or a willingness to form an intimate relationship with their revealed deliverer. They told Moses, "We don't want God to speak to us anymore! Please give us an intermediary."

We too sometimes remain aloof from God Almighty so we don't have to embrace an all-powerful God with intimacy.

God has offered to join each of us in an intimate, personal relationship through Jesus Christ. We must not let fear—of our sinfulness before a holy God, of our weakness before the omnipotent Creator—prevent us from accepting this offer. God has chosen, by grace, to accept us and sent Jesus Christ to die on our behalf to make it possible. Therefore, let us not hesitate to turn to God.

God, sometimes I find myself fearful of you, just like the Israelites.
Help me acknowledge the presence of the Holy Spirit and desire tender
fellowship with my Savior, Jesus Christ, so I might break down any
barriers between my Creator and me. Help me live in freedom and
without fear, surrounded by your love and grace. In the name of Jesus I
pray. Amen. ❧

56

A Cross to Choose

"Whoever wants to be my disciple must deny themselves and take up
their cross and follow me."
MARK 8:34

How different are these words from those of many prosperity preachers on television! The latter often say things like, "If you listen to my sermon and believe in Jesus and send me $25 a month, you'll get a promotion—or maybe even *win the lottery*!"

Too often in church, we say an easier thing: "If you believe in Christ, you'll have everlasting life." We present it as a giveaway. "Do you want to live after you die? If so, then accept Christ." It all sounds very simple, and it's a very attractive device to get people to say (at least superficially), "I'm a Christian."

But Jesus never said anything about an easy giveaway. He said, "If you want to follow me, take up your cross." His disciples didn't know the full meaning of "taking up your cross." They knew only that the Romans used the cross as a brutal way to execute slaves and foreigners.

What does "taking up your cross" mean for us today? I think it requires us to forsake our own pride and to submit to God through complete faith in Jesus Christ. We make Jesus paramount in every aspect of our lives, regardless of the personal cost in wealth or pleasure. It doesn't mean we should spurn all enjoyment or give up everything we care about. It simply means that Jesus becomes our highest value.

Christ tells us to put our human problems into proper perspective. Yes, they still cause us pain; but compared with Christ's love for us, such tragedies become relatively insignificant. We must never allow *anything* to become equal in importance with knowing and serving Christ—and that means we must renounce self-centered living. That is, we must pick up our cross and follow Christ and there find true peace and joy.

O God, embed in my soul the meaning of taking up the cross for Christ,
and help me substitute the standards of a genuine Christian for those of
the constantly changing secular world. Give me wisdom and strength to
build my life on the things that never change, especially a humble and
subservient commitment to my Savior, Jesus Christ, in whose name I
pray. Amen. ❧

What's the Cost?

*"Suppose one of you wants to build a tower. Won't you first sit down and
estimate the cost to see if you have enough money to complete it? For if you
lay the foundation and are not able to finish it, everyone who sees it will
ridicule you, saying, 'This person began to build and wasn't able to finish.'"*
LUKE 14:28 – 30

Is it possible to know how strong a commitment we have to Christ until it
gets seriously challenged?

During my presidency, Idi Amin was the leader of Uganda and the most
brutal dictator I had ever known. He lied and killed his way to power and
then executed tens of thousands of his own people to stay there. We later
saw vultures, called Marabou storks, hanging around a prominent hotel in
the capital city. Why? Amin often killed his opponents and had their bodies
thrown from the hotel's balcony. The birds ate their corpses.

Amin hated me because I had a strong policy of human rights and had
condemned him publicly. One time, to embarrass me, he rounded up fifty-
one Christian missionaries and announced to the world that he would execute
them. I didn't know what to do. Finally, I talked with some Muslim friends
in Saudi Arabia, who called Amin and threatened to cut off foreign aid in an
effort to convince him to let the missionaries go.

Amin relented and told the missionaries they could go free. But every one
of them refused to leave their service for Jesus Christ in Uganda. When I
received word of their decision, I went off by myself and wept.

God has given each of us the power and autonomy to make our own
decisions. As Christians, we can choose how deeply we commit ourselves to
follow in the footsteps of Jesus. Let's count the cost of full commitment and
resolve to sacrifice everything in the cause of Christ.

*O Lord, thank you for reminding me that my greatest privilege is to form
a proper relationship with you through my Savior, Jesus Christ. Also teach
me how to create better relationships with those around me. Enable me to
gauge accurately the true strength of my commitment to you and to make
whatever improvements are necessary. I pray this in the name of Jesus my
Lord. Amen.* ❧

58

Whom Will We Serve?

"Choose for yourselves this day whom you will serve."
JOSHUA 24:15

As the Hebrew people got ready to enter the Promised Land, their celebrated leader, Joshua, told them they had to make a decision about whom they would serve in their new homeland. Joshua's words could just as well be addressed to us today: "Choose whom you will serve."

Joshua did not *command* the people to serve God. Instead, he said, "You have to make a choice. You are independent and free human beings, and must decide whether you will serve God or someone else." As our Creator, God has given all of us the privilege—and responsibility—of making our own choices.

As we go through a day's experiences, we make thousands of choices. Many of them are quite minor, such as what time to get up, whether to bathe and brush our teeth, what clothes to wear, what to have for breakfast, what time to go to work, and so forth. We make countless individual decisions, most of them relatively trivial.

But we also have to make major decisions of the kind Joshua presented to his people. We have to decide whether we will serve the Lord or something else.

It's easier to make the little decisions because they are largely shaped by habit and have few serious consequences. But the much more important decision of whether to serve God is often not made, or is just put off until next Sunday. But if we don't consciously make that decision every day of our lives, then we are likely to set other priorities and serve all kinds of things besides God—without even realizing it. So we have to decide: Whom will we serve?

Lord, I'm blessed in so many ways, as were the Hebrews who finally reached the Promised Land. I have almost everything I want and need, and now I must decide: Is Christ my guide, my leader, my example, the perfect pattern for me to emulate as best I can? Help me make the right choice, and strengthen me in my resolve to follow Christ. I pray in the name of my Savior. Amen. ❧

A Drastic Change

Saul got up from the ground, but when he opened his eyes he could
see nothing. So they led him by the hand into Damascus.
ACTS 9:8

The moment Jesus confronted Saul on the road to Damascus, the Pharisee's world shattered. Saul had gone to the Sanhedrin, the Jewish ruling council, and received permission to imprison or kill any Christians he might find. In effect, he said to the council, "I'm the most fervent anti-Christian in Judea. You just give me the authority, and I'll take care of these people."

Saul was a proud, impatient man. But in the twinkling of an eye, this hyper-orthodox religious leader was transformed into an apostle of Christ. All these changes took place when Saul came face-to-face with Jesus. Before that moment, he had few, if any, self-doubts. Had you asked him, "Are you willing to be remembered as the man you are right now?" he would have replied, "Certainly! I'm the leading proponent of the orthodox Jewish faith. I'm doing God a big favor by doing away with these evil people."

We too are radically changed when we come face-to-face with Jesus. We might be going our own way, proud of ourselves and feeling self-satisfied — but then Jesus turns our world upside down. God has made an enormous investment in us, much as he did in Saul (who became Paul, the apostle). After his conversion, Paul immediately "began to preach in the synagogues that Jesus is the Son of God. All those who heard him were astonished and asked, 'Isn't he the man who raised havoc in Jerusalem among those who call on this name? And hasn't he come here to take them as prisoners to the chief priests?'" (Acts 9:20–21).

People noticed an immediate difference in Paul. Does a similar thing happen with us? Do people notice a difference in how *we* live? Do they see Christ alive and at work in *us*?

O Lord, thank you for orchestrating this dramatic event in the life of Saul
and for making it into a major turning point in the history of the Chris-
tian church. While my conversion was not nearly so dramatic, use me
to reshape my own world for your glory, just as you did with Paul; and
make me into a pliable, humble servant. I pray in Jesus' name. Amen. ❧

A Permanent Condition

In his great mercy [God] has given us new birth into a living hope
through the resurrection of Jesus Christ from the dead, and into an
inheritance that can never perish, spoil or fade.
1 PETER 1:3 – 4

At age eleven I walked down the aisle at a revival and gave my hand to the pastor. At that moment, I accepted Christ as Savior, and I was baptized a few nights later.

I have to admit, however, that I have not always recognized this as the second birth of Jimmy Carter — that at that moment I became a different person, a new entity in the eyes of God, an individual set aside to live for God in all my words and actions.

God offers all Christians a completely new life, different from what we had before we placed our faith in Jesus Christ. God gives us a "living hope" and an unchanging, permanent, never-ending "inheritance." There's nothing temporary about this new alignment we accept as Christians! It won't go away, no matter how mistaken, sinful, or forgetful we might be about our obligation to Christ. That new hope and inheritance within us is something like a plant, always growing, though it may suffer setbacks along the way and at times may even fade. We never lose it; God implants it permanently in our hearts, minds, and souls.

Therefore we should never think, *I'm not much different now than I used to be*, or *I'm nobody special; I have no special opportunities as a Christian*. In the eyes of God, we are *all* special, and one day we will all see the truth.

Peter reminds us of the profound nature of our faith, which establishes an everlasting relationship between God and us. The Holy Spirit dwells in our hearts and never moves out — and nothing can be any more permanent than that.

O God, give me a full appreciation for all you gave me when I placed my faith in your Son, Jesus Christ. Open my eyes to see the countless changes you are offering to make in my life, and give me the courage and strength I need to make whatever additional changes may be required in order to emulate more closely the perfect example of my Lord. I pray these things in Jesus' name. Amen.

A New Name, a New Man

The man asked him, "What is your name?" "Jacob," he answered. Then the
man said, "Your name will no longer be Jacob, but Israel, because you have
struggled with God and with humans and have overcome."
GENESIS 32:27 – 28

After a lifetime of deception and trickery, Jacob made his way back to Canaan, despite deep fear about what his brother, Esau, might do to him. Years earlier, Jacob had tricked Esau out of his birthright and his blessing.

Just before meeting Esau, Jacob had a life-changing encounter with God. The Lord (or an angel in human form) wrestled with Jacob. As dawn approached, this mysterious "man" wanted to call it quits, but Jacob refused. The man then touched Jacob's hip and threw it out of joint, leaving Jacob with a lifetime limp. "I will not turn you loose until you bless me," Jacob had said. He finally got a blessing—painfully.

At that moment, Jacob became a new person. God changed his name from Jacob ("supplanter" or "deceiver") to Israel ("he perseveres with God"). God told Jacob he would become the father of a great nation; and in fact, the twelve sons of Jacob sired the twelve tribes of Israel. God gave Jacob a new life—the same thing he offers us. Through faith in Christ, we can have our sins forgiven and can embark on a new life, filled with peace and joy.

Jacob never did become perfect, and none of us will either. Yet we *will* find liberation. As we give our lives increasingly to Christ, our lives will expand in amazing ways.

Jacob, this very strange Old Testament man, made many mistakes. He was a liar, a cheater, and a thief—and yet God used him to establish the nation of Israel, through which came our Savior, Jesus Christ. What might God be able to do with you?

Lord, I come from an ordinary place and background, with hopes and
dreams and aspirations and concerns and tears and disappointments
unknown to others but intimately felt by me. Stretch my mind to embrace
the future offered to me by my King, Jesus Christ, and open my heart to a
new and constantly expanding life as I walk side by side with my Savior.
In his name I pray. Amen. ❧

62

The Ultimate Question

*Now faith is confidence in what we hope for and assurance about
what we do not see.*
HEBREWS 11:1

A group of liberal academics calling themselves "the Jesus Seminar" meets annually to discuss the "search for the historical Jesus." Their stated purpose is to discover the "real" Jesus. But apparently these scholars consider *any* biblical statement about Jesus false if they can't prove it through their own iconoclastic methods of inquiry. These "scholars" have voted that only *one sentence* in Mark's entire Gospel, and just a few phrases in the Sermon on the Mount, are authentic, and they urge us to disregard completely the Gospel of John.

These professionals do not believe in the resurrection of Christ and have imagined all kinds of alternative explanations. Some claim that the apostles had visions of a risen Christ after his death, perhaps out of guilt over abandoning Jesus. One theorizes that Jesus' corpse was thrown into a common grave and eaten by wild dogs. Another claims that Jesus, still alive, was buried by mistake in a cave by the Dead Sea, was revived with a purgative, married Mary Magdalene, had three children, divorced, remarried, and finally died in Rome.

The Jesus Seminar theories sound ridiculous, but at times we too may have experiences that seem to contradict our basic Christian beliefs. When this happens to me, I prefer to rely on my personal faith, confident that further discoveries will never disprove what I believe or change what makes Jesus' impact on my life so profound.

The ultimate questions are these: If there is no basis for our faith, as the Jesus Seminar suggests, then how do we account for the presence of Jesus Christ in hundreds of millions of lives across the globe? How could Jesus still be alive to me? How could so many hearts be touched and minds stimulated by Jesus to seek ultimate truths about life and the world around us?

*O Lord, thank you for the impact of your grace in my life and for sending
the Holy Spirit into my heart to bring the living Christ into each day of
my existence. When doubts trouble me, help me remember all the times
you have shown yourself to be strong, real, and active in my life. Thank
you for the truth of the resurrection. I pray in Jesus' name. Amen.* ❧

Becoming Whole

And he said unto him, Arise, go thy way;
thy faith hath made thee whole.
LUKE 17:19 (KJV)

All of us tend to divide our lives into fragments. If we look back on last week, for example, we probably have compartmentalized our existence, separating some pieces from others. As a result, we might be a different person when we're at work than we are at home. We may act differently with a stranger than we do with someone familiar. We may have a different attitude toward someone who depends on us than toward someone on whom we depend. And many of us seem to be different persons while at church than we are the rest of the week. We all tend to fragment our lives, at least to some degree.

While this is not necessarily a bad thing—I'm guessing that some compartmentalization is necessary to function effectively in this world—some of us may be excessively "two-faced." If we act artificially to benefit ourselves as circumstances change, this can harm us, our loved ones, and others.

It is significant that Christ said to the Samaritan leper, "Thy faith hath made thee whole" (KJV). In effect, he was saying, "Your faith has brought together the various jumbled pieces of your life." Genuine faith has an integrating and healing effect on the human personality.

It's not possible for us in our earthly existence to be perfect, of course, to combine all the facets of who we are in order to live a wholly consistent life. But when we submit ourselves to the almighty power of God, in a spirit of humility and love and gratitude, the Lord can make us whole. He can fill us with humility and peace as we grow in our relationship with Jesus Christ, the source of all power and wisdom.

That is true integration and true health.

O God, help me look at my life without fear or trepidation, but with confidence that you will take the pieces of my life and integrate them into a single, healthy whole. Make me a blessing not only to my friends and loved ones, but also to others who might need my help. Through me, may they know of your saving grace. I ask this in Jesus' name. Amen. ❧

64

It's Not Up to Us

The person without the Spirit does not accept the things that come from the Spirit of God but considers them foolishness, and cannot understand them because they are discerned only through the Spirit.
I CORINTHIANS 2:14

I once participated in an inner-city outreach to mostly Spanish-speaking people from Puerto Rico. My partner was Eloy Cruz, a Cuban Baptist missionary who had a tiny church in Brooklyn. I could speak enough Spanish to read the Bible, but unfortunately, I had learned my Spanish in the Navy, and it was not exactly the vocabulary I needed on this trip. So I read the Bible, and Eloy gave a message of salvation.

On that trip I saw Christianity in its purest, most beautiful form. I felt the presence of the Holy Spirit in a way that totally exceeded anything I'd ever known. It was an earth-shaking experience for me.

These dear people were living in old, dilapidated, abandoned high-rises. I'll never forget one encounter. We knocked on a shabby door and a woman answered. We said, "We're Christians who have come to talk to you for a few minutes about Jesus." We could see her husband in the background, slipping a bottle of beer under a sofa cushion. Eloy began to tell this mother, five children, and husband the story of how Jesus raised Lazarus from the dead (John 11). When he came to the end of the story and spoke Jesus' words, "Lazarus, come forth," the whole family broke into applause and cheers. They could envision the love of Jesus Christ for this devastated family. It was an unforgettable experience for me and reminded me forcefully that it's the Holy Spirit who uses us to bring change to human hearts. It's not up to us.

It's not easy for us to give the Holy Spirit total responsibility for the fulfillment of our ambitions or successes. But great things can happen when we humble ourselves enough to let God decide what comes after we do our best.

Dear Lord, what a relief it is to remember that I am not ultimately responsible for whether people accept Jesus as Savior. Rather, you make it clear that my responsibility is to speak the message as boldly and plainly as I can, and then your Holy Spirit assumes responsibility. In Jesus' name I pray. Amen. ❧

A Statue of Responsibility

"Now I will tell you what I am going to do to my vineyard: I will take away its hedge, and it will be destroyed."
ISAIAH 5:5

When I was a boy, I loved listening to the chain gangs that often worked on the road and railroad tracks in front of my house. They had learned to make rhythmic music that extolled freedom even while enduring punishment for their crimes. Their songs sounded beautiful to me.

The prophet Isaiah once sang a very different kind of song to the people of Judah. His lyrics described a vineyard, prepared and nurtured with care. The owner had selected the best land and given it proper cultivation, but it produced only bad grapes, so the owner decided to destroy his vineyard.

Isaiah used this disturbing song to communicate God's condemnation of the people of Judah, because while they accepted all of God's benefits — special protection from enemies and a comfortable life — they repaid the Lord with injustice and idolatry. They had abandoned God, and Isaiah's song brought God's threat home to them.

What do *we* do with our gifts from God? We have been reconciled with God through Jesus Christ, but the Lord expects us to obey heavenly laws and to follow Christ's example. If we ignore this responsibility, we also will be disciplined, as the New Testament assures us: "My son, do not make light of the Lord's discipline, and do not lose heart when he rebukes you, because the Lord disciplines the ones he loves" (Hebrews 12:5–6).

Some have suggested that in addition to having the Statue of Liberty, Americans should also have a Statue of Responsibility. While we gladly accept freedom, security, and other blessings, too often we avoid any responsibility that might interfere with pursuing the "good life." As Christians, we must perform our duties and accept God's discipline out of love and in good spirits.

God, I thank you for the message of Isaiah's song. Help me analyze how I respond to the bountiful gifts you give me. I praise you for giving me your only Son, Jesus Christ, to be my Savior, and I ask you to help me follow as closely as possible his perfect example. In his name I pray. Amen.

An Honest Question

"How will this be," Mary asked the angel,
"since I am a virgin?"
LUKE 1:34

As an elderly priest named Zechariah ministered in the temple, the angel Gabriel appeared to him and told him that he and his wife, Elizabeth, would have a child together. Zechariah responded with incredulity, asking, "How can I be sure of this, since both of us are very old?" Gabriel answered by striking him dumb.

A few months later, Gabriel visited a young girl named Mary and told her that she would bear a son named Jesus. As the Son of God, her newborn child would be the long-promised Messiah. Mary responded with bewilderment, because she was a virgin.

Now, here is a puzzle. Mary appeared to respond just as Zechariah did; so why did Gabriel strike Zechariah dumb for his question but answer Mary kindly with a full but startling explanation?

I think part of the answer is that Mary was young and innocent, and her question natural and inevitable. Also, Elizabeth and Zechariah knew from Scripture that Abraham had reached a hundred years of age, and Sarah ninety, when Sarah gave birth to Isaac. The priest should have understood God's miraculous power that let old people have babies long after their normal time of childbearing.

Mary, on the other hand, was no Bible scholar. And for a virgin to have a baby! That was unprecedented. And so Mary's question was not considered cynical, like Zechariah's, but honest (if puzzled).

God takes into account not only our actions but the state of our hearts and the circumstances of our lives. Gabriel blessed the young and innocent Mary and helped relieve her honest confusion about how she could bear a child as a virgin. God deals with all people on their own terms.

Jesus also said, "Of those who have much, much will be required" (Luke 12:48). We Christians are expected to measure up to a very high standard of ethical standards and conduct. If Gabriel were to visit you tonight with surprising news, how do you think you would react?

O Lord, help me realize that because I have received the special blessing
of salvation, based on your love and grace and my faith in Jesus Christ,
great responsibilities are mine. Let me, therefore, faithfully serve your
Son, the Prince of Peace, in whose name I pray. Amen. ❧

No Condemnation

*Therefore, there is now no condemnation for those
who are in Christ Jesus.*
ROMANS 8:1

This is one of my favorite Bible verses, because to this point in his letter, Paul has been emphasizing torture, anguish, alienation, and a total absence of joy and hope. And now, suddenly, he switches to complete acceptance and reconciliation. What a transformation!

Christ lived among us. He understood sin yet did not commit it. He loved those around him as well as loving those of us who would come later. He took on himself the penalty of sin for all who believe. Therefore, there is no condemnation for those who live in Christ.

No matter how sinful we might be, by God's grace and through our faith we can have a full life. God does not overlook our sins, but fully recognizes them and places punishment on his willing Son.

Romans 8:1 doesn't mean only that God no longer condemns those who believe; it also implies that "in Christ Jesus" we will not condemn others. If we love Christ, who cleansed us, then we will be careful not to drift into habits of sin. We must never forget that our sinfulness fell on the shoulders of Christ, whom we love.

Imagine if every time I committed a sin, my daughter, Amy, had to take the punishment for it. And suppose I had to witness her punishment. Do you think I would be more careful not to sin? If I had to come home every night and go in my little girl's room and watch her suffer the punishment for all the "little white lies" I told that day, you can be sure I would be very careful to be completely truthful!

Do we love Christ any less than we love our own children?

It lies almost beyond our comprehension that there is now no condemnation for those who are in Christ Jesus. Fabulous! But that very recognition ought to inspire us to live for the one who died for us.

O Lord, I ask that you drive deep into my heart the conviction that Jesus died to reconcile me with you and that I can rely on the spiritual resources you make available to me. Help me grasp what "no condemnation" means, and empower me to help others grasp for themselves the wonder of your grace. In Jesus' name I pray. Amen. ❧

Called by God

*"Before I formed you in the womb I knew you, before you were born
I set you apart; I appointed you as a prophet to the nations."*
JEREMIAH 1:5

Some time ago *USA Today* published one of the most interesting nationwide poll results I've ever seen. "If you could come face-to-face with God," people were questioned, "what would you ask?"

Six percent replied, "How long will I live?" Seven percent answered, "Is there intelligent life elsewhere?" Sixteen percent said they would ask why bad things happened. Nineteen percent would ask, "Is there life after death?" But the largest group, 34 percent, asked, "What is my purpose in life?"

People wanted to know, "Why was I created? What should I do with my life?"

The Lord's words to the prophet Jeremiah intimidated the young man, and he objected, "But I'm only a boy!" God answered that he would be with him wherever he went.

Several centuries later, before Jesus ascended into heaven, the Lord gave his followers the Great Commission, in which he promised: "I am with you always, to the very end of the age" (Matthew 28:20).

Just as God had told Jeremiah, "I knew you in the womb, and even then I had a purpose for you," so God knew *us* in the womb and has a unique purpose for *us*. Our purpose is to glorify God by emulating the life of Christ and by carrying out the Great Commission. We are to tell other people, "This is what Jesus Christ, the Son of God, means to me."

*O Lord, empower me to exhibit through my actions, words, and thoughts
the message that "this is what Christ would do." I confess that too often
I want to live in a world of my own making, but you call me to break
through barriers with confidence as I rest on your promise that you will
be with me. In Jesus' name I pray. Amen.* ❧

Confidence in Faith

*"God has helped me to this very day; so I stand here and testify to
small and great alike. I am saying nothing beyond what the prophets
and Moses said would happen."*
ACTS 26:22

When Paul faced trial in Caesarea, he sat under a possible sentence of death, yet he felt compelled to witness about Christ. He had confidence that he spoke the will of God.

By this point, Paul had been preaching for almost twelve years, no doubt often repeating the same story. Perhaps he had almost memorized the words as he described to people all over Greece and Turkey and elsewhere his remarkable experience with Christ on the road to Damascus. And now he proclaimed the same message to powerful government leaders.

Never again would Paul have a free day in his life. He went from Caesarea through a circuitous route around the Mediterranean Sea to Rome, where as a Roman citizen he stood trial in the capital. He spent the rest of his days in the heart of the empire. Yet none of that worried him. His only concern was to proclaim the gospel of Christ's resurrection to whoever would listen.

Once Paul made a commitment to Christ and became more knowledgeable about him, the apostle knew he had found his life's calling. He dedicated his whole life to proclaiming the good news of Jesus' death and resurrection. Whatever disappointments or frustrations or suffering would come, he never seriously questioned his calling.

Do you have a similar confidence? Despite serious tests and challenges, the apostle Paul remained convinced about the purpose of his life. He had received Jesus Christ as Savior, and he had total confidence that his Lord would cause his mission to succeed. His confidence lay in his Lord, not in himself. Do you have the same confidence in your Savior to help you succeed so long as you remain loyal to him?

O God, help me to remember the teachings of Christ as explained by Paul and to use them to guide me through my daily life. I pray for some of the boldness of this apostle, who suffered so much for Jesus' sake but who yet counted it all as nothing compared to knowing Christ and being found in him. Give me such a champion's spirit, for I pray in Jesus' name. Amen. ❧

Patience in Love

Love is patient.
1 CORINTHIANS 13:4

While I have a great love for Rosalynn, she would readily note that I lack the patience to go with my love. God's *agape* love, on the other hand, is perfectly patient. It accommodates the incompatibilities between people without straining itself. It expresses affection consistently and in a perfect way.

Patient love transcends the vicissitudes of human life. It doesn't dissipate just because someone does something to hurt us or annoy us. Two married people may really care for each other, but they will differ in both character and personality and will have distinct priorities and views of life. This will inevitably lead to some trying times in their relationship. The same holds true for all of us, whether married or single.

Each of us is deeply individualistic; we see life as it revolves around us. To some degree, we understand only ourselves, so we tend to measure others by how *we* think they *should* be. The apostle Paul insists we should do the opposite and instead try to understand how others think, feel about things, or view the world. We need to love them patiently and not become alienated or annoyed with them because they act or believe differently than we do.

Patient love is, indeed, a difficult goal to reach!

Patient love applies to more than just two people in love, of course. By comparison, lovers have it much easier. The greater challenge is to have a patient love for people for whom we don't care very much, who do not seem very attractive to us, or who might be so different from us in their basic life concepts, habits, and manner of speaking that they aggravate us. How do we reach out to *these* people with a patient love?

The answer is that on our own, we can't. We can do so only with God's help. And thank God that's exactly what he offers.

O God, I admit that patience seems like a great thing when I need others to express it toward me, but it doesn't seem nearly so wonderful when I find myself annoyed by the failure of others to live up to my expectations. Lord, help me be as generous and universal in my patience with others as I desire them to be when I'm the irritating or annoying one. In Jesus' name I pray. Amen. ❧

Throwaways

*"Now then," said Joshua, "throw away the foreign gods that are
among you and yield your hearts to the LORD, the God of Israel."*
JOSHUA 24:23

Joshua reminded his people that loyalty to God included two things: serving God and putting away anything that came between them and service to God. Sadly, although the people did pledge to serve God, they did not put away other gods.

All through the book of Judges and the Prophets, repeatedly we see the same people (and their descendants) profess to serve God, especially when a crisis came along. But after God saved them and they grew more affluent and self-sufficient, they again adopted other gods that they hoped might bring them pleasure or more wealth. These other gods also seemed much easier to manipulate than the living God of Israel, and they liked that.

Although most of us don't worship pagan gods, we do serve other things in God's place. And yet as Christians, we have, in effect, promised to comply with the standards of God Almighty as exemplified in the words and actions of Jesus Christ. This is not an easy promise to keep! Often we don't try to keep it at all; more often we just gradually ignore it. We start to revere our money or our career, or maybe a loved one, in preference to God. We make a multitude of small decisions, day by day, that slowly move us away from God and a life modeled after that of Christ.

Sometimes this happens because we live in a society that doesn't share our morals and commitments, as happened to the ancient Hebrews. As they intermarried with the pagan peoples around them, they succumbed to the strong temptation to worship their pagan gods.

We must be careful to serve God alone and not fall into the trap of serving "other gods" or pursuits that blunt our commitment to Jesus Christ. As in Joshua's day, God calls us to throw away all competitors of the Lord.

*O Lord, throughout all facets of my life, help me retain my faith and my
reverence for you. Remind me that you are my Creator, filled with love,
grace, and forgiveness, and that you sent your perfect Son, Jesus Christ,
to be my Savior. Give me the courage and dedication I need to share this
wonderful message with others. I pray in Jesus' name. Amen.*

Save or Stamp Out?

*"If someone slaps you on one cheek, turn to them the other also. If
someone takes your coat, do not withhold your shirt from them."*
LUKE 6:29

A slightly built truck driver eating a hamburger at a restaurant saw the
members of a motorcycle gang drive up outside. Four men entered and soon
began to harass the truck driver. They took his French fries, dipped them in
ketchup, and smeared them all over his face—and worse. Finally the truck
driver left.

One guy from the motorcycle gang said to the waitress, "He's not much
of a man, is he?"

"No," she replied, "and he's not much of a truck driver, either. He just ran
over four motorcycles."

Most of us enjoy this kind of joke because we automatically put ourselves
on the side of the abused person. Our natural reaction is to want retaliation.

A situation like this existed on a much larger scale in Jesus' day. The
Romans had occupied Palestine, and revolution was in the air. Many wanted
to overthrow Rome violently; one group called the Zealots had committed
themselves to this goal. The Romans considered them terrorists.

If some foreign force occupied the United States and imposed its rule
on us, many of us would be ready to fight for our freedom. As a submarine
officer in the U.S. Navy, I was prepared to defend my nation.

But Jesus tells us to turn the other cheek, which seems contrary to human
nature. What are we to make of it?

Many thought the Messiah would be the leader to overthrow the Romans.
Instead, the Prince of Peace made forgiveness and love preeminent and, for
our sakes, submitted willingly to death on a cross. He could have retaliated
with a massive, overwhelming strike (Matthew 26:53); instead, he forgave
his executioners. Jesus' top priority was peace, not war—reconciliation, not
hatred. And he calls us, as Christians, to follow his example.

*Dear God, equip me to face the challenges of life and respond to them as
Jesus commanded. Give me the strength to love those whom I am more
inclined to consider my enemies. Enable me to act as Jesus would, relying
not on my natural human reactions, but on your Spirit's power. I ask
these things in the name of my gentle Savior. Amen.* ❧

73

A Simple House

This is what the LORD Almighty says: "... Go up into the mountains
and bring down timber and build my house, so that I may take
pleasure in it and be honored."
HAGGAI 1:7 – 8

Jews returning from Babylonian exile planned to build a new temple but quickly faltered. They knew that whatever they built would seem paltry compared to Solomon's temple, now in ruins. The first temple had been constructed out of marble, gold, silver, and cedars imported from Lebanon. It became a source of pride, attracting foreigners to see its wonders.

After the exile, however, God declared that his new house of worship should be built of wood from trees on nearby hills. And the Lord made no mention of mounds of gold or piles of silver; God wanted the Jews to begin immediately to worship together and, thus, to begin their national redemption.

We also build houses of worship. Some are ornate, while others are simple, constructed of wood and Sheetrock. Both provide a sanctuary dedicated to God. While it is nice to honor God and attract people with a beautiful building, the important thing is the spirit of those who worship there.

In fact, God gives us *no* New Testament instructions about building a church facility. Some of the most spiritually alive congregations I've seen worshiped in vacant storefronts or homes of new believers. I've also visited large, ornate churches that lacked a spirit of welcome, harmony, and love.

We tend to emphasize the material side of things: not only buildings, but elaborate furnishings, ceremonies, and fancy choir costumes. Perhaps we extend this even to special requirements for membership; we exclude certain kinds of people who don't measure up to our high "ethical" standards. Unless we are careful, we violate scriptural reminders that *all* people are equal in the eyes of God, and we forget that Jesus reached out to the lowliest and most despised people of his day.

Haggai teaches us that a simple house can honor God just as well as a palace, if our hearts are right.

O God, thank you for the opportunity to gather as your people, to worship
you and learn from your Word. Help me focus on what is important, not
on standards based on pride or self-righteousness. Remind me that the
church is a group of redeemed people, reaching out to neighbors whom I
never should consider unworthy. I pray in Jesus' name. Amen. ❧

Honor and Responsibility

When I consider your heavens, the work of your fingers, the moon and the stars, which you have set in place, what is mankind that you are mindful of them, human beings that you care for them? You have made them a little lower than the angels and crowned them with glory and honor.
PSALM 8:3 − 5

When I look at the awe-inspiring panorama of the heavens, I often wonder why I was created. Why should God care about a tiny, insignificant speck in the vast universe? The psalmist also wondered but knew that human beings have a special status in God's creation.

Each of us has been made "a little lower than the angels." What an incomprehensible compliment! But it's not only a compliment; it's also a responsibility, for our special status equalizes us with other people in the eyes of God. The Lord has exalted not only me or some special group; God has exalted *everyone*. It's the people of Burkina Faso and Niger and Guyana and Haiti. It's people who never learned to read and write or who live on fifty cents a day. *All* human beings have been made a little lower than the angels, and we have a responsibility to treat them accordingly.

Because God has given us dominion over the earth, we also have a responsibility to nurture and protect God's creation. When I was a child, at least once a year we heard a sermon on "stewardship." It reminded people (nearly all of them farmers or timber workers) that they had a responsibility to care for God's creation and to pass it on to their descendants in better shape than when they got it.

Incredibly, God has honored us by making us a little lower than the angels, giving us dominion over all creation. We therefore have a responsibility to treat each other with respect and to care for the earth that God has given us.

O Lord, thank you for this psalm, reminding me that you created the universe and gave me the mental capability to understand certain facts about your creation. I'm grateful that you gave me the exalted capability to share in your honor and glory. And because we're all created equal, just a little lower than the angels, we also have almost unlimited opportunities to serve you. I thank you in Jesus' name. Amen. ❧

An Unnecessary Schism

You, Lord, are forgiving and good, abounding in love
to all who call to you.
PSALM 86:5

In 1968 I joined a group of volunteers to share our faith with area families. On our way to a back-alley address, my partner and I heard a woman's voice shouting the filthiest language I'd heard since my Navy days. We knelt down and prayed, then knocked on the door. She flung it open. It was obvious she ran a brothel.

When we told her why we had come, this madam thought it quite funny but invited us in. She told us her father had abused her as a young girl, and when she told her mama about it, her daddy denied all guilt. Then both parents condemned her for dreaming up such a fantasy, and she left home as soon as possible.

After we explained the plan of salvation, she said she had no alternative but to continue her occupation, but she asked us to return the next day. She let me place a call to her parents, and we left while they were talking.

These kinds of schisms happen. Maybe our parents demand something unsuitable for us, or we expect something of our own children that they can't accept. By refusing to make any accommodation, we drive a wedge between us. Sometimes such a schism can even separate us from God, as with the abused madam.

In my inaugural address as president, I quoted Micah 6:8: "And what does the LORD require of you? To act justly and to love mercy and to walk humbly with your God." If we have failed in this and wonder how a perfect heavenly Father could ever accept us, we should remember Psalm 86:5. God has none of our failings and wants us to maintain loving relationships with others through the power of Jesus Christ, our Savior.

O Lord, I pray that I might remember the gentle admonition of the
prophet Micah regarding what you expect of me — things that all of us
can achieve regardless of talent, ability, physical appearance, or financial
status. Help me remember that no obstacle can ever prevent the easy,
constant, and intimate relationship I desire with you. I ask these things in
Jesus' name. Amen. ❧

A Life Built on Promises

"Fulfill your vows to the Most High, and call on me in the day of
trouble; I will deliver you, and you will honor me."
PSALM 50:14 – 15

Promises shape our existence. We base our lives on them. In effect, we live on the promise that the government will provide us with security, clean water, and crucial services. Our employers depend on our promise to show up for work. As merchants, we make a promise to our customers: "This item I'm selling is what you think it is." Before I became president, I raised the best seed peanuts in Georgia. I promised my customers that my seeds were exactly the variety they thought they were buying and that they had a high likelihood of sprouting, growing, and flourishing.

But the most important promise of all is the one *every* Christian has made to live in a Christlike way. When we place our faith in Christ, we declare, in effect, "I promise that in accepting Jesus as my Savior, I will use Christ's works and actions to guide my life. I'll try to pattern my own existence after the example he set. I will endeavor to keep God's commandments, as Jesus did."

It's a serious thing to make a promise—or to break one. When we cheat in a marriage or decide not to show up for work, we let people down. But when we keep our promises, our friends and acquaintances say, "That is a person of his word." It's one of the most admirable things we can say about someone.

God *always* keeps his promises, and these promises should shape our lives. Because God has promised to remain with us always, we have the resources to honor and keep biblical commandments, as explained by Christ. What a powerful assurance we have, something unshakable we can depend on throughout our lives!

> *Lord, thank you for reminding me about the importance of promises.*
> *Help me honor my promises, especially the central one I made when I*
> *accepted your offer of salvation through faith in Jesus Christ. Give me the*
> *strength I need to keep my promise to serve you and to glorify you with*
> *my life, and so allow me to bless those around me. Help others see your*
> *faithfulness through my glad obedience. I pray in Jesus' name. Amen.* ❧

Don't Get Screened Out

Love never fails. But where there are prophecies, they will cease;
where there are tongues, they will be stilled; where there is
knowledge, it will pass away.
I CORINTHIANS 13:8 – 9

What would you name as the most important Christian quality? Faith? Hope? Kindness? Generosity? Paul picks none of them. He says it's love. Why?

Imagine you had died and were in the presence of Christ. Would you still need hope then? No. The thing you'd hoped for stands right before you. Would you still need faith? No. In the presence of Christ, you will see your Lord and all your expectations will be fulfilled. While in this life you do need faith, hope, knowledge, and sound judgment, without love, they become all meaningless.

My good friend John Moores, owner of the San Diego Padres baseball team, once sent me a great story. It recounts how a man and his dog were walking along a hot paved road when suddenly the man realized that he was dead and that the dog beside him had been dead for several years.

The pair came to a tall arch glowing in the sunlight, with a gate that resembled mother-of-pearl. They saw a man at a desk and a sparkly sign that read "Heaven." The traveler requested to come in for some water for his dog, but the man said they didn't accept pets. So the traveler and his dog walked on.

Eventually they came to a narrow dirt road leading to a farm gate and saw a man leaning against a tree. When the traveler asked for some water, the man gave both him and the dog a cool drink. The traveler learned that *this* place was heaven, and the first place was hell. "Doesn't it make you angry that they use your name like that?" he asked.

"Nope," said the man, "we're just happy that they screen out the folks who would leave their best friends behind."

O Lord, thank you for this reminder about the preeminence of love. Help me explore more deeply and in all ways how I can demonstrate Christian love in my daily life. May the lives of others be enhanced as I explore the boundaries of love. I pray this in the name of my Savior, Jesus Christ. Amen. ❧

An Exemplary Life

*For we know, brothers and sisters loved by God, that he has chosen
you, because our gospel came to you not simply with words but also
with power, with the Holy Spirit and deep conviction.*
1 THESSALONIANS 1:4 – 5

While in Thessalonica, Paul didn't win converts just through his speaking prowess; men and women placed their faith in Christ as the Holy Spirit worked within their hearts and minds. The presence of God led them to faith and strengthened them in perseverance and self-confidence.

Almost immediately, these young believers were persecuted for their belief. They didn't know what would happen and couldn't be sure what the future held. They felt isolated, weak, and alone. But Paul says that their faith emboldened them enough and the presence of Christ in their hearts so strengthened them that even though they may have felt alone, and despite their fears or anxieties, they still acted in a way that pleased God.

As we go through life, with all its temptations, trials, threats, and disappointments, we must remember that the Holy Spirit is with us, and that with God's aid, there is no limit to what we can accomplish or endure. As we persevere in a Christlike way through challenges and sorrows, we become examples to other believers and witnesses to those who don't yet know Jesus.

Because of their faith, the ancient Thessalonians felt inspired to do good works, following the model of Christ—and everyone in the region noticed.

Let us discipline ourselves to do the same. We have been set free from our sins by the sacrifice of Jesus Christ. Now, by the power of the Holy Spirit, let us endeavor to live in a way that pleases God, to act as Christ acted during his ministry on earth, so that by our example we can encourage fellow believers and draw others to a saving faith in Jesus.

O Lord, I'm thankful for Paul and for his clear teaching that our relationship with God is based completely upon faith in Jesus Christ. Help me follow the example of Christ, and give me the strength to reshape my life in his image. Enable me to demonstrate to my family and community what it means to be a "little Christ." I ask this in the name of my Savior. Amen.

A Chance to Renew

*"Come, all you who are thirsty, come to the waters; and you who
have no money, come, buy and eat! Come, buy wine and milk
without money and without cost."*
ISAIAH 55:1

This seems like a very mysterious statement to make to Jewish captives in Babylon. What is Isaiah saying?

He is telling these people, "Even though your sin resulted in your exile, the Lord is not through with you yet. Come and have a good life, whether you're rich or poor. You can have a productive life by turning your back on your rebellion and choosing to follow and obey the Lord."

The ancient Hebrews believed themselves to be the chosen people of God because of the Lord's covenant with Abraham (followed by other covenants, as with Moses and David). They believed that these covenants meant they would ultimately triumph.

But sometimes they forgot that these covenants came with provisos. "I will be loyal to you and will protect you," said the Lord, "*if* you remain loyal to me." Time after time, however, the Hebrew people betrayed God, violated the covenants, worshiped idols, and abandoned biblical principles of justice, truth, and compassion. In response, God gave them over to their enemies, just as promised.

Through these words of Isaiah, God was saying to his disobedient people, in effect, "I'm offering you a chance to renew your covenantal relationship with me. But you must choose to renew it. You must choose life and not death."

We too must make a foundational choice that will shape our entire life. Will we serve the Lord? Regardless of what we have done in the past, will we now cast our lot with Christ? If so, we can enjoy a life of happiness, joy, and fulfillment.

O Lord, you gave your ancient Hebrew people a chance to choose whether they would honor their covenantal relationship with you. Now you give me the same choice to cast my lot with you. I pray that as I choose you first, that choice will shape all the other decisions of my life, for your glory and the benefit of others. In Jesus' name I pray. Amen.

80

Easy to Fall Away

Moses went back and summoned the elders of the people and set before them all the words the LORD had commanded him to speak. The people all responded together, "We will do everything the LORD has said."
EXODUS 19:7 – 8

Rosalynn and I first visited Israel in 1973. We got up early every morning to wander though Jerusalem, before everyone else woke up, just to see how it might have been when Jesus walked those streets.

We also visited a kibbutz. One Sabbath we got up early, went to the synagogue, said a prayer, and waited for other worshipers to arrive. Although about 150 people lived there, only two came to the synagogue. We asked our young guide, "Aren't you worried about the Jews not worshiping God in this place?"

"Oh, it's not important," he replied.

Later, when I met Prime Minister Golda Meier, I said, "I'm concerned about the future of Israel because I've studied the Bible, and it seems to me that every time the Hebrews turn away from God, they get punished."

She also replied, "Oh, it's not important. We have some political factions that are very religious; they take care of our worshiping for us." Later these more religious political believers became top leaders.

When Moses read aloud the Ten Commandments, the Israelites eagerly responded, "We accept everything God has said! We will observe it for the rest of our lives!" But of course, they didn't.

How often do we follow their example? During an emotional moment, we say, "I accept Jesus Christ with all my heart and will follow his example for the rest of my life." But that deep commitment sometimes lasts only days or a few minutes. Then we revert to a secular life — just like the Hebrews in the wilderness with Moses.

It's human nature to fall away, so we must take special care to maintain our wholehearted commitment to Christ.

O God, I recognize my own tendency to abandon my deep commitment to you. I am prone to let pressures of everyday life seduce me into a secular lifestyle. Help me take time each day to renew my commitment to you and to Jesus. Let me follow his example as I come into contact with others. In his name I pray. Amen.

A Second Chance

*"Simon, Simon, Satan has asked to sift you as wheat. But I have
prayed for you, Simon, that your faith may not fail. And when you
have turned back, strengthen your brothers."*
LUKE 22:31

In the last week of his life on earth, Jesus set his face toward the cross. Yet his disciples, as usual, misunderstood his intentions. He spoke plainly about his coming arrest, flogging, crucifixion, and resurrection, but his followers debated among themselves what he might mean by "rising from the dead." Peter, especially, did not accept the idea that Jesus would die on a Roman cross, and in his typical bragging and excessive fashion, he declared, "Lord, I'm ready to go with you to prison and to death!"

Clearly, Peter was still thinking about an earthly kingdom. If there were going to be a glorious battle between the forces of evil and good, he felt fully prepared to give his life for Christ. I think he was being both honest and sincere. But in fact, Peter would betray Jesus before that day had ended.

It's easy for us to look down on Peter for his betrayal. Yet most of us are inclined, like Peter, to say, "I will always be staunchly loyal to my Savior, Jesus Christ." And then the daily challenges of life and temptations of the world lead us to make poor choices. We abandon a pure and dedicated relationship with Jesus Christ—and so we fail, as Peter did.

The good news is that our failure doesn't have to be fatal. Peter came back to Christ and helped to found the early church.

Just as Jesus prayed for Peter that he wouldn't lose his faith, so he prays for us that our faith will remain steadfast and strong. Yes, we will fail just as Peter did. But in Christ we all have a second chance.

*O Lord, thank you for recording Peter's adventures and for showing
me that he was a simple human being just like me. He failed as I do,
and yet in your grace you continued to use him to bring about your
kingdom's purposes. Give me the courage to align myself permanently and
unshakably to the Holy Spirit's power, through faith in my Savior, Jesus
Christ, in whose name I pray. Amen.* 🌿

Failure and Fulfillment

But he replied, "Lord, I am ready to go with you to prison and to death." Jesus answered, "I tell you, Peter, before the rooster crows today, you will deny three times that you know me."
LUKE 22:33 – 34

The failures of the apostle Peter make him a very interesting man. The Lord never said to him, "You are my super-disciple, and the others will report to you." Yet Christ recognized something in Peter that would one day make him the leader among a group of equals.

Many people have fears and doubts but never express them. They remain timid and fearful of failure, and so they never try anything extraordinary. So they avoid failure by failing to do much of anything.

Peter failed because he tried *a lot*. He wasn't timid. He bragged that he would never forsake Christ, in effect saying, "I'm so strong in my love for you, Jesus, that I don't need God to help me withstand temptation." Despite his confidence, of course, Peter failed. *Spectacularly*. Three times he denied publicly that he even knew Jesus. He failed in a huge way; and yet, because he knew that Christ loved him, ultimately Peter made a decision to become a great witness, a great disciple, and a great example for us.

It can be the same with us. We have the ultimate choice to follow Christ or not, to stand with Christ or not, to try to resist temptation on our own or to recognize our human fallibility and turn to God for help. If we strive for greatness and fail, we know that God will forgive us, just as he did Peter.

Peter devoted the rest of his life to serving Christ, and he did it so effectively that today, almost two thousand years later, his life still inspires and reassures us. Peter teaches us that through Christ we will succeed. But without Christ, even our "great boasts" amount to nothing.

Thank you, God, for the example of Peter, a strong man who had many weaknesses. Help me, Lord, to try new things for you, even if I risk failure. When I fall, help me get up and keep moving toward the goal of becoming more like Christ. In Jesus' name I pray. Amen. ❧

The Door Is Always Open

*"The son said to him, 'Father, I have sinned against heaven and
against you. I am no longer worthy to be called your son.'"*
LUKE 15:21

Nothing we do can alienate us permanently from God. No matter how despicable our actions, no matter how we deliberately withdraw ourselves from a relationship with God, no matter how badly we treat others—none of those things can ultimately separate us from God. Through the sacrifice of his Son, Jesus Christ, God is always willing to embrace us, if only we will return.

Jesus vividly demonstrated this truth in his parable about a father who eagerly embraced his prodigal son. This dad welcomed his son in a spirit of love and forgiveness, not based on what the son might do to be reconciled, but based on the father's grace.

Through faith in Christ, we have this same relationship with God. We may try to separate ourselves from the prodigal by saying, "I haven't demanded from my father that he give me my estate! I haven't gone off and eaten with hogs!" But these are merely details. All of us tend to lust after material things, elevate ourselves over others, endanger ties of friendship or loyalty to "get ahead," and forget the basic premises of Christian morality on which we have pledged to base our lives.

God has given us the freedom to do so, just as the father in the parable gave his youngest son his freedom. God allows us to decide how to use the inheritance given to us. Unfortunately, we often use it badly. We fail to measure up to the perfect standards set for us by our Savior, Jesus Christ. And yet, despite it all, nothing we do can alienate us permanently from God, who asks only that we return. The door is always open.

Thank you, Lord, for giving me some of your most profound messages through simple stories, not wrapped up in abstract concepts hard for me to understand. I can envision myself as the young man coming home in disgrace to his father, who receives him with open arms and with total forgiveness. Renew my faith in Christ, and elevate my own commitment to act as a genuine Christian. I ask these things in the name of my Savior. Amen. ❧

84

Return to the Lord

*"Even now," declares the LORD, "return to me with all your heart, with
fasting and weeping and mourning." Rend your heart and not your garments.
Return to the LORD your God, for he is gracious and compassionate, slow to
anger and abounding in love, and he relents from sending calamity. Who
knows? He may turn and relent and leave behind a blessing.*
JOEL 2:12 – 14

After the prophet Joel finished prophesying dire warnings of doom and condemnation to God's people, he stopped and declared that, despite all the evil
the people committed, despite their long history of turning away from God,
even now — if they repented — God might send them blessing rather than
judgment. Remarkable!

In ancient days, people often tore their clothes and put ashes on their
heads as a sign of grief and repentance. But God says, "Don't merely rend
your clothes; rend your hearts." In other words, "It's not the outward show
that interests me, but the inward change."

And why would Joel say nobody knew whether God would relent, that
such a welcome possibility was still up in the air? Why didn't Joel know if
the Lord would show mercy? Because he didn't know how the people would
respond. They had to make a choice.

If we reject God's mandates, then we'll receive God's discipline; Christ
repeatedly warned us about this. But if we comply with God's will by drawing
on the power of God's Spirit — if we follow the principles of our faith and
emulate Christ in our lives — then we will receive God's blessing, forgiveness,
mercy, love, compassion, and intimacy through Christ.

Joel insists that God is not a stern, condemnatory judge who delights in
keeping track of all the bad things we do. Rather, he says, "Remember two
things: God is holy and will send judgment if you depart from his ways; but
God is gracious and forgiving and has no desire to punish." God *much* prefers
reconciliation over judgment!

*O Lord, help me apply the words of the ancient prophet to my own
experience, because you say that regardless of my circumstances, the Holy
Spirit can partner with me to expand and fulfill my life. Help me make
the wise choice to walk with you daily, rather than follow the crowd and
go my own selfish way. Thank you for your grace and forgiveness! I pray in
the name of my Savior. Amen.* ❧

85

The Big Picture

"For my eyes have seen your salvation ... a light for revelation to the
Gentiles, and the glory of your people Israel."
LUKE 2:30

An old man named Simeon, a righteous and devout believer, had lived in Jerusalem for many years. He had waited even longer for the redemption of Israel—the arrival of the Messiah. Like the pious remnant of Jews who survived all previous national captivities, Simeon kept alive the hope that God would send a Savior, according to the covenant.

The Holy Spirit revealed to Simeon that he would see the Messiah before he died. When Jesus' parents brought their infant son to Jerusalem for the purification ritual, Simeon met them at the temple, took Jesus in his arms, and praised God. Jesus' humble mother and father had heard from angels what their precious son would do, but Simeon's words still amazed and disturbed them. For in addition to blessing them, Simeon said, "This child is destined to cause the falling and rising of many in Israel, and to be a sign that will be spoken against, so that the thoughts of many hearts will be revealed. And a sword will pierce your own soul too" (Luke 2:34–35). Simeon strongly hinted that though they had an important part to play in human history, some future event would bring them sorrow and pain as well as triumph and joy.

In each generation since, atrocities and tragedies have defied explanation. Some of them plague us with a profound sense of hopelessness. But whenever we get beaten down by circumstances and wonder how things can be so bad, let's remember the Big Picture. When Simeon praised God, he said, "For my eyes have seen your salvation." God has made possible, through Christ, the redemption of all humankind—and one day the Lord will turn all mourning into joy and laughter. Until then, we wait in confident hope.

Dear God, I praise you for changing world history with the birth of
the baby Jesus, who fulfilled your promise of a Messiah, a descendant of
David who would rule forever. Help me mimic the confidence and joy of
Simeon and the faith and love of Joseph and Mary. I ask these things in
the name of Christ my Savior. Amen. ❧

86

A New Life

As it is with the good, so with the sinful; as it is with those who take
oaths, so with those who are afraid to take them. This is the evil in
everything that happens under the sun: The same destiny overtakes all.
ECCLESIASTES 9:2 – 3

The author of Ecclesiastes thought that whether someone lived a good or bad life, made wise or ignorant decisions, really made no difference: at heart, everyone was evil and so suffered the same fate. He saw being alive as the one good thing: "Anyone who is among the living has hope — even a live dog is better off than a dead lion! For the living know that they will die, but the dead know nothing; they have no further reward, and even their name is forgotten" (Ecclesiastes 9:4 – 5).

Not exactly a positive thinker, was he? But we should recognize that before the time of Christ, the Hebrews did not have a fully developed belief in the afterlife. For them, life on earth was the main event. They mentioned Sheol, a shadowy place of the dead, but said little about it. I'll paraphrase a bumper sticker I've seen that sums up this perspective: "Life's bad, and then you die."

As Christians, however, we know that Jesus Christ transformed the relationships among human beings, God Almighty, and eternity. God loves us so much that he sent his only Son to take the punishment for our sins, so that if we put our faith in him, we are totally forgiven. And that's just the beginning! When Jesus rose from the grave and appeared to many individuals and groups, he proved that this life is not the end. If we want a new life, we can have it.

"I am the resurrection and the life," Jesus said. "The one who believes in me will live, even though they die; and whoever lives by believing in me will never die" (John 11:25 – 26). That's life — and afterlife — worth having.

O Lord, sometimes I find it hard to face unpleasantness and the prospect
of death. Yet all of us will endure unpleasantness, and all of us will die.
May the truth of the resurrection seep so deeply into my heart that it
transforms every day of my life. As I consider what lies ahead — eternity
with you — let me live boldly and courageously for you. In Jesus' name I
pray. Amen.

Beyond the Wonder of Life

*Jesus said to her, "I am the resurrection and the life. The one who
believes in me will live, even though they die."*
JOHN 11:25

Sometimes on my farm I walk to the top of a hill late in the afternoon. I see
the sun setting behind beautiful clouds, with green trees in the foreground
and a pasture next to me. And at times I wonder how many more years I will
see all of this.

That's not necessarily a morbid or unpleasant thought! Yet one of the most
difficult issues that human beings have to face is death. It's a subject we often
don't like to ponder, particularly when we get to be senior citizens (like me).
Too often thoughts of death inspire an element of dread, sorrow, uncertainty,
or unpredictability. And yet death is inevitable; every one of us is moving
toward it in an unstoppable, unavoidable way.

Christ teaches us that we can look upon death, this very troubling inevitability, with hope and expectation.

After the death of Lazarus, Jesus said to Martha, "I am the resurrection
and the life. The one who believes in me will live, even though they die; and
whoever lives by believing in me will never die." Then he asked: "Do you
believe this?"

All our concerns about the inevitable can be eased by faith in Jesus Christ.
I don't mean that if you are ill or lose a loved one, it's not serious. But Christ
urges us to put these things into perspective.

Lazarus might have been fifty when he died the first time, and just a few
years older when he died again. His age is not the point. The point is, we have
two choices. One is a life of doubt and fear built on the shaky foundation of
human emotions. The other is the solid rock of faith in Jesus Christ. Which
will we choose?

*O Lord, I don't know how many additional years or months of life I have
ahead of me, but I do know that I will follow Jesus to the grave. Help me
face this inevitability not with fear, but with faith that Jesus will bring
me into a full experience of eternal life. In his name I pray. Amen.* ❧

88

Justice Will Prevail

"I will keep you and will make you to be a covenant for the people and
a light for the Gentiles, to open eyes that are blind, to free captives from
prison and to release from the dungeon those who sit in darkness."
ISAIAH 42:6 – 7

These remarkable words describe in vivid detail God's anointing of a special chosen servant who will spread justice over all the earth. This is God's
promise to the world, the fulfillment of the promise God made to Abraham,
Moses, and David. God declared that one of David's descendants would
become a ruler whose kingdom would last forever.

That ruler, we know now, is Jesus Christ.

Jesus is the saving link between God and us, sent to all nations to open
blind eyes, release prisoners from jail, and give light to those who sit in
darkness.

At first, this text doesn't seem to be talking about us. We're not blind or
in prison or in darkness. But God is not speaking literally here. In fact, the
Lord is talking about everyone on earth, for all of us are afflicted with spiritual blindness or sorrow or despair, hopelessness or grief. God's description
includes people who suffer oppression or who feel hopeless because society
treats them unfairly. It also includes people who feel alone or are in some
spiritual need. Therefore, this description is all-inclusive. *Every one of us* has
suffered and has a spiritual need for God.

It boggles the mind to consider Isaiah's words. God Almighty, the Creator
of the universe, has promised to send a humble, beloved, and chosen servant
to offer justice and salvation to every person on earth. And in this task, he
will never be deterred. The perfect example set by Jesus Christ still prevails,
and salvation through faith in him is available to all people.

O God, I'm grateful for this lesson from the Scriptures, describing in the
most vivid and evocative terms the characteristics of my Savior, who gives
hope to the hopeless, courage to the weak, and ambition to the timid. I
pray that you will expand my own horizons of service to you as I depend
on the Holy Spirit to help me emulate the words and actions of Jesus
Christ, in whose name I pray. Amen. ❧

Days of Anticipation

I am torn between the two: I desire to depart and be with Christ,
which is better by far; but it is more necessary for you that I remain
in the body.
PHILIPPIANS 1:23 – 24

When I was a child, almost every new thing we got came from Sears Roebuck and Company. On Christmas, we got new things from Santa Claus, but before we got ready to ask him for something, our parents put very strict limits on us. The requests had to be reasonable. So, if you'll excuse the expression, the Bible for our Christmas requests became the Sears catalog.

One of the biggest events in our year occurred whenever the Sears catalog arrived—thick, crisp, and new. The old one quickly landed in the outdoor privy. If our family needed something—either my daddy for the farm or my mother for the house or my two sisters for themselves—the place to go was the catalog. We could order new appliances, guns, fishing tackle, clothes, and books. It had *everything*. In fact, even the farmhouse in which we lived came from Sears.

When preparing to order, we excitedly filled out the forms, put them in the mailbox, and watched as the mailman picked them up. The next morning, we'd stand by the mailbox—a week prematurely—hoping our stuff had come.

If we ponder our lives from earliest childhood through today, we see that the expectation of receiving a gift and its actual receipt provide almost equal excitement. In fact, expectations sometimes exceed the arrival.

When it comes to being with Christ for eternity, however, I think the realization will *far* outweigh any expectations we may have. Just as Paul joyfully envisioned the day he would be with his Lord, so we too should do whatever we can *now* to make that day a real celebration. Let us therefore work to make our remaining days of life full, productive, and fully compatible with the teachings of our Savior, Jesus Christ.

O God, I look forward with excitement and joy to the time I will be with
you forever. I ask that the anticipation of that wonderful day will shape
my conduct here on earth, especially that I will look for innovative ways
to bring the good news of Jesus Christ to my neighbors, friends, and new
acquaintances. I ask these things in Christ's name. Amen.

The Final Celebration

Then I heard what sounded like a great multitude, like the roar of rushing
waters and like loud peals of thunder, shouting: "Hallelujah! For our Lord
God Almighty reigns. Let us rejoice and be glad and give him glory!"
REVELATION 19:6 – 7

Passover was the first regular celebration ordained in the Bible. God told the Israelites, recently liberated from Egyptian slavery, that every year they should remember how the angel of death "passed over" them. This religious ceremony has been observed for about 3,500 years.

Christmas is an important annual celebration on the Christian calendar. On that day we remember the birth of our Savior, Jesus Christ. And there is Easter, of course, when we rejoice in the Lord's resurrection.

In our secular lives, we celebrate Mother's Day, Father's Day, birthdays, weddings, anniversaries, and graduations. Sometimes we have class reunions to renew old friendships. I've been attending reunions with classmates from my high school and the Naval Academy for many years.

We have these celebrations so we can be joyful together in honor of some significant event or person. We also have celebrations to reflect on and think about the past. And we have celebrations to reaffirm attachments of love.

The ultimate celebration described in the book of Revelation has all three of these key elements: joy, reflection, and a bond of love. All of us who profess faith in Christ — including about two billion Christians alive today — will someday have a marriage feast with Jesus Christ. This is going to be a wonderful occasion, after the earth's sinfulness has been eliminated. There will be nothing but purity, honesty, service, decency, justice, forgiveness, compassion, and love. The characteristics of Christ will prevail.

What a celebration that will be! The justice of Christ will reign forever, and the intimate union of love and joy we have with him will never be dissolved!

O Lord, as I look ahead to that great day when we will celebrate
your ultimate triumph over evil and the establishment of your eternal
kingdom, my heart fills with praise. Always remind me that the presence
of Christ on earth now is demonstrated by my life as a Christian. Help
me live as closely as I can to my Savior, Jesus Christ, in whose name I
pray. Amen. ❧

Looking Forward to a New Creation

Then I saw "a new heaven and a new earth," for the first heaven and
the first earth had passed away, and there was no longer any sea....
"God himself will be with them and be their God. 'He will wipe
every tear from their eyes. There will be no more death' or mourning
or crying or pain, for the old order of things has passed away."
REVELATION 21:1, 3 – 4

One day, John tells us, God will create a new world for human habitation. The earth as we know it will pass away and the sea will be no more. That last detail is just one of many in Revelation that puzzles us. Why does John emphasize it?

For one thing, all the way through the Bible, we read of roaring waves, sinking ships, uncertainty, and destruction. The ocean is pictured as fearsome. As someone who served in the Navy, I don't share that feeling, although I've seen the ocean in turbulent storms. But John was sure that if our future habitation has no ocean, then something better will replace it.

More importantly, in eternity, the separation between God and us will vanish. God will dwell with us and "will wipe every tear" from our eyes. Death, mourning, and pain will cease to exist, for the "old order of things" will pass away.

John wrote Revelation to encourage us and urge us to prepare ourselves for this amazing future with God. Our present world is only temporary. That doesn't mean we forget about taking care of it or helping those in need! Rather, no matter how bad things get, God will create a wonderful future for us.

We cannot separate the symbolisms from the actualities in the book of Revelation, but we are constrained to order our lives to prepare for the future by drawing ourselves closer to the perfect example set by Jesus Christ.

O Lord, give me an open heart to grasp the words and images of John,
and enable me to apply them to my life as I minister in a troubled
world. Remind me of your promise to be with me forever, and remind
me that no matter what fearsome challenges arise, they fade into relative
insignificance compared to your grace and love. I ask these things in the
name of my Savior, Jesus Christ. Amen. ❧

PART 2
GROWING

We still farm the land that has been in our family since the 1830s, and I know that it takes a lot of work to keep a farm running and even more effort to increase yields and profits. All this becomes much easier if the land is fertile and rainfall is dependable — if a good foundation makes growth and improvements possible. This is true both in agriculture and in the cultivation of the soul.

The apostle Peter urges us to "grow in the grace and knowledge of our Lord and Savior Jesus Christ" (2 Peter 3:18). But what sort of work is involved in nurturing and expanding our fullest human lives as Christians? What must we *do*?

In this section, we'll explore the opportunities of wholehearted commitment to Christ, the desire to listen to God and to please God, the role of prayer and the church, the often missing jewel of thanksgiving, the crucial place of forgiveness, the need for obedience, and the power to do all things through the Holy Spirit. Human and spiritual growth occurs not through a passive process, but an active one, and we'll consider how to achieve it.

Does this sound like a wonderfully challenging agenda for us? Well, that's because it is! But God doesn't just point a divine finger to a pile of work and say to us, "That's it. Now do it!" Instead, out of love and mercy, the Lord forms a partnership to "strengthen you with power through his Spirit in your inner being, so that Christ may dwell in your hearts through faith. And I pray that you, being rooted and established in love, may have power, together with all the Lord's holy people, to grasp how wide and long and high and deep is the love of Christ, and to know this love that surpasses knowledge — that you may be filled to the measure of all the fullness of God" (Ephesians 3:16–19).

Total Commitment

*He answered, "'Love the Lord your God with all your heart and
with all your soul and with all your strength and with all your
mind'"; and, "'Love your neighbor as yourself.'"*
LUKE 10:27

During the brutal Nazi regime of Adolf Hitler, a German pastor named Dietrich Bonhoeffer became a martyr for Christ. He had led several churches — one in Spain and two in London — before returning home for the last time. Regardless of where he served his Lord, his heart always remained in Germany.

Bonhoeffer had a friend named Reinhold Niebuhr, a German theologian living in the United States. Just before the outbreak of World War II, Bonhoeffer accepted Niebuhr's invitation to lecture in America. During that time, Hitler rose to power and began to persecute his dissenters, including some in the church. Niebuhr tried to induce Bonhoeffer to stay in the United States where he would remain safe, but Bonhoeffer refused. "I have to be among other Christians who are being persecuted in Germany," he declared. So Bonhoeffer returned to his beloved homeland.

Once there, he preached against Nazism, racism, and white supremacy. Predictably, Hitler had him arrested. Bonhoeffer remained in prison until just a few days before the Allies liberated Germany, when Hitler ordered his execution. This brave German pastor died as a dedicated disciple of Jesus Christ.

One of Bonhoeffer's most famous books carried the title *The Cost of Discipleship*. In it he condemns what he calls "cheap grace." He insists one cannot follow Christ without full commitment, wherever that commitment might lead. In his case, it led to a Nazi gallows.

While our sinful tendencies prevent any one of us from living fully for Christ and never capitulating to the world's temptations, we should all strive for total commitment, regardless of where it may lead.

*O Lord, help me avoid the kind of cheap grace that would encourage me
to put aside the responsibilities of my faith. Give me courage to ask myself,
"How can I more vividly personify the words and actions of my Savior,
Jesus Christ? What can I do to be a successful Christian, as measured
by the priorities and standards of my Savior?" I ask these things in his
precious name. Amen.* 🌾

Halfhearted Is Wholly Repugnant

*"At that time I will search Jerusalem with lamps and punish those
who are complacent, who are like wine left on its dregs, who think,
'The LORD will do nothing, either good or bad.'"*
ZEPHANIAH 1:12

At the time of Zephaniah, many people in Judah worshiped God because of the influence of good King Josiah; but it definitely was not their top priority. While they professed loyalty to God, they didn't let their "faith" interfere with conflicting cultural institutions, personal ambitions, or the worship of false gods.

In response, the Lord vowed to find the proud, smug, and self-satisfied people and punish them. Dregs are what's left at the bottom of the barrel—bad tasting and useless. We sometimes see dregs left after drinking a cup of coffee. Dormancy is no virtue when it comes to convictions about God's influence and power in our lives.

Our own times seem not unlike Zephaniah's. While we might in theory acknowledge God as the Creator of the universe—all-powerful, all-knowing, and everywhere—often we think we can get along just fine on our own. We doubt God will intervene and see no tangible, provable relationship between God and us. We see ourselves as self-sufficient, with no need for an active, intimate, subservient connection to God.

When Jesus encountered such a complacent attitude, he declared, "Because you are lukewarm—neither hot nor cold—I am about to spit you out of my mouth" (Revelation 3:15–16). Christ loathes indifference toward him! This applies to Christians who feel no obligation to be a witness to our faith. What a sad state of affairs! Let's not be indifferent, but rather seek God wholeheartedly and assume our Christian obligations with eagerness and delight.

God, remind me that you designed the prophet's words for me, even in this modern, fast-changing world. Give me the courage to acknowledge parallels between the complacent people of ancient Jerusalem and me, and help me realize that you call me to a different standard, one exemplified by my Savior. Let me respond in a spirit of meekness, humility, truth, and love. I ask this in Jesus' name. Amen. ❧

While He May Be Found

Seek the LORD while he may be found;
call on him while he is near.
ISAIAH 55:6

The prophet Isaiah advised his countrymen—and us—to prepare for the coming of the Messiah by doing just one thing: Seek the Lord. This is not a passive strategy. It doesn't invite us to sit by quietly, take care of our own affairs, meet our own crises, see how much money we can acquire, get as big a home as possible, and strive for success in our community. That's not it at all.

So what is it? What does it mean to "seek the Lord"?

The word *seek* is an active term, both intentional and energetic. Seeking the Lord is the most foundational, important decision we can make. It plays a central role in forming a dynamic relationship with God that shapes our entire existence. We must seek aggressively, no matter what age we might be, regardless of our life experiences. Down through the centuries, Isaiah is calling us, even at this very moment, to seek the Lord.

But the last part of his famous phrase is equally important: "while he may be found." What does *that* mean? Does it mean that the Lord might disappear, never to be found?

While God will never wander away from us, we can, through our own inaction, lose opportunities to form a working partnership with the Creator. We can fritter our chances away, day by day, by postponing our decision or involvement and turning our attention to other things, as the ancient Hebrews often did. If we choose that foolish route, we'll come to the end of our lives having wasted our chances for a vigorous, adventurous, exciting, and gratifying partnership with the King of the universe.

There are two kinds of people in the world. One follows Isaiah's advice and says to God, "Thy will be done," while the other says, "My will be done." That's the decision before us.

Lord, I confess that too often I find it very easy to put off seeking you.
Too easily I say, "Someday I'll become a wonderful Christian," or "Next year my life will mirror the words and actions of Jesus—but not yet."
Lord, help me seek you right now, right where I am. In Jesus' name I pray.
Amen. ❧

Unfaithfulness

Hear the word of the LORD, you Israelites, because the LORD has
a charge to bring against you who live in the land: "There is no
faithfulness, no love, no acknowledgment of God in the land."
HOSEA 4:1

From where do we get the concept of faithfulness or commitment? Where do we first begin to learn and commit to the codes by which we live?

Our parents normally become our first teachers. Our mother and father teach us what is right and wrong. We quickly learn that if we do something wrong, we either get warned or punished. My mother usually warned me three times before doling out punishment; at the most, my daddy gave one warning. The point is, we learned a standard of conduct as youngsters: "Don't hit your sister," "Don't lie," "If you take something on your plate at dinner, eat it." I learned that last one from my parents, and I taught it to my children. My grandchildren totally ignore it.

When I went to the Naval Academy, I had to abide by the school's very rigid standards. One of them prohibited lying. If you were caught lying, you were dismissed in disgrace, with no appeal. Truthfulness was the most important thing; and when we returned from leave or vacation, we had to sign a little form that declared, "I have not done these things." You weren't expelled for doing those things; you were expelled for lying about them.

If you're reading this book, you probably have committed yourself to Jesus Christ and pledged to adopt the standards by which he lived. That's the deal we make when we say, "Lord Jesus, I accept you as my Savior." When we let *anything* come between us and that commitment, we are being unfaithful. Is there anything more important than remaining faithful to Jesus Christ? I can't think of it. God is completely faithful to us; and that kind of unbending commitment demands our faithfulness in return.

O Lord, help me remember the countless ways you are faithful to me.
Encourage me to remain faithful to you, regardless of the difficulties,
not somehow to repay you (which is impossible), but rather as a form of
thankfulness and worship. I pray these things in Jesus' name. Amen. ❧

Aim to Please

Am I now trying to win the approval of human beings, or of God?
Or am I trying to please people? If I were still trying to please people,
I would not be a servant of Christ.
GALATIANS 1:10

I used to be a politician; I'm not anymore. When I ran for the Georgia state senate, 75,000 people lived in my 14ᵗʰ district. As I went out campaigning, I wanted to please them. After I got to Atlanta, I wanted to please them even more.

One day I decided that I wanted to be governor. So I began trying to please not just those 75,000, but all the people of Georgia.

Later I ran for president, and I wanted to please all the citizens of the United States.

I doubt that Paul would have made a good politician. In effect he wrote, "I don't write to please people. I'm not trying to ingratiate myself with anyone. I don't travel around the Roman world just to make friends. I don't work to gain a reputation as a great preacher or a great writer. I travel and speak and write for one reason only: to please God."

When we read Paul's words, it's not hard to see whom he thinks we ought to labor to please, and it's not the people around us. Most of us, including me, have in the back of our minds pleasing other people. Paul says, "Not me."

It's not that we should try to irritate people by acting badly and mistreating them. Just the opposite! But Paul made it clear that when we set "pleasing people" as a primary goal, we're in for trouble. That's not the territory we should claim in life.

Let's make it our goal, instead, to emulate as closely as possible the words and actions of Jesus Christ. As Paul might say, "That's all I'm trying to do: please God."

O Lord, while I serve people in the name of Christ, help me never to make pleasing them my primary consideration, for this might lead me to the "lowest common denominator." Give me the superior and ultimately more effective goal of pleasing you, whatever that means and wherever I am. Help me live in accordance with Jesus' life and words, his teaching and example. I ask in his name. Amen.

Act in a Way That Pleases God

There are six things the LORD hates, seven that are detestable to him:
haughty eyes, a lying tongue, hands that shed innocent blood, a heart
that devises wicked schemes, feet that are quick to rush into evil...
PROVERBS 6:16 – 18

Notice that the first five of the "detestable" things listed above involve the human body: eyes, tongue, hands, heart, and feet. When God gave us life and the biological mechanisms to see, speak, hold, think, and move, he did not grant us complete moral freedom to use them in any way we chose. God put very clear restraints on our behavior.

In a similar way, when we buy something, we put ourselves under certain restraints. If we spend a lot of money on a finely embroidered tablecloth made by expert artisans — a cloth that a woman may have worked on for two years — we wouldn't bring it home and scrub the floor with it. Or if we bought a brand-new automobile, we wouldn't dump our wet garbage in the backseat to haul the trash away. But when God gives us an amazing, unspoiled body, what do we do with this possession, something far more precious than fine lace or a new automobile? Sometimes we use it to do hurtful things that God despises.

The mandates of God and the standards of Jesus Christ never change. No matter what society accepts, no matter what we see happening in the movies or on television, no matter what our neighbors have adopted as common practice or our friends have decided is acceptable, as Christians we must hold to the way set for us by God. We must make a decision to accept God's laws as our laws, to use our bodies and minds in a way that pleases God, and to refrain from breaching the standards of Christ.

O God, I praise you for your wonderful gifts. I marvel that you love
me and want only the best for me, even though I sometimes fail to
understand what is truly good for me. Give me the wisdom and strength
to do your will in all areas of my life, and so bless not only myself but also
those around me. In Christ's name I pray. Amen. ❧

Faithful Despite the Turmoil

Then God said, "Take your son, your only son, whom you love—
Isaac—and go to the region of Moriah. Sacrifice him there as a
burnt offering on a mountain I will show you."
GENESIS 22:2

Since we know how much we love our own children or grandchildren, we can imagine how precious a possession Abraham and Sarah considered Isaac to be. Isaac had arrived as the fulfillment of God's personal promise after his father and mother were very old, long after their normal childbearing years. Abraham and Sarah must have loved Isaac dearly.

But then, out of the blue, God said, "Abraham, offer me a sacrifice." Abraham replied, "I'll do anything you ask, God." And God said, "Take Isaac and your sacrificial knife and go to this remote place, and there sacrifice your son." The command must have stunned Abraham, but he obeyed, although in great sorrow. When father and son reached the appointed place, Isaac looked around and said, "Where's the goat?" Abraham said that God would provide the sacrifice, and then proceeded to tie up his son.

At the last moment, however, as Abraham raised his dagger to plunge it into Isaac's heart, an angel stopped him and showed him a ram with its horns entwined in vines. "You've proven your faith," said the angel. "Sacrifice the ram instead."

This test transcends anything any of us ever have experienced. Abraham was so dedicated to God and so convinced of the Lord's omnipotence, omniscience, and love that he obeyed. He considered God so wise that whatever the Lord commanded was the right thing to do, even if he didn't understand it.

That is the sort of faith for which we should all strive. We don't always understand why things happen the way they do or why God commands us to live in certain ways, but we should have unshakable faith that God knows best. And so let us follow the Lord's commandments as we learn them from the Bible and from the perfect example set by Jesus Christ.

O God, I can only wonder what Abraham was thinking as he climbed
that mountain with his son. The book of Hebrews says that he reckoned
you could raise Isaac from the dead; but even so, the pain must have been
excruciating. He obeyed because he had faith, which is as important to
me as it was to Abraham. Increase my faith, in Christ's name. Amen. ❧

Seeing God in Creation

For since the creation of the world God's invisible qualities—his eternal
power and divine nature—have been clearly seen, being understood
from what has been made, so that people are without excuse.
ROMANS 1:20

If we had never read a Bible or heard a sermon, and never heard about Moses or the prophets or Jesus Christ, still we would know about God. God is there to be seen in the vast reaches of space, in the invisible atom, in the intricacies of the human brain and eye, and in the wondrous birth of a child. In all these things, the miracle of creation points to God.

We wonder how a tree grows from an acorn, how a flower blooms, or how DNA can shape the appearance and character of a living creature. And it's almost incomprehensible to us that our Milky Way galaxy alone contains *billions* of stars equivalent to our sun.

At the other end of the scale, I marvel that the "indivisible atom" I learned about in high school is really a collection of remarkable components—matter and antimatter, rotating in different directions, yet held together by forces of immense power. Some subatomic particles can pass through the entire earth without being deflected.

Some people look at all of this and see nothing but a cosmic accident. They maintain that the universe, with all its grand and glorious mysteries, has no Maker. Yet if we ask sincerely whether God exists, all we have to do is look around us.

The fact of creation is by itself a potent proof of God. That's a foundation on which we can comprehend the correlation of science and faith—based on awareness and knowledge. In both there are transformation and growth, as when a tiny seed blossoms into a beautiful rosebush or even an enormous tree. That's also the way our faith in God should grow.

Dear Lord, as I read these verses from your Word, implant your wisdom
in my heart so I can grow to maturity in faith. Teach me and challenge
me to stretch the boundaries of my spirit, to expand the blessings I bring
to others, and to enlarge the scope of my forgiveness. Bind my heart
together with other believers in the kind of love you have for us. In Jesus'
name I pray. Amen. ❧

100

Return to the Scriptures

*Ezra the priest brought the Law before the assembly, which was made up
of men and women and all who were able to understand. He read it aloud
from daybreak till noon as he faced the square before the Water Gate in the
presence of the men, women and others who could understand. And all the
people listened attentively to the Book of the Law.*
NEHEMIAH 8:2 – 3

After the return to Jerusalem of many Jews from Babylonian exile, God impressed on Nehemiah the need to remind his people about the Word of God. Very few of them, if any, remembered the Scriptures.

So one day Ezra the priest delivered a Bible-based message to a large crowd, reading selected passages from the first five books of the Bible. Ezra taught for six hours. He would read a carefully selected portion of the text, and then he and his scribal colleagues would walk through the crowd, explaining what it meant. They also answered questions and then repeated the process.

It took a long time, but the people of Judah eventually got reacquainted with the Holy Scriptures. Since the people themselves were the repository of God's covenant and the guardians of the divine revelation, it was important for them to understand and then reaffirm the covenant made with Abraham, which later evolved into the final covenant about Jesus as the Messiah. The people of Judah had an enormous responsibility.

Today, where is the repository of God's covenant and divine message of salvation through faith in Jesus Christ? It's with all of us. What a sobering thought! The very essence of God's divine message to humanity rests with us. Therefore it's incumbent on us to understand this message, interpret it accurately, and deal with the questions of those who may not completely understand it.

We have an obligation—not only to ourselves and to our children, but also to those outside the church—to read the Bible, analyze its message carefully, and then apply it to our lives in practical ways.

*O Lord, help me not only read your Holy Word, but understand and
demonstrate its meaning in my daily life. Give me a thirst for wisdom
and a longing to see my faith in Jesus Christ bear fruit in my everyday
experience. In his name I pray. Amen.* ❧

Wisdom Calling

Does not wisdom call out? Does not understanding raise her voice? At the
highest point along the way, where the paths meet, she takes her stand;
beside the gate leading into the city, at the entrance, she cries aloud.
PROVERBS 8:1 – 3

God's wisdom is neither passive nor dormant; it searches for us, seeking to implant within us the ability to comprehend life more completely and accurately. Like accepting a lover, these verses say we must choose to accept wisdom. Otherwise, it may never become ours.

To gain divine wisdom, we must keep our minds open and listen to others. Unfortunately, this is not a universal human characteristic! Some people (we call them "know-it-alls") refuse to listen to others. They think, *Why should I listen to others, when I know I'm right? I'm correct in my habits and in my political, philosophical, and religious opinions; I have no need to listen to any outside voices.*

If we are to follow Christ faithfully, however, we must remain willing to stretch our hearts and minds in search of further divine instruction. We need to work hard to develop sound judgment and establish priorities that please God. And we can't do those things while remaining proud, arrogant, prejudiced, or unwilling to listen.

Most important of all is to ask God for the Holy Spirit's help. Through prayer, we ask God for wisdom and then yield ourselves to God's will. Wisdom calls us actively to assess ourselves, perhaps by asking the Lord, humbly and maybe in solitude, "God, what in my life needs to be corrected or improved? What wisdom should I seek today? Do I have any lifetime habits that you find unacceptable?" It takes a lot of willpower, humility, and courage to do this! But effective followers of Christ do it every day, knowing that only then can they acquire the wisdom of God.

Lord, I know I lack your wisdom in many areas of life. But I also
acknowledge that you offer it to me, if only I will open my mind to
whatever I need to learn, however you might want to teach it. Give me
listening ears, a humble heart, and the will to discover and then do your
will. Help me follow in Christ's footsteps, for I pray in his name. Amen.

102

The Big Picture

*As he was praying, the appearance of his face changed, and his
clothes became as bright as a flash of lightning. Two men, Moses and
Elijah, appeared in glorious splendor, talking with Jesus.*
LUKE 9:29 – 31

Sometimes in studying the Bible we are too inclined to look only at individual episodes. We fail to see the Scripture as one great, panoramic story of human existence. But God designed the Holy Word to show the continuity and the fulfillment of heaven's plan for all of us.

In the story of the Transfiguration, for example, what was the significance of Moses and Elijah being present? Moses represented the law, while Elijah represented the prophets. Jesus represented the completion of both Old Testament strands, the perfect fulfillment of the law and the very embodiment of the gospel, the good news of salvation. God designed the whole scene to show a continuity of the divine plan throughout biblical history.

We also see a diversity of circumstances surrounding the departure of each of these men from the earth. When the time came for Moses to die a natural death, God took him up on Mount Nebo and allowed him to gaze upon (but not enter) the Promised Land. Elijah did not die but was transported directly to heaven, a foreshadowing of the ascension of Jesus into the clouds. Jesus died while suffering in anguish on a cross, but with the full realization of all his life's work would accomplish. These are just a few examples of the intriguing linking threads we find throughout Scripture.

We must not become fixated on individual Bible stories, lest we miss God's point. Peter committed exactly this mistake when the confused apostle asked permission to build three shelters, one for Jesus and two for his heavenly guests — thus completely missing the point of the Transfiguration. Let us strive to grasp the greater and continuing story of God's redemptive plan for humanity!

God, thank you for the treasure trove of divine insight you give me in the Holy Scriptures! I confess that too often I miss the significance of what you say in your Word, and I ask your help in reading it with understanding and wisdom, and applying it with vigor. Help me grow in grace, as did Peter, and be a partner in your divine agenda. I pray in Jesus' name. Amen. ❧

A Forehead of Stone

"But I will make you as unyielding and hardened as they are. I will make your forehead like the hardest stone. Do not be afraid of them or terrified by them, though they are a rebellious people."
EZEKIEL 3:8 – 9

Ezekiel was a doomsday prophet who hammered away on two negative facts in his prophecies: (1) Judah will go into Babylonian captivity; (2) Jerusalem will be destroyed. Not pleasant messages!

But it got worse. God told Ezekiel to deliver this difficult message to his own people, a stiff-necked group that would refuse to listen to him. Nevertheless, Ezekiel was to continue speaking, for then they would know there had been a prophet among them. I like that! "No matter whether you succeed or fail in what you attempt, Ezekiel, let them know that there has been a man of God among them."

God instructed Ezekiel to "eat" some words written on a scroll—to absorb them into himself. In effect, God was telling the prophet, "Accept me *totally*. It's the only way you'll succeed in this difficult task."

We too should absorb the Word of God and thereby take Christ into *our* very selves. How else can we hope to live a more transcendent, dedicated, useful, and joy-filled life? We don't know what lies ahead. We don't know the challenges, difficulties, or obstacles. But God does, and so it makes sense to take both God and his Word along with us.

We need foreheads like flint if we are to accomplish what God sets before us. Without such determination, it's too easy to fall back, give up, and sink to the lowest common denominator. Let's not worry about the reactions of other people when we attempt to do something remarkable in the name of Christ. Let's just do it anyway and let God take care of the results. If we fail to try, we already have failed.

Lord God, please give me confidence that I have within me the ability to do your will. Teach me how to "absorb" your message, like Ezekiel, and then share it with others—not in an arrogant, boastful manner, but with humility. Be with me this week as I seek to do your will, and let me be bound close to you, in the name of my Savior. Amen.

A Gnostic Confusion

See to it that no one takes you captive through hollow and deceptive philosophy, which depends on human tradition and the elemental spiritual forces of this world rather than on Christ.
COLOSSIANS 2:8

Long ago, a problem arose in the Colossian church. The founder of this little fellowship, a Christian named Epaphras, didn't know how to deal with the challenge and so went looking for Paul, who sat in prison at the time. He told the apostle that the Colossians were being confused by the teachings of a group later known as the Gnostics.

Gnostics taught that spiritual things were absolutely holy, pristine, and without sinfulness or any sort of unpleasantness, but that all earthly, physical things were vile and sinful and embarrassing. Therefore there was no way to bridge the gap or join the spiritual with the physical. Since it was inconceivable that God could be involved in worldly sordidness or sinfulness, Gnostics taught that Jesus Christ could not be both God and also a human being. He could not be spiritual and also associate with earth's immorality or unpleasant things.

The Gnostics grew very powerful and persuasive, not only in Colosse, but all over the Roman world. These deep thinkers held public debates where they promoted their beliefs. As a result, the Colossians became very confused. Despite their devout faith, this errant message had thrown them into disarray.

While the Gnostics are long gone, sometimes we still get confused or disturbed about various religious claims. Some may make us doubt the purity and essence of Christianity. It's important to realize this is going to happen, even to devout followers of Christ. We must prepare ourselves for it by studying the Bible, seeking advice, and going to God in prayer with our confusion. We may be in for struggles, even prolonged ones; but God uses even these challenges to strengthen our faith and help us to mature in our personal relationship with Christ.

O God, I'm grateful that you included Paul's words to the confused little church of Colosse, for I also have to face and overcome challenges to my faith. Equip me to meet those questions with courage and humility, and remind me that I do not stand by my own strength or knowledge, but by relying on your power and wisdom. In Jesus' name I pray. Amen. ❧

Our Shepherd's Voice

"The one who enters by the gate is the shepherd of the sheep. The gatekeeper opens the gate for him, and the sheep listen to his voice. He calls his own sheep by name and leads them out."
JOHN 10:2 – 3

If you were to visit Galilee, in the northern part of Israel, you would see a lot of farmlands, most of them not even requiring irrigation. Wheat fields and fruit orchards dot the landscape. Farther south in Judea, however, the land becomes quite arid. Little will grow without extensive irrigation, and instead of farmlands, you'll see sheep and goats and those who tend them. These people live as nomads, much like the Bedouins, who move around with their flocks and camp out in tents.

Rosalynn and I have visited Saudi Arabia several times. On one occasion, we flew about two hundred miles north of Riyadh to visit King Fahd in the desert. From our helicopter we looked down on many Bedouin camps. Saudi Arabia is a wealthy country, but most Bedouins still live in their goat-hair tents, just as their ancestors did. Nowadays, of course, you might also see a British Land Rover next to the tent and a satellite antenna so the family can watch Al Jazeera, CNN, or cartoons.

When different flocks come to a central water hole, the sheep all mix together. When the shepherds get ready to move along, they stand aside and call or whistle, and their sheep come to them. An intimate relationship exists between sheep and their shepherd.

Jesus used this image to encourage us to get to know his voice. Often we struggle to get answers to life's complexities; one voice says this, and another says that. How do we recognize what's right? By recognizing the voice of our Master. Therefore we need to know what he says and commit ourselves to his words. That is the way to truth.

O Lord, in our loud and raucous world, many voices shout at once, each claiming to declare "the truth." Through the din, help me listen carefully for the voice of my Savior and then comply with his words and example. Let me realize that this will guide me to a more abundant, significant life. In his name I pray. Amen. ❧

106

Are We Listening?

*"We are going up to Jerusalem," he said, "and the Son of Man will
be delivered over to the chief priests and the teachers of the law. They
will condemn him to death and will hand him over to the Gentiles,
who will mock him and spit on him, flog him and kill him. Three
days later he will rise."*

MARK 10:33 – 34

On the first Sunday at his new church, a pastor gave a very dynamic sermon, urging the congregation to undertake some bold mission work. The elders and deacons felt thrilled with what the pastor said about improving the church's ministry.

The following Sunday, the pastor preached the same sermon, word for word. "Well," said the elders and deacons, "he probably just forgot he'd already preached that one; or maybe he got his notes mixed up."

The next Sunday the pastor preached the identical message once again. Now the elders and deacons began to grumble. "We made a mistake in hiring this guy," they groused.

Fourth Sunday, same sermon. After the service, the lay leaders confronted their pastor. "Why do you keep preaching the same sermon?" they demanded.

"I figured I should keep preaching it," he replied, "until you act on it." No one had done anything the pastor had urged them to do. Everyone just listened to his sermon, applauded it, and then ignored it.

I think something like this was going on when Christ told his disciples about his dying and rising again. He said these things over and over, but they didn't want to believe it. So he repeated the message.

Let's not make the same mistake. When we read the Bible and hear Christ commanding us to help the poor, forgive each other, or love God and our neighbor, we must take care not to treat it superficially. Let's allow Jesus' words to sink deeply into our consciousness and direct how we live. A wonderful sermon does no good without attentive listeners.

*Sovereign Lord, open my ears to hear your Word, and give me
understanding so that I might grasp your meaning. But also, Lord, give
me the insight, the conviction, and the courage to move ahead and do
your will, whatever that might be. Give me humility and a commitment
to serve others in your name, to reach out to those in need. I ask all of this
in Jesus' name. Amen.* 🦋

107

Open Your Eyes!

*Now that same day two of them were going to a village called
Emmaus, about seven miles from Jerusalem. They were talking with
each other about everything that had happened. As they talked and
discussed these things with each other, Jesus himself came up and
walked along with them; but they were kept from recognizing him.*

LUKE 24:13 – 16

With the death and burial of Jesus, the disciples entered a dark time of grief,
fear, disillusionment, and despair. The two discouraged men Luke describes
were perhaps plodding back home with nothing to relish about the future.
When Jesus joined them and struck up a conversation, they didn't even recognize him.

Does that sound familiar? Jesus is with us all the time, but sometimes we
don't recognize him. Sometimes our eyes and minds remain closed to his
presence, even though he's there.

In Revelation Jesus says, "Here I am! I stand at the door and knock. If
anyone hears my voice and opens the door, I will come in and eat with that
person" (Revelation 3:20). That's a simple, little thing: "I'll have supper with
you." Jesus appears to us in the most mundane ways—when we're walking
down a road, when we're with a friend, when we see somebody in need, when
we hear about an opportunity to show kindness, when we have a special problem. Jesus appears to us in ordinary things. But to recognize his presence,
we have to be receptive, alert, and eager to welcome him into the occasion.

Sometimes we get slapped down with a tragedy or a setback and we
feel abandoned by or alienated from God. But a Christian is never alone,
even when overpowering feelings of loneliness hit. Jesus is present, not only
through the Holy Spirit, but in the presence of God's people. We need to
open our eyes to find Jesus in the everyday circumstances of our lives.

*O God, how often have I missed your presence simply because I have not
sought that possibility? Give me a new determination to remain sensitive
to your Spirit so I might respond to you and to your will, wherever and in
whatever form you might appear to me. Help me serve you with genuine
humility. I ask these things in the name of my Savior. Amen.* 🌾

108

Never Stop Learning

The wise prevail through great power, and those who have knowledge
muster their strength.
PROVERBS 24:5

As we grow older, many of us feel reluctant to ask questions and reveal our need for answers. We may not wish to look ignorant or as though we know less than the person we're asking. Sometimes this happens at age eighty-five; sometimes at forty-five; and sometimes when we're fifteen. I've been a professor at Emory University since 1982, and I've met some college students who have decided they already know it all. They've closed their minds to expansion.

We're never too old to learn. Every morning when my mother got out of bed, even at eighty, she was eager to learn, whether about the Brooklyn Dodgers, something in politics, or what makes a good pecan crop. She was always probing for answers. My uncle did the same thing, unlike my father. Whenever I came home from the Navy, my father normally asked me the same three questions. "Jimmy," he would ask, "are you getting along okay?" I would reply, "Yes, sir." "You need anything?" "No, sir." "You like the Navy still?" "Yes, sir." And that would be it. But then I'd go see my uncle, and he'd pepper me with questions for two hours. By the time he got through with me, he knew how many people were on my submarine, what kind of food we ate, how much money I made each month, and how big a torpedo was. He was always trying to expand his mind.

We Christians need to be lifelong learners, because the depth of meaning in the Scriptures is so vast that we'll miss important truths if we fail to continue to ask probing questions and seek answers about God's world, our relationship to Christ, and our relationships with each other. God says his Word lasts forever, which implies we should study it forever. Are we ready for that?

O Lord, give me an unquenchable desire to learn all I can about your world, your Word, and the people and things you've put in both. Let me use this thirst for knowledge to bless those around me and to prepare me for that glorious day when my faith will be realized. In Jesus' name I pray. Amen. 🌿

Why Go to Church?

And let us consider how we may spur one another on toward love and good
deeds, not giving up meeting together, as some are in the habit of doing, but
encouraging one another—and all the more as you see the Day approaching.
HEBREWS 10:24–25

"Although I believe in God and in Jesus Christ," I've heard people say, "I don't see any reason to attend services regularly. I can get just as much from my religious faith by staying at home, taking a walk in the woods, reading Bible verses, or saying a prayer." All these things were available in biblical times—so why does Scripture instruct us to attend church services?

First, at church we gain deeper insight into the meaning of Scripture. We need to hear from those who have studied the text in depth, who can point us to things we could not get merely by reading the Bible on our own.

Second, we attend church to gain correction. Do we learn how to live righteously as we walk in the woods, go to work in a factory, or plow a field? Probably not. It's more likely that at work or alone we get into a rut and our world becomes smaller. It is unlikely that anything in these environments stretches our minds to a greater awareness of God's world. Nothing in them is designed to teach us how to live as Christians.

Third, we attend church in order to worship God collectively, to acknowledge as a group the sovereignty of God, the one who gave us life and the many blessings we enjoy. In congregational worship we recognize the beauty of God's creation and the spiritual companionship that blesses our lives. And we also demonstrate our obedience to God—after all, it's his Word that instructs us to gather as a congregation for worship.

And finally, church services are a wonderful way to learn who might be in need so we can volunteer to serve them.

God, I recognize that you have reasons for the instructions you give me.
Whether I always understand your reasons or not, I pray that you might
give me the will to obey you, for my own good. When we gather as the
church, grant us all the grace to bless others, even as we seek blessing for
ourselves. I ask this in the name of my Savior, Jesus Christ. Amen.

Have a Great Time

How good and pleasant it is when God's people live together in unity!
PSALM 133:1

Once a year, in November, Rosalynn and I attend one of the finest events held in South Georgia. Bruce Johnson, a good friend of ours, has a hunting club and conducts field trials for bird dogs. He rents part of our land for that purpose and raises money throughout the year to support a hospice operation.

For friends and financial supporters of the hospice, he holds a noonday quail dinner. (I still call it dinner.) Bruce invites about 250 guests and cooks 850 quail, five different ways, with biscuits, grits, sugarcane syrup, and desserts. The food is wonderful! It makes my mouth water just thinking about it. These people get together yearly for a common cause, despite their different points of view about politics, religion, and other issues. We share old times, talk about our varying interests, and meet each other's family members. I find few events as enjoyable as this one, and its essence is fellowship.

Rosalynn and I have four children, twelve grandchildren, and six great-grandchildren, living in different places. For many years we've gathered our whole family the week after Christmas and gone somewhere attractive enough to encourage our college-age and high school kids to accompany us. We have a good time—but the point of the trip is to enjoy fellowship with members of our family, people who really care for each other.

Each week we have the same binding experience in our small church. Fellowship means togetherness, the sharing of common memories, ideals, hopes, dreams, fears, doubts, and suffering; it's a sharing of entire lives on an equal and intimate basis. All of us, as believers in Jesus Christ, need to be strengthened in fellowship with each other and with God Almighty, our Creator. It really *is* good and pleasant for God's people to live together in unity!

O God, thank you for creating me with a deep need for intimate relationships, both with you and with those made in your image. Give me the time and creativity needed to pursue true fellowship—not merely superficial get-togethers, but times when I can really connect with you and with others, and therefore times of mutual blessing. In Jesus' name I pray. Amen. ❧

The Church as Family

Do not rebuke an older man harshly, but exhort him as if he were
your father. Treat younger men as brothers, older women as mothers,
and younger women as sisters, with absolute purity.
1 TIMOTHY 5:1 – 2

Rosalynn and I have a large and growing family. For our diverse group to function well, all of us need to develop a willingness to understand and forgive. I often do things contrary to what Rosalynn would prefer, and vice versa.

We've also had to deal with rebellious children who have occasionally disobeyed us or even violated the law. Our three boys were independent and fun-loving teens, and in her college days Amy was arrested three times for demonstrating against apartheid in South Africa. One Massachusetts court also tried her for opposing an American government policy with which she disagreed; the court found her not guilty. To maintain our family's harmony, we've all had to forgive and accommodate our idiosyncrasies.

The same is true of a church family. If we disagree with someone or they do something wrong, we can't isolate them or become bitter against them. We have to be willing to forgive them, to approach them and say, "What can we do to make things right again?" That is why Paul set down some high standards for conducting life within a congregation. He said, in effect, that a church group should function as a family by honoring each other regardless of age—just as parents and children do in a family. That's a very high standard, requiring *a lot* of forgiveness and understanding.

We must recognize that just as our families are bound together by blood, so our church family is bound together by the Holy Spirit and the blood of Christ.

Dear Lord, thank you for teaching me about my duties to others, whether in the church or in my family. I admit that some of the differences among us seem insuperable, but I also confess that through your grace and love, we can be drawn closer together, regardless of the difficulties. Forgive my sins and bind our hearts together in Christian love, as demonstrated by the life of our Savior, Jesus Christ. Amen.

Worthy to Worship

LORD, who may dwell in your sacred tent?
Who may live on your holy mountain?
PSALM 15:1

How do we assess a Sunday worship service? Often I may say, "The sermon was too long," or "The choir did a beautiful job." Most of us ask whether the sanctuary felt comfortable or whether we received a warm greeting.

But that is *not* the biblical way to judge a worship service. Instead, we must make two key assessments that focus on *participation* and the *presence of God*. And where do these two factors place the responsibility?

When we talk about the quality of the choir, the responsibility lies with the choir, doesn't it? So when we speak of participation and the presence of God in a worship service, then it should be clear that the responsibility lies squarely with *us*.

In today's text the people ask, "Lord, who may abide in your tent? Who may dwell on your holy hill?" In other words, who is worthy to worship? I wonder, do we often ask ourselves these questions as we prepare to participate in a worship service? This is important, because too often we approach God without any preparation at all. We say, "Since God loves me, I'm going to ask him a favor, and I expect him to listen." Too often we fail to approach God humbly. We fail to engage in self-assessment. It's more convenient to avoid the question and assume, "I am always worthy."

But the apostle Paul *did* ask the question, and he instructed us to do the same (see 1 Corinthians 11:27–32). So ask yourself, "Am I worthy to come into your church, Lord? Am I worthy to dwell on your holy hill?"

We shouldn't ask merely, "Am I worthy to pray in church?" but we should always ask ourselves, "How can I be sure I am worthy now, here, wherever I am and whatever I'm doing?"

O God, I ask that your presence within me might foster a self-searching attitude that prompts me to ask, "What can I do to represent Jesus Christ more worthily as a Christian?" Lord, I pray that this penetrating question will be on my heart, not only as I seek to worship you in church, but also as I walk with you throughout the day. In Jesus' name I pray. Amen. ❧

Humility Before Worship

"If you are offering your gift at the altar and there remember that
your brother or sister has something against you, leave your gift there.
First go and be reconciled to them; then come and offer your gift."
MATTHEW 5:23 – 24

The center of worship in the Old Testament was the Jerusalem temple, and at the center of the temple worship stood sacrificial offerings. And yet Jesus could say, "Before you offer your sacrifice, clear up anything that stands between you and other people."

Notice that Jesus addresses not the aggrieved person, but the one who committed the offense. He tells us, as the parties who caused the hurt, to stop our worship and immediately go and seek to reconcile with those we have hurt. "Until you take care of the problem," he tells us, "don't even try to worship me! Get reconciled first, and afterward come back with your heart cleaner so you can more fully participate in the kingdom of God."

I had a good friend, an Episcopalian, who sometimes skipped communion because he couldn't be reconciled with some other person.

Jesus was indeed revolutionary, but most of the time he tried simply to open his audience's mind to God's will for them. He called us to expand our vision of the familiar words *forgiveness* and *love* and *honesty* and *justice* and *fairness* and *compassion* and *service*, and then apply them in a humane and practical fashion.

As Christians, we profess to worship Christ. We claim to seek and to do the will of God. In this passage, Christ gives us very practical guidance on how we might do just that. It takes an open mind and a humble spirit to comply! He's simply not interested in worship from closed minds and proud souls.

Holy God, forgive me for the times when I have circumvented or ignored or deliberately misinterpreted the words of my Savior in order to make my life more convenient. Guide me into a fuller, more joyful, more peaceful existence in companionship with other Christians, as together we worship and serve our Lord. Bind our hearts together in Christian love and let us go forth in the power of your Spirit. In Jesus' name I pray. Amen. ❧

114

After Discipline

*The punishment inflicted on him by the majority is sufficient. Now instead,
you ought to forgive and comfort him, so that he will not be overwhelmed
by excessive sorrow. I urge you, therefore, to reaffirm your love for him.*
2 CORINTHIANS 2:6 – 8

A serious problem plagued the Corinthian church: some angry member was attacking Paul, lying about him and alleging that the apostle was trying to establish churches for his own benefit. Paul heard about the conflict while in Ephesus, and he quickly sat down to write a letter to deal with the situation.

He singled out this man and said, "This member of your church has done wrong and you cannot ignore his misdeeds. The church must discipline him." Church discipline is a very difficult thing for Christians to do, but Paul said sinful acts cannot be ignored and allowed to fester.

Paul sent his earlier letter to Corinth by a young man named Titus, and then he worried as he waited for a response; he could hardly sleep because of the harsh words he'd written to Christian friends he dearly loved. He didn't know how they would respond. Titus finally returned and said that the Corinthians had done what Paul asked; they had disciplined the man.

Now, when he wrote again, Paul instructed the church to forgive this man so that he wouldn't feel "overwhelmed by sorrow." We have to assume, although it never is stated clearly, that the man accepted his punishment and repented. If he hadn't, then Paul probably would not have written this letter.

Since he did repent, Paul laid out a second step to be taken after any kind of discipline: reconciliation and further steps toward harmony and forgiveness. Those who honestly repent of some sinful act and who accept punishment shouldn't be ostracized and condemned permanently for their error. I believe this principle has broad applications, including even our prison system, for Jesus said, "I have come to proclaim freedom for the prisoners" (see Luke 4:18).

*O God, give me the courage to continue reassessing my commitment
to you, and grant us as a church the wisdom to know when and how
to exercise discipline. Help me commit myself to peace, justice, and
forgiveness, and enable me to effectively use the spiritual gifts you have
granted me. I pray these things in the name of my Savior. Amen.* ❧

Love Rules

And now these three remain: faith, hope and love.
But the greatest of these is love.
I CORINTHIANS 13:13

If you were asked, "What is the key to a perfect life?" you might answer, as many of us would, "Faith." The apostle Paul, however, says that if you had enough faith to move mountains but lacked love, it would profit you nothing.

And what about benevolence or generosity? Paul answers, "If you gave all your goods to feed the poor and offered your body to be burned, but still lacked love, it means nothing." How about professional ability? Paul replies, "If you can speak with tongues of men and angels but still lack love, you're like a noisy brass band or a clanging cymbal." Paul goes down a long list of things and concludes that *nothing* compares with love.

One of my greatest theological heroes is Eloy Cruz, the Cuban American pastor of a small church in Brooklyn. Years ago, in the late sixties, I joined him for a week of Christian witness and ministry to Puerto Rican immigrants in Massachusetts. He let me read the Bible in Spanish to them, and then he would speak to these poor and often lonely immigrants, some of whom were "illegals." Eloy was not the most eloquent of speakers, but the obvious presence of the Holy Spirit in his life amazed me and greatly impressed his listeners.

At the end of the week, I embarrassed him by asking for the secret to his success. Finally he said that he was not a theologian, but he did know that you must have two loves in your life: love for God, and love for whoever stands in front of you. I don't know of a more profound and practical way to describe the essence of the Christian faith!

It's easy to say, "I love God and, of course, those poor people in Haiti." But to love the person in front of you is a serious challenge. Making such a commitment, however, can transform a Christian in profound and significant ways.

O God, I know that Jesus welcomed strange people in front of him at nearly all times: tax collectors, lepers, adulterers, Samaritans, Gentiles. Although I can't be perfect like Jesus, help me escape from the constraints that limit my love, and let me prize love above every other virtue. Amen. ❧

116

Love from the Heart

Now that you have purified yourselves by obeying the truth so that you
have sincere love for each other, love one another deeply, from the heart.
I PETER 1:22

There is no Christian duty, Peter says, like the obligation to love one another. In saying this, he simply reiterates a theme found throughout the Bible.

Jesus said, "A new command I give you: Love one another. As I have loved you, so you must love one another. By this everyone will know that you are my disciples, if you love one another" (John 13:34–35). Paul wrote, "Love does no harm to a neighbor. Therefore love is the fulfillment of the law" (Romans 13:10). John declared, "Dear friends, let us love one another, for love comes from God. Everyone who loves has been born of God and knows God" (1 John 4:7). And listen to my favorite verse in the Bible: "Be kind and compassionate to one another, forgiving each other, just as in Christ God forgave you" (Ephesians 4:32).

If we are to follow Christ, we must put aside animosity, hatred, a lack of forgiveness, and a tendency to ignore others. Jesus could have walked down the dusty roads of Palestine keeping to himself, but he didn't. He could have enjoyed the company of Martha, Mary, and his disciples, never bothering with a leper or a blind person, never eating with a tax collector or drinking water with a troubled Samaritan woman; but he didn't. Christ could have ignored all these people. But he didn't.

For us to walk our narrow way, therefore, with blinders on, is a colossal failure to emulate Christ. We *must* demonstrate our Christian faith by loving people from the depths of our hearts—even those who may not love us back, who are not very lovable. Jesus calls us to love them even when we get no credit for doing so. Our duty is to love them deeply, as Christ would.

My loving God, I thank you for reminding me of the centrality of Christian love. How easy it is for me to talk about loving others, and how hard it is in actual practice! So help me, Lord, to be Jesus' hands and feet in this hurting world. Give me his eyes to see the suffering and his heart to minister to the needy. In his name and for his sake I pray. Amen. ❧

The Key to Intimate Relationships

If we claim to be without sin, we deceive ourselves and the truth is not in us. If we confess our sins, he is faithful and just and will forgive us our sins and purify us from all unrighteousness.
1 JOHN 1:8 – 10

The key to close relationships with others is an unconditional, forgiving love. We simply must not underestimate the importance of forgiveness. Relationships thrive when people know we love them so much that we will forgive them anything—and they shrivel in the absence of such love.

If you have a spouse, for instance, to whom you cannot admit a mistake for fear of severe condemnation and punishment, communication becomes very difficult and love dissipates. Or if your children don't feel safe to confess to you that they have done something wrong, you drive a wedge between you or make liars out of them.

I once wrote a poem titled "I Wanted to Be in My Father's World." In it I described how I hungered for my father to express his love for me in terms I could never doubt. I longed for the kind of relationship in which I would never have to prove myself or be afraid to tell him I'd done something wrong. Only after I had written the poem did I realize that I had created the same kind of stern relationship with my own children. As my children have grown older, they have pointed out that I was quite harsh as a father.

We just can't do without God's forgiveness, because we all fall short of perfection. We all sin. And yet God unconditionally promises us that if we acknowledge our sins and turn away from them, we will be forgiven. This is possible because Christ, on the cross, freely accepted the full punishment for our sins. Through faith in him, we can have a clean life, to be lived in the name of Christ.

Lord, make the knowledge of your forgiveness a central part of my existence. As Christ has forgiven me, so give me the grace to forgive others—not grudgingly or partially, but willingly and emphatically. Help others know that I love them because I stand ready to forgive them. In Jesus' name I pray. Amen. ❧

118

Fundamental Faith

[Jesus said,] "Everything is possible for one who believes."
Immediately the boy's father exclaimed, "I do believe; help me
overcome my unbelief!"
MARK 9:23 – 24

I've written two books with the word *faith* in the title. One, called *Keeping Faith*, describes my service in the White House. Later I wrote *Living Faith*, which describes my experiences with religious belief.

We build our entire existence on faith. As infants, we depend on faith to get us fed, clothed, and nurtured. Our confidence builds in our mother, then our father, then perhaps in siblings and friends. Later we have faith in ourselves, our nation, the laws that protect us, and the principles that guide us. So when our faith gets shattered, it's a very troubling experience.

One day a man brought his demonized son to Jesus' disciples — and they couldn't help him. Their faith failed them. Jesus asked the father, "How long has this been happening?" The man replied, "From childhood. But if you are able, then have pity on us and help him."

If you are able?

We have a similar kind of faith, don't we? We know that God Almighty, the Creator of the universe, is omnipotent. But we don't know if God will take care of our particular problem. Jesus told the man, "Everything is possible for one who believes." Immediately the father cried out, "Help me overcome my unbelief!" — in effect, "Lord, I want to believe, but I need you to help me eliminate my doubts, to become more intimately associated with you."

In point of fact, merely professing our faith in God is not enough for any of us. We need a constant and intimate relationship with God Almighty, which we build through prayer. The disciples had forgotten about this connection. They still had Jesus' authorization to heal, but they failed. Why? They lost faith and forgot to pray, and so turned their responsibility over to God.

Faith grows only through prayer and the deepening intimacy with God that prayer brings.

Lord, I thank you for this story about the handicap of a faltering faith. I also thank you that, after the resurrection, the weak disciples grew in their faith and through the power of the Holy Spirit spread the Christian faith far and wide. Help me remember that my strength must come not only from my faith, but through my continued relationship with you through prayer. I ask this in Jesus' name. Amen.

119

Embracing God's Will

Is anyone among you sick? Let them call the elders of the church to pray
over them and anoint them with oil in the name of the Lord. And the
prayer offered in faith will make the sick person well; the Lord will raise
them up. If they have sinned, they will be forgiven.
JAMES 5:14–15

Rosalynn and I own a little mountain cabin with some friends in North Georgia. One Sunday we attended a worship service near the cabin in which the husband and children of a very sick woman brought her to church so that the congregation's leaders could minister to her. The eldest deacon of the church brought some oil and they anointed the woman's head with it, while the entire congregation prayed for her.

Is this the kind of ceremony that James had in mind? And if so, what result does James promise for such a prayer? James is *not* saying that any sick person who comes to church to be anointed with oil will be physically healed. Rather, James wants the whole congregation to come together so that everyone might experience the sustaining strength of a common commitment to God's will. He encourages Christian people to bind together in love for a common purpose.

I've learned that God's answers to prayer are sometimes yes, sometimes no, and sometimes "You've got to be kidding!" So often God uses our prayers to reorient our ambitions. Whenever we pray, we should seek the fulfillment of God's will and not our own.

My sister Ruth Carter Stapleton became a very important and famous evangelist before she died. Ruth believed in the ceremony described by James because it brought people together in a spirit of humility. She asked her friends to pray, not that she would recover from her fatal disease, but that she'd be strong enough to accept the will of God. She wanted to embrace God's will with joy and not as a tragedy.

Dearest Lord, you know that all of us want healing from whatever
illnesses plague us. Most of all, however, I want to be cured of the disease
that makes me value my own will above yours. Grant me the grace to
accommodate your will, whatever it happens to be. And give me joy as I
follow you, above all else. In Jesus' name I pray. Amen.

120

Ask Him for Anything

At Gibeon the LORD appeared to Solomon during the night in a dream, and God said, "Ask for whatever you want me to give you."
1 KINGS 3:5

God had promised David that his son Solomon would succeed him as Israel's king. Once Solomon took the throne, God made the young man an amazing offer: he could ask God to give him anything he wanted.

Imagine that God Almighty came to you with the opportunity to ask for whatever you wanted. What would you do if given the same amazing offer? Solomon asked for wisdom and discernment so that he could govern his people well. The king's request pleased God so much that he gave Solomon not only wisdom but also great wealth and influence and a long life. It is important to note that Solomon's wish lined up with God's will.

The fact is that every Christian *has* received the same divine offer that Solomon accepted. John records Christ as saying, "If you remain in me and my words remain in you, ask whatever you wish, and it will be done for you" (John 15:7). What difference is there between that offer of Christ and the offer of God to Solomon? Some may reply, "There is a caveat in the case of Jesus' offer: '*If* you remain intimate with me.'" But in fact, that same proviso appears throughout Scripture whenever God makes such a generous offer.

Christ has promised that we can have anything we ask for, provided that we remain "in him." *Every* Christian has this promise. It doesn't matter if we are rich or poor, smart or ignorant, prominent or unknown. We have the same exciting promise given to Solomon. If we remain faithful to God, we can ask of him *anything*.

God, help me grasp the full meaning of your offer, and give me the wisdom to take full advantage of it, not only for my own blessing, but for the benefit of others. Give me a vision of what you want to accomplish through me, and then give me the strength, through your Spirit, to reach this goal. I pray this in the name of my Savior, Jesus Christ. Amen. ❧

121

The Power of Righteousness

The prayer of a righteous person is powerful and effective. Elijah was a human being, even as we are. He prayed earnestly that it would not rain, and it did not rain on the land for three and a half years.
JAMES 5:16 – 17

James reminds us that the Old Testament prophet Elijah was a human being, just like us, but also a righteous man. A righteous person is one who has a proper relationship with God Almighty—and James says that the prayer of such a person can bring about miracles.

When Elijah prayed for a drought, he prayed in alignment with God's will (1 Kings 17:1). In effect, God directed Elijah to pray in this way in order to demonstrate the power of God over those who worshiped idols. As a result, Elijah proved that God alone is the Almighty.

If we want our prayers to have the kind of power that Elijah's did, then we need to be righteous and comply with God's will. A righteous person knows the will of God through faith in Christ and understands the proper relationship that should exist between himself or herself and God.

It would be difficult to understand God's character and know God's will if it weren't for the life of Jesus Christ! I, at any rate, have a hard time envisioning an omniscient, omnipotent, omnipresent being who created the universe. So that we might better comprehend the Almighty, however, God sent his Son to earth. Through his ministry, words, and actions, Christ gave us practical examples of the nature, desires, and priorities of God. He showed us how the will of God could be expressed in the lives of common, ordinary human beings.

In order to genuinely seek the will of God through prayer, like Elijah, we must first understand God's nature. Then we can become strong enough and wise enough to develop a life compatible with God's will.

Lord, I long to have a prayer life that gets the kind of results Elijah had. Thank you for showing me that this is indeed possible, although not by following a formula. Teach me what it means to be righteous, as Elijah was, and then give me the courage to stand out in the crowd for you, just as he did. In the name of my Savior, Jesus Christ, I pray. Amen. ❧

122

Be Honest with God

[Moses] asked the LORD, "Why have you brought this trouble on your servant? What have I done to displease you that you put the burden of all these people on me?"
NUMBERS 11:11

Everyone, even those of deep faith, will face disappointment, failure, sorrow, and loss. All of us will have ambitions that somehow remain out of reach. All of us will suffer temporary setbacks or alienations from loved ones. Moses was no exception.

One day he asked God, "Why give me such a burden and then abandon me? Why haven't you rewarded me for my good work?" Moses assumed that God had turned against him because of all the unpleasant experiences he had while trying to lead the Hebrews through the wilderness.

We all have our own desert experiences, when we feel spiritually dry. Sometimes the glowing, growing, enthralling relationship with God we once had shrivels up, and we don't quite know why. At such times, we may struggle with our faith. That is the time to cry out to God with honest, soul-bearing, anguished prayers: "God, why do I no longer find favor with you? Why have we lost our intimacy? Why are we alienated from each other?" We should not feel afraid to pray honestly in times of doubt or distress! It is okay to pray for understanding.

All of us should pray honestly, especially in times of doubt or distress. God will not be hurt by anything we do, and we will not alienate God by our crying out for understanding, wisdom, correction, or help. Therefore, let's not be afraid to bare our souls to God. If we have doubts about our faith, about the hereafter, or about any other aspect of life, let us confront those doubts and share them with God. An answer will come to us, although not always the one we might prefer.

O Lord, thank you for teaching me that I should never try to conceal anything from you. Help me be honest in the midst of troubling experiences, and use them to bind me to you and to your strength, power, wisdom, and judgment. And then, Lord, enable me to reorient my priorities to more closely parallel the perfect example established for me in the words and actions of my Savior, in whose name I pray. Amen.

123

Not for Show

"And when you pray, do not be like the hypocrites, for they love to pray standing in the synagogues and on the street corners to be seen by others. Truly I tell you, they have received their reward in full."
MATTHEW 6:5

Jesus' disciples constantly saw their Master in prayer: sometimes in thanksgiving, and at other times asking God to take care of his disciples, to provide enough food to feed a hungry crowd, or to heal a leper or cure a blind man. The disciples saw Jesus pray in times of happiness, need, sorrow, and uncertainty. In the garden of Gethsemane, they heard Jesus ask God for some alternative to the cross.

The disciples knew that Christ's strength came from his intimate prayer life with God. They saw it sustain him at all times. And here, in the Sermon on the Mount, Jesus offers us a key to effective prayer.

"Do not be like the hypocrites," he says. The word *hypocrite* comes from the Greek term *hypokrites*, which means "stage actor." In those days, actors wore masks. So Jesus is saying, "Don't put on a false mask when you pray." If you do, the only reward you'll get is the praise of onlookers. You'll receive nothing else from God.

Jesus doesn't mean, of course, that we shouldn't pray in public; it's perfectly proper to have public prayer. But whenever we pray, whether in private or in public, we should do so humbly and sincerely. Make sure your heart and mind are intimately attached to God and that you're speaking to God and not thinking, *Oh boy, all these people see me praying, so I must be very important.* Jesus himself often prayed in public, as did the apostles and other early Christian leaders. It's really a matter of connecting ourselves to God in humility. Whenever we pray and however we pray, we should do so to God and not for show.

God, what a blessing it is that I can come to you in prayer—wherever I am, whatever is happening around me. Whether I pray in private or in public, I ask that you might grant me the humility that comes from seeing you in your majesty and me in my role as a worshiper. I thank you, Lord, that you invite me to come to you in Jesus' name. Amen. ❧

124

The Value of Unceasing Prayer

Pray continually.
I THESSALONIANS 5:17

I admit it; sometimes it's hard for me to pray. My mind wanders and I have to really concentrate, because if I don't, all of a sudden I'm wondering about what I'm going to do after church and how long the photograph line will be and what Rosalynn is preparing for dinner. Sometimes it's a real challenge to make sure that every word I pray intentionally expresses my thoughts to God.

And yet God established prayer as a means by which we can communicate about every circumstance of our lives. Success, failure, happiness, despair, ambition, uncertainty, significance—God invites us to pray about all of these concerns. How can I repair the fractures between myself and another human being? How can I capitalize on a current opportunity? How can I stretch my mind to know more about God's world? How can I stretch my heart to encompass more people and thus discover the true meaning of love? How can I overcome some persistent difficulty? How can I make the day now dawning more meaningful? How can I assess my life's priorities to make sure they jibe with the priorities of Jesus Christ? Communication with God through prayer benefits every aspect of our existence.

Whenever Jesus faced any kind of challenge—when he was called upon to heal someone, or when he faced crucifixion, or when he felt deeply grateful for God's blessings, or when he wanted to feed five thousand hungry men—Jesus turned to God in prayer.

Prayer is invaluable because God is omnipotent. While we are weak, we can find strength by forming a partnership with God. While we are ignorant, we can find wisdom by asking God for it. If our prayer life has become superficial, then perhaps it's time to strengthen our commitment to pray more consistently. For when we pray without ceasing, we get help without interruption.

O Father, how patient and kind you are with me, even though I struggle to keep my mind focused on you as I pray to you. Give me the strength I need to communicate openly and honestly with you, depending upon you for divine wisdom. You know everything, Lord, and so you know what I will face today and what I will need to meet the challenges ahead. In Jesus' name I pray. Amen. ❧

Don't Give Up

*"Even though I don't fear God or care what people think, yet because
this widow keeps bothering me, I will see that she gets justice, so that
she won't eventually come and attack me!"*
LUKE 18:4 – 5

The early Christians had grown discouraged. They had anticipated Jesus'
quick return, but he hadn't come back. They wondered why the church
should be so persecuted if Christ were sitting at the right hand of God. And
most of all, they felt discouraged about prayer. They thought that since they
belonged to Christ, the miracle worker, their prayers should be answered in
miraculous ways. But too often, when they prayed for a sick person to get
well, the individual died. Perhaps this is why Luke quoted this parable about
a judge who neither feared God nor cared what people thought.

In those days, there were no juries or appellate courts. Whatever a judge
ruled, that was it. No doubt this judge oriented his decisions toward the rich
and influential. Widows had the lowest social status, since they inherited
nothing from their husbands and had no rights under the law; quite often
they became homeless or beggars. Yet one widow kept coming to the judge
and saying, "Grant me justice against my adversary!" Imagine him in his
house at night, maybe having a party for some prominent friends — and this
widow rattles his window and says, "I want justice!" Every time he goes to
bed, there she is, banging at the door: "I want justice!" Every time he walks
down the street, she follows him, waving a placard for all to see. Finally the
judge gives in, perhaps concerned about his reputation.

Jesus counsels us, "Be persistent in your prayers. Don't give up! If even an
unjust judge will give in to a persistent widow, then how much more will a
just and loving God answer the persistent prayers of the ones he loves?"

*O Lord, may this widow's persistence teach me constantly to turn to God
in prayer. As I meet with a friend or a stranger, prompt me to pray, "Let
me cement this relationship more deeply and fill it with more love." Help
me understand how I can live a transcendent life, striving always to
emulate my Savior. I ask these things in Jesus' name. Amen.*

126

Persistence and Faith

When the wine was gone, Jesus' mother said to him, "They have no more
wine." "Woman, why do you involve me?" Jesus replied. "My hour has not
yet come." His mother said to the servants, "Do whatever he tells you."
JOHN 2:3 – 5

One day Jesus visited a little village named Cana, just south of the Sea of
Galilee. There, at a wedding feast, he performed his first public miracle.
Sometime after the feast began, the wine ran out. The embarrassed host
apparently approached Jesus' mother and said, "We've run out of wine." Mary
then went to Jesus and told him about the problem. Jesus replied, "Woman,
my time has not yet come"—in effect, rebuffing her.

Mary reacted in an interesting way; she paid no attention to Jesus' negative response but simply told the servants to carry out her son's instructions.
And then Jesus, seeing that his mother had ignored his rebuff, told the servants to fill the jugs with plain water, which then turned into the best wine of
the party. The people who witnessed the miracle were filled with wonder, and
the disciples recognized that Jesus was indeed divine. God was among them!

Jesus' creation of about forty gallons of excellent wine is painful for some
Baptists. In fact, if there were one part of the Bible that many Baptists would
like to delete, it probably would be this incident when the water turned into
wine. If only he had changed it into grape juice!

The interesting lesson is that when we ask God for something, we have
to persist in our faith. When Mary turned to Jesus for help, clearly she had
complete faith that he could resolve the problem. Even after he declined, she
expected him to act; she even ordered the servants to prepare for it. It is this
kind of persistence and faith that God loves to reward.

Dear God, thank you for this scriptural story about the water turned into
wine and for using it to remind me to persist in my faith. When I believe
I am following your will and yet answers to my prayers seem delayed, help
me persist in my faith and continue to feel confident that you will act for
your glory and my benefit. I pray these things in Jesus' name. Amen. ❧

127

For All People

I urge, then, first of all, that petitions,
prayers, intercession and thanksgiving be made for all people.
I TIMOTHY 2:1

When a problem develops or some action must be taken, the number one priority for Christians is prayer. Prayer attaches us to our all-powerful God. So Paul reminded Timothy that no matter the difficulty, no matter the challenge, no matter the disappointments, sorrows, or opportunities, the wisest thing we can do is to align ourselves with God Almighty through prayer. And we are not to pray only for a few chosen people; Paul says we should pray for *everyone*.

Rosalynn asked me at breakfast one morning if I had difficulty praying for the poor children we see every time we travel to Africa (we had just returned from Ethiopia). Did I feel a little uncomfortable or hopeless in asking God to make their lives better, when deep down I felt their lives probably never would get much better? It was a legitimate question.

Suppose that every American Christian (we won't even count the ones worldwide) who prayed for the children in Africa to have a better life, would also say, "I'm not only going to ask God to help them, but I'm also going to do my part." How would the resulting flood of people visiting from rich countries (and the flood of money with them) affect the lives of those who suffer? It would immunize those children against disease, give them a home in which to sleep, make available more food to eat, and create money for better education and health care. We would see a dramatic change. As we ask God for some blessing, we have an obligation to participate ourselves in the fulfillment of those dreams, aspirations, hopes, and ideas.

O Lord, thank you for the encouragement to expand my prayer life
and for the reminder that you give me the opportunity to intercede for
others. As I pray for those in need, keep me aware of my own obligations
to improve their lives. Equip me to live with and for Christ in an
exemplary, dynamic, adventurous, exciting, joyful, and peaceful way. I
ask in his name. Amen. ❧

128

The Right Words?

We do not know what we ought to pray for, but the Spirit himself
intercedes for us through wordless groans.
ROMANS 8:26

Sometimes we just don't know how to express strong emotion. This happens even in marriage, where perhaps a husband feels intense love for his wife but has no words to express it. Little poems that begin with "Roses are red" just don't meet the need of the moment.

No doubt many of us lack the command of language necessary to communicate with passion the strong emotions that, at times, we all feel. Even if we did, how often do we have two or three hours to sit down and laboriously put poetic words together in a meaningful, lovely, and well-coordinated way? Many of us have trouble enough using words to express our *simple* feelings! And it is especially aggravating to be unable to express in words how we feel about someone, or to communicate our inner doubts, fears, or frustrations, or to convey sorrow over some failure or loss.

The same problem can plague our prayer lives. At times we're in anguish and desperately need God, but we find it impossible to find the right words to express our desire for comfort, forgiveness, or even reconciliation. When times of deep confusion, despair, alienation, or loneliness burden our hearts, our emotions well up inside us and we feel almost that they will explode. Rarely do we know how to express all of that pent-up emotion, which makes the experience all the more disheartening.

But Paul tells us not to worry. The Holy Spirit will help us pray! In fact, the Spirit will pray in our stead. We don't have to worry about being spiritually inarticulate. If a sincere yearning burdens our heart, it will reach God. We have to acknowledge and sincerely feel it, but we don't have to spell it all out with eloquent words. The Holy Spirit will intercede for us.

Dear God, I am grateful for the Spirit's ministry of intercessory prayer.
When words escape me, even though strong emotion does not, I thank you
for giving me a heavenly prayer partner who knows exactly how to present
my inarticulate longings before your throne of grace. Help me grow closer
to you as you enable me to walk with Jesus. In his glorious name I pray.
Amen. ❧

How Do Our Prayers Get Answered?

Paul and his companions traveled throughout the region of Phrygia and
Galatia, having been kept by the Holy Spirit from preaching the word in
the province of Asia. When they came to the border of Mysia, they tried to
enter Bithynia, but the Spirit of Jesus would not allow them to.
ACTS 16:6 – 7

After Paul's successful missionary journey in Asia, he felt eager to return there to strengthen the churches he had established. He prayed and made careful plans, but all of them fell through. As he pondered his next move, Paul dreamed of a man in Macedonia who said to him, "Come over here and help us!"

Paul and his companions accepted the dream as a divine directive and traveled to Philippi. There they met Lydia, a wealthy woman who became the first Christian convert in Europe. They soon established a church in her home.

Paul's earlier redirections by the Holy Spirit could have been caused by illness, orders from Roman soldiers, or other difficulties. Whatever the case, he accepted these unexpected barriers as instructions from God.

We too seek God's will through prayer—but how do we receive God's answers? Most of our guidance tends to come in the form of doors opened or closed. We may wish and pray to be a lawyer, professor, business executive— or to marry a certain sweetheart—but what if none of these ambitions come true? God often reveals his will for us through life circumstances. We must respond by accepting what the Lord gives with thanksgiving.

Garth Brooks is a friend and a dedicated Habitat for Humanity volunteer. One of his greatest hits is "Unanswered Prayers," which describes his gratitude when he meets a former sweetheart (who chose someone else) many years after he had married his "second choice." He thanks God that the Lord denied his earlier prayer. Garth says, "Happiness isn't about getting what you want; it's wanting what you've got."

Dear Lord, help me recognize your hand in the circumstances of my
life—not only in the pleasant and welcomed circumstances, but also in
the ones I didn't expect and didn't perhaps want. Remind me that you
see much more than I do, and give me the grace to accept your superior
wisdom. In Jesus' name I pray. Amen.

130

Thank God in Prayer

Praise the LORD, my soul; all my inmost being, praise his holy name.
PSALM 103:1

Rosalynn and I thank God every time our grandkids come for a visit. Before we eat, we hold hands and say a simple blessing, which often is this: "God is great, God is good, let us thank him for our food. By his hands we all are fed; give us, Lord, our daily bread."

As good as that is, however, Psalm 103 admonishes us to reserve times just for blessing God. How often do we express our thanks with such fervent commitment? I doubt we do this nearly enough; I know I don't. Perhaps we should strive to do so once a day.

Let's bless and thank God with all our soul and being—wipe away everything else from our minds and describe in detail the many things for which we give the Lord thanks. Let's not say merely, "I thank you for all my blessings," but instead try to mentally list them. How about eternal life or the essence of love or the forgiveness of our sins? How about the proven promise that, through faith, we always have access to our Creator, who will receive us for the sake of his Son? It should not be hard to find many things for which to thank God; in fact, we owe the Lord our very lives.

When I was four years old, I developed colitis. At the time, the disease was nearly always fatal. Doctors told my mother, a registered nurse, that I couldn't recover. But I *did* recover. Later, when I served on Navy submarines, three times I thought my life was about to end; each time, God spared me. No doubt you've had similar experiences. The point is that God has given us the very life we enjoy. And isn't *that* a good reason to give thanks?

O Lord, by giving you thanks, help me turn a potentially dull and uninteresting existence into a life of joy, exuberance, gratification, and exaltation, with a peace that passes understanding. Help me develop a plan and a dream that can lift me above my daily existence to reach new heights in furthering your kingdom—aspirations that can outstrip any I had considered before. I thank you for all of this in Christ's name. Amen.

A Forgotten Element

Sing and make music from your heart to the Lord, always giving
thanks to God the Father for everything, in the name of our Lord
Jesus Christ.
EPHESIANS 5:19 – 20

Think back on your life for a moment and ponder the things that have happened to you, both the good and the bad. Think especially about your life over the last year or the last month. Can you thank God for "everything" you recall?

Paul instructs us to give thanks "for everything." No matter how serious our problems or how bad the circumstances, he counsels us to find a way to give thanks to God. It's easy to forget this element of Christianity, isn't it?

Those who don't give God thanks tend to fall into two categories. Christ addressed one of them when he encountered a young ruler addicted to his wealth. This sort of person rarely prays or gives thanks because his ego keeps him feeling self-satisfied. He doesn't need outside help and all his achievements are his own; so why should he thank God for them? Such an individual struggles with more than giving thanks; Jesus said it's more difficult for him to get into heaven than for a camel to squeeze through the eye of a needle.

The second sort of thankless person is one who feels unfairly afflicted. He believes that God causes his problems, not himself, human nature, or mere accident. He blames God for most of what goes wrong in his life, and so he does not give thanks.

Let's strive to avoid becoming like either person. When success or joy comes our way, let's thank God. And when loss or suffering enters our lives, let's give thanks for other blessings and for God's promise to work out all things for good. Let's try to maintain an attitude of thanksgiving, as Paul did, who eventually gave his life in service to his heavenly Master.

O God, while most of us find it easy to thank you during good times, I
admit it's a different story during darker times. I pray that you give me a
thankful heart for life itself and other gifts, and for the opportunities and
responsibilities I have, even when my tasks are unpleasant or challenging.
Fill my lips with praise, Lord. I ask these things in Jesus' name. Amen.

132

Our Sustainer

I lie down and sleep; I wake again, because the LORD sustains me.
PSALM 3:5

Most of us lean toward self-sufficiency. We want to stand on our own two feet, make our own way, heal our own wounds, and take care of our own needs. We don't want to depend on anyone but ourselves.

Every Mother's Day we reach out to our mothers, if they're still living. I wear a white flower, because my mother has died. Had she lived, she would have been 101 years old this year. Mothers are just one special example of those to whom we should show our gratitude, since we have so heavily depended upon them for so much.

But many others we know—from work, as neighbors, at church, or at school—also deserve our thanks and probably receive almost no expression of gratitude. Sometimes just to say, "I'm really grateful to you," feels like a big stretch for our hearts—and our pride. It doesn't come easy for us because by saying, "I'm grateful," we imply that we needed what the other person gave. And that makes us feel somewhat dependent.

I wonder if we fail to show God enough gratitude, for the same reason. We may say grace at the dinner table for every meal—my family does, and I like it when our little grandchildren hold hands with us and say, "God is great, God is good, let us thank him for our food"—but many times, we say these prayers without thinking much about them. We usually prefer a brief prayer because we're ready to eat.

How would our lives change, I wonder, if we tried to do a better job of giving God thanks for the many ways he sustains us every day? In how many thousands of ways has God blessed us? Have we told the Lord "thank you"?

Without hurrying?

O Lord, may I take time during each day to give you thanks for all the ways you sustain me. Help me realize how much I depend on you for everything, including every breath I take. Grant me an additional vision of how much others help me, and let me express my gratitude to them. Grant me a thankful heart that delights in showing gratitude. I pray in Jesus' name. Amen. ❧

133

When to Be Thankful

Give thanks in all circumstances; for this is God's will for you in Christ Jesus.
I THESSALONIANS 5:18

On my boyhood farm, we had no electricity or mechanical devices, no trac-
tors or self-propelled combines or anything like that. We used kerosene lamps
and worked with our hands and with mules. We had one gasoline engine
that we cranked up once a day to pump water for the livestock. We also had
a hand pump, so if we couldn't get the engine to start, we could put a bolt
through the pump handle and spend an hour pumping water.

Technology has changed radically in a very short period of time. The
backbreaking work that used to consume so much of our days has given way
to motors, machines, vehicles, and systems that make our lives much easier.
We have so much for which to be thankful!

But *are* we thankful for it?

How often do we take a few minutes to thank God for provision, care, and
blessing? Too often we limit our thanksgiving to particular situations where
a crisis gets resolved. Perhaps we pray for a loved one to be rescued from a
dangerous situation. When rescue comes, for a brief time, we're deeply and
sincerely grateful to God, and we express our thanks, sometimes out loud.
Or perhaps we thank God for allowing us to escape some tragedy that befell
others, or for peace when our country has been at war. Maybe we pause to
give thanks, on occasion, for the people around us whose love shows itself in
their nurturing care.

That's all to the good. But would our lives not be richer and our relationship with God more dynamic and satisfying if we learned to give thanks in
all circumstances, as Paul instructs us? We all know how many thousands of
blessings we have received. Do our actions and words express our gratitude
to God?

*O God, thank you for taking care of my needs. I am grateful for a nation
in which freedom of religion is a given, where I can come to you at any
time to seek help, to worship and praise your goodness. Let me show my
gratitude in prayer and in following Christ more closely. In Jesus' name I
pray. Amen.* ❧

134

Sin and Thanksgiving

*Then I acknowledged my sin to you and did not cover up my
iniquity. I said, "I will confess my transgressions to the LORD." And
you forgave the guilt of my sin.*
PSALM 32:5

We don't generally like the ugly word *sin*. Most of us prefer to say, "I'll admit
that sometimes I'm selfish and not very aware of the suffering of others;
sometimes I'm not very compassionate or loving or forgiving; sometimes I
bear grudges. I'm willing to admit that—but it's not who I really am." For
many of us, to acknowledge we're *sinners* (that ugly word again) feels like
going a bit too far.

I wonder, though. Can we *truly* be thankful to God for forgiveness unless
we are willing to acknowledge the sins that the Lord has forgiven?

We know from the Bible that everybody is a sinner: "All have sinned and
fall short of the glory of God" (Romans 3:23). But unless we are willing to
connect that statement to our own lives and personalize it—"*I* am a sinner"—
we can't truly be thankful to God for his grace and mercy. Why not? Why
can't we say, "I can be thankful and still keep my sinful ways"? Why can't we
feel thankful for life itself, for a nice house, for the chance to worship together,
for a healthy family or for exciting opportunities, all without embracing that
ugly word *sin*?

The main problem is that we *have* sinned, and to deny it or ignore it is
to live in falsehood. Jesus said, "I am the Truth," and no lie can coexist with
him. Without admitting our sin, we can never reach that feeling of reconciliation or intimacy with God that is necessary for true thanksgiving.

It takes courage to acknowledge our transgressions. But if we confess our
sin and seek forgiveness, then we know God's grace is abundantly there for
us. And then our hearts can express genuine, sincere, and joyful thanksgiving to God.

*O Lord, I'm thankful for this potent reminder from David about the
close relationship between repentance, confession, forgiveness, and
reconciliation—a healing process that leads to thanksgiving. And may I
express, often and genuinely, my thanks to you for your great work in my
life. In Jesus' name I pray. Amen.* ❧

Divinity Not Divinely Acquired

*What a wretched man I am! Who will rescue me from this body that
is subject to death? Thanks be to God, who delivers me through Jesus
Christ our Lord!*
ROMANS 7:24 – 25

For a few years, my grandparents lived on a hill near our house. A young friend named Rembert Forrest and I once visited their house right after Grandma had cooked up a batch of divinity candy. "How many folks at your house, Jimmy?" she asked. "Eight," I replied. And she laid out sixteen pieces of candy.

On the way home, Rembert and I stopped along the road and thought, *Does everybody really need two pieces of candy?* So very carefully we counted out eight pieces and ate them. When we arrived home, we proudly presented to my mama and daddy eight pieces of candy from Grandma.

Unfortunately, the next Sunday my grandparents ate dinner with us. Mama said to her mother, "Thanks a lot for the piece of candy." Grandma answered, "*One* piece? I sent two pieces for each person."

All eyes focused on Rembert and me, and we had no alternative but confession.

We all do wrong, and it's not easy to acknowledge it, as Paul did. We may say, "I go to church on Sunday. I put a little of what I earn in the collection plate. I don't hurt anybody. I don't break into people's houses or endanger the lives of others. I'm not a drug addict, and I stay away from people who are." And so we imagine ourselves to be acceptable in God's eyes. But if we *really* took a look at our lives, we'd see that we fall *far* short of righteousness. We tend to remain blind to our own sin, thus separating us from a vital relationship with God.

Knowing the depth of our sin should remind us of our salvation in Christ and then spur us to live more vibrantly and enthusiastically for God.

*Dear God, since I love Jesus, help me consider his life and actions and
words and then use that model to shape my behavior. I confess that I come
up far short of your glory, but I thank you for making it possible for me,
through Christ, to have a fuller and better and more gratifying existence.
I pray in the name of my Savior. Amen.* ❧

136

Cherry Picking Sins

*"Why do you look at the speck of sawdust in your brother's eye and
pay no attention to the plank in your own eye?"*
MATTHEW 7:3

Religious leaders in Jesus' day treated rules about the Sabbath with special reverence. On that day they would not allow any secular activity; people could walk only a certain number of steps; they could not pick up anything; they couldn't prepare food. These leaders condemned anyone who broke their multitude of meticulous rules; they even condemned Jesus for healing people on the Sabbath.

Sadly, at times, we do very similar things in our churches. When I was a child, the churches in Plains lived by three basic rules: don't dance; don't drink; and don't associate with anybody who does. One of the biggest scandals in the Methodist church occurred when two prominent members, including my uncle, broke the dancing rule. The church kicked them out, and they joined the Baptist church, which was more lenient about dancing.

We tend to interpret Scriptures and define Christianity in ways that seem most convenient for us. If we don't drink, we emphasize drinking as a sin. If we don't dance, we equate dancing with being a bad Christian. We take certain faults or habits that we don't have and escalate their importance.

But if we have a "little" sin, like selfishness or gossip, we downplay it as relatively unimportant. Or if we lie or cheat on occasion, uncaringly ignore someone we know to be in need, or consider ourselves superior to people who are female, imprisoned, black, Arab, or Hispanic, then we don't count those kinds of things. That is *exactly* the kind of attitude Jesus warned us about.

We must never forget that all of us are sinners, that we all fall short of the glory of God, that the wages of sin is death, and that we are saved by the grace of God through our faith in Jesus Christ. God gives us no room to "cherry pick" sins.

*O God, keep me from the arrogance of considering myself superior to
others. Help me look my sin square in the face, give me an insatiable
desire to do your will, and grant me the strength to follow through on my
commitments. In Jesus' name I pray. Amen.* ❧

Taking Responsibility

"For everyone belongs to me, the parent as well as the child—both alike belong to me. The one who sins is the one who will die."
EZEKIEL 18:4

The people of Judah irked Ezekiel when they began quoting the proverb, "The parents have eaten sour grapes and the children's teeth are set on edge," which meant, "When Daddy does wrong, the children pay for it."

The people had used this bad theology to excuse themselves from personal responsibility for their nation's subjugation. If they were guilty of worshiping a golden idol, they'd explain, "It's because our leaders set up the golden idol and even the king said it was okay. So I'm not responsible for God's anger." But God made it plain that individuals are responsible for their personal actions—and the consequences that may follow.

Let's look at our own lives. Clearly we are affected by our culture. Our habits and way of life are shaped by our encounters with others and by the standards and ideals that prevail within our society. These things can drag us down or inspire us. They can push us to reach for great things or lower our moral standards and make it easy to rationalize wrongdoing. In the latter case, we say, "Hey, if most others are doing it, then it must be okay." And so we cut corners, cheat, ignore the needs of others, or perhaps damage someone's reputation through gossip. We might condone our leaders' decisions to unnecessarily antagonize others, leading to war instead of peace; or maybe we excuse injustice and oppression.

Let's hear Ezekiel again: "The one who sins is the one who will die." We must not blame our nation, parents, friends, Hollywood, Wall Street, or anyone else for our own deviation from God's will. When we are guilty of ungodly behavior, instead of shifting blame, we must repent and turn to God for forgiveness.

Lord, once again I am thankful for Old Testament passages designed for your people two or three thousand years ago, but which still apply to me. I pray that I might have the courage to look into my own heart and ask, "How can I be a better Christian? How can I more clearly demonstrate my faith in a perfect Savior?" I ask these things in his holy name. Amen. 🌱

138

Be Honest about Your Sin

*Blessed is the one whose transgressions are forgiven, whose sins are
covered. Blessed is the one whose sin the LORD does not count against
them and in whose spirit is no deceit.*
PSALM 32:1 – 2

Shortly after arriving in a small town, a pastor new to his church had to
conduct a funeral. In preparation for the service, he made the rounds of the
barbershop, the grocery store, and elsewhere asking for nice things to say
about the deceased. But he couldn't find anyone who would say anything
good about the man.

In desperation, when the funeral service started, the pastor decided to
invite the members of the congregation to speak up for the deceased. A long
silence followed, and finally he said, "Can't anyone say *anything*?" At last
somebody stood up in the back and said, "His brother was worse."

If we're honest with ourselves, how many of us might be concerned about
comments made at our own funerals? David's psalm admonishes us to make
sure we're absolutely honest in confronting our sinfulness. There can be no
deceit, no covering up; we can't pray in generalities, "Lord, forgive me all
my sins." True repentance requires honest confrontation. We must freely
acknowledge *our* guilt in deviating from the teachings of Jesus Christ.

We might pray, "God, at times today I have failed to do the things you
have commanded. I did not take the opportunity to help someone, although
I saw her needing assistance. I refused to share my possessions with others,
although I saw their need. I said unkind things about a coworker. I did not
reconcile with my wife after an argument."

We must be brutally honest with ourselves and not try to hide anything
from God, who knows the truth anyway. We need to acknowledge what we
have done wrong, confess it, and pledge not to repeat the improper acts or
sinful habits.

*O God, allow David's words to produce in me a deep sense of humility.
Give me the courage to look inside my heart to see what kind of person
I really am. Help me strive each day to expand my heart and serve those
in need. Enable me to remember how Jesus dealt with people whom his
society despised and to follow his example of loving action. In the name of
Christ I pray. Amen.* ❧

139

Blanket Pardons?

In those days John the Baptist came, preaching in the wilderness of
Judea and saying, "Repent, for the kingdom of heaven has come near."
MATTHEW 3:1 – 2

When we ask God to forgive us our sins, most of us probably are conscious of certain "hazy sins" we've committed. We seldom specify them, even in our private thoughts. And yet we want God to forgive them. We recite by rote, "Forgive us our sins," and probably don't stop to inventory the sins we want forgiven because we hate to face them. So we say, in effect, "Lord, whatever sins I might have committed—I don't want to think about them right now—please forgive me for all of them." We ask for a blanket pardon.

On the other hand, no doubt we can easily enumerate the injuries others have inflicted on us. If we were given a sheet of paper and asked to list the five sins in our life that we consider the most serious and habitual, that would be a torturous exercise. We might not even be able to do it. But if we were asked to list five people who have harmed us in some way, we would find making that list much easier.

Christ demands that we confront our sin before God. That's a requirement for repentance. I'm no theologian and I don't know whether it's valid just to say, "Whatever sins I've committed, I repent," but such a declaration doesn't seem to fulfill what John the Baptist meant when he said, "Repent!"

I believe that we need to confront, in specific terms, our sin. So we must say, "God, I hurt my wife," or "God, I have cheated another human being," or "God, I have told a lie," or "I've turned away from a needy person." That's the beginning of true repentance. Anything less is just a sham.

O God, give me the courage to examine my heart, confess my sins, and
ask myself, "How well have I lived as a Christian? How much do I strive
to imitate the perfect life of Christ as I immerse myself in the world
around me?" Give me the grace to be honest with myself and with you. In
Jesus' name I pray. Amen. ❧

140

A Willingness to Face Our Sin

You came near when I called you, and you said, "Do not fear." You,
Lord, took up my case; you redeemed my life.
LAMENTATIONS 3:57 – 58

The author of Lamentations looked around at a devastated Jerusalem and struggled to come to terms with the consequences of Judah's terrible sin. He does not cry out against God's judgment; rather, he calls for enlightenment, for instruction, for inspiration. He hungers for reconciliation with God and expresses a complete willingness to look into his own heart and say, "How have I sinned?" and then repent from that sin.

That is a very difficult thing to do. It's certainly difficult for me to do. But we are told that when we confront our sins, we have no need to fear. Why not? God is with us and has redeemed us. The phrase "do not fear" is the most frequent admonition to us from God in the Bible; it's used 350 times in both testaments. We don't have to fear, for if we turn to God, the Lord will take up our cause.

Nevertheless, it can be hard to face the ugly truth that we have been in the wrong, that our troubles might have resulted from that wrong, or that God might be punishing us. I'm sure that was difficult for the Israelites! But we all must do it if we want to begin the reconciliation process with our Lord.

If we have faith that God is in control and knows everything about us — if we trust that God has redeemed us and that we can return to him and be forgiven — then we can face the fear of confronting our sin and accepting God's discipline. In fact, we can face *any* suffering, adversity, or punishment, so long as we enjoy a personal relationship with God through faith in Jesus Christ. What a great blessing!

O Lord, as I look at the difficult circumstances around me, let me see what part I might have played in creating the problems. Give me the strength of character to face my sins squarely and repent sincerely. Let me turn to you without fear, even knowing the necessity for your righteous discipline in my life. Help me increasingly to reflect the glory of Jesus Christ, in whose name I pray. Amen. ❧

Don't Hide Away

She thought, "If I just touch his clothes, I will be healed." Immediately her
bleeding stopped and she felt in her body that she was freed from her suffering.
MARK 5:28 – 29

We tend to conceal two things about our character: the embarrassing mistakes we've made and the personal needs that might make us blush. Often the two are interlinked. Why do we feel so reluctant to reveal these things?

Usually it's because we fear that by living more transparently, we become vulnerable. Being honest about ourselves might make us uncomfortable, so we tend to hide those things away. When we go to church, we put on a happy face, or maybe a devout expression, to let people know, "I am okay in the eyes of God. I'm not ashamed of any of my habits, actions, or failures." I do this myself. We put on our "best face" to show people what we want them to see.

The woman who had been hemorrhaging for twelve years couldn't afford that. She felt desperate and had enough faith to overcome her natural inclination to conceal her need. She reached out to Jesus—a remarkable act, for in those days women were severely oppressed. The birth of a baby girl was considered evidence that the prayers of that family had not been answered. Boys were looked upon as breadwinners of the future, a kind of Social Security for the family. Girls were merely a burden who needed large dowries to get married.

Also, this woman had a disease that, in the Jewish faith, made her unclean. She could not participate in any religious ceremony. She could not visit the temple, even its outer reaches. And anyone who touched her was considered unclean.

But when Jesus walked by, she took a chance. She revealed her most embarrassing secret to him. Jesus rewarded her honesty and her faith, as he will reward yours. Hiding your faults and needs from Christ never brings healing.

O Lord, give me the courage to reveal who I really am and to share with
Jesus Christ the parts of me that are most private and embarrassing. Let
me also be available to help others who might have confidence in me to
share their pain. I pray this in Jesus' name. Amen. ❧

Publican or Pharisee?

"For all those who exalt themselves will be humbled, and those who humble themselves will be exalted."
LUKE 18:14

Jesus once told a parable about a Pharisee and a publican. In those days, a "publican" usually was a tax collector who worked for the Romans. (I'm not trying to equate publicans with Republicans, if that's what you thought.) Jews despised publicans but revered Pharisees, the religious and secular rulers of that era.

Jesus described how both men began to pray. The loud and proud Pharisee said, in essence, "God, I'm thankful that you made me a good man. I'm thankful that you let me have my special religion. I'm thankful that you let me be so right, even about tithing. I'm glad that you made me want to attend synagogue every Saturday. And I *sure* am thankful that you didn't make me a disgusting publican."

Meanwhile, the publican uttered a very different prayer. With a voice full of contrition, he said, "Forgive me, Lord, for I have sinned. I am not worthy of you."

Jesus told the crowd (of proud people) that while God forgave the publican, the Pharisee went home still in his sins.

Jesus clearly thought it important to give this stiff warning against pride and self-righteousness. We all tend to say (or at least think), "I am better than most other people," or "I'm okay the way I am. I don't need repentance. I don't need to change the way I relate to God Almighty. I don't need to change the way I relate to other human beings." Christ continually preached against any such kind of smug attitude.

In condemning the Pharisee and exalting the publican, Jesus wanted us to see that public reputation is no guide at all to a person's heart. I think he wants each of us to ask, "Am I more like the Pharisee or the publican?" And then, "How might I need to change?"

Dear God, give me the strength to look at myself and see the true status of my pride or ego. Grant me the humility to associate gladly with those whom others may consider "inferior," and remind me that the blessings of a Christlike life are available to all people on an equal basis. Bind my heart together with others in Christian love, for I pray in Jesus' name. Amen. ❧

143

What God Desires

"Come, let us return to the LORD. He has torn us to pieces but he will heal us; he has injured us but he will bind up our wounds."
HOSEA 6:1

It's hard to imagine that God can totally forgive our sins, making it as though we had never sinned. It's hard for us to believe, because we know how difficult it is for *us* to forgive others.

Do you harbor some resentment or grudge against anyone, either for hurting you or for doing something you detest? The truth is, we just don't like some people. We disapprove of their actions or their attitudes, and we simply dislike them.

Sometimes such resentments exist within families. Rosalynn and I have been married for over sixty years, but we still have had our troubles and sometimes go to bed angry with each other. Ordinarily we read aloud the Bible as a couple every night, but in years past we have even refused to follow this habit.

One day we had a very serious argument. I went to my woodshop and sliced off with my finest band saw a very thin piece of beautiful walnut. I sanded it smooth and wrote this message on it: "To Rosalynn: each evening forever, this is good for an apology or forgiveness, as you desire." She has used it several times, and so far I've been able to honor it. Rosalynn has a permanent check, you might say, signed by me, whereby anytime we have an argument we can't resolve, she can bring that check to me and get her choice of an apology or forgiveness. While a lack of understanding or agreement can tear us apart, forgiveness can bring us back together.

Who may God be calling you to forgive? Who may need to forgive you?

O Lord, I'm grateful for your love and mercy. I marvel at the forgiveness you offer me through Jesus Christ, and I recognize that you have called me to forgive others. I pray that forgiveness might become an integral part of my life. I ask this in the name of Jesus Christ. Amen. ❧

A Debt to Forgive

"Forgive us our sins, for we also forgive everyone who sins against us."
LUKE 11:4

Many of us do not find it easy to forgive. We assume that if we get into an argument, we are right and our opponent is wrong. Or if we get into a fight (or a war), we assume the fault lies with our antagonists.

When did we last hear gossip that offended us? While it may have been a false report, for a while we tended to think the worst about the person so slandered. Sometimes we hold grudges against those whom we don't naturally like, even if we don't really know them. We harbor an ugly collection of petty grievances in our hearts, resulting in a tendency to condemn.

Because Christ recognized this sinful inclination, he reminded us of God's unrestricted love, grace, and forgiveness. The Lord loved us so much that "he gave his one and only Son, that whoever believes in him shall not perish but have eternal life" (John 3:16). In his total innocence, Christ paid the full penalty for our sins. Even if we lie, cheat, commit adultery, or commit murder, Christ has taken our deserved punishment upon himself. As a result, he has miraculously wiped away our guilt, making it as though we had never sinned.

We are forgiven! And that is why we must forgive others.

Jesus once told a story about a servant who owed his master a staggering debt. In mercy, the master forgave it all. Yet no sooner did the forgiven man leave his master than he threatened his own debtors with prison. When the master heard about it, he reversed himself, threw the man in jail, and insisted that he repay his enormous debt.

Each of us has been forgiven a mountain of debt. And that is why each of us must freely forgive the molehill of debt that others may owe us.

O God, help me gain a better understanding of the enormous debt you have forgiven me, and let me constantly remember the enormity of Jesus' sacrifice on the cross. Drive deep into my heart the recognition that it is my calling as a Christian to forgive those who have hurt or offended me. Help me change my life and draw closer to my Savior, in whose name I pray. Amen. ❦

145

How Often Should We Forgive?

Then Peter came to Jesus and asked, "Lord, how many times shall I forgive my brother or sister who sins against me? Up to seven times?" Jesus answered, "I tell you, not seven times, but seventy-seven times."
MATTHEW 18:21 – 22

One of the most intriguing books in my home library is *The One Hundred* by Michael Hart. Hart consulted scholars and identified the one hundred people who had the greatest impact on human history. I don't agree with many of his conclusions, but I've read the book several times because I find his thoughts both provocative and intriguing.

The first person on his list is Mohammed, and the second is Isaac Newton. Hart claims that Newton's theories provided the basis for modern science, which affects almost every aspect of life. The third person is Jesus Christ. Hart explains that Mohammed appears on the list above Jesus because Mohammed not only founded the Islamic faith but also wrote its central religious text, the Qur'an, and was the political and military leader who spread his teachings to many nations. Christ, on the other hand, didn't write any Scripture and, according to Hart, Jesus shares the credit for the spread of Christianity with others, including Paul (number six). Nor was Jesus a political or military leader during his time on earth.

Hart says, however, that the teachings of Christ are the most transforming, interesting, and revolutionary words in history. As an example, he cites Christ's commands to love our enemies and to forgive those who sin against us. He concludes that if Christians actually practiced Christ's teachings, Jesus would have topped his list.

Love and forgiveness are not easy. First-century Jews thought it generous to forgive someone three times; Peter upped the ante and suggested seven times. Jesus replied, "Multiply that number by seventy." The point is to avoid keeping score. Through the power of the Holy Spirit, God calls us to develop an *unlimited* capacity to forgive.

O Lord, open my eyes so I might see the beauty, peace, and joy that can be mine when I choose to obey you gladly. Help me turn to you in complete submission and confidence, knowing that when I sin and repent, you will forgive me—provided that I also forgive others. I ask these things in Jesus' name. Amen. ❧

A Guilty, Honest Man

Then David said to Nathan, "I have sinned against the LORD."
2 SAMUEL 12:13

One evening as King David looked out from his palace rooftop, he saw a beautiful woman bathing. He sent for her and slept with her, even knowing that she was married and that her husband was away fighting a war. Some time later, she sent a message to David informing him that she was pregnant with his child.

Trying to cover up his sin, David thought, *I'll invite her husband, Uriah, back from the war; he can go home and sleep with her. Then, when the baby comes, everybody will consider it to be his.* But Uriah, instead of returning home, curled up on the ground in front of the palace, feeling that he shouldn't enjoy such pleasure while his fellow soldiers remained on the battlefield.

Desperate, David wrote a letter to the commander of his army, instructing him to place Uriah at the battlefront and then withdraw from him so he would be killed.

It seemed like a perfect crime. But God sent the prophet Nathan to confront David—and when David was forced to face his own sin, he confessed, repented, and cried out in remorse, "I have sinned against the LORD." Nathan described David's punishment, then added, "The LORD has taken away your sin."

What a depraved series of acts David committed! And it all began with a simple look from a balcony at a beautiful woman. If even David, whom the Bible describes as a man after God's own heart (1 Samuel 13:14), could become guilty of such terrible crimes, then we are all susceptible to sin. The good news is that if we genuinely repent of our sins, God will forgive us, just as God forgave David when the king admitted his wrongdoing and repented sincerely.

Dear God, I thank you for the privilege I have to come to you in prayer and worship. I praise you because you are a faithful, loving God who makes a way for me, through faith in Christ's suffering on the cross, to enjoy a living relationship with you, despite my failures. Help me be a blessing to those who have been injured by sin, whether mine or that of others. In Jesus' name I pray. Amen. ❧

147

Be Reconciled

"In your anger do not sin":
Do not let the sun go down while you are still angry.
EPHESIANS 4:26

During a Seattle book signing for my presidential memoirs, *Keeping Faith*, a woman said to me, "I hope you will write a note to my brother in your book. He hasn't spoken to me for eight years, but after he gets the book, I'm going to call him on the phone. I hope you'll ask him to talk to me." I honored her request, and they spoke to each other.

For a long time, my own brother and sister were alienated from each other. Billy refused to speak to my older sister and her husband; only toward the end of his life were they reconciled. How sad! If one of the most wonderful things we can do is to have fun as a family, then one of the worst experiences is when a family divides.

The writing of *Keeping Faith* required careful research into the details of my years in the White House. As I examined six thousand pages of personal diary notes and many official documents, my faulty memory surprised me. I could hardly recall the details of some historic events.

But recently I joined my small grandson, Joshua, on a little two-person paddleboat. As captain, he sat in front, pushing two foot pedals that made the boat go right or left. Despite our erratic course, we caught a nice bass — just the two of us. After one long period of silence, Josh looked at me and said, "Papa, this is the life."

That incident won't appear in any history books, but I'll never forget it. This is the kind of event that really counts and is worth cherishing. It is also the kind of pleasure that unresolved grudges can prevent or negate. We must never let that happen! Let's reconcile with our loved ones while we still have the chance.

Father, sometimes I don't cherish the gentle, simple things that compose a life—small acts of humanity and sharing that bring me peace, gratification, and joy. Sometimes I see success in life as having earthly possessions such as a large bank account, a big house, fancy new automobiles, or public acclaim. Help me instead measure my life by the standards of my Savior, Jesus Christ. In his name I pray. Amen. ❧

148

Godly Sorrow

*Godly sorrow brings repentance that leads to salvation and leaves no
regret, but worldly sorrow brings death.*
2 CORINTHIANS 7:10

All of us have to work out the differences we surely will have with others.
Even if a young couple is madly in love and each person considers the other
absolutely perfect and above the angels, still they likely will have to deal with
some significant differences between them once they get married. The odds
of this occurring approach 100 percent.

None of us are immune to strife. Even if I have a friend whom I look upon
as a bosom buddy and who has meant the world to me, times will come when
that friend and I will differ on some important issues. It's an inevitable part
of life.

Knowing this, let's forget the idea that we can steer clear of all confronta-
tions. That's impossible. Instead, we must live so that when the unavoidable
disagreements come, we can resolve them in a healthy way, with mutual
acceptance of responsibility. Grieving in a godly way over things we might
have done to harm others — or vice versa — leads to repentance and healing.
I think that may be what Paul means by "godly sorrow."

Worldly grief, on the other hand, perpetuates feelings of animosity and
pain. It shows itself when we think, "I was aggrieved by this event, but I know
I'm right. Although I have been made to suffer, I can compensate by feeling
resentment." "Worldly sorrow" reveals a lack of repentance and the absence
of a desire for reconciliation.

Today we see so many conflicts, not only in world affairs, but even within
the kingdom of God. Too often misunderstanding, division, and lack of
mutual respect prevail. We must not let worldly grief keep these divisions
alive, but instead must try to abandon resentment and alienation and work
to be reconciled with those who have disagreed with us.

*O Lord, thank you for the chance to consider these words from Paul about
the growth and vitality of the early Christian church. Let his message
inspire me to overcome animosity and resentment and division, despite
whatever differences of opinion may exist. Help me value others and love
them sincerely in Jesus' name. In his name I pray. Amen.* ❧

149

Secure in God's Love

Whom have I in heaven but you? And earth has nothing I desire
besides you. My flesh and my heart may fail, but God is the strength
of my heart and my portion forever.
PSALM 73:25 – 26

Rosalynn and I once saw a movie called *East of Eden*, patterned after the biblical drama of Cain and Abel. The star was James Dean, who played a young Californian named Cal, tortured because his father loved his brother, Aron, but seemed to have no love for him. So Cal lashed out, misbehaving in every way to aggravate his father.

Finally Cal borrowed some money, invested it, and made a small fortune. He decided to give the money to his father, who had no way to repay a crushing debt. Cal laid the money at his father's feet—and his father flatly rejected his gift.

The movie illustrates how difficult it is to love unless we have the security of love in return. Who likes to be embarrassed or take the risk of getting hurt? Even as Christians, we find it difficult to express our love or to forgive unless we have strong assurance of being loved or forgiven in return.

Yet Christ instructs us not to wait to love or to forgive. If we've gotten into a nasty disagreement, we must not wait until we think the other person will forgive us. We are not to say, "I can't risk forgiving him until I'm sure he will forgive me. I won't put myself in a vulnerable position by offering to become friends, only, perhaps, to be rebuffed again!"

That is not how Christ lived. He did not wait to love and forgive others until he felt sure they would accept him. Neither should we. No matter who has hurt us, we always have the security of being loved and forgiven by God. We always do right by following the example set by Jesus. From that secure position, we can forgive and love others freely.

O Lord, thank you for displaying your love for me, through countless declarations in Scripture and especially through the ultimate sacrifice of Jesus Christ on the cross. Always let me remember the love of Christ as expressed on Calvary. And as I am loved, so enable me to love others. I pray this in Jesus' name. Amen. ❧

Maintain Your Integrity

The LORD detests dishonest scales,
but accurate weights find favor with him.
PROVERBS 11:1

A woman visited a store and told the grocer, "I need a large chicken." The man replied, "Yes, ma'am," and went to a back room. This took place in the days before refrigeration, when chickens were kept in a back-room barrel filled with brine.

The grocer brought out his only chicken and put it on the scales. It weighed a pound and a half. "No," the woman said, "I have company coming, and I need a larger one." So the grocer returned to the back room, dipped the chicken in the brine, and then placed it back on the scale while pushing down with his thumb.

"Okay," he said, "two pounds. Is that enough?"

"That's great," the woman replied. "I'll take both of them."

A survey by the University of Virginia analyzed forty-two business leaders, only half of whom had succeeded in their careers. Researchers assessed what had made the difference and discovered that all the businessmen had adequate charisma and competence; but those who failed lacked integrity. Personal honesty made the others into successes.

No doubt each of us has been hurt by someone's lack of integrity. Maybe we placed our trust in a close friend and discovered later the friend had lied, cheated, or damaged our reputation. All of us have seen news media reports about the imprisonment of business leaders who betrayed their investors and employees, bilking them out of millions or even billions of dollars. And of course, political leaders and church leaders have been found guilty of similar crimes.

It is especially important for those of us who call ourselves Christians to maintain our integrity and not give in to the temptation of lying, cheating, or hurting others to get ahead. God detests dishonesty—and has an unbending commitment to correcting the balance sheet.

O Lord, give me the desire to look deep within my heart and ask, "How can I improve the way I live? How can I have a more peaceful life, a more honest life, a more generous life, a more adventurous life, a more gratifying life, a more joyful life, as I yield to your leadership and let the Holy Spirit fill my heart and soul?" I ask this in Jesus' name. Amen. ❧

151

Live Consistently

But Daniel resolved not to defile himself
with the royal food and wine.
DANIEL 1:8

At the Camp David peace talks, I invited about fifty Israelis and fifty Egyptians to accompany their leaders, Menachem Begin and Anwar Sadat. Begin, a devout Jew, always insisted on eating kosher food, so our Filipino cooks made sure that all the utensils for cooking were cleaned properly and that the food was prepared under the supervision of a rabbi. But they couldn't figure out how much kosher food to make for each meal.

They soon learned that if the prime minister chose to eat in the large mess hall, they needed to cook a lot of kosher food, because all the other Israelis would eat kosher too. But when he ate in his cabin, most of his associates didn't worry about dietary rules.

Many centuries before, Daniel and his three close friends lived as captives in Babylon. The king felt very eager to have these young men trained to serve in his palace, so he took a keen interest in their education and health. He ordered his top servants to make sure they had the best possible food, but unfortunately, some of this food wasn't kosher. Daniel and his friends could have been killed for refusing to eat what the king had generously offered them, but they stayed firm in their convictions—and benefited physically from their strict diets.

Hundreds of years later, Jesus put aside many of the dietary and other ceremonial Jewish restrictions and instead emphasized our personal relationships with God and with our neighbors. If we choose to accept the leadership of Christ and, therefore, decide to live in a specific way because of our religious beliefs, we need to live that way consistently, even if nobody is looking. And if we do, we will be blessed, as was Daniel.

O God, thank you for showing me how, like Daniel, I can remain firm
in my convictions, heroic in my actions, wise in my daily conduct, and
dedicated in my habits. Implant in my heart a determination to observe
my faith and thus demonstrate every day that I am following Jesus Christ.
Help me be as nearly like him as possible. In his name I pray. Amen. ❧

152

Do You Gossip?

A gossip betrays a confidence.
PROVERBS 11:13

Many of us tend to separate our lives between the secular and the religious. Some of us go so far as to divide our lives into seven parts; six parts go to the secular, while one part goes to the religious. Sunday is the religious time, and the other six days we live according to a more worldly standard.

This often happens with gossiping, which the Holy Scriptures roundly condemn. While in church or when studying our Bibles, we consider gossip to be a sin and try to refrain from doing it. But the rest of the week, somehow we turn a blind eye to it.

Probably all of us have friends who gossip, and maybe we gossip a little ourselves, every now and again. I know I do. Sometimes it may feel exciting when our gossiping friends are coming for a visit, because we know they will bring some titillating information. Unfortunately, the degree of enjoyment or excitement over the gossip is usually proportional to how much it hurts others. That's because gossips don't go around telling a lot of good things about people; they move around telling all the bad things they've learned about others.

When we welcome this kind of talk, we contribute to the problem. So how do we confront gossips? I admit that's a difficult situation to handle. Often they're nice people, so we may not feel like chastising them directly, which might threaten our friendship with them.

Our daughter, Amy, always has felt uncomfortable with gossip. Often she will say, "I don't want to hear this," or will interrupt the conversation so as to defend the person damaged by the negative words. Sometimes she will physically leave the room. Her influence has been quite effective in combating gossip. Amy sets a good example for the rest of us to follow—even if that means missing some interesting conversations.

Dear Lord, few people like to be known as gossips, and most would be appalled to have earned that reputation. Forgive me, God, for the times I have gossiped, and give me the determination to guard my tongue and say only what builds up others. I pray this in Jesus' name. Amen. ❧

153

Be Fair

"Do not defraud or rob your neighbor."
LEVITICUS 19:13

An old man ran a small country store. He maintained a pious image but didn't hesitate to put his thumb on the scales. One day his small grandson came for a visit; and wanting to make a good impression, the man thought, *Whenever I make a sale, I'll say a Bible verse.*

A woman came in and ordered a loaf of bread and a pound of cheese. He rang up thirty-five cents and said, "Every perfect gift cometh from above." A few minutes later, the woman returned and said, "This cheese is moldy and the bread's too hard. Give me my money back." The store owner reluctantly complied and then said, "The Lord giveth and the Lord taketh away."

Soon a big Cadillac drove up in the rain, pulling a horse trailer. The rich driver wanted a blanket for his horse. The shopkeeper had three cheap blankets; blue, yellow, and red. The man asked the price for the blue blanket. "Five dollars," the owner said. "No, I can't put a five-dollar blanket on a horse as valuable as mine," the man said.

"I have another one," said the owner, pointing to the yellow blanket. "This one's forty-dollars." The man replied, "No. My horse is worth fifty thousand dollars. I couldn't use a forty-dollar blanket." The store owner said, "Wait! I have one more blanket." He grabbed the red one and said, "How about this one? It's one hundred dollars."

The fellow answered, "I'll take it." After he left, the little grandson, who knew the true price of the blankets, said, "He was a stranger and we took him in."

We must try always to be fair and honest in our dealings, whether in business or in personal matters. We represent Jesus to the world, and how we treat others reflects on our Lord. Based on our actions, what will they think of our Savior?

O Lord, help me remember that I represent you through all my actions and words, and so enable me to follow the perfect example of my Savior in my dealings with others. I pray these things in Jesus' name. Amen. ❧

154

A Simple Yes or No

"All you need to say is simply 'Yes' or 'No';
anything beyond this comes from the evil one."
MATTHEW 5:37

One day Rosalynn and I went to Atlanta to see our first great-grandchild, who weighed in at a whopping 9.2 pounds. He's a cherished little boy — the first son of a first son of a first son of a first son. I doubt that means anything, but all four generations, including the infant, gathered for a picture just after his birth.

While the medical staff weighed and measured him, they let us come in to watch. The nurse said he was twenty and a half inches long; but I'm a fisherman, and I kind of stretched his leg out a little bit and invoked my presidential authority. So she wrote down twenty-one inches, and everyone laughed.

Was that a "white lie"? I suppose it was. I hope that in such a context, I can be forgiven. But truth (and telling the truth) is crucial for us as followers of Christ. When Jesus told us, "All you need to say is simply 'Yes' or 'No,'" he meant that our reputation for integrity should be so absolute that when we say something, we don't have to swear by God or by anything else to verify our word. We just say, "This is it," and that's enough. If we have Christlike integrity, there's no doubt that what we say is true.

Think about your own situation for a moment. Do you find yourself constantly adding some kind of oath after you make a statement? If so, then you might want to take a look at your "integrity quotient." Jesus says to let your yes be yes and your no be no. If you find that you need more than that to be believed, then it's time for some serious soul-searching. Better now than when you stand in judgment before Christ!

O Lord, thank you for the freedom that speaking the truth brings. When I feel tempted to cut corners, embellish details, or fabricate some account to make things more pleasant for myself, remind me of these words of Jesus and give me the courage to speak only the truth. I pray in Jesus' name. Amen. ❧

The Seriousness of a Broken Oath

"As surely as I live, declares the Sovereign LORD, he shall die in Babylon, in the land of the king who put him on the throne, whose oath he despised and whose treaty he broke."
EZEKIEL 17:16

After conquering Judah, King Nebuchadnezzar of Babylon didn't want the responsibility of ruling so far from home. So he approached an Israelite named Zedekiah and said to him, "I'm going to put you on the throne of Judah; you are to rule my way." Zedekiah therefore became a puppet king. He swore before God that he would remain loyal to Babylon and carry out Nebuchadnezzar's commands.

But after Zedekiah had ruled for about eleven years, he decided to betray Nebuchadnezzar — despite the warnings of the prophet Jeremiah, who strongly advised him to honor his oath before God. Nebuchadnezzar quickly returned in wrath to punish this man who had betrayed his oath of loyalty. Zedekiah was taken captive and made to watch as Babylonian soldiers slaughtered all of his sons and then plucked out his own eyes.

Most scholars believe that Zedekiah was executed while in Babylonian captivity, and so the southern kingdom of Judah came to a tragic and inglorious end.

Giving our word is a solemn thing, even when it is done to gain a definite advantage. We make many such commitments during a lifetime — to our customers, our employers, our spouses, and when we accept Christ as Savior. It is wrong to violate such a solemn promise, even when it seems convenient to do so.

Taking an oath such as Zedekiah's goes against the teachings of Jesus Christ, who tells us not to swear any oaths at all, but simply to say yes or no. Anything beyond this, he says, "comes from the evil one" (Matthew 5:37). An earned reputation for integrity should be more than enough.

O God, this sobering story reminds me of Psalm 15:4, which praises the one who "keeps an oath even when it hurts." Help me be a person who can be trusted to keep my promises and who is known for integrity and telling the truth. Let me be trusted because I follow Jesus. In his name I pray. Amen. ❧

156

Humility

But when you are invited, take the lowest place, so that when your host comes, he will say to you, "Friend, move up to a better place." Then you will be honored in the presence of all the other guests.
LUKE 14:10

Very serious questions exist about the order of seating among those who belong to some established organizations. In the Navy, I never had any doubt about who was a superior on a ship. Even at the Naval Academy we had a definite order of seniority, based on our final class standing. If I stood at 84 and somebody with me stood at 85, I was his superior, no questions asked.

We learned quickly that the senior officer spent the least amount of time in a small boat. So if your battleship came in and anchored and a small boat arrived to take people ashore for leave, then everybody got in the boat in reverse order of seniority: enlisted men first, then NCs, and so on, until finally the captain boarded. The senior officer always was the last one in an elevator as well, and the first one out.

As a former president, I see a regular protocol for state dinners and things of that sort. On those occasions, a protocol officer has complete control over who sits where and who does this and that.

By contrast, Christ told his disciples *not* to take the best place (just to the right of the host); instead, they were to take the lowest place. Once the host arrived, he might move them up to a higher place and then exalt them in the presence of the others. To seat yourself to the right of the host, however, might mean a humiliating reassignment to the bottom of the table.

Jesus was trying to make a point that applies to God's kingdom. Humility is both difficult and crucial. It's one thing that distinguishes Christianity from other ways of life.

O Lord, build into us the humility we need to represent you well. Enable us to emulate the life of Jesus as best we can, and give us a more adventuresome spirit so that we might take a few more chances for you. Strengthen our commitment to you and help us overcome our weaknesses, timidity, and reluctance, so that we might be more effective disciples for you. In Jesus' name we pray. Amen. ❧

Beware the Trap of Pride

Pride goes before destruction, a haughty spirit before a fall.
PROVERBS 16:18

Many people consider Theodore Roosevelt to be one of this nation's greatest presidents. I too would put him in that category, although he was a very proud man, boastful of his many accomplishments. Even in his own lifetime, his pride gave birth to a lot of stories.

One tale goes that Roosevelt went to heaven and there met Saint Peter, who acknowledged that Teddy had been a very important person on earth and had done some good things. So Peter asked Roosevelt if he had any special requests. "Yes," Roosevelt said, "I want to be in charge of the heavenly choir."

Peter thought that sounded reasonable and asked, "What can we do to help you?" Roosevelt replied, "I want ten thousand sopranos, ten thousand altos, and ten thousand tenors."

Saint Peter asked, "And how about the basses?"

"I'll sing bass," Roosevelt replied.

The Bible records several stories in which pride preceded the downfall of a powerful person. When Moses approached Pharaoh to demand that the Hebrews be released and allowed to return to their homeland, Pharaoh refused to listen. Instead, he pridefully insisted that he didn't need advice from anyone on what to do. His arrogant refusal brought disaster upon his own Egyptian people.

King Herod Agrippa I, for another example, ruled Jerusalem during Jesus' earthly ministry and remained king for a few years after Christ's death and resurrection. Eventually, he became filled with his own pride, and when people began to worship him as a god, he accepted their worship. Immediately, the Bible says, "he was eaten by worms and died" (Acts 12:23).

God hates human arrogance, which often ends in punishment or a fall of some kind. Yet God invites us to achieve what we can, provided that we give thanks for our accomplishments and give God credit for what he enables us to do.

O Lord, remind me never to feel superior to others, for in doing so I end my efforts to improve myself. Help me instead to acknowledge my own shortcomings, sinfulness, and deviations from the perfect life of Jesus Christ. Give me the humility to relate to others on an equal basis, one heart to another, and strengthen me in my commitment to your humble Son. In his name I pray. Amen. ❧

158

The Main Task

*Always be prepared to give an answer to everyone who asks you to
give the reason for the hope that you have.*
I PETER 3:15

Rosalynn and I regularly attend church services, as you may. But the rest
of the week, like us, you probably are busy with other duties involving your
work, family, or studies. While it is natural for us to pursue our daily lives
with dedication, sometimes we let those daily duties become paramount, even
all-consuming.

I wonder, how many of us spend a few minutes every day in private or
family worship, or each week preparing for Sunday school or worship service?
Are we prepared to explain the simple plan of salvation to interested friends
or acquaintances?

We often feel inclined to separate our daily routines from the religious life
we enjoy. We naturally seek personal and financial security, try to enhance
our professional achievements, and seek enjoyment in private pursuits and
relations with others, sometimes at the expense of the ministry of the gospel
of Christ. In doing so, we miss the main responsibilities and opportunities
of Christianity.

Let's think about where we stand in our Christian commitment to follow
in the footsteps of our Savior. Have we refrained from ministering to those
who are in need or who hunger for the gospel of Christ? Our primary goal
is not to hoard for ourselves the mercy of God, the forgiveness of sin, or the
knowledge of Christ. We are to share the gospel, and we need to prepare
ourselves with a deeper relationship with Jesus Christ and the Scriptures. We
need to make our faith paramount and pursue it with excitement and energy.
When we do so, we will find our professional achievements enhanced and
our secular lives expanded and more enjoyable.

*O Lord, help me carve out times each week to evaluate where I stand in
my Christian commitment and ways to increase it. Give me courage and
strength to look honestly at my daily life and make accurate judgments
about the real state of my relationship with Christ. And then help me
make whatever changes may be necessary, through the power of the Holy
Spirit. I pray in Jesus' name. Amen.* ❧

Strong Consequences

"This is what the LORD, the God of Israel, says: There are devoted things among you, Israel. You cannot stand against your enemies until you remove them."
JOSHUA 7:13

Joshua had destroyed Jericho and was marching toward Bethel. The Israelites planned to take a small town called Ai, and since it seemed insignificant, Joshua sent just a small contingent of soldiers to destroy it.

But they got whipped. The few men of Ai chased the invaders down the mountain, killing thirty-six Hebrew soldiers. This struck a devastating blow to the Israelites' self-esteem.

Joshua tore his robes, fell on his face, and cried out to God. He thought God had abandoned Israel. Soon the Lord told Joshua that someone in his camp had committed a crime and that therefore the Israelites had themselves become devoted to destruction.

Joshua moved quickly. He identified a man named Achan, who admitted stealing an imported coat and some money. Joshua then had Achan and his entire household stoned to death.

It's hard for us today to understand the harshness of this act. And while I can't explain it, I can say that God wanted this lesson to be very vivid for the nation. Achan's greed affected everyone around him.

We tend to think that as we depart from the teachings of Christ, it affects only us. But Paul reminds us that we are part of a community and that everything we do affects everyone else ("If one part suffers, every part suffers," 1 Corinthians 12:26).

Each of us has a role to play in the kingdom of Christ. When we faithfully play it, we become, in effect, an army for good. If we fail, our failure is magnified. That is what community means: sharing with others the blessings of life in the name of Jesus Christ.

O God, some Old Testament stories disturb me, and sometimes I feel discouraged by the demands posed by the example of Christ. So I ask you to give me courage to seek out your will for me and to strip away the barriers that I erect in my life. Help me be not so disturbed by new ideas, new demands, and new challenges from you. In Jesus' name I pray. Amen. ❧

160

They're Depending on Us

"I have not hesitated to proclaim to you the whole will of God."
ACTS 20:27

In general, it's hard for us to understand how difficult it was for Paul to evangelize and minister, as well as what it takes to be a Christian missionary in other parts of the world today. We often forget that each day Christians are severely persecuted and even lose their lives at the hands of oppressive governments or neighbors hostile to personal faith in Christ. In some places where Hindus or Muslims dominate, it's actually against the law for someone like you or me to tell a person about Jesus and suggest that they accept Christ as Savior.

Habitat for Humanity workers were excluded from India until I signed an official declaration to the prime minister that they would not promote Christianity. It's also against the law in Greece to convert an Orthodox believer to Protestantism. When I was president, I had a serious problem because one of our mercy ships docked in Greece, and an officer gave some Protestant pamphlets to a teenager who came on board. His mother learned about it and told the authorities, and they arrested the officer and put him in prison. Fortunately, I was able to use my presidential influence to get him released, but it was a surprising thing to see happen.

Most of us Americans don't face these kinds of challenges, and most countries do not have such policies in opposition to Christianity. We have our own challenges, of course. Being a devout Christian isn't always popular in the United States. People often want nothing to do with us if we start sharing our faith.

Whenever we face such challenges, we should remember Paul's words: "I have not hesitated to proclaim to you the whole will of God." Christ calls us to overcome our fears and share our faith with others, for people are depending on us.

O God, it is my privilege to tell others about your love and about the amazing sacrifice Jesus made on the cross to enable us to have a vital relationship with you. Too often I remain silent when I should speak up, or I mumble when I should clearly declare your Word. I ask for courage and wisdom in sharing the gospel. I pray in the name of Jesus my Savior. Amen. ❧

161

A Purpose in Life

Fear God and keep his commandments, for this is the duty of all mankind. For God will bring every deed into judgment, including every hidden thing, whether it is good or evil.

ECCLESIASTES 12:13 – 14

Some think the author of Ecclesiastes was Solomon, while others believe the book was written centuries after his time; but whoever wrote this book of wisdom was clearly both a great teacher and a fine scholar. We read that the author had many wonderful achievements: builder, philosopher, theologian, deep thinker, and pleasure seeker. He had amassed far more wealth than most of us ever will—and yet he judged it all meaningless. In fact, he concluded that *everything* human beings do "under the sun" is totally without meaning. In his view, none of our "success" ultimately has any significance.

This attitude afflicts many in our society today. Many people who enjoy riches, fame, and success see no ultimate purpose in their existence. They realize that most famous people are soon forgotten—certainly after a few years have passed—and that none of their own successes will save them from growing old and dying. Such morbid and hopeless thoughts can lead to despair.

Yet toward the end of his pessimistic little book, the author of Ecclesiastes expresses one final conclusion: we have a duty to obey God's commandments, for every one of our deeds will be judged. This is the only thing, he says, that matters.

For Christians, this verse has great meaning because we know that our Savior commanded us to make disciples of all nations, teaching them to obey everything that he had commanded us. *This* is our purpose in life, as defined in some of the last words of Jesus Christ. *This* gives our lives meaning: speaking and acting as an example for others, based on the perfect life of our Savior.

Dear God, thank you for this reminder that a life lived outside of a deep, personal connection to you ultimately has no meaning. But thank you even more for reminding me that by fulfilling your will, through faith in Christ, my life gains both immediate and eternal meaning. Help me remember this and to live each day in light of the calling you have given to me. I pray in Jesus' name. Amen. ❧

Boldness over Safety

*"Sovereign Lord," they said, "you made the heavens and the earth and
the sea, and everything in them.... Now, Lord, consider their threats
and enable your servants to speak your word with great boldness."*
ACTS 4:24, 29

The Jewish religious authorities in Jerusalem wanted, at all costs, to prevent
the message about Jesus from spreading. So when they heard Peter and John
preaching about the resurrection of Christ, they took the apostles into custody. Then they sternly warned them—and in effect, all believers—to cease
preaching in Christ's name. They forbade the apostles from telling others
about Jesus' victory over death.

So what did the apostles do? Immediately they returned to the rest of their
small congregation and huddled together, not to argue about homosexuality, or
whether women could preach in church, or the meaning of "priesthood of all
believers," or the proper role of pastors, but to gain strength for the task ahead.
They knew the message they had to proclaim about the risen Christ greatly
transcended their fear and any differences they might have with each other.

So they gathered, and so they prayed to seek God's guidance. Notice that
they did *not* pray for safety or that God might protect them from the very
real threats of the Sanhedrin. No, they prayed for boldness in speaking to
others about Christ. In other words, they prayed that God would aid them
in being effective witnesses for Christ and that their ministry would be filled
with courage and inspiration and innovation.

These were ordinary folks like us. But filled with the Holy Spirit, they
wanted to elevate their Christian service to the highest possible point. As a
result, their faith in God strengthened them, and the presence of the Holy
Spirit transformed them. Oh, may we follow their example of proclaiming
Christ—in unity!

*Lord, I confess that too often I tend to worry so much about personal
status and prevailing over others that I forget the importance of serving
boldly for you—and in harmony and partnership with fellow Christians.
Forgive me this error, and grant me the courage to represent Jesus with
the same boldness and unity that you gave the apostles two thousand years
ago. Give me wisdom and courage. In Jesus' name I pray. Amen.* ❧

Obedient in Little Things

*Jesus sent two of his disciples, saying to them, "Go to the village
ahead of you, and . . . you will find a colt tied there, which no one
has ever ridden. Untie it and bring it here."*
MARK 11:1 – 2

What factors make for a successful Christian life? Do you see any parallels
between a successful marriage and the kind of productive life that Christ asks
us to pursue?

In relating to a spouse, it's probably the small things that have the greatest
power to destroy a marriage or make it successful. Marriages grow as loved
ones respectfully relate to each other, dozens of times each day.

The same thing is true of spiritual growth. It happens best as we do the
little things that Christ asks us to do, over and over.

Two kinds of events characterized Christ's life: the glorious, the historic,
and the revolutionary; and the mundane, the down-to-earth, and the apparently
insignificant. He brought both sides together and "married" them.
Jesus' apparently insignificant command to bring a stranger's donkey to him
led to the memorable event we call the Triumphal Entry.

Too often, perhaps, we search for the glorious. We want the profound,
the dramatic. We think of ourselves jumping into a swollen river to save
a drowning child—maybe with TV cameras rolling. Or maybe some dramatic
event will permit us to demonstrate our Christian character. And while
that might happen someday, it's no excuse for failing to respond to everyday
opportunities.

Mark is telling us, "Don't wait for a dramatic event. Do the little things
now." So if we find ourselves beside a stranger in an airplane, we might find
a simple way to love that person. If we have neighbors we rarely see, we may
look for opportunities to demonstrate to them the Christian message.

What donkey is Christ asking you to untie and bring to him?

*God, I pray that these words from Mark might find a place in my life.
Through little things, help me draw closer to Christ, not just on rare
occasions or in the distant future, but a dozen or more times each day as I
relate to those around me. Let me develop and enjoy an expansive Christian
life, following the lead of my Savior, in whose name I pray. Amen.* ❧

164

His Commands Are Not Burdensome

This is love for God: to keep his commands. And his commands are
not burdensome, for everyone born of God overcomes the world.
1 JOHN 5:3 – 4

In many ways, these verses sum up the Christian faith. But why does John say it is not burdensome to obey God's commandments? It certainly feels that way sometimes.

Imagine that you are reading in the Sermon on the Mount about turning the other cheek, loving your enemies, and putting others first. These things certainly *seem* burdensome; so how can John say that human beings, who are sinful, weak, and self-centered by nature, can find God's commands anything other than burdensome?

In the first place, if we believe in God, we don't resist temptation on our own. Instead, we form a partnership with God Almighty, who changes our hearts and helps us discipline ourselves to live according to his ways. The Spirit of God helps us love those alienated from society, who may seem less lovable than others.

Have you ever been in love? I have. In fact, I still am. At the height of that love, we can't see anything wrong with our beloved. Even if the individual has some unpleasant characteristics, you automatically forgive them. And if you find out that your loved one really *needs* something, then you go and get it. That's a bit how God helps us feel toward others. And once we experience this divine love, it really is true that following God's commandments — such as loving our neighbors and our enemies — is not burdensome.

But the main reason it's not a burden to obey God's commandments is because we were created to comply with them. When we do so, we are happiest and most content. The more we comply, the happier we realize we are, and the easier it becomes to obey.

O Lord, thank you for showing me how your love is the connecting link
between me and you, between me and Jesus Christ, and between me and
other human beings. Let me proclaim the message of your love in ways
that embrace ever-increasing numbers of people around the world in a
true, divine experience of that word. I ask these things in the name of the
champion of love, my Savior, Jesus Christ. Amen. ❧

An Obedient Servant

"Brother Saul, the Lord—Jesus, who appeared to you on the road as
you were coming here—has sent me so that you may see again and
be filled with the Holy Spirit."
ACTS 9:17

A follower of Christ named Ananias lived in Damascus. After Paul encountered Jesus on the road and was led into the city as a blind man, the Lord appeared to Ananias in a vision and told him to go to a street called Straight. At the house of a man named Judas, Jesus said, Ananias was to look for a man named Saul, who would be expecting him. Rosalynn and I have visited the house where this occurred, according to Syrian Christians.

At the very mention of the name "Saul," Ananias's heart probably stood still. How could he visit a dangerous, hate-filled man who had dedicated himself to stamping out the church? But God insisted; so Ananias got up, found the house, entered, and laid his hands on Saul, addressing him as *"Brother* Saul." Imagine his calling this feared man his "brother," thus demonstrating his belief in the transforming power of God's salvation! Through Ananias, Saul regained his sight and was filled with the Holy Spirit.

Ananias clearly had real trepidation at the thought of going to Saul, regardless of any conversation with the Lord. But he didn't argue with the Lord (except briefly). He did what Jesus commanded.

Ananias is never mentioned again in the Bible, and Paul never referred to him in his letters. The call of God to Paul was blazing, dramatic, and unforgettable. The call of God to Ananias, on the other hand, was quiet and private. Yet because Ananias obeyed God's most uncomfortable call on his life, Paul went on to convert thousands and spread the gospel throughout the Roman Empire.

Obeying God, even when difficult, has rewards that we might never foresee.

O Lord, as I remember the dramatic call to Paul and the mundane call
to Ananias, remind me that I too am called in various ways and my
responses shape my life. Give me a searching heart to seek your will and
the wisdom and strength to obey. In Jesus' name I pray. Amen. ❧

Difficult Decisions

After David had finished talking with Saul, Jonathan became one in spirit with David, and he loved him as himself. From that day Saul kept David with him and did not let him return home to his family.

I SAMUEL 18:1 – 2

Many of us feel reluctant to form strong friendships. If you're a woman, how many intimate female friends do you have? Whom do you love having in your home, just to share some coffee? If you're a man, with how many male friends do you like sharing a few hours, or even a day or two? How many friends do you have with whom you are willing to share your life and let down your guard, even to the point of admitting your shortcomings, doubts, and fears?

If I went down my list of friends, I'd have to say that one of my most cherished friends at this moment is an African-American woman whom I met more than twenty-five years ago. We helped Jessica build a Habitat for Humanity home in New York City. She worked side by side with Rosalynn and me, and in later years she joined us in other cities to build homes for other poor people. I saw within Jessica the characteristics of a very valuable friend.

The adventure of seeking new and intimate friends is a life-enriching experience, but one that must be based on some common interest or commitment. Jonathan and David developed such a friendship, but it required a lot of effort. They had to cross huge social barriers to make it work. But when they based their friendship on a mutual commitment to God, they found a solid foundation and both came away as men changed for the better.

Lord, help me follow the example of Jonathan, who pursued a friendship with David even though it meant a step down in social status. Enable me to reach out to those who may be different, lonely, poor, and so enrich both their lives and my own. Despite all obstacles, bless those bonds of friendship. In Jesus' name I pray. Amen. ❧

167

A Condemning Compliment

Make every effort to add to your faith goodness, and to goodness,
knowledge, and to knowledge, self-control, ... perseverance, ...
godliness, ... brotherly kindness, ... and love.

2 PETER 1:5 − 7

I really thought I had it made at the Naval Academy, and that's why I relaxed. Someone wrote in *The Lucky Bag*, the Naval Academy annual book, "Jimmy never studied except when he was helping a classmate." It was an exaggeration and maybe a compliment, but also a condemnation.

I sometimes *was* lackadaisical about my studies. I read many books, raced sailing boats, traveled across Chesapeake Bay, learned how to fly seaplanes, and did many other enjoyable things. I did well academically, but my lax study habits probably cost me a Rhodes scholarship. Only later in life did I realize my mistake. Now I see that each of us has opportunities to excel in life through self-control and perseverance.

The same is true of our Christian lives. If we persist in serving Jesus wholeheartedly, we can do much for the sake of God's kingdom. Because we are human beings, however, we naturally find it difficult to control ourselves. We tend to do the same kinds of foolish things that Peter did in his worst moments: we succumb to temptation and depart from Jesus' teachings.

We must be courageous enough to recognize this fault and determine that, through self-control, we will orient our entire life's purpose, as much as possible, in the path that Jesus prescribed. In that determination, we must be tenacious, sticking to it even when it becomes difficult.

Most of us struggle with perseverance because we limit or underestimate our capabilities. We become discouraged and think there is no possible way we can live full lives for Christ. But Peter tells us that since God has given us everything we need, we really can persevere. Therefore, why limit yourself?

Dear Lord, I'm grateful to have the privilege of considering the words of Peter, one of the most interesting persons in the Bible. I am thankful that he wrote these letters to faithful Christians, giving me instruction and inspiration, as well as needed criticism. Help me put his words into action in my life through the power of the Holy Spirit and to the glory of your Son. I pray in Jesus' name. Amen. 🕊

168

Only What's Required

Offer your bodies as a living sacrifice, holy and pleasing to God—
this is your true and proper worship.
ROMANS 12:1

A small company was contemplating a new health-insurance plan. Everyone in the company supported it, except one man, named Rudolph. This was a problem because everybody needed to accept the plan for it to move forward. So every company employee wrote a message to Rudolph asking him to change his mind. He refused. Then they invited a special salesperson to come and explain the benefits to Rudolph, but still Rudolph said no. Finally, his boss called him in and said, "Either you approve the plan or your job is terminated." Immediately Rudolph agreed. Later, when asked what changed his mind, he replied, "Well, the boss was the first one to explain it to me clearly."

Paul tried to accomplish something like that in this passage. In his day, the sacrifices offered at the temple were all dead. You killed a lamb or an ox or a similar animal, burned the carcass, and the priests divided up the remaining meat. We're not used to such religious practice today; we would be shocked if this Sunday our pastor sacrificed animals on a church altar. But that's how it was in Paul's day; so when he writes, "Offer your bodies as a living sacrifice," he means that we should live for God in vital, growing, expanding service, with the *same degree of devotion* those animals gave in death.

"Listen, this is just what you owe to God," Paul tells us. "This is not above and beyond the call of duty; it's what we're obligated to do, since we've received the love of God through Christ."

We owe God *everything*. And while we don't "pay back" anything by offering ourselves totally to God as living sacrifices, that's what is required. Anything less is an insult to the Lord.

O God, although most of us have no experience in seeing animals
sacrificed on an altar, yet we understand that such total commitment
should characterize our lives as people who have trusted Jesus Christ. I
belong to you, as do my possessions, my time, my body, and my talents.
Help me demonstrate my love for you by loving and serving those you put
in my path. I pray in Jesus' name. Amen. ❦

A Slow Slide

It is actually reported that there is sexual immorality among you, and of a kind that even pagans do not tolerate: A man is sleeping with his father's wife. And you are proud! Shouldn't you rather have gone into mourning and have put out of your fellowship the man who has been doing this?
I CORINTHIANS 5:1 – 3

Recalling how religion used to be in the United States can surprise us. Before World War I, trains didn't run on Sundays. After both world wars, no baseball games took place on Sunday. In Georgia, stores could not legally open on the Sabbath. In my childhood, I never went to movies on Sunday, although some kids did, provided they attended Sunday school and church that morning and more church at night. And people *never* fished or played cards on Sunday. How times have changed!

Today we take permissiveness for granted. And it's not just that stores open on Sunday or that we can play cards whenever we wish. Today we can't watch television or a movie and hope to see any sort of biblical standard of morality. We see extreme violence, sexual promiscuity, even the exaltation of extramarital affairs—which bring benefits, not punishment, to the people portrayed. Divorce has become common and acceptable. When I left home for the Naval Academy, I didn't know of a divorced person in Plains. A few wives no longer lived with their husbands, but they never divorced.

While I'm not advocating a return to the culture of yesteryear, we Christians need to guard against becoming morally permissive. We tend not to notice how much we've come to accept. Perhaps the Christians in Corinth to whom Paul wrote didn't think they were being so bad. Each of us is responsible for maintaining our commitment to obey God, regardless of what our society may do. Our best guide is the example of Jesus.

Dear God, help me make this life you've given me meaningful, significant, and pleasing to you—not measured by the standards of a constantly changing society, but by the things you value, which never change. Help me demonstrate to quizzical, skeptical, or cynical observers that this is what a Christian life means—that is, that I become more and more like my Savior. In his name I pray. Amen. ❧

Should Gold Be Most Precious?

*On reaching Jerusalem, Jesus entered the temple courts and began
driving out those who were buying and selling there.*
MARK 11:15

In Jesus' day, the temple complex in Jerusalem spread out over thirty acres. At its heart stood the Holy of Holies, containing the ark of the covenant. Around this holiest place was the courtyard for the priests, and around that stood another courtyard, for Jewish men. Another was for Jewish women, and the remaining area belonged to anyone else. It was that outer courtyard that the priests were treating as anything but a holy place.

All visitors to the temple were expected to contribute money and sacrifice a creature of some kind, like a dove or a lamb. But the priests had ordained that only animals and coins they had personally approved could be used to fulfill these obligations. So if you visited with your own gold coin or with your own doves or lamb, you couldn't offer them; you had to exchange them for the ones sold by the priests, which cost many times more than a lamb you could buy at the local market. The religious leaders obviously made an enormous profit.

The money changers also charged a high percentage to swap a gold coin that you could spend downtown for a temple coin you could present as your religious obligation for the year. By Jesus' day, the whole place had become a mass of corruption.

When Christ saw this holy area being used for making money, he chased out the money changers and overthrew their tables. He said to them, "It is written, 'My house will be called a house of prayer,' but you are making it 'a den of robbers'" (Matthew 21:13).

We should take heed. Whenever our life's priorities focus more on money than thankful prayer and good deeds, we have adopted the same attitude as the money changers.

O Lord, I live in an affluent society, where concerns about money seep into every unguarded crevice; so make me especially vigilant about keeping my faith pure and free from the love of money. May my prayers and my service to you both reflect the holiness of Jesus. In his name I pray. Amen. ❧

A Liberating Slavery

You have been set free from sin and have become slaves to righteousness.
ROMAN 6:18

When we lived in the White House, Rosalynn and I had a chance to meet some of the world's consummate performers. Andrés Segovia once came to play some of my favorite songs on the guitar, including "Recuerdos de la Alhambra." When he performed, it seemed as though four separate musicians played that one instrument!

Vladimir Horowitz, perhaps the greatest pianist of our lifetime, came to the White House one afternoon. I helped him arrange the stage for his performance. As he tried out the piano with a little of Rachmaninoff's third piano concerto, he thought the sound failed to reverberate appropriately, so he demanded some carpeting. White House stewards retrieved several carpets, and Horowitz and I dragged them all over the floor in the East Room to prepare for his concert.

And there was the time Mikhail Baryshnikov, one of the greatest ballet dancers in history, visited the White House. During practice, he leapt so high that we had to lower the stage by about a foot so he wouldn't bump his head on the chandelier!

What made these performers so wonderful? They had the talent, obviously; but they couldn't have become superb unless they had devoted themselves to a lifetime of improvement. What would have happened to Baryshnikov, Horowitz, or Segovia if they had practiced only once a week?

As Christians, each of us is called to a life of devotion; Paul called it becoming "slaves of righteousness." When we accept God's grace through faith in Jesus Christ, we should attune our entire heart and soul to resonate with the perfect life of Jesus Christ. It's not easy! But it's also not oppressive. We gain a peace that passes understanding and a joy that liberates the soul. When we become slaves to Christ, fear and despair lose their grip on us. We are set free!

Dear Lord, show me more each day what it means to be a "slave of righteousness." Help me understand how I may better cooperate with you to reflect the compassion and grace and mercy of Jesus Christ, my Savior. Train me to devote myself, in both heart and soul, to you and to your kingdom, and give me the strength to act like a "little Christ." I ask these things in Jesus' name. Amen.

172

Train for Godliness

Having nothing to do with godless myths and old wives' tales;
rather, train yourself to be godly.
I TIMOTHY 4:7

We all have noticed the huge popularity of diets. Diet books often top the bestseller lists in the United States. Millions of people are concerned about looking trim and physically attractive, although usually health isn't our primary concern. We just don't want to look fat.

While caring about our looks is not wrong, an overemphasis on physical appearance can get in the way of training ourselves to comply with God's laws — and *that's* what will count in the long run. As Paul says, while physical training is of some value, godliness has value for all things, holding promise for both the present life and the life to come (1 Timothy 4:8).

Being godly doesn't mean turning into someone who thinks he's better than everyone else. It doesn't mean living with a "holier than thou" attitude. Being godly simply means happily conforming to the laws and wishes of God. Godly people dedicate themselves to pleasing God through willing obedience to heaven's laws and directions.

Unfortunately, godliness doesn't come naturally to any of us. We have to train for it and dedicate ourselves to acquiring it, much as an athlete trains for a big game or a college student prepares for a future career. Many things can get in the way, which is why Paul warns us not to get sidetracked from such critical training by "tales" and "myths" of no value.

Let's not make the mistake of thinking that since we are Christians, we will automatically become godly. *No one* becomes godly without training hard for it. And how do we train ourselves to keep the laws and wishes of God? We begin by studying the life and teachings of Jesus Christ, by reading other parts of the Bible, and by striving and praying to God daily for strength.

O God, while I want to be godly, I confess that too often I try to take shortcuts to get there. Thank you for reminding me that godliness comes only with dedication, training, and a continual reliance upon the Holy Spirit's strength and guidance. Implant Paul's words in my heart and mind, and help me as I strive to emulate Christ as best I can. I ask in Jesus' name. Amen. ❧

JANUARY 10, 1999

Rule Over It

"If you do what is right, will you not be accepted? But if you do not do what is right, sin is crouching at your door; it desires to have you, but you must rule over it."
GENESIS 4:7

When we read the Bible, we tend to put ourselves in the role of the good characters. In the parable of the Good Samaritan, we like to see ourselves as the hero, not as those who walk past a man in great need. In the case of the prodigal son, we want to put ourselves in the role of the forgiving father. And in the case of Cain and Abel, we *certainly* do not want to equate ourselves with Cain.

But since one of our main purposes in studying the Holy Scriptures is to improve our relationship with God and not to congratulate ourselves, then perhaps we should try to understand how even sinful characters can help us learn from God's Word.

While Cain was a farmer, his brother, Abel, was a shepherd. Both brought an offering to the Lord. God accepted Abel's offering, but not Cain's. The reason is not explained, but instantly, Cain grew furious. "Why are you angry?" God asked. "Why is your face downcast?" Then God added, "If you do what is right, will you not be accepted? But if you do not do what is right, sin is crouching at your door; it desires to have you, but you must rule over it" (Genesis 4:6–7).

Here, in one of the earliest messages of God to human beings, Cain is told (and we are told through him) that even though he might be contemplating some sin, he can turn from it and do what is right. The Lord warned that sin is constantly "crouching at the door." In other words, we must recognize that we are tempted to give in to pride, self-congratulation, complacency, selfishness, envy, resentment, laziness, wasting of talents or opportunities, avoidance of responsibility, and other sins. It is a very long list.

But we do not have to succumb to such temptations! Sin is not inevitable. Through a commitment to follow in the footsteps of Jesus Christ, and by the power of God's Spirit, we *can* master it. Sin is strong, but with God's help, we can prevail over it.

O Lord, help me realize that, as with Cain, none of my thoughts or attitudes are hidden from you. Give me courage to confess my shortcomings and correct them by depending on your help. In Christ's name I pray. Amen.

Must We Be Right?

*We know that "We all possess knowledge." But knowledge puffs up
while love builds up. Those who think they know something do not yet
know as they ought to know. But whoever loves God is known by God.*
1 CORINTHIANS 8:1 – 3

Are you superstitious? It bothers some people, even Christians, when a black cat walks across the road in front of them. Whenever that happens to me, I try to get around the fact by saying to Rosalynn, "Look at that dark gray cat."

Some superstitions have very logical origins. When my father served in World War I, for example, soldiers would never light three cigarettes from one match. On the front lines, if you kept a light going long enough for three cigarettes, the enemy might see you and shoot. That very logical practice turned into a superstition that he kept his whole life.

One of Rosalynn's pet superstitions concerns her aversion to us walking on opposite sides of a post. I didn't know about that one until we got married, but now I'm always aware of it. If it weren't for her saying, "Bread and butter," every time we accidentally did it, we may not have had such a good and safe time together!

The point is that despite our Christian faith, remnants of other beliefs remain. Such "knowledge" can cause divisions between people if some who "know better" try to force others to comply with their own beliefs. Perhaps Paul had this in mind when he said, "Knowledge puffs up." Without love, knowledge puffs us up with self-importance, superiority, and arrogance. Loveless knowledge can destroy harmony among Christians. That's why Jesus insisted on humility (see Matthew 23:11).

We must balance what we know or believe with respect and love for others. Is it really so important we demonstrate that we are right and others are wrong? Let's give humility—and harmony—its proper place.

*O Lord, teach me to value my relationships over my need to be "right."
Help me remember all the times I thought I had something absolutely
correct, only to learn later that I had made an error. Use my life
experience to build humility within me, and help me value true Christian harmony over the skill of winning silly arguments. In Jesus' name I
pray. Amen.* ❧

Why Do the Wicked Prosper?

I envied the arrogant when I saw the prosperity of the wicked.
PSALM 73:3

You may know of the bestselling book that asked, "Why do bad things happen to good people?" Well, an ancient writer named Asaph asked the other side of the question: "Why do good things happen to bad people?"

Has this question ever crossed your mind? There is no easy answer to it. I wonder why powerful people who commit terrible atrocities often get off with barely a reprimand, while some of the best people I know suffer terribly. Some of the most devout, dedicated, humble, and God-serving Christians see their children die at an early age, lose their spouse prematurely, or develop cancer or some hideous illness. Meanwhile, other people with no faith in Christ enjoy great health. It doesn't seem right or fair.

Asaph did not doubt the goodness of God; he just approached God to say, "It bothers me to see the wicked prospering when, in my opinion, they ought to be punished. They are the ones who should be poor and starving and diseased. Instead, they're sleek and fat and prosperous and seem to have all the material benefits."

There's nothing wrong with asking this kind of question. We shouldn't avoid it and say, "It's not Christian to ask such troubling questions." In fact, it's healthy to confront such a problem. We could pray, "God, I don't understand this. Why do these things happen? Please give me insight." In effect, that's what Asaph did in Psalm 73.

Some of our greatest theologians have encouraged us to bring our doubts to God. Theologian Paul Tillich said that religion is a search for the truth about our relationship with God and with fellow humans. Self-satisfaction or a lack of inquiry means we think we have it all figured out—and therefore have no need to go to God for understanding. Asaph knew better. So should we.

Dear Lord, when troubling questions come to mind, I pray that you would give me the courage to face them frankly, to get them into the light, and to come to you for insight. Prompt me to constantly reassess my Christian life and ask questions about how to orient myself to get more in alignment with the perfect life of Jesus Christ, in whose name I pray. Amen. ❧

A Difficult Teaching

Do not repay evil with evil or insult with insult. On the contrary,
repay evil with blessing.
I PETER 3:9

We have three basic options for how we choose to deal with people. First, we can badly treat those who are good to us or who are weak or under our authority. It's wrong, of course, but we're all guilty of it sometimes.

Second, we can reciprocate, doing to others what they have done to us. If others treat us badly, then we can treat them badly; or if someone does us a good deed, we can repay her with a good deed. This option seems reasonable—but apparently not reasonable enough for Peter.

The apostle urges us to choose the third option: if people do something bad to us, then we repay them with a blessing. This is a very difficult lesson.

Peter wrote to the early Christians in Rome who suffered for their faith under the persecution of Caesar. Every day they lived with the threat of imprisonment or even death. How do you think they reacted to Peter's exhortation? They couldn't have found it any easier to accept than we do.

Of course, Peter didn't invent this teaching. Paul had said exactly the same thing (Romans 12:17), and so did Jesus before him: "You have heard that it was said, 'Love your neighbor and hate your enemy.' But I tell you, love your enemies and pray for those who persecute you" (Matthew 5:43–44).

We tend to respond to this as Saint Augustine did, who spent his first fifteen years of adulthood as a philanderer. At one point he prayed, "Give me chastity and continence—but not yet."

Does this strike home to us? Don't many of us say to ourselves, "When I reach a certain stage in life, when it's more convenient, *then* I'm going to be a better Christian"? Peter says to us, "Don't wait. There is no more convenient time. Live like this now—*beginning today.*"

O Lord, let this difficult message from Peter prompt me to ask, "What is my actual relationship with God? What is my relationship with sin? What is my relationship with mercy, goodness, grace, and forgiveness? How can I follow more closely the perfect life of Christ?" I pray this in Jesus' name. Amen. ❧

177

Father Knows Best

*My son, do not forget my teaching, but keep my commands
in your heart, for they will prolong your life many years and bring
you peace and prosperity.*
PROVERBS 3:1 – 2

One day when I was about twelve years old, my father, a very domineering person, said to me, "Jimmy, I want to talk with you." Now, my father never called me Jimmy; he always called me Hot (short for Hotshot). I didn't know what I had done wrong; or maybe more accurately, I wondered what my father might have uncovered.

He and I went into the bathroom, and he closed the door. This was unprecedented, and I felt deathly afraid. He said, "I want to discuss something with you that is very serious." I said, "Yes, sir, Daddy." "There's something I want to make sure that you don't do," he stated. By that point, I was willing to promise *anything*. Then he said, "I don't want you to smoke cigarettes until after you are twenty-one years old."

With great relief, I immediately responded, "I promise, Daddy." I kept my promise—and still am keeping it, some sixty-three years later.

Daddy smoked two or three packs of cigarettes a day, a habit he acquired in World War I. Later, he died from cancer, as did my mother, both of my sisters, and my brother—all of whom were smokers.

While we don't always understand why our parents ask us to do certain things, honoring their instruction can literally save our lives. The same principle holds true with our heavenly Father. We do not always understand God's commandments or why things turn out as they do, but we can be sure that God knows what's best for us.

We Christians know that Jesus set a perfect example for us to follow. Actually following it will change our lives for the better.

*O Lord, grant me the wisdom to trust what you say in your Word and the
strength to obey your commands, even when I can't always understand
the reason behind your instruction. I ask these things in the name of my
Savior, Jesus Christ. Amen.* ❧

178

Knowing Ourselves

As iron sharpens iron, so one person sharpens another.
PROVERBS 27:17

Have you ever tried to evaluate yourself by assessing what other people think of you? This can be a very valuable exercise because observers sometimes have better insight into your behavior and character than you do.

I experienced this in the Navy when my superiors made regular assessments of me, both brutally honest and supposedly fair. Perhaps even more accurate were the opinions of voters when I became a candidate for state senator, governor, and president.

We usually try to shape carefully the impression we make on others, either in private business or in casual encounters at home or in church. In a way, we turn into a salesperson marketing a product. We hope to impart what we consider a good image of ourselves.

But sometimes our efforts to create "a good image" don't succeed. To indicate that we have succeeded in life, for example, we might make a remark about the size or location of our home, which schools we've attended, or some famous person we know. We do this to make a good impression—but sometimes we end up alienating people instead. They might consider us to be bragging or trying to feel superior.

Despite our best efforts, our negative human traits tend to come through one way or another. And sometimes it is a best friend or spouse who is willing to tell us the truth about ourselves. I can usually depend on Rosalynn to take the wind out of my sails when I most need it. This can feel disconcerting, but it is very valuable.

Prayer gives us another means of self-improvement, provided we have the courage to bare our innermost thoughts to God in frank confession. As we acknowledge our shortcomings and failures, we may be inspired to correct what we have been doing wrong. And while this is never easy, it can be very rewarding.

O Lord, I don't like to have my life assessed in a brutally frank fashion, nor do I always know how to reach the goal of a better life. Let me appreciate my friends and loved ones who have the courage to tell me the truth about myself. And let me also turn to you for your own accurate assessment. In Jesus' name I pray. Amen.

179

Keeping the Faith

"We have been unfaithful to our God by marrying foreign women from the
peoples around us. But in spite of this, there is still hope for Israel. Now let
us make a covenant before our God to send away all these women and their
children, in accordance with the counsel of my lord and of those who fear
the commands of our God."

EZRA 10:2 – 3

God intended for his chosen people to remain pure. This was important, not to preserve the purity of the Hebrew bloodline, but because the devout Israelites worshiped the one true God, while the tribes around them worshiped false deities. God knew that as the Hebrews mixed freely with pagans, before long their intermarriages would dilute the purity of the Jewish religion. Marriage would inevitably bring some exchange of religious beliefs, and marrying into pagan families would unavoidably weaken the nation's exclusive commitment to God Almighty.

At God's command, therefore, Ezra intervened, and because of his transforming leadership, most of the Jewish people have retained their identity to this day.

Ezra forced the Jewish men who had married pagan wives to divorce their spouses and to send both them and their children away. While that honestly makes me uncomfortable — I can't envision breaking up whole families — it was important that the Jews honor the special covenant between them and God. What they had done blatantly violated the promises they had made.

We Christians can learn from this ancient event. We too have made solemn promises to our Savior, Jesus Christ, and we must let nothing and no one violate or weaken those promises. There simply is too much at stake.

O Lord, help me understand this admittedly uncomfortable episode from
Israel's history. And help me see that my commitment to you must remain
the paramount concern of my life. In my own relationships, help me keep
you first in all things, and enable me to encourage others to open their
hearts to accept Christ as Savior. In Jesus' name I pray. Amen. ❧

180

Don't Dismiss Discipline

Folly is bound up in the heart of a child,
but the rod of discipline will drive it far away.
PROVERBS 22:15

My father had no problem keeping discipline in his family. I knew I had some punishment coming whenever I did something deliberately wrong and my father learned about it. I still remember four of the most severe whippings I got from my daddy, and I can't deny all were well deserved.

My mother tried to stand between Daddy and me, and when she knew I did something wrong, she would punish me in a very mild way. When Daddy came home, Mama would say, "Jimmy did such and such, Earl, but I've already punished him, so you don't have to."

I treated my three boys in a similar way. If they directly violated my orders or if they lied to me or did something unacceptable at school, then they knew I would punish them when they got home. While my daddy used a switch to punish me, I used a board to give my boys perhaps three licks on their rear end.

When my grandchildren came along, I was amazed when my sons didn't exercise similar discipline. I used to squirm when I saw my grandchildren deliberately violate their father's command and then say, in effect, "I'm not going to do what you tell me." My sons would reply, "I wish you would obey me, but ..." Sometimes they would deprive their children of watching television for an hour, but there were no spankings. I have to admit, however, that their mild approach worked as well as mine.

While I'm convinced that all children need discipline from their parents, it doesn't need to be physical punishment. And in any case, it should be done with justice, mutual understanding, and love.

O Lord, while none of us especially likes discipline, your Word makes it clear that children beloved by their fathers will receive whatever correction and discipline may be necessary for their proper training. Help me recognize and accept discipline and proper conduct in my own life, and give me wisdom in exercising authority over those for whom I am responsible. I pray these things in Jesus' name. Amen. ❧

181

Be Happy and Do Good

*I know that there is nothing better for people than to be happy and
to do good while they live.*
ECCLESIASTES 3:12

If I hadn't been a square dancer, I never would have become president.

When Rosalynn and I returned home from the Navy in 1953, we wanted
to become involved in our former community as much as possible. I had left
home when I was seventeen and returned after being away for twelve years,
and we wanted to get to know as many people as we could. So we joined a
square dance club in nearby Dawson. About fifty people met every Friday
night to dance. Through square dancing, we got to know people from several
counties. Together we learned new steps, practiced them, and looked forward
to the next Friday night.

Nine years later, on the spur of the moment, I ran for the Georgia State
Senate. I hadn't planned to become a politician, and I faced an election
unfairly stacked against me. On Election Day, 126 people were listed as having voted alphabetically for my opponent, down to the third letter in their
name; some of them were dead, others in prison. The list was fraudulent. I
finally won, by 66 votes. If I hadn't received support from our square-dancing
friends, I would have lost and never become a state senator. And if that had
occurred, I never would have run for office again.

People make innocent decisions, often reaching out to new people, and
these choices sometimes change their lives. That's why it's important, regardless of our circumstances, to stretch our hearts and have an expansive life.
Rosalynn and I enjoyed the square dancing—but we've probably enjoyed a
lot more what's happened since. You just never know.

*O God, thank you for the happy surprises you scatter throughout my life
and for using them to bless me and distribute your grace to others. May
I realize that all of my choices, regardless of how unimportant they may
seem at the time, can become your chosen means to bring me to the place
you have for me. Let me also make choices to bring happiness to others. In
Jesus' name I pray. Amen.* 🕊

A Good Inheritance

I am reminded of your sincere faith, which first lived in your
grandmother Lois and in your mother Eunice and, I am persuaded,
now lives in you also.
2 TIMOTHY 1:5

Many of us are blessed with ancestors, parents, or grandparents who had vital relationships with Christ. They passed along their faith to us. Since birth we've been immersed in the life and teachings of Christ. Paul would tell us, "Take advantage of that godly, spiritual heritage! Don't let it go to waste. God did not bless you with cowardice or timidity, but with power and strength. Take an inventory of what you have to offer!"

Paul specifically reminds Timothy about "love and self-discipline." Self-discipline doesn't refer only to the avoidance of sinful acts; it also helps us grow in effectiveness and use wisely the talent and opportunities we have. It's easy to say, "I'll just let other people do it. That's the preacher's job. I leave it to those who are more articulate than I am. I'll let the missionaries take care of it." Paul warns us against that sort of attitude. Whatever talents or abilities or opportunities we have, we must take advantage of them in the service of Jesus Christ. Each of us should aggressively pursue this and say, "This is where I live, these are the people I know, and this is what I have to offer." Whatever we've inherited, let us use it well, in Jesus' name.

And we can do so with love! How can we truly help people without caring for them? We mustn't do "good works" out of a sense of competition or because we think (mistakenly) it will help us earn our way to heaven. No, we help others because we love them as people made in God's image. It's not always easy, but God will help us. It's God's idea, after all.

Dear God, help me glorify you by using whatever spiritual inheritance
I might have. Give me the understanding I need to analyze my own
situation and gifts, and then help me to depend on your Spirit and your
power to guide me do what most pleases you. And, Lord, help me create a
good spiritual inheritance of my own. In Jesus' name I pray. Amen. ❧

Walk by the Spirit

*So I say, walk by the Spirit,
and you will not gratify the desires of the flesh.*
GALATIANS 5:16

When I was a child, I lived on a farm in the country, although I spent some time in the town of Plains. One night I joined some other boys in doing a curious thing: we went down to South Hudson Street to visit what we called a "Holy Roller church."

If you were anywhere in the small community at night, you could hear the Holy Rollers, singing loudly and shouting in strange languages as the Holy Spirit moved them to do so. When we got to the church, we put a few coins into the offering plate. The people welcomed us warmly, glad that we could see how deeply committed they were to worshiping Christ in their own way, which to us seemed quite strange.

My sister Ruth Carter Stapleton, a famous evangelist and author, herself spoke in tongues. One time I questioned her about it, and she replied, "Jimmy, I think you should speak in tongues as well, because it's a matter of total relationship with God. You shouldn't be timid; you should completely relax and let the Holy Spirit fill you and not try to be so proper and cautious, like an engineer or a farmer." I tried, but I never could bring myself to speak in tongues.

Whether we speak in tongues or not, it is imperative that we "walk by the Holy Spirit." As the third person of the Trinity, the Holy Spirit is a powerful presence who wants to work in our lives. If we cooperate with the Spirit, we will be in a proper relationship with ourselves and with God. Therefore, let us walk by the Holy Spirit, the presence of Jesus Christ in our lives. This will bring us both joy and peace.

O God, the words of Paul prompt me to ask, "Have I opened my heart fully to the presence of the Holy Spirit? Am I reconciled, through Christ, with my Creator? Do I really live as a Christian, as a 'little Christ'?" Teach me, Lord, how to be filled each day with your Spirit, and through his power enable me to live in harmony with you. In Jesus' name I pray. Amen.

PART 3
❦SERVING❦

Contrary to what many private citizens (and some candidates) think, holding political office is not about wielding power, but about public service. It's not about making others do what we want them to do, but about doing for others what they need us to do. This is easy to forget in a me-first, get-ahead-at-any-cost culture, but we neglect service to others at a great cost to ourselves—not just in politics, but even more in the Christian life.

As the Messiah and Son of God, Jesus had more right than anyone to have his way, and yet we know that Christ "did not come to be served, but to serve, and to give his life as a ransom for many" (Matthew 20:28). Christians who desire to please their Lord and enjoy a vibrant life also will choose the way of service; it's in our divine DNA. The very word *Christian* means "little Christ," and Jesus calls us to copy his example, to "follow in his steps" (1 Peter 2:21). In this section, therefore, we'll explore what it means to serve in this deeply hurting world. We'll ponder the example of Jesus; discuss justice and injustice; focus on compassion; discover what it means to be ambassadors of Christ; see how creativity, happiness, and service go hand in hand; note the role of humility; strive for peace; and more.

This section and the previous one overlap, of course, because no one grows in faith merely by absorbing from outside. Growth comes when we achieve a balance of taking in and giving out. Most of the time, our "giving out" comes in the form of service to others. God designed us for service (always gratifying) and destined us for an ultimate reward when we fulfill our divine design. Imagine Jesus speaking the following words to us at the end of history: "Well done, good and faithful servant! You have been faithful with a few things; I will put you in charge of many things. Come and share your master's happiness!" (Matthew 25:21).

184

Little Christs

*The Spirit of the Sovereign LORD is on me, because the LORD has
anointed me to proclaim good news to the poor. He has sent me to
bind up the brokenhearted, to proclaim freedom for the captives and
release from darkness for the prisoners.*
ISAIAH 61:1

One Sabbath day in his hometown of Nazareth, just after he had launched his public ministry, Jesus went to the synagogue to worship. Leaders asked him to read from the holy scrolls, and he turned to the first few verses of Isaiah 61. He read them, then said, in effect, "Today you have witnessed the fulfillment of these words through my life."

These words of Isaiah sum up the crucial elements of Christ's ministry—and many Christians have a hard time accepting their reality.

One meaning of the word *Christian* is "little Christ." When we acknowledge Christ as our Savior, we announce to the world, "I will follow Christ. I will emulate, as best I can, his words and actions. Through the power of God's Spirit, I will be a little Christ."

Many of us stray from this commitment to the oppressed, the persecuted, the lonely, the prisoners, and the sick. But if we claim to be "little Christs," then we can't build a cocoon around ourselves and devote our whole existence to caring for our own needs or those of our immediate family. Christ calls us to reach out to those in need.

A chasm exists between most affluent American families and their needy neighbors or people in the rest of the world who live on less than a dollar a day. Although God loves them equally as much as he loves us, they feel abandoned and sometimes turn against us in resentment when we fail to recognize their plight.

We do not find this truth easy to accept. But if we claim to be Christians, "little Christs," then we must acknowledge that we have inherited this ministry from Christ. Like him, we have been anointed by God's Spirit to share in his work.

*Lord, let my heart and mind expand so I can live closer to Christ.
Strengthen me to remain in the presence of the Holy Spirit, so that God
Almighty—the Creator of the universe—will bring joy and happiness
and light into my life, and through me into the lives of those around me.
In Jesus' name I pray. Amen.*

Our Leader, the Servant

"Whoever wants to become great among you must be your servant,
and whoever wants to be first must be your slave."
MATTHEW 20:26

What are the qualities of a good religious leader? Most of us would say we want someone who is fair and trustworthy, who inspires our confidence with eloquence, and who follows the edicts of God. We want our leaders to reassure us and give us helpful answers. Often we want a visionary, someone to challenge us and raise our expectations and ambitions.

While these things are all good, none matches Christ's definition of a spiritual leader. Jesus said a leader must be the servant of all — and he taught by example. At the Last Supper, after he had equated himself with God Almighty, he took off his outer clothes, wrapped a towel around his waist, and washed the feet of his disciples. In so doing he provided a vivid, dramatic demonstration of his definition of leadership.

The self-exaltation of some contemporary pastors concerns me. They tend to set themselves up as the unchallenged superiors in their congregations and sometimes expect (and almost receive) the adulation of their church members. I also question the construction of church facilities that seem more like mammoth country clubs. I am aware of one church complex that cost $32 million to build. The congregation left a fairly poor neighborhood in a downtown urban area and moved out to the suburbs, where its enormous new center boasted squash courts, tennis courts, and a swimming pool. "If you join our church," went the appeal, "you'll be with people just like you. You will have the use of all these wonderful facilities, and you'll have a pastor who can pray directly to God for your welfare."

Such ostentatious self-exaltation contradicts what Christ said about leaders. We must be humble servants to those who trust us in Christ.

Eternal, almighty God, I confess that it feels more natural for me to
act like a superior than it does to function as a servant and a slave.
How grateful I am that my Lord and Savior, Jesus Christ, willingly
chose the way of the servant! Help me follow his example and welcome
opportunities to be the least in my service to others. I ask this in Jesus'
name. Amen. ❧

The Power of Presence

*"When you pass through the waters, I will be with you; and when you pass
through the rivers, they will not sweep over you. When you walk through
the fire, you will not be burned; the flames will not set you ablaze."*
ISAIAH 43:2

My mother was a registered nurse; and when she was sixty-eight, she became
a Peace Corps volunteer in India, where she served the poorest of the poor in
a small village near Bombay. She worked in a small clinic side by side with a
doctor. I once wrote a poem derived from a letter that Mama wrote to us. I
wrote the poem in her voice.

Miss Lillian Sees Leprosy for the First Time

When I nursed in a clinic near Bombay, a small girl, shielding all her lep-
rous sores, crept inside the door. I moved away, but then the doctor called,
"You take this case!"

First I found a mask, and put it on, quickly gave the child a shot and
then, not well, I slipped away to be alone and scrubbed my entire body red
and raw.

I faced her treatment every week with dread and loathing—of the chore,
not the child.

As time passed, I was less afraid, and managed not to turn my face away.

Her spirit bloomed as sores began to fade. She'd raise her anxious, searching eyes to mine to show she trusted me. We'd smile and say a few Marathi
words, then reach and hold each other's hands.

And then love grew between us, so that, later, when I kissed her lips, I didn't
feel unclean.

So let me ask you: Do you think Mama gave up more than she got? Do
you suppose she made a real sacrifice by going to India? She didn't think so.

*Lord, as I think about the word presence, give me the courage to look
at how I extend or restrict my own presence. Help me think about these
things and then take appropriate action. Most of all, help me remember
the perfect example given to me by my Savior, Jesus Christ, and give me
the strength to walk, however feebly, in his steps. In his name I pray.
Amen.* ❧

The Standard of Success

... who despises a vile person but honors those who fear the LORD; who
keeps an oath even when it hurts, and does not change their mind.
PSALM 15:4

Scripture implies that vile people are despised. To modern ears, that doesn't sound very positive, does it? But the verse is talking primarily about hating what God hates and loving what God loves. It encourages us to admire truthful people who love God.

Who are our heroes? Whom do we consider a success? What kind of standards are we establishing for ourselves as we observe or relate to those around us? Whom do we want to emulate? As Christians, we have a perfect standard laid out for us in the life of Jesus Christ. Often we can imagine how Jesus might react to various temptations or deprivations.

But how do we set standards for ourselves in order to lead a successful life? What do we perceive as "success" in our modern-day, technologically oriented, fast-paced, ever-changing world?

Some would say, "Success means making a lot of money." Others would list having social prestige or owning a big house or gaining fame—or enjoying a long life. While none of those things is morally wrong, they all fail to represent the standard of Christ, who is our perfect example. In fact, he had none of these things.

As followers of Christ, we need to search our own hearts and ask, "How do I measure up in the eyes of my Savior, Jesus Christ? Does *he* think I am a success?" The successful people we ought to emulate are those who fear the Lord.

Most of us Americans already have just about everything we need. Most of us have food, security, education, health care, and citizenship in a great nation, while most people around the world lack those things.

The question for us is this: Do we have a "good life," as measured by Jesus Christ? That's the only kind of success that ultimately matters.

O God, help me live a "good life" according to your standards. Teach me
to know what you mean by "success," and then give me the wisdom and
strength I need to succeed. I ask these things in the name of my Savior,
Jesus Christ. Amen.

The Essence of Christianity

*Be kind and compassionate to one another, forgiving each other,
just as in Christ God forgave you.*
EPHESIANS 4:32

One morning I asked members of my Sunday school class to name a Bible verse that, in their opinion, described the essence of Christianity. After hearing many good suggestions, I quoted Ephesians 4:32, which theologian Reinhold Niebuhr considered his favorite verse.

I believe that this text, coupled with John 3:16, encapsulates the essence of Christianity. It's not broad in scope. It's not a philosophical treatise. It's about relationships between people. Each of us is precious in God's sight, and we are urged to act toward others as God acts toward us, even though we are sinners.

Christ had a special relationship with *individual* human beings. *Every* person was important to him, and he loved them *all.* Jesus personified a ministry focused on individual lost sinners. We know of this personal aspect of his love even in regard to the Pharisees, who often opposed Jesus. It shocked people when a leper approached Christ, falling on his knees, and Jesus responded with affection and even physical contact. What a radical departure for religious leaders of those days! They simply didn't behave in this way. Jesus, however, healed the leper with a touch and told him to go to the religious authorities to certify his cure, because only then could the man be accepted back into society.

While Christ cared for the despised, too often we think that outcasts deserve their ill treatment. It wasn't only the Pharisees who thought that people suffered because God had rejected them!

Christ ministered to real human needs because he saw the harm that deprivation causes. The lack of education, health, social equality, justice, freedom, and love—these human afflictions provided the occasion for Christ's ministry. As Christians, we should respond as Jesus did.

O God, I see in the Gospels how Christ responded to human need and departed radically from the religious teachings and practice of his day. Help me learn from his perfect example and then emulate it. Let the kind of words and actions that epitomized his life—peace, humility, concern, forgiveness, and compassion—permeate my own life as his disciple. In Jesus' name I pray. Amen. ❧

Who Are You?

Now we ask you, brothers and sisters, to acknowledge those who work
hard among you, who care for you in the Lord and who admonish
you. Hold them in the highest regard in love because of their work.
I THESSALONIANS 5:12 – 13

How do we define ourselves? We might reply, "I'm a school teacher," or "I'm a farmer," or "I'm retired." Or we might say, "I'm a wife," or perhaps "a Georgian" or "a Baptist." Our intent is to say, "I am a special person, with certain talents, interests, and commitments."

But notice that all of these self-definitions tie us to other people in some way—as a partner or as a respectable part of some distinguished group. We are not necessarily trying to brag, but we don't tend to relate ourselves to people who are not very admirable, like the poor, homeless, or prisoners. When Jesus described himself to his fellow citizens in Nazareth, he said, "I am the one who came to preach the good news to the poor, to proclaim freedom to the prisoners, to recover sight for the blind, and to release the oppressed."

I would be embarrassed to say, "I am one who helps to build Habitat houses," or "I am one who teaches Bible lessons in my church." Some of these things may be true, but it is better to let others know, in an appropriate way, that "I am a Christian." In fact, this is a necessary part of carrying out the Great Commission, to declare ourselves followers of Jesus Christ and to explain why we have made this commitment.

Our challenge is somehow to put together these two things: to describe our secular lives, but also to acknowledge our faith in Jesus. The best approach may be through our actions and life priorities.

Paul confirmed this approach when he told church members to respect dedicated people because they worked hard at serving others in Christ's name. Now, *that's* a good goal for a church member, don't you think?

Lord, I'm grateful that you have given me this Scripture, and I ask that
you expand my heart so that I might be flexible and receptive to apply
these words to myself. Let me learn how to merge my secular and spiritual
lives. In the name of Christ. Amen. ❧

190

First or Last?

*Sitting down, Jesus called the Twelve and said, "Anyone who wants
to be first must be the very last, and the servant of all."*
MARK 9:35

Jesus had just told his disciples that he was going to suffer and lay down his life for others. But no sooner had he made the announcement than his followers began arguing with one another.

"What were you quarreling about?" Jesus asked, but they remained silent. Since Jesus already knew they had argued about who was the greatest, he said to them, "So you want first place? Then take the last place. Become the servant of all."

This remains a revolutionary idea, even two thousand years later, because it violates the very premise under which the modern world operates: "Get on top and stay there." When Jesus says we must become the servant of all, he doesn't mean that we must not use our talents and abilities to the fullest. He means, rather, that we are not to dominate others or strive for superiority at their expense. Serving others is the essence of Christ's ministry: "The Son of Man did not come to be served, but to serve" (Mark 10:45).

Christ opened to his disciples—and to us—a challenging way of life. Which is easier, for us to succeed by human standards or by Jesus' standards? How must we change if we are to start measuring up to his mandate?

Just as he asked his disciples, so Jesus asks us to think about our goals in life. "I know you want to be the closest one to me," he says, "but don't forget the most basic element of my life, which I have just explained to you. If you want to be first, then you must be last, and servant of all."

This is not a superficial principle or a matter of casual interest. Rather, it goes to the very heart of Christianity itself.

*Jesus, I ask that you forgive my self-centeredness and grant me the
power to change. Let me realize that what made your own ministry so
significant is that you reached out to those who were not attractive, who
were most in need. Help me do likewise, in your holy name. Amen.* ❧

Are You Great?

"Those who are regarded as rulers ... lord it over [others].... Not so with you. Instead, whoever wants to become great among you must be your servant, and whoever wants to be first must be slave of all."
MARK 10:42 – 44

One day while Jesus and his disciples walked to Jerusalem, James and John argued over who would sit at the chief places of honor in his coming kingdom. When the other disciples heard about it, they grew angry because they thought these two brothers were trying to secure the top spots.

Do you see any parallel between what happened there and the attitude of many of us today? Christ is saying that we are to share our abilities, influence, wealth, and time—not to get public acclaim or for any other self-gratifying motivation, but rather to benefit others. In Jesus' words, "The Son of Man did not come to be served, but to serve, and to give his life as a ransom for many" (Mark 10:45).

Do you wish to be great? Then you must become the servant of all. Christ says to us, "This is my measurement of life's success, of human greatness. This is heaven's measurement of loyalty to me as your Savior."

It is a very big step, however, to subjugate our own human aspirations and priorities to those of Jesus! And yet this is necessary if we are to become great in the eyes of God.

Jesus built his church on the foundation of the apostles—but not until they had learned this crucial lesson of serving others. The crop of greatness grows only from the seeds of servanthood.

Lord, again in your Word I confront lessons that are difficult for me. It's easy for me to relate them to James and John, but it's not so easy for me to acknowledge that they also apply to me. Help me admit that my own life needs to be transformed, as were those of the disciples. They showed us, through your Spirit, what Christianity means—a faith full of heroism and courage and dedication and humility and service and love. So help me apply their lessons to my life. I ask these things in the name of my Savior. Amen. ❧

192

Your Greatest Achievement

*Therefore, my brothers and sisters, you whom I love and long for, my
joy and crown, stand firm in the Lord in this way, dear friends!*
PHILIPPIANS 4:1

What does Paul mean when he calls his friends in Philippi "my joy and
crown"? A "joy and crown" is something of ultimate importance, so when
Paul used this term to refer to his Philippian family, he was saying, "You are
the most important thing in my life."

Now, consider that Paul was talking about a tiny church in a poor back-
water town, a group that today we would likely write off as inconsequential.
Although the church had few members, Paul looked upon its people as the
culminating achievement of his life. Why? Because into that tiny church
Christ had breathed life through his servant Paul. The apostle reckoned that
his evangelistic achievement, his winning people to faith in Christ, was the
greatest thing he had ever done. In effect, he was saying, "When my life ends,
you are what I want to leave as the memorial to my efforts."

I'm sure that most of us have given at least some thought to what we want
inscribed on our gravestone. Would we like to record how many people we
led to Christ? If so, would our surviving family members feel embarrassed
by what it said?

Our lives need to have the right purpose. We need to look upon our service to Christ as the greatest achievement of all. And when we start thinking
this way, we'll start shaping our lives differently. We'll spend more time and
energy on spreading the gospel and furthering the cause of our Savior. And
Jesus assures us that such a choice will bring us greater adventure and satis-
faction, not less.

*O God, help me remember that your love for me never wavers, your
forgiveness of my sin is absolute, and your mercy toward me remains genuine
and unwavering. Teach me to realign my life according to your priorities,
not someday in the future, but now. And so lead me into a more joyful,
transcendent, and successful way of living. And instruct me to pour my life
into others so that I too can point to them and say, "There's my crown." In
Jesus' name I pray. Amen.* ❧

A Liberating Commitment

*"Therefore go and make disciples of all nations, baptizing them in
the name of the Father and of the Son and of the Holy Spirit."*
MATTHEW 28:19

The Great Commission is great not only because of its massive extent ("all
nations"), but also because of its vast importance ("make disciples"). "Go,"
Jesus says, "and do as I have done. Go and act as I have acted."

Those are the marching orders of a Christian. We must work in our own
communities and do what we can in Christ's name among all nations. Our
strength will come from the presence of Jesus Christ, for he promised, "I will
be with you always."

We can't all go to Peru or to the Philippines to build homes with Habitat
for Humanity. But we *can* ascertain who among our acquaintances seems
lonely or suffering. We *can* minister to them in a spirit of Christian love.

We can also ask, "Against whom do I have resentment or animosity in my
heart?" We can ask God to give us a forgiving spirit so that we can remove
that hatred or resentment from our lives. Then the Lord can open a spirit of
friendship and even love between us, even if in the past we considered the
individual unworthy of forgiveness.

God has given us the opportunity to be aggressive and adventurous in
how we demonstrate our faith in Christ. With such a commitment and demonstration, we can find fulfillment. It's not a matter of restricting ourselves,
a common fear when some hear these words. "I don't want to change *too*
much," they say, or "I don't want to restrict my life to some rigid definition
of Christianity."

Much to the contrary, Christ promises that when we partner with him, we
will achieve a *higher* degree of freedom that transcends anything we have ever
known, along with joy and a peace that passes all understanding.

*God, may my commitment to follow Christ come not as a restriction, but
as a divine liberation. Help me become more innovative and aggressive
in looking for opportunities to serve others, so I may find and enjoy a life
far better than anything I've ever known. May my relationship with God
through Christ sustain me and change me for the better. Amen.* ❧

Do Not Remain Silent

Hate evil, love good; maintain justice in the courts. Perhaps the LORD God
Almighty will have mercy on the remnant of Joseph.... "But let justice roll
on like a river, righteousness like a never-failing stream!"
AMOS 5:15, 24

The Patriot Act, as a reaction to terrorist activity, took away some of the historical freedoms of our nation. While one can make an argument for taking such action, I disagreed with it.

It's generally known that the United States was torturing prisoners. Sometimes we try to redefine torture so we can say, "I don't torture anybody; I just hang them upside down and pour buckets of water over their faces so they think they're drowning." That practice is called waterboarding, and our leaders admitted doing it.

This is the first time in history since George Washington outlawed torture that our nation has condoned it. We have claimed that the Geneva rules regarding treatment of prisoners do not apply. We even passed a law that does away with *habeas corpus*, a basic principle that applies to all prisoners. Individuals have a right to know why they are in prison; charges must be brought against them, or they must be released. That started with the *Magna Carta* in 1215. Because Congress removed *habeas corpus*, some prisoners have languished at Guantanamo Bay for many years without a single charge lodged against them. They have no direct access to an attorney and can't speak with their parents, wives, or loved ones.

What is our responsibility, as Christians, to see that justice is done? We cannot keep silent just because the injustice doesn't affect our own families or friends. In fact, that's when we should speak up most of all. It might be a risk; it might not be prudent; it might endanger our own well-being or popularity. Yet we must speak up for justice in the name of Christ.

O Lord, I pray that our nation might refrain from adopting the policies
of a rich, successful, and self-congratulatory society that Amos condemned.
Rather, give us grace and strength to follow the perfect example set by
our Savior in both his words and actions. In our dealings with family,
businesses, and local and national affairs, teach us how to strive for peace,
justice, and righteousness. I pray this in Jesus' name. Amen.

Speak against Injustice

Then two scoundrels came and sat opposite him and brought charges
against Naboth before the people, saying, "Naboth has cursed both God and
the king." So they took him outside the city and stoned him to death.
1 KINGS 21:13

An evil king of Israel named Ahab wanted the land of his neighbor Naboth for a vegetable garden. But when he asked for it, Naboth refused the king's request. The king pouted and sulked.

Ahab's wife and queen, Jezebel—a wicked and ruthless pagan woman— saw her husband lying on his bed, blubbering, and learned the cause of his grief and anger. She said to him, "Don't worry; get up, have a good meal, and enjoy yourself. I will get the land for you." She ordered that Naboth be greatly honored, but then she had false charges brought against him, claiming that he cursed God. After his conviction, he was stoned to death, and then Ahab claimed the land he wanted. (Later, Elijah pronounced a curse on Ahab for his complicity in the incident.)

Why did Jezebel first honor Naboth? Perhaps it was to turn others against him. Although his neighbors knew him to be a righteous man and had never heard him criticize God or the king, perhaps they had become jealous. In any event, Jezebel's plan worked.

In this tragic story, we see the sinfulness of a whole group: Ahab, his wife, Jezebel, the elders who held the trial, the false witnesses, and the silent neighbors who refrained from testifying on Naboth's behalf. They all sinned by failing to speak up against injustice.

It is just as sinful for us to remain silent in the face of injustice. We who follow Christ *must* represent the cause of justice and speak up for those suffering from poverty, helplessness, or racial discrimination. That is a big part of what it means to follow Christ.

Dear Lord, while I quickly condemn the injustice of Jezebel, Ahab, and the false witnesses, it is more uncomfortable for me to realize that I may share the same kind of guilt as Naboth's neighbors, who out of fear or jealousy failed to speak up for him in his time of need. Give me wisdom, Lord, to know what is right, and the courage to speak and act for justice, just as Jesus always did. In his name I pray. Amen. ❧

196

Living Faith

*"Is not this the kind of fasting I have chosen: to loose the chains of
injustice and untie the cords of the yoke, to set the oppressed free and
break every yoke?"*
ISAIAH 58:6

When we fast, we usually think of refraining from food or drink. But God
favors a very different kind of fasting: a turning away from injustice and
oppression.

All of us feel tempted to choose a life of easy access to family, friends, or
people who seem very much like us and who won't make too many demands
on us. But by being so restrictive, we betray the basic mission that Christ
established for us as his followers.

In Matthew 25:31 – 46, our Savior warned us that in the judgment to
come, each of us will stand before him. He will say to his faithful ones,
"When I was hungry, you fed me; when I was thirsty, you gave me something
to drink." His followers will reply, astonished, "Lord, we never had a chance
to help you." But Jesus will answer, "Inasmuch as you did it unto the least of
these, you have done it unto me."

We could respond, "Well, my Christian faith is strong. I'm an active member of a congregation. I go to church every Sunday. I give regularly." But Isaiah said we could do all these things, and yet our prayers won't reach heaven.
God may not even know us as true believers, despite our religious activity.

The essence of a proper relationship with God is to assume the role of
a supplicant or a sinner who seeks forgiveness while acknowledging the
supremacy of our Creator. Because we worship and love Jesus, we strive to
emulate him by demonstrating peace, justice, humility, service, generosity,
compassion, and love toward others. That is the kind of "fasting" Isaiah says
God has chosen for us.

*O Lord, help me see that my relationship with my Savior is not expressed
in some prescribed form of worship or in being religious, but in reaching
out to others to prove that I love them. Help me, Lord, to embrace those
things in my heart as a foundation for my day-to-day life. Amen.* ❧

197

Love Reaches Out

"And if you spend yourselves in behalf of the hungry and satisfy the
needs of the oppressed, then your light will rise in the darkness, and
your night will become like the noonday."
ISAIAH 58:10

I grew up in Archery, Georgia, about two miles from Plains. Our family had a party-line telephone, one of three in the whole area. Whenever we answered our ring, we knew that three people were listening, plus the telephone operator.

Today I have several telephones—in my home, in my office in Atlanta, and in my office in Plains. I have a cell phone, a fax machine, and email.

The instantaneous nature of communication today shows how our lives have improved in material ways, but this does not mean we are communicating as we should. Isaiah tells us that we are to reach out to others and discover how we might help them.

My hometown of Plains has 635 citizens, 60 percent of whom are black and 40 percent white. In addition, we have about 85 Latinos, who have little money. They either ride around town on bicycles or walk, since the State of Georgia will not grant them driver's licenses. But they're wonderful neighbors and dependable employees, showing up every morning for work.

Historically, our church members have had very little communication with them, since the Latinos have a close-knit community and few of them speak any English. So not long ago we organized regular visits to their homes to deliver food, clothing, and other things that they needed. Although the adults still prefer to worship with a visiting priest, their children have become the most enthusiastic participants in our vacation Bible school. This exchange has enlivened and strengthened our church.

Isaiah is telling us that it is time to reach out to those around us in a spirit of love and understanding. As we do, we demonstrate the reality of our faith. And that pleases God.

O Lord, I come before you again, searching for a more gratifying and
fulfilling existence. Help me walk with Jesus as I should and reach out in
his name to others. Help me communicate in ways that bless those around
me. In his name I pray. Amen.

A Good Life

"I, even I, am the LORD,
and apart from me there is no savior."
ISAIAH 43:11

We often don't look at God as our Savior, and yet that is how our Creator describes himself. Just as God created the world through Christ, so he saves us through Christ. The important thing is to consider from what we were saved—and *for* what we *are* saved.

We *were* saved from condemnation and alienation from God, even though we are not promised a life without trial or pain. We tend to look for security, for comfort, for a good life, and all too often that becomes our primary goal. But what is a good life? Certainly, the average American's life looks good to most of the rest of the world.

But do we strive to live intimately with Christ, or do we tend to live within a gilded cage, cautious about who might want to penetrate our personal sacred grounds? Are we careful that only our friends or people similar to us come into our presence? It's a natural human trait. We want to protect ourselves. We don't want unsavory people of unpredictable behavior to encroach upon our personal privileges or priorities.

How very different was the life of Jesus Christ, our Savior! He was condemned and questioned by his own people because he reached out to tax collectors, hated by the Jews and used by the Romans. Jesus even ate with them in their homes! He embraced both lepers and prostitutes. Christ expanded his life and in the process gave us an example to follow—we *are* saved to continue his ministry in the world.

For the Christian, a good life is measured by the standards of Jesus Christ. It's a life of sharing, of humility, of unselfishness, of peace and joy. It's a life of adventure and gratification. It's a life that transforms the sacrifices we thought we were making into great blessings. That is a "good life," and no other.

God, help me see that the good life I seek must embody divine love,
Christlike compassion, and unselfish concern. I remember that I can love
like this only because you first loved me. Empower me, Lord, to be your
hands and feet in this needy world. And in that way, help me live the
good life. In Jesus' holy name I pray. Amen. ❧

199

Share with the Poor

The generous will themselves be blessed,
for they share their food with the poor.
PROVERBS 22:9

In a high school graduation speech, I once told a joke about a churchgoing man who died. When he got to the pearly gates, Saint Peter said, "I'm glad you taught Sunday school for years, but what have you ever done for poor people?"

The man replied, "Back in the Depression, my neighbor's house burned down. I had a table on my back porch that we didn't need, so I gave it to him without any charge." Saint Peter asked, "How much was it worth?" The man answered, "At least fifty cents."

Saint Peter nodded and asked, "Any other times?" The man answered, "Yes, once a homeless family came by, asking for food. I gave them two sandwiches and a glass of tea each." Saint Peter said, "That's very nice. How would you value that?" The man replied, "That was at least fifty cents."

Saint Peter turned to an angel and said, "Go down to earth and see if what he claims is true." So the angel went down and back and said, "Yes, he really did those things." Saint Peter asked, "What do you think we should do with him?" The angel answered, "Give him his dollar back and tell him to go to hell!"

Sharing what we have with the poor is not just an option or a onetime duty appended to the Christian faith. It is *essential*. Our Savior, Jesus Christ, always cared for the unfortunate around him, the poor, the despised, the outcast, the condemned, the sick, and the impoverished. He said, "As you did unto the least of these, you did unto me. " How we deal with "the least of these" is a very important and serious issue. We *must* remember to serve the poor. It is God's command, and it is our Christian duty.

O God, you remind me that I have constant opportunities to serve you
by sharing what I have with others. I pray that this lesson will implant
itself in my heart in such a way that I'll look at my circumstances and
say, "How can I personally demonstrate my faith in Jesus Christ through
generosity and service to those in need?" I ask this in the name of my
Savior. Amen. ❧

200

Invest in the Kingdom of Heaven

*"For whoever has will be given more, and they will have an
abundance. Whoever does not have, even what they have will be
taken from them."*
MATTHEW 25:29

Jesus once told a parable in which a master gives differing amounts of gold to his servants before leaving on a long journey. He gives to each man according to his ability: five bags of gold to one; two to another; one to the last. When he returns, he discovers that the first two servants doubled their money, while the last servant merely buried his gold in the ground.

The master praises and generously rewards the first two servants, but he rebukes and condemns the third man. He takes away the last servant's gold and gives it to the first man, and then says, "Throw that worthless servant outside, into the darkness, where there will be weeping and gnashing of teeth" (Matthew 25:30). This story is not easy for us to understand.

The master here represents God, and we are the servants. Some of us have been given much talent, ability, and opportunity; others less. But in each case, what is given is precious and valuable. We Christians have been given freedom also, to decide how we will serve our Master, Jesus Christ, to whom we have committed our lives with a solemn oath before our Creator.

God does not treat us as puppets or automatons, nor manipulate us with strings. We alone decide how we will use our gifts to benefit the kingdom of Christ.

We must ask ourselves, "What have I done? What am I doing? What will I do to serve God in the name of my Savior, Jesus Christ?" Are we investing our resources and time for the sake of Christ and his kingdom, for the benefit of those around us who are in need? What a sobering thought!

The stakes are large, and the decision is ours.

*Lord, show me how to use the talents you have given me to serve my
Savior. Help me work for you and your kingdom with an eye toward the
future and in a spirit of adventure. Make me courageous enough and wise
enough to serve you in a way that pleases you, and thus find eternal joy in
my labor. In the name of Jesus Christ I pray. Amen.* ❧

Arm's-Length Charity

Jesus put his fingers into the man's ears.
Then he spit and touched the man's tongue.
MARK 7:33

Some time ago, Rosalynn's mother went to the hospital with heart trouble. One night she asked Rosalynn to remove her false teeth and put them in a glass of water; my wife told me later that she hesitated a moment before reaching into her mother's mouth and pulling out those dentures.

Sometimes we feel reluctant about certain kinds of intimacy, even with those we love. We avoid being near someone guilty of a serious crime, who is mentally ill, or who suffers with leprosy or AIDS or river blindness.

One day, while on his way back from Tyre and Sidon, Jesus met a deaf and mute person. The townspeople had brought the man, hoping the Lord would heal him. After they got alone, the Lord put his fingers into the man's ears and then put *his own saliva* in the man's mouth.

Frankly, this disturbs me a little and involves the kind of intimacy that troubled Rosalynn. The question arises: Why? Jesus could have said, "Touch the fringe on my garment," or even "Go home, and you'll be healed." Why did he stick his fingers in this man's ears and in his mouth?

He probably wanted to create a close personal relationship and, perhaps, to teach *us* not to avoid intimacy with other human beings. While it's good to donate money to charities that help the homeless and it's wonderful to pack Christmas boxes for poor families, we also should be willing to make a more direct connection with the needy. Jesus wants us to invest ourselves *personally* in their lives and sorrows. Helping others is not a hands-off, arm's-length experience. At times, it calls for a certain intimacy, or personal sharing, with those in need.

O God, I confess that too often I like to see people helped at a distance so I don't have to become too intimate with those suffering from a contagious disease, or who are criminals, drug addicts, or mentally ill. But your Word teaches me that these are the kinds of people to whom Christ devoted his ministry. Help me, Lord, to follow his example, regardless of the discomfort. In his name I pray. Amen. ❧

Compassion Takes Action

Dear children, let us not love with words or speech
but with actions and in truth.
I JOHN 3:18

I read recently in the *New York Times* that thirty thousand Christians got permission to demonstrate in the name of Christ against the continuation of the Iraqi War. On a related issue, the National Association of Evangelicals, which claims to represent forty thousand American churches, issued a statement condemning torture of inmates by Americans in Abu Ghraib prison in Iraq, and opposing torture and indefinite incarceration without trial of prisoners in Guantanamo Bay, Cuba.

These news reports of admirable concern remind us that Christians must not be satisfied with just words or a temporary demonstration. While compassionate concern about others is an important factor in a Christian's thought process and an admirable attitude, it isn't enough.

The apostle John tells us not to stop there, but to use all our available resources to bring an end to the problem. It is not enough to say, "I am concerned about people in need, about those who suffer from war, people who don't have enough to eat, or families who lack an adequate place to live. I am *really* concerned and will even pray for them." That's all very good; but John says it's not adequate. We can't let ourselves feel complacent and self-satisfied just because we have the right attitude toward others or because we feel compassion for them. We must find ways to put that concern into action—by using the truth.

If we're concerned about people who suffer from war, then we should promote peace strongly and persistently, reminding others that this is the commandment of the Prince of Peace. Because of a false sense of patriotism, too few Christians are willing to express themselves as free and influential citizens. Jesus says, "It's time for a change."

O Lord, too often I assume that feeling compassion is adequate. Give me the will and the courage to take tangible, specific actions to relieve the suffering, poverty, and pain of the people of the world around me. Allow that compassion to stretch beyond my pocketbook, to take shape in my own hands and feet. Lead me, Lord, and strengthen me. In Jesus' name I pray. Amen. ❧

Doing Good

"They must turn from evil and do good."
I PETER 3:II

The key word in this verse is "do." Why is "do" so important? It's important because it's active.

Most of us are basically dormant. We measure our success as Christians by how well we comply with Christ's teachings, but in a negative way. We say, "I try not to kill or condemn others; I try not to steal; I try not to be selfish; I try not to dwell on materialistic things; I try not to be disloyal to my wife or husband; I try not to gossip about my neighbors."

Many of us live our whole lives in this way. We let the hours, days, weeks, months, and years go by while doing little that is active. And then we rationalize our inactivity by saying, "I'm a pretty good Christian. I'm a member of a church. I accepted Christ when I was a child and I've tried to refrain from doing evil."

We *should* avoid evil, obviously. But is that enough? Is a negative approach to our religion sufficient? Peter didn't think so. He said we must move to the positive, active side of the ledger and be eager to do something good. That might be quite a change from our normal habits. David wrote the same counsel in the Psalms, centuries before Peter's time: "Turn from evil and do good; seek peace and pursue it" (Psalm 34:14). That sounds to me like a consistent divine standard.

Let's think about our own lives for a moment. As we look at the challenges and opportunities and prospects before us, how can we actively search for ways to do good things in the name of Christ? What "good things" can we do in our home, at work, at church, in our neighborhood, or with family and friends to make a difference for the Lord? How can we exercise our creativity in actually *doing* good?

> *O Lord, help me change from "How can I keep from doing evil in this situation?" to "How can I do good for Christ in this situation?" Bring within me a new habit of thought so that I become active in my faith rather than passive, creative rather than reactive, advancing rather than retreating. I pray this in the name of Jesus, my active Savior. Amen.* ❧

A Blessing for Everyone

*[Jesus said,] "There were many widows in Israel in Elijah's time, when
the sky was shut for three and a half years and there was a severe famine
throughout the land. Yet Elijah was not sent to any of them, but to a
widow in Zarephath in the region of Sidon. And there were many in Israel
with leprosy in the time of Elisha the prophet, yet not one of them was
cleansed—only Naaman the Syrian."*

LUKE 4:25 – 27

During almost ten decades in the South—and throughout America—very
few of us, even in our churches, condemned or criticized total racial segregation. We accepted the legal premise of "separate but equal." In fact, in
our Plains Brotherhood meeting, every year or two, some distinguished
Bible scholar from a prestigious seminary would come to "prove" to us from
Scripture that God had ordained the separation of the races. Even the most
enlightened pastors would say, "Well, that's a social problem. We just preach
the gospel." We shake our heads now, but that's the way we lived back then,
and that was the way we had lived for generations. We accepted the "fact"
that we white folks were "superior" and that people of a different color were
"inferior."

In the time of Christ, the Jews believed that Gentiles stood outside the
purview of God's covenant with Abraham. Naturally, this caused the Jews to
feel superior. But in this encounter with the people of Nazareth, his hometown, Jesus emphasized that God wants to bless *all* of us, simply because
God loves us. God's blessing is available to everyone through the sacrifice
of Christ, who offers himself as Savior to all who will receive him. Sometimes we forget this and so discriminate against those toward whom we have
some grudge or animosity. We therefore mentally relegate them to an inferior
position.

Jesus says, "Love others, regardless of who they are." Let's pray that we
might eliminate discrimination, animosity, and grudges from our lives as
followers of Jesus Christ.

*Dear God, I pray that you would expand my heart so that I seek to
worship you alongside others who may be different from me or with
whom I might disagree. Help us, Lord, to be your people—all of us,
together. In Jesus' name I pray. Amen.* ❧

The Weak and the Strong

Accept the one whose faith is weak, without quarreling over disputable matters. One person's faith allows them to eat everything, but another person, whose faith is weak, eats only vegetables. The one who eats everything must not treat with contempt the one who does not, and the one who does not eat everything must not judge the one who does, for God has accepted them.

ROMANS 14:1 – 3

A sharp division arose in the early church over what a believer could and could not eat. The Old Testament forbade the Jewish people from eating certain kinds of meat, and one day an altercation erupted among Christians over whether one could eat meat offered to idols.

Knowing that idols were just pieces of wood or metal, Paul labeled as "weak" the individuals who refused to eat "unclean" meat or meat sacrificed to idols. The "strong" he considered those who ate without constraint. What did he mean?

Apparently, if we start narrowly defining Christianity according to our own tastes — setting up our own extrabiblical rules — then we are weak, because we have limited the breadth and scope of the blessing of God. This passage admonishes us against trying to prescribe a human definition of Christianity by adding purely man-made rules about right and wrong.

Yet Paul insists that "strong" individuals should not judge the weak and that "weak" individuals should not despise the strong. How easily we fall into both errors! We must remain very conscious of these harmful tendencies and try to fight them whenever we discover them in ourselves. That means, first, we must not devise our own extra rules of right and wrong. And second, we should avoid judging others who don't follow every ritual that we do. Nor should we think badly of those who follow rituals that we consider superfluous.

God accepts people in both groups, so who are we to reject them?

Dear God, I'm grateful for the warning that I'll answer to you for the times I wrongly judge or condemn others as my inferiors. Give me strength to resist this temptation and to live in accordance with the teachings of Christ, who valued justice and peace, and always with humility and forgiveness. Help me aspire to these characteristics in my daily life. I ask these things in the name of my Savior. Amen.

Who Are the Prisoners?

*"The LORD looked down from his sanctuary on high, from heaven he
viewed the earth, to hear the groans of the prisoners and release those
condemned to death."*
PSALM 102:19 – 20

As the new governor of Georgia, I visited all out state prisons with an enlightened prison director. We entered cells and assembly areas, spoke with the prisoners and guards, and discovered some shocking things.

Some inmates in the Reidsville State prison had been in solitary confinement for as long as ten years. No prisoners had received any career planning and about 35 percent of them were mentally retarded. In response, other Southern governors and I set a goal of seeing how much we could improve the prison systems.

In Georgia, we started giving every new prisoner a psychiatric test, an aptitude test, and an IQ test. Counselors learned what all prisoners wanted to do after their release and so arranged training for their future careers. Those eligible for parole were given the opportunity to participate in an early release program. I personally held training courses in the state's senate chamber for service club members who had volunteered to serve as probation officers. They had to visit prisoners and their families before release and agreed to find a job for the prisoner. We governors competed over who achieved the lowest prison populations.

Today, by contrast, the competition throughout America is over which governor can have *more* inmates in prison and who can have the most severe penalties for crimes. The result? We have more of our people in prison than any nation on earth.

Jesus said, "He has sent me to proclaim freedom for the prisoners" (Luke 4:18). Where is our Christian influence? We increasingly look upon prisoners as inferior, permanently condemned, and unworthy of our concern. We must remember that *all* of us are guilty of sin, and yet God thought us worthy of forgiveness and sent Jesus to save us.

We have an obligation to show that same concern to others.

*Dear Lord, the Scriptures remind me that I stand before you as guilty
and worthy of condemnation. Yet in your love and grace, you sent your
innocent Son, Jesus, to accept my punishment, so I might be pardoned
and rehabilitated. Let me demonstrate my gratitude by treating others as
you have treated me. In Jesus' name I pray. Amen.* ❧

Who Cares for the Despised?

A man came along who was covered with leprosy. When he saw Jesus, he fell
with his face to the ground and begged him, "Lord, if you are willing, you
can make me clean." Jesus reached out his hand and touched the man. "I
am willing," he said. "Be clean!" And immediately the leprosy left him.
LUKE 5:12 – 13

In the time of Christ, lepers were outcasts because of their contagious and feared disease, and also because religious leaders saw them as divinely condemned. If we had lived back then, the mere approach of a leper would have filled us with loathing. We would have protected ourselves and removed our children. That is why lepers had to walk alone and cry out, "Unclean, unclean!" to warn people of their disease.

But when one leper saw Jesus, he fell on his face (probably disfigured) in front of the Lord. Jesus did not back away. Rather, he stretched out his hand and touched the man. It seems natural to us, doesn't it? If you had never read this story and I asked, "How did Jesus react when the leper approached?" you would have said, "He reacted with love."

But back then, no one expected it. The crowds looked upon Jesus as a great religious teacher, and they thought, *He's going to act like all the other religious leaders.* It shocked them when Christ responded with love and affection — and actual physical contact. A radical departure from the religious elite!

Christ cares for the despised; do we? In fact, we may think that drug addicts, alcoholics, the mentally ill, those with AIDS, and the homeless all deserve their pitiful lot in life. We may "show compassion" to prisoners but still consider them inferior to us; after all, they committed some crime and were found guilty.

Jesus aggressively cared for the despised. And he calls us to do the same.

O Lord, I easily applaud your loving care and touch, even as I shrink
from doing those things myself with "unsavory" people. I confess that my
actions often do not measure up to my ideals — and I pray that you might
cure me of this disease, just as Jesus cured the leper. Grant me compassion
to move beyond tender emotion to an eagerness to do your will. In Jesus'
name I pray. Amen. ❧

All Things to All People

Though I am free and belong to no one, I have made myself a slave
to everyone, to win as many as possible.... I have become all things
to all people so that by all possible means I might save some.
I CORINTHIANS 9:19, 22

When I was running for office, I had to be careful *not* to be "all things to all people." News reporters followed me around like Georgia gnats and wrote down exactly what I said at various locations and then compared my exact words from place to place to make sure I had not contradicted myself. If I said one thing to one group and a conflicting thing to another group, it would demonstrate that I was merely after votes.

Paul meant something very different when he said, "I have become all things to all people." He meant that he would put aside his own preferences and priorities and habits in order to tie himself in friendship and spiritual concern with the people he was trying to win to Christ. He wanted to build up the most intimate, personal, and honest relationship between himself and both Jews and Gentiles. In doing so, he did not violate the principles of his faith or deviate from the purity of the gospel, but merely put aside insignificant things that divide people in order to concentrate on the essence of Christianity. He said, in effect, "To serve all people in the name of Christ, I've put aside all commitment to my past, my heritage, my old beliefs, and my geographical orientation." Paul put his life in the hands of Christ and so became his slave—and thus a slave to all.

Whose slave are we? What are we willing to do to "save some"? May we follow Paul's example of remaining faithful to Jesus Christ while accommodating whatever cultural or social circumstances might separate us from others.

Lord, help me listen to Paul's words so that within my own sphere of
influence I can demonstrate what Jesus Christ means to me. Help me put
aside the relatively insignificant details that separate me from others, and
help me act in unity to better represent you. In the name of my Savior,
Jesus Christ, I pray. Amen. ❧

Undiscriminating Mercy

*One of them, when he saw he was healed, came back, praising God
in a loud voice. He threw himself at Jesus' feet and thanked him—
and he was a Samaritan.*
LUKE 17:15–16

I find it interesting that Samaritan lepers traveled together with Jewish lepers. Jews normally despised Samaritans, but their common disease broke down the normal walls of prejudice and so they traveled as a group, shouting, "Unclean, unclean!" so that no one would inadvertently get anywhere close to them and thus risk defiling themselves or contracting the disease.

Nowadays we don't have many lepers, but we still have a lot of outcasts. Dr. Jimmy Allen, a former president of the Southern Baptist Convention, told me about one. Not too long ago Jimmy attended a conference at the Carter Center and told us that his grandson, Mark, became HIV positive through a tainted blood transfusion. Mark's father served as pastor of a large church, and when Mark contracted HIV, the boy became an outcast within his father's own congregation. Finally, a deacon approached Jimmy's son and told him the deacons would prefer that Mark not attend their church anymore.

All of us have a strong tendency toward prejudice. Many of us might have the same attitude toward those with HIV that the people in Jesus' time had toward lepers. Consciously or not, we think they must be more sinful than we are, or at least that they must have separated themselves from God. Otherwise, how would they contract such a horrible disease?

Jesus reminds us that all of us stand in need of God's mercy, Christians and non-Christians alike. Christians, however, have a special duty to give mercy, even as they have been shown mercy. None of us can comprehend all of the mercy God has shown us; but we don't need to understand it completely to act as Christ did.

*O God, let me, a sinner, remember that only through faith in your Son
do I become reconciled with you, whereas on my own I deserve death.
Having been blessed with your mercy, let me avoid prejudice and the
human tendency to feel superior to others who may be suffering or whom
our society may condemn or deem unacceptable. I pray in Jesus' name.
Amen.* ⁂

Rich toward God

"I'll say to myself, 'You have plenty of grain laid up for many years.
Take life easy; eat, drink and be merry.'"
LUKE 12:19

At the beginning of this millennium, I was asked to make speeches in both Asia and Norway on "The Greatest Challenge Facing the World." I focused on the growing chasm between the rich and poor—not merely that such a gap exists, but that it's growing every year.

There is a great and increasing disparity in our own country between the rich and the poor, and the same thing is happening in most nations on earth. There's also a growing disparity between the richest countries and the poorest ones. This presents us with a great challenge. Most of us have no awareness of what goes on in the lives of desperately poor people—many have incomes of a dollar or less per day—so we don't feel greatly concerned about helping them. But as Christians, we must do so.

In the time of Christ, the rich and poor were separated, as they are today. Most people who came to hear Jesus preach were poor peasants looking for a better life. The rich and powerful, on the other hand, were the ones who ultimately plotted to kill Jesus, because he disturbed the status quo. If you have everything you want in life—plenty of wealth and political influence—and you run the temple and decide who gets religious privileges, then you don't want to change anything. You do not welcome a revolutionary message.

Jesus' parable about the rich man gives us a practical reason to help the poor: we cannot take our wealth with us when we die. Our material wealth neither impresses nor influences God. How we treat the poor—whether we follow God's commandments—is what counts. To be stingy toward God is the ultimate poverty ... and it has no remedy, except repentance.

O God, may I accept Jesus' words as just as applicable to me as they were to those who first heard them. Stir in my heart a concern for the poor, first for those who live near me, and then for those who may live far away. Help me avoid the error of the rich man in Jesus' parable, who tended only to his own comfort. I pray in Christ's name. Amen. ❧

Let's Not Be Selective

*"Therefore anyone who sets aside one of the least of these commands
and teaches others accordingly will be called least in the kingdom of
heaven, but whoever practices and teaches these commands will be
called great in the kingdom of heaven."*
MATTHEW 5:19

Jesus warns us against acting selectively as we seek to follow God's will. He knows that we tend to choose the divine commandments that resonate most with our natural desires, the ones that seem most convenient. Those that make us feel uncomfortable, however, we tend to ignore.

Jesus instructs us to reject any such practice.

Christ constantly warned us against saying to ourselves, "I have measured myself by my own standards and I find myself to be okay!" He consistently condemned pride, self-exaltation, and self-congratulation, for such an attitude implies, "I do not need to change. I do not need to expand my heart. I do not need to care for a larger group. I will restrict my community to the smallest and most convenient size possible. I will love those who love me. I will reach out to those who look like me, whom I know best, whom I understand most. I won't strain myself to love the unlovable."

Many in Christ's day assumed that lepers suffered because of their sin. These shunned people were considered not only dangerously unhealthy, but also terrible sinners. Many of us, unfortunately, regard in a similar way those who are mentally ill or addicted to drugs or alcohol. Many self-described Christians despise these people because they are considered to be inferior. These believers think, surely *God has condemned these sinners, so why should I care for them?*

Christ, however, loved the lepers, touched them, and healed them. He reached out to the most hated outcasts of his society. He loved the "least" in his culture precisely because he honored the "least" of God's commandments — even when those commands entailed deep personal discomfort.

*Lord, I ask that you grant me the love of Christ as I seek to do your will
in this hurting world. Challenge me with the greatness of your mission
and with the humility it takes to fulfill it. Enable me to reach out to those
whom I might ordinarily dismiss as unworthy of your grace, and cause me
to remember that your grace never makes any such distinctions. In Jesus'
name I pray. Amen.* ❧

One Child

"Whoever welcomes one of these little children in my name welcomes me;
and whoever welcomes me does not welcome me but the one who sent me."
MARK 9:37

The great thing about following Jesus' counsel here is that we don't have to be great in talent, education, income, or fame to comply with it. All it takes is a willingness to minister in a tangible way to "the least" among us, which in Jesus' day meant children or those who were innocent.

To "receive a child" means to look for ways to exhibit our dedication to Christ. Rosalynn and I have discovered that one way is to help build houses for those who have never had the funds to own a home. Or we might get the names of widows or elderly people in our neighborhood, take them something, and say to them, "I was just thinking about you and wanted to let you know that I'm available to help when needed. Here's my phone number." Or perhaps we could say, "Would it be okay if I give you a call each morning, just to make sure you're okay?"

If we have not been concerned about the homeless, the needy, or lonely individuals, then we *must* break through this isolation, in the name of Christ. Learning to serve others will not weigh us down with sacrifice but will open up a whole new life of adventure, marked by a feeling of righteousness, peace, and joy (see Romans 14:17).

When Jesus tells us to serve the "least of these," he is not saying to us, "Punish yourself," but rather "Reward yourself!" When you reach out to others as Jesus did, you will discover an important new reason for your existence.

O Lord, I know it's difficult to make this kind of change in my life, but I also know that with you, nothing is impossible. Through prayer, help me analyze my priorities, commitments, and habits. Show me how I can use the time you give me to gain a more exhilarating life by serving others in your name. In the name of my Savior. Amen. ❧

213

Correcting Injustice

*Do not exploit the poor because they are poor and do not crush the needy in
court, for the LORD will take up their case and will exact life for life.*
PROVERBS 22:22 – 23

Thomas Jefferson famously wrote, "We hold these truths to be self-evident,
that all men are created equal ..." But Jefferson owned slaves, as did George
Washington. For eighty-nine years after the signing of the Declaration of
Independence, our country was legally committed to slavery. Then, at the end
of the Civil War, for another century America maintained a policy of racial
discrimination, with approval by both churches and courts.

Today we still have elements of such discrimination. Crack cocaine and
powder cocaine, for example, have the same narcotic effect; but the penalty
for possession of crack is about fifty times as severe as the penalty for powder.
Why? Because crack cocaine is used by poor people. If rich persons are caught
with the more expensive white cocaine, they normally receive a very minor
sentence, or just a warning. Poor persons caught with crack cocaine typically
receive long prison sentences.

The poor often are assigned court lawyers for trial. This happened to
Mary Prince, who has helped my family ever since my days as governor. One
day when she took a short trip to see her aunt, a shooting occurred. As Mary
was the only stranger in town, she was arrested for the crime, although she
had nothing to do with it. On the day of her trial, her court-appointed attorney met her (for the first time) and said, "Mary, just plead guilty, and we'll
get you a minimum punishment." She did so and received a life sentence.

When I became president, the original trial judge agreed to look into
Mary's case; soon she was found completely innocent, but by then she had
served six years. After receiving a full pardon, she was released.

As Christians living in a democracy, we are responsible for taking steps to
correct our society's injustices.

*God, I recognize that many kinds of prejudice plague our society and
other places around the world. Help me become more aware of the
injustices and then have the courage to condemn them boldly and strive to
right the wrongs. Bless me as I seek to be the hands and feet of Jesus. I ask
this in my Savior's name. Amen.* ❧

214

Avoid Injustice

*"He defended the cause of the poor and needy, and so all went well.
Is that not what it means to know me?" declares the LORD.*

JEREMIAH 22:16

Throughout the Bible, from Genesis to Revelation, we hear the call for those in power to be honest and just with the poor, to treat them equally, and not to use their authority to subvert justice. The prophet Jeremiah, for example, speaks out strongly against injustice: "Woe to him who builds his palace by unrighteousness, his upper rooms by injustice, making his own people work for nothing, not paying them for their labor" (Jeremiah 22:13).

Some time ago, a war nearly erupted on the Ivory Coast because the president wanted to build a huge cathedral, as large as Saint Peter's in Rome. He insisted on it, even though he led a poverty-stricken nation. To finance the enormous project, he harvested a major portion of his country's precious timber—and even then he ended up in debt. It was a project built at the expense of the people, for the sake of a powerful leader who wished to glorify himself.

Jeremiah insists that those of us who have inherited from God *any* position of authority or influence have a responsibility to use it justly. This includes not just kings and presidents but police, parents, a dominant spouse, or business leaders. My dictionary defines justice like this: "the quality of being righteous." All leaders must possess this quality and reflect it in their behavior.

Although in America we have a relatively just government, we can't afford to rest on our laurels. We can't ignore the injustices that persist—in our nation or our own community—against minorities, the poor, or the mentally ill. And we have an obligation to try to correct them. Insisting on treating others fairly will serve as an attractive testimony to our living relationship with Jesus Christ.

*Dear Lord, help me become a more fervent and effective witness
for Christ. In my daily behavior and in my every action, help me
demonstrate that I serve a righteous and just God, who has commissioned
me to carry on his work of compassion in this deeply hurting world. In
the name of Jesus Christ, my Lord, I pray. Amen.* 🕊

Defend the Innocent

Speak up for those who cannot speak for themselves, for the rights of all who are destitute. Speak up and judge fairly; defend the rights of the poor and needy.
PROVERBS 31:8 – 9

For thirty years I've served as a professor at Emory University. One week I was teaching in the law school and there met with a famous theologian named Martin Marty. He and I formed a partnership to address some of the social issues affecting our country. One of those issues concerned the death penalty and the rights of children.

After I left the White House, an assembly of leaders at the United Nations drafted a commitment known as the "Convention on the Rights of Children." Although the American president signed it in 1995, the U.S. Senate, under pressure from religious and political conservatives, has refused to ratify the convention. The only other nation that has rejected the covenant is Somalia, which has no functioning government.

One of the primary reasons for our nation's refusal to endorse the Convention on the Rights of Children is its prohibition against the death penalty or life imprisonment of children. In 2005, the United States Supreme Court finally ruled against imposing the death penalty on children, but it is still legal to give a child a life sentence. [*Note added in 2011*: The United States is the *only* Western nation that still imposes the death penalty (it is prohibited in sixteen states), and only China, Iraq, Iran, and Saudi Arabia executed more people in 2009.]

One of the basic premises of Christianity is that everyone has certain basic rights, especially children — even if the U.S. government fails to agree. Christ reached out to people in need, to the suffering and abandoned, and to those who had lost hope. And who could be in more need or more vulnerable than a child? As followers of Christ, we have an obligation to protect and promote basic human rights, regardless of what our government may do.

O God, thank you for the perfect example of Jesus, who reached out to the poor, needy, defenseless, and vulnerable. I am thankful that Christ had great compassion for children and showed them far greater respect than his society expected. Help me follow his example and do what I can to protect the precious lives of the world's children. I pray in Jesus' name. Amen. ❧

God's Political Agenda

Endow the king with your justice, O God, the royal son with your righteousness. May he judge your people in righteousness, your afflicted ones with justice.
PSALM 72:1 – 2

What divisive issues have provided the most highly publicized controversies among Christian denominations in modern-day America? I'd suggest these: inerrancy of Scripture, imposition of creeds, exaltation of pastors, financial and other material rewards for worship, condemnation of homosexuals, women's role in church leadership, abortion, separation of religion and politics, support for military adventures, and prayer in schools. Unfortunately, some of the debates have deteriorated into a total lack of harmony or even personal animosity. I am sure that you could add other issues.

Holy Scripture gives us many ideas about God's "political" agenda. Psalm 72 probably was written for the coronation of some Israelite king. The Hebrews looked on their king as God's servant, the connecting link between God and the people. So when the king wasn't right with God, neither were the people. When the king violated God's covenants about justice and righteousness, Israel lost battles and her people went into captivity.

I find it somewhat reassuring to realize that similar issues caused dissension among members of the early Christian churches. They involved arguments over such things as how to observe communion, circumcision as a prerequisite for being a Christian, eating of meat sacrificed to idols, treatment of the Sabbath, and ranking of Jesus' disciples.

Jesus, Paul, Peter, and other leaders advised strongly that such human differences of opinion, no matter how important they seem, should never be permitted to divide believers from each other. We should accept our differences and serve harmoniously together by accepting the overall premise that we are all equal in God's sight. All of us are saved by God's grace through our mutual faith in Jesus Christ. So why not work together?

O Lord, help me realize that when my voice espouses and demonstrates peace, justice, compassion, humility, service, forgiveness, and unselfish love, it can help bring healing of differences and blessings to others. Forgive me for my failure to recognize inequities and dissensions that exist in our society, and grant me the wisdom to encourage harmony among all Christians. In Christ's name I pray. Amen. ❧

217

Let Justice Roll On

"I hate, I despise your religious festivals;
your assemblies are a stench to me."
AMOS 5:21

Only twice in the Old Testament does God combine the words "hate" and "despise." One instance appears here in Amos. The Scripture continues: "Even though you bring me burnt offerings and grain offerings, I will not accept them. Though you bring choice fellowship offerings, I will have no regard for them. Away with the noise of your songs! I will not listen to the music of your harps" (vv. 22–23).

What brought such severe condemnation? The Israelites were observing the ordained feasts, attending worship services, giving nice offerings to God, and singing appropriate religious songs, some written by King David himself. And yet God said he "despised" all these things. Why?

He did so because their hearts were not in tune with the divine covenant. Many wealthy Israelites observed festivals and offered sacrifices to a God of justice but then turned around and behaved unjustly with their fellow countrymen. Their wicked actions revealed their corrupt hearts. And God hates hypocrisy.

We must take care not to repeat their mistake. How do we respond to injustice? Do we accept it with equanimity? Do we rationalize it by saying, "I don't want to rock the boat," or "I'm just one voice among many, so I wouldn't make any difference"? It's easy for us to withdraw from responsibility by blaming our government.

Amos would disagree. Since we worship a God of justice, every one of us must speak up for justice in our society. Each of us is responsible.

In many instances, America's civil and criminal laws strongly favor rich and prominent people. We have more people in prison than any other nation on earth, and most of them are poor, members of minorities, or mentally ill. We are the only industrialized society that still imposes the death sentence, and we have learned that many of those on death row are innocent. It's hard to imagine a wealthy white man being executed.

How can we remain silent?

O Lord, grant me the courage to speak as Christ would speak. Help me live out the righteous characteristics of Christ by the power of your Spirit. May my neighborhood, community, and world be a better place because of my presence in them. In Christ's name I pray. Amen. ❧

Administer Justice

"This is what the LORD Almighty said: 'Administer true justice; show mercy and compassion to one another. Do not oppress the widow or the fatherless, the foreigner or the poor. Do not plot evil against each other.'"
ZECHARIAH 7:9 – 10

The Carter Center recently sponsored a conference about corruption in the world's governments. Corruption is one of the most unaddressed and persistent problems in this hemisphere. In fact, when Jim Wolfensohn first became president of the World Bank, instead of writing out the word *corruption*, he just wrote the letter *c*. He decided that in official papers it was best not to connect corruption with any particular country.

We are now addressing the problem more openly, primarily because social inequality and poverty cannot be successfully addressed if governments and the private sector are corrupt. Wealth and power will dominate, and the powerless and the poor will suffer.

Business leaders in Third World nations rarely have enough money to bribe outsiders, so most such bribes come from the world's rich nations. I saw this clearly during my presidency, so during my early months in office we passed a law called the "Foreign Corrupt Practices Act." This made it a serious crime for any American business to bribe a foreigner in order to make a sale or gain an advantage. Many objected to the act, even good friends, who thought they would be at a severe disadvantage if they couldn't offer bribes. And in fact, after the act passed, Delta Airlines had to cancel all its flights to Mexico and Jamaica, partly because airport officials there wouldn't service its planes unless the airline bribed them.

Unfortunately, few other nations have passed laws like ours, although several European nations recently signed a treaty pledging that within the coming years they'll pass antibribery laws.

The best solution is for individuals in government and private life to be honest. Christians, of course, don't need to wait for laws that require them to act justly. We simply need to heed the instructions of our Lord.

O Lord, help me realize that I have a responsibility to spread the word about what it means to be a Christian. Help me be both a fervent evangelist and a dedicated supporter of truth and justice so I can make a good case for committing one's life to Jesus Christ. In Christ's name I pray. Amen. ❧

Cultural Barriers

When a Samaritan woman came to draw water, Jesus said to her,
"Will you give me a drink?"
JOHN 4:7

When I worked in the fields for my father, it would have been inconceivable for a white person to drink from the same dipper as a black worker in the same field. Even if we played with them, went fishing with them, worked in the same field, and plowed with the same mules, we would *never* drink out of the same cup.

So when Christ asked this Samaritan woman for a drink of water, he was actually doing something extremely significant. He didn't have a cup with him, so clearly he intended to drink out of her cup. Remember that the Jews typically hated all Samaritans, and this person was a woman ostracized by her own village—in effect, a whore. What a startling demonstration against racial or ethnic or religious prejudice!

We all have innate, natural prejudice in our hearts. How can we deal effectively with it? We don't *want* to be prejudiced; we don't *want* to be insensitive—but it's almost ingrained in us to look down upon people different from us. We naturally think our religion or our race is superior, or our way of life is more correct than that of those who differ from us.

Jesus visited this well not just because he was thirsty, but also so that he might have a life-changing encounter with this woman. Christ is telling us, "If you follow me, then do as I did with this despised Samaritan woman." In other words, reach out to the people who are isolated, different, most in need, and even the most sinful. Christ asks us to change by breaking down our prejudices.

Christ showed us how to break down deep prejudice by using a single cup of water—a little symbolic gesture. Who would have imagined that you could tear down a whole wall using just a small cup?

O God, again I find that a simple story I have known since childhood has depths of meaning and application to my own life that I didn't expect. I pray that you might open my mind, that I might open my heart to those who seem very different from me. In Jesus' name. Amen. ❧

The Advantages of Listening

Everyone should be quick to listen.
JAMES 1:19

Are you a good listener? Be honest, now. When someone else is talking, do you normally start thinking about what you're going to say next?

In fact, it's *very* difficult to be a good listener. But consider two great advantages of listening.

First, we learn things we wouldn't have known otherwise. If we walk by a homeless person living under a bridge and stop to listen to his story—even if he may be an illiterate alcoholic—we might learn something new about life and begin to understand others. By understanding them better, we may begin developing a love for them and a desire to learn how we can help them, thus beginning to put into practice the teachings of Jesus Christ. Is that not a great advantage?

Second, listening breaks down the barriers between people. When we listen, we start to understand people who differ from us, and that helps us overcome prejudice. I learned a lot during a week I spent on the Cheyenne River Indian Reservation in the northern part of South Dakota, where the Lakota Indian tribe lives. We worked alongside tribal members to build thirty-six Habitat for Humanity houses. During that time, I was able to listen to the people, even the chief when he found some free time to work on our house. Most of the time, his duties did not permit him to join us. He had a lot of entertaining to do! About 1,400 volunteers came to this small village that normally boasts a population of 3,500. We listened to these delightful Lakota men and women tell us about their challenges, opportunities, culture, frustrations, and ambitions for the future, and it was all very exciting to me.

Listening instead of talking is a good habit for learning about others—and about ourselves.

O Lord, I remember that one of Jesus' favorite phrases was "He who has ears to hear, let him hear." May my ears be opened to hear not only what you say in your Word, but also the men and women with whom I meet every day. Help me think of these encounters as divine appointments and help me listen for your voice above all other voices. In Jesus' name I pray. Amen. ❧

The Wall Came Down

For he himself is our peace, who has made the two groups one and has destroyed the barrier, the dividing wall of hostility.
EPHESIANS 2:14

Oaxaca, Mexico, is a beautiful city inhabited mostly by indigenous peoples. The average man is about five feet tall; the average woman about three inches shorter. Rosalynn and our family spent a week there, visited its beautiful churches and cathedrals, and met with some of the region's most noted religious leaders.

One of the area's earlier archbishops induced the pope to declare that Indians were fully human. Historically, the Spanish conquistadors, fervent in their religious belief, considered the Indians to be animals and thought that God approved of exterminating any who would not accept Christ as Savior. This debate on the equal status of Native Americans goes back to the fifteenth and sixteenth centuries.

The Mideast has its own serious problems of racial division. In the Holy Land, for example, Jews comprise a dominating force, both militarily and politically. The Palestinians, of both Muslim and Christian descent, have little influence or power. Bethlehem is almost completely surrounded by a high Israeli wall, and in this birthplace of Jesus, many Christians are leaving their homes under pressure, abandoning the place where their families have lived for two thousand years.

In cases like these, one group usually imagines itself as having a special favored relationship with God and therefore condemns and views as inferior anyone else. The result is discrimination, hatred, and often violence.

Christ came, in part, to do away with this sort of ugly division. In Jesus' day, the wall separating Jews from Gentiles seemed nearly impenetrable. Through his death and resurrection, however, Jesus demolished that wall so it could never be rebuilt. A big part of our responsibility is to preserve and promote the peace and equality that Christ won on the cross.

O Lord, thank you for reminding me that I'm no better than anyone else, that men are not better than women, that neither Jews nor Greeks are better than the other, that masters are not better than slaves. Within our often discriminatory and contentious society, let me as a Christian condemn any distinctions that cause division and animosity. In Jesus' name I pray. Amen. ❧

Through the Gate Together

There are different kinds of gifts,
but the same Spirit distributes them.
I CORINTHIANS 12:4

All too often, at a certain time in our lives, we start comparing ourselves to others and judging ourselves superior. Over time we adopt an attitude of segregation, whether by race or social status or neighborhood or level of intelligence. It's not always easy to identify the time or event when this starts to happen.

As a farm boy growing up during the days of racial segregation, I drew no distinction between me and my African-American playmates. I had two black friends, A.D. and Johnny, and we worked together as equals in Daddy's fields, hunted, fished, flew kites, wrestled, and fought together, all without any deference to one or the other. But one day, as we approached the pasture gate, they went ahead to open it—and then stood back to let me go through first.

Somehow, I guess, they had gotten word from their parents that a distinction was to be made between white and black people. We saw it only vaguely then, but our relationship was transformed that day; a silent line was drawn between friend and friend, race and race.

In a similar way, as the early church grew, divisions began to arise between Christians based on race, gender, age, wealth, social status, and interpretation of Scripture. This became one of Paul's major concerns, and he insisted that despite these inevitable differences, they were all one in spirit and they all served the same Lord, Christ Jesus.

A major challenge to the modern Christian church is fragmentation because of differences in interpretation of Holy Scripture. We argue about forms of worship, status of women, authority of pastors, acceptance of homosexuals, the death penalty, and other social and religious issues.

We must resist divisions between ourselves, whether based on superficial differences or on more substantial ones. As Paul insisted, we are bound together as equals by one common belief: We are saved by the grace of God through our faith in Jesus Christ.

O God, regardless of when I had my own "pasture gate" experience, give me the wisdom and grace to treat others as equals, as we truly are in your sight. Help us together become the living embodiment of Christ's love for all people, and grant us a spirit of oneness in his holy name. This is our prayer. Amen. ❧

Equal in God's Sight

*"So if God gave them the same gift he gave us who believed in the Lord
Jesus Christ, who was I to think that I could stand in God's way?"*
ACTS 11:17

When I was leaving the Navy in 1953, Rosalynn and I traveled through
Washington, D.C., where a racist congressman named Tic Forester hosted
us. He represented our district and was famous for despising Jews, Catholics,
and "Negroes" (though that's not what he called them).

During a tour of the Capitol he gave us, the congressman deplored the
passing of a law that allowed public housing to be built in his district. It upset
him because some government housing in his hometown, just twenty miles
south of Plains, was in the "white folks'" community.

"You and I both know that as soon as these cheap houses are built," he
said, "the wrong kind of people are going to come in and destroy our town."
We said nothing because we ourselves had just been accepted to live in public
housing. We had little money; in fact, our total income was only $280 our
first year back home.

That unpleasant experience made me realize that human beings have a
strong tendency to exclude others who are unlike themselves. When that happens in Christianity, it significantly damages the church's ability to spread
the word about Jesus Christ.

When God sent Peter to Cornelius's house and then gave these Gentiles
the Holy Spirit, it surprised everyone. Peter then had to return to Jerusalem
to explain to disapproving church leaders why he had visited this Roman in
Caesarea. Through that episode, God began to break down the barriers that
people build around themselves. From then on, it has been clear that God
makes no distinction about who can be saved.

Today, since God has broken down racial and other barriers, we must do
what we can to make sure they never get erected again.

*Dear Lord, I thank you for breaking down the barriers that long had
separated people. I confess my innate prejudices, and I ask you to help
me accept all people as equal, even as you do. Make me into an agent of
divine reconciliation. I ask these things in the name of my Savior, Jesus
Christ. Amen.*

The Fundamentalist Affliction

There is neither Jew nor Gentile, neither slave nor free, nor is there
male and female, for you are all one in Christ Jesus.
GALATIANS 3:28

When Iran took American hostages in November 1979, the affliction of Islamic fundamentalism hit me as president. One of the basic principles of the Qur'an is that visitors are to be treated with the utmost respect. Some passages say that if diplomats visit your country, you treat them with absolute courtesy. Yet the fundamentalist Iranian leader of that time violated these principles by holding our hostages for fourteen months. I thank God that eventually they all returned home, safe and free; but through that experience I learned an unwelcome lesson on fundamentalism.

As the crisis unfolded, I made a study of the principles of fundamentalism. Almost invariably, such movements are led by authoritarian males who consider themselves superior to others, who subjugate women as inferior, and who dominate their fellow believers. They see the past as better than the present but retain only certain aspects of history—namely, whatever benefits *them*. They draw clear distinctions between themselves as true believers and others, and believe that anyone who contradicts them is ignorant and possibly evil. They use any means to defend their beliefs. Fundamentalists usually make increasingly narrow definitions that tend to isolate themselves, and they view negotiation or other efforts to resolve differences as signs of weakness. Three words characterize fundamentalism: *rigidity*, *domination*, and *exclusion*.

Paul made this discovery when he visited the churches he had founded on his first missionary journey. Some fundamentalists insisted that God favored certain kinds of people and that salvation depended on keeping particular rules. Paul said, "Nonsense! All you need is faith in Jesus. In Christ, there is no distinction or superiority between Jew and Gentile, slave and free, male and female."

Differences are bound to exist among us—but they don't have to divide us.

O Lord, help me learn from the early church, its struggles and successes,
its mistakes and the lessons it learned. It encourages me to know that
the healing process enforced on the early church by the apostles actually
worked. I pray for the same spirit of reconciliation, friendship, respect,
and love. I ask this in Jesus' name. Amen. ❧

225

The Image of God

Then God said, "Let us make mankind in our image,
in our likeness."
GENESIS 1:26

What does it mean that human beings are made in the image of God? It doesn't mean that we have the physical appearance of God. We can't say, "God looks like that kind gentleman sitting over there on the park bench," or "God looks like me." It has nothing to do with physical appearance.

God is invisible and a spirit, so we can have no idea what God really looks like, or whether the Lord "looks like" anything at all. We know how the Sistine Chapel depicts God. When we stand there and look up at the ceiling, we see a distinguished old gentleman with a long beard reaching out to touch the finger of a much younger human being. But that's just an artist's imagined representation, in paint; it's not meant to be an accurate portrait of God.

So if our being created in the image of God doesn't mean that we *physically* look like God, then that must mean that the image is some other attribute — perhaps an ability to communicate with or relate to others, to assess oneself, the capacity for self-awareness, or an ability to look into our hearts and souls and say, "What am I doing in my relationships that might need to be improved?"

Whatever the image of God is, Genesis says that God created all of us with it. And that means, at the very least, that *every* human being has enormous value. We must take great care to respect that value!

The Scriptures also remind us that all people are equal in the eyes of God, whether Jew or Gentile, male or female, slave or master. This explains why human rights are so important to me and to others. When we mistreat other human beings, we are mistreating our peers, created in the very image of God. And that is a *very* serious thing.

Lord, it is an honor to know that you made me in your image — unlike other creatures. Although I cannot fully comprehend what this means, help me remember that this also applies to other people. Remind me that as I treat the least of them, so I treat you. I pray this in Jesus' name. Amen. ❧

226

Sweet One

The Samaritan woman said to him, "You are a Jew and I am a Samaritan woman. How can you ask me for a drink?" (For Jews do not associate with Samaritans.)
JOHN 4:9

Years ago Rosalynn and I saw a superbly performed play called *The Man of La Mancha*. It's based on the book *Don Quixote* by Miguel de Cervantes. In the story, Don Quixote enters a roadside tavern and finds a prostitute. In his twisted and idealistic mind, he sees a woman of purity and glory, so he calls her Dulcinea ("sweet one"). She slaps him and scorns him and spits on him and derides him. But later as he lies on his deathbed, she reappears, and we discover that her brief contact with him had transformed her life. This old, decrepit man with a wandering mind had confidence in her, much more than she deserved. He exalted her out of her sinfulness—resulting in her transformation.

As a Baptist church member and a deacon, I've gone out to witness to people alienated from our churchgoing society. I've seen their lives transformed—not because of me or the other Christians with me, but because of a new awakening of the Holy Spirit in their hearts. They realized they meant something to us and to God.

That's what happened to the woman at the well. Jesus showed kindness and treated her as a person of value, and she moved from an attitude of alienation to casual conversation, then budding friendship, and finally to the stunning realization that, despite her sins, Jesus cared for her and might even be the Messiah. She ran to the town, exclaiming her joy and excitement.

Jesus calls us to treat all people with dignity and respect, seeing them as people of great worth. They need to know that we care about them, and so does God. What "sweet one" needs some kindness from you?

Lord, help me grasp the wonder of your calling me a "saint" and "worthy" and a "priest" and "much loved" and "holy." Let me embrace my exalted calling and live up to it in my daily life as I submit to your will by the power of the Holy Spirit. May my genuine kindness lead others to you. In Christ's name I pray. Amen. ❧

God Calls Ordinary People

"Alas, Sovereign LORD," I said, "I do not know how to speak;
I am too young."
JEREMIAH 1:6

Despite his doubts about himself, Jeremiah became God's spokesperson anyway. I think most of us, like the young prophet, have a feeling of inadequacy.

But how big a house do you need to be compassionate? Do you require a college degree to forgive someone who has hurt you? What talents are necessary to do good things in the name of Christ?

As governor of Georgia, I was honored one day to get a personal request from Norman Vincent Peale. I quickly agreed to his request because of my respect for this famous man.

"We're giving a prize to a church in Macon as the outstanding church in America," he said, "and I hope you will join me in speaking to the audience." The church to be honored had only thirty members, all of them mentally handicapped. It was called the Church of the Exceptional.

Mr. Peale gave his usual extraordinary speech to an audience of about seven thousand; I followed him, hoping for accolades. The ceremony concluded with the lighting of a big candle, which a small woman with Down syndrome was to light. The church's members came down the aisle, the woman holding a small torch. She tried to light the candle, but her hands shook so badly that she failed, again and again. When the pastor tried to help her, she pushed him away. The audience held its breath ... and finally the candle lit!

I'll never forget the look on that woman's beaming face. No one in the audience would recall a word that I or Norman Vincent Peale said, but they would remember the woman who, with persistent faith, lit the candle.

How much talent does it take to make a difference for God?

O Lord, give me the same spirit of determination that I see in Jeremiah, personified by the woman who lit the candle. That's all she did — but through her simple faith, she inspired thousands and let us all know that our lives can also count for a great deal. Help me light my own candle for you in the advancement and growth of your kingdom, for I pray in your Son's name. Amen. ❧

Instruments of God

"I am the Lord's servant," Mary answered. "May your word to me be
fulfilled." Then the angel left her.
LUKE 1:38

What kind of person was Mary, the mother of Jesus? She was a young girl, perhaps fifteen years old, who lived in a small town in a backward region of the world. There seemed nothing special about her. She was not a princess and was not expected to do anything especially notable in her lifetime.

Nevertheless, God chose Mary to give birth to the Savior of the world.

In 1976, I was running for president and was pleased to speak to the Southern Baptist Convention. I followed Billy Graham, and a truck driver was to follow me. While Billy Graham spoke, the truck driver kept saying, "I'm leaving; there's no way I can get up and speak to all these folks." I restrained him and tried to calm his nerves. The truth is, I didn't want to be the only one compared to Billy Graham.

When it was the truck driver's turn to speak, he hesitantly began, "Most of my life I've been a drunk. A few years ago, I heard about Jesus and began to study the Bible. But I still couldn't break away from whiskey and spent most days in the local barroom with my old friends. But I would take my Bible there sometimes and read it. The other men teased me about it, but I kept studying and asking questions of a Christian friend of mine. Eventually, the men who made fun of me began to ask me about Jesus Christ. And finally, in addition to me, fourteen of my friends accepted Christ as Savior."

The whole audience stood up and cheered. I imagine his is the only speech that anyone remembered. God can use us in many places where, with faith and an element of humility, we can make a difference—and many times, truck drivers more than former presidents.

God, thank you not only for using Mary to bring your Son into the
world, but also for letting me know something about her. She helps me
realize that you can do great things with anyone, so long as that person
is willing and humble and flexible. Use me, Lord, to do your work, even
though I am so small. I ask this in the precious name of my Savior, Jesus
Christ. Amen.

229

Who's Thaddaeus?

These are the twelve he appointed: Simon ... James ... John ... Andrew,
Philip, Bartholomew, Matthew, Thomas, James son of Alphaeus,
Thaddaeus, Simon the Zealot and Judas Iscariot, who betrayed him.
MARK 3:16 – 19

Jesus' ministry attracted such huge crowds that it became hard for him to get away. Only rarely could he get alone by himself to pray, relax, or fish beside the Sea of Galilee. The crowds demanded to be near him, to touch him, to bring their sick relatives to him. Jesus needed a way to redistribute the ministry load.

So one day he got alone with his closest followers and chose a few of them to become his specially designated associates. Mark says, "He appointed twelve that they might be with him and that he might send them out to preach and to have authority to drive out demons" (3:14 – 15).

If we tried to list the disciples, probably we'd write down the same names that most people remember. No doubt we would name Peter, and certainly Judas. Maybe we'd list the names Andrew and John and James and Matthew (who wrote the first gospel). But very likely, that would be the end of it. We might not even *recognize* the names Thaddaeus or Bartholomew or Simon the Zealot or James the son of Alphaeus.

We should understand that not every successful follower of Christ becomes famous. While some who make full-time commitments to serve the Lord become well known, others who do just as much good work remain unknown, except by their family and friends.

Recognition and public acclaim are not the point! Whether people remember our names is no measure of success in Christ's service. The *only* thing that matters is that God knows how you and I live and serve. So long as we follow his commandments faithfully, we receive the description "successful."

Dear God, help me remember that I do not have to become rich,
powerful, or famous to be successful in your sight. Remind me that you
measure achievement not in terms of public recognition, but in terms of
faithfulness to you and your cause. Let me not underestimate my ability
to serve you in whatever capacity you call me, and give me the wisdom to
make the most of every opportunity. In Jesus' name I pray. Amen. ❧

Representing the King

"Therefore say to the Israelites, 'This is what the Sovereign LORD says:
It is not for your sake, people of Israel, that I am going to do these
things, but for the sake of my holy name.'"
EZEKIEL 36:22

God selected the Israelites to be the chosen people, not only to give them a better life as the Holy Spirit filled their hearts, but also to generate within them the ability to glorify God before others. Because the Lord wanted the whole world to comprehend God's omnipotence and grace, the Israelites were chosen to show the surrounding countries what kinds of good things happen to those who willingly accept God as their Creator. But Israel failed completely.

The people had grown utterly wicked and the surrounding nations saw Israel fall into impotence. The chosen people lost their gracious living, their power, and their national sovereignty, and eventually ruthless conquerors obliterated their country.

In the midst of this devastation, God explained the message. The Lord decided to do something for Israel that would highlight both human need and divine grace. God would use fallen human beings to demonstrate divine glory, omnipotence, grace, benevolence, love, and omniscience—not because the people deserved it, but rather for the sake of God's holy name.

It is important to remember that our character as Christians, in a similar and very significant way, demonstrates the character of God. How we act suggests to others what God is like. Of course, we know that God's character never changes, regardless of how we behave. But so far as others are concerned—Muslims, Jews, Hindus, Buddhists, nonbelievers—they judge the essence of our faith by looking at Christians.

What a sobering realization this should be, to recognize that our words and actions as individuals represent in the eyes of onlookers the very character of Jesus Christ! That's a great responsibility—and also a wonderful opportunity—for us all.

God, I tremble at the idea that my behavior as a Christian can either attract others to you or repel them. How awesome to realize that people get an idea of who you are by watching me! So, Lord, help me represent you well. Strengthen me to reflect your holy character in all that I do, and in that way bind me most intimately to my Savior, Jesus Christ, in whose name I pray. Amen.

In Jesus' Name

We constantly pray for you, that our God may make you worthy of his
calling, and that by his power he may bring to fruition your every desire for
goodness and your every deed prompted by faith. We pray this so that the
name of our Lord Jesus may be glorified in you, and you in him.
2 THESSALONIANS 1:11 – 12

Some ideals have been with America since the very beginning. We have a basic commitment to freedom, equality, and the service of others. These are moral values on which our country was founded.

But as Christians, we must remember that we commit ourselves to these principles *in the name of Christ.* Whenever we do good works, we should nurture an inner spiritual attitude that says, "I'm doing this in the name of my Savior, Jesus Christ."

And it doesn't hurt to say it out loud.

Sometimes before Thanksgiving, we sit around in our Sunday school room and say, "Why don't we give a nice Thanksgiving dinner to some poor families?" Everybody says, "That sounds like a great idea! Who knows some needy people we could help?" And to our embarrassment, we actually know few of the poor people in our community.

So maybe we call a welfare office and get the names of some families in need, and we go out with a delicious Thanksgiving meal and give it to them. Now, that's a very nice thing to do. But we should take care we do it for the right reason, namely, that we do this in the name of Jesus Christ. So when we deliver the Thanksgiving turkey, we should say, "We bring this to you as members of Maranatha Baptist Church, because we are servants of Jesus Christ. We do this in his name."

In fact, we should know and serve all the needy families, all through the year. That is what it means to serve "in the name of Jesus."

Dear Lord, sometimes I use the phrase "in Jesus' name" as if it were simply
a nice way to end a prayer. Thank you for reminding me that it is much
more than that! When I serve in Jesus' name, I do so for his glory and in
his strength. Help me give you control of my life so that love and justice
and forgiveness will become part of my very existence. Amen. ❧

232

Ambassadors for Christ

We are therefore Christ's ambassadors, as though God were making
his appeal through us. We implore you on Christ's behalf: Be
reconciled to God.
2 CORINTHIANS 5:20

When I was president, I had more than 120 ambassadors stationed around the world. Each of them represented the authority of the United States of America; their actions, in effect, were the actions of our nation. It's a huge responsibility. All ambassadors have to realize that they represent, or stand in for, a superior authority.

Ambassadors also move within the countries they're serving and immerse themselves among the people of that land, treating them with respect. They do this to convey important messages more effectively about the policies and desires of the authority they represent.

While few of us will ever become U.S. ambassadors, the Bible says *all* Christians are ambassadors for Christ. God makes his offer of salvation to the world through us. As ambassadors for Christ, we represent God's authority, and as such we are commissioned to spread the message that a way has been provided for sinful human beings to be reconciled with God Almighty, Creator of the universe. Although everyone is a sinner who deserves punishment, we have the opportunity to be saved because Jesus Christ took our sin upon himself when he died on the cross. When we repent and put our faith in him, it is as though we had never sinned. And thus we become acceptable to God.

As Christ's ambassadors, we are to take this message to all people around the world. We must not exalt ourselves as superior to those who don't yet know Christ, but rather recognize that each person is a spiritual being, extraordinarily valuable to God. So we must reach out in a spirit of love and care and compassion, treating others with utmost respect. We are to be champions of peace for the sake of the gospel.

O God, I am grateful that I worship the Prince of Peace! As an
ambassador of Christ, help me reach out to the poor, the afflicted, the
weak, and the abandoned. Equip me to represent you to them effectively,
and give me a genuine love for those you bring into my life, a love that
will flow out in compassion. I pray in Jesus' name. Amen. ⟩⋆

Beyond the Wonder of Healing

The royal official said, "Sir, come down before my child dies." "Go,"
Jesus replied, "your son will live." The man took Jesus at his word
and departed.
JOHN 4:49 – 50

Many years ago a little girl fell into a Texas well, and for days the story of her rescue remained the top headline around the globe. Some of our most emotional relationships are with little children.

One day Jesus returned to the town of Cana, where he had turned water into wine. A desperate local official sought him out and said, "Sir, come down before my little boy dies!" John shows us that here is a divine Savior who is eager and able to change lives — not merely to extend life or help people get well, but to transform those lives after the miracle ends.

Jesus replied, "Go, your son will live." Now, if Jesus had said that to me, I'd probably have some doubts: "But, sir, can't you at least come and see him? Maybe you can bless him with the same miraculous power you showed at the wedding." But Jesus didn't have to visit the boy, so he told the man, "Quit worrying about it. Go home and see for yourself." Once that father got home and learned that his son recovered at exactly the time Jesus spoke, you can bet that he started witnessing to his servants and his neighbors!

All of us face challenges. Maybe they involve children; maybe they don't. Maybe they're life-threatening; maybe they're not. But we can always let those around us know of our faith. We must not remain quiet out of fear of embarrassment but must be willing to testify, "Jesus Christ is the Son of God. He is my Savior and he has transformed my life." Jesus gives each of us the opportunity to make our lives count, through our actions and testimony.

Lord, help me remember the faith of the nobleman whose boy was dying, as well as the miraculous way that Christ answered his request. As I remember, help me not to merely wonder about medical details, but to see the potential of changing my own life for the better as I seek to show the compassion of my Lord to hurting people in my world. I ask these things in Jesus' name. Amen. ❧

A Great Work

*But they were scheming to harm me; so I sent messengers to them with
this reply: "I am carrying on a great project and cannot go down.
Why should the work stop while I leave it and go down to you?"*
NEHEMIAH 6:2 – 3

After Ezra arrived in Jerusalem to begin restoring Israel to a right relationship with God, everyone expected the result to be wonderful — but it wasn't.
Thirteen years later, the walls of the city still remained in ruins.

About this time, Nehemiah, who served the Persian king, asked his boss
for permission to travel to Jerusalem to finish rebuilding the city's walls. He
wanted his people to regain their self-respect, dignity, and hope. The king
let him go.

When Nehemiah arrived in Jerusalem, he told the people, "We're going
to rebuild the walls." Nobody thought they could do it. They had a lot of
enemies, who, over the previous century, had established their own enclaves
of power and influence. These enemies didn't want any changes to alter their
privileged position, whether economically or politically. They resented Nehemiah, a stranger, arriving to alter the status quo.

To stop him, they called for a meeting outside the city, intending to harm
him. But Nehemiah saw through their plot and wrote back, "I am carrying
on a great project and cannot go down. Why should the work stop while I
leave it and go down to you?"

Why was Nehemiah's work "great"? Because it was God's work. To build
a wall may not have looked like much to outsiders, but it bore the mark of
heaven. And Nehemiah had committed himself to it.

As Christians, we also have a great work to do. Our great work is to obey
God's commandments and spread the gospel of Jesus Christ. Will each of us
remain as committed to our great work as Nehemiah was to his?

*O God, thank you for recording the acts of Nehemiah, whose efforts
to repair the ruined walls of Jerusalem not only encouraged his own
people but helped prepare for the coming of our Savior, Jesus Christ, a
few centuries later. Help me learn from his example of persistence and
courage, through my faith in you. Give me strength each day to perform
your great works. In Jesus' name I pray. Amen.* ❧

Our Christian Mission

Woe to me if I do not preach the gospel! If I preach voluntarily, I have a reward; if not voluntarily, I am simply discharging the trust committed to me.
I CORINTHIANS 9:16 – 17

Paul was a man on a mission, armed with a mandate from God. In effect, he put himself in the position of a slave for Christ, a servant carrying out the will of his master. So as he preached, established churches, wrote letters, or theologized on the meaning of Christ's ministry on earth, Paul acted in the name of his Savior. As a full-time evangelist, he made this the total commitment of his life.

I believe that, as Christians, all of us have been given a similar mission of sharing our relationship to Christ with the world. Most of us also have other duties to which we are committed: to foster healthy family relationships, to become better educated or trained in our profession, to succeed in our endeavors, to elevate our social or economic status. And while there's nothing wrong with pursuing these things, we must not forget our main task and our mission as Christians: to spread the word of Christ, to demonstrate our faith by our words and actions, even, if necessary, to sacrifice our social status or our wealth.

Are we willing to go so far?

Paul reminds us to be careful how we live, to ensure we make the most of our time here (Ephesians 5:15). Our lives are brief, and it is easy to postpone or ignore our Christian mission. And while not everyone has to be a preacher or a missionary in some far-off nation, all of us are called to acknowledge the mandate we have voluntarily assumed as Christians.

Within our own circle of influence, let us dedicate ourselves to the service of others in the name of our Savior, Jesus Christ. It is our privilege to share how God has blessed us, whether in happiness, material blessings, or time.

O God, I ask that you help me share the message of Jesus wherever I go, and that my life might be inspired and invigorated with a heavenly mission for his sake. Help me reach out to those in need around me in the true spirit of Christ, and let that be my freely adopted mission. I ask this in his holy name. Amen. ❧

A Carter Stayed Here

"Whenever you enter a house, stay there until you leave that town."
MARK 6:10

During my 1976 presidential campaign, none of us had any money—and yet we had seven family campaigns we had to keep going at once: Rosalynn, me, our three sons (with their wives), my mother, and her sister. To cover more territory, we all visited different places. Rosalynn and I never campaigned together; I would go to one state while she went to another. The same held true for our family members and other volunteers who helped us.

Because we were so strapped for cash, we had one simple rule: no one stayed in a hotel without paying the bill personally. Whenever we got to a town, therefore, we looked for a host family willing to take us in for the night. Our practice helped us form wonderful and long-lasting friendships with our many generous hosts. Had we stayed in costly hotels, we never would have made such delightful personal connections.

The first week after I moved into the White House, we had a reception for all the gracious people who had acted as hosts for my family. We invited no one else. More than seven hundred people came. We gave each of them a small brass plaque that said, "A member of the Carter family spent the night here."

Perhaps Jesus had something like this in mind when he told his disciples to stay with individual families when they visited a village. He knew that if we want to fulfill his command and spread the gospel, we can't do so from a distance. We have to get to know people and build relationships with them. We have to share our lives with them. Only such a personal approach will authenticate our message.

O Lord, help me remember that you have called me into a living community that you call the church, and that healthy relationships are what make that community function and thrive. Keep my fellow human beings at the forefront of my consciousness, and never let me forget that you have commissioned me to share the gospel with them in the service of Jesus Christ, in whose name I pray. Amen.

Look Out for False Prophets!

*"From early times the prophets who preceded you and me have
prophesied war, disaster and plague against many countries and great
kingdoms. But the prophet who prophesies peace will be recognized as
one truly sent by the LORD only if his prediction comes true."*
JEREMIAH 28:8 – 9

When people called Jeremiah a false prophet, he replied, in essence, "The false prophets are those who oppose the Word of God." Jeremiah gave bad news as well as good. But the prophets speaking to King Zedekiah craved popularity. "Everything will be okay," they said. "We are good people. We don't know why God allowed Nebuchadnezzar to overthrow Judah, but it certainly wasn't our fault."

Likewise, we have to watch out for modern-day false teachers who tell us we are basically good people, living well and pleasing God. They tend to say, "We are grateful for our material blessings and for God's wisdom in recognizing how much we deserve them."

We must recognize and accept God's true messages, rather than those that may gratify us more. We must continually search the Scriptures for things that God considers important. This may not always bring good news; we may not find that God values big church buildings or homogenous congregations. We may find God does not condone the way people glorify their wonderful nation for its security, wealth, and influence, sometimes to the detriment of other nations. We may find that God's message makes us uncomfortable.

Jesus warns us that at the final judgment, some will think they belong to him—but Jesus will say he never knew them, for they refused to give him a drink of water when he was thirsty or bread when he was hungry. Those listening will ask, "When did you ever need our help in these things?" And he will respond, "Whatever you did not do for the least of these, my brothers and sisters, you did not do for me."

*God, often I am taken aback when I read your Holy Word and see how
it applies to me. But eventually I come to realize that the message is one
of glory and inspiration and challenge, which can make my life more full
and joyful and peaceful—if I remember the perfect pattern given us in the
life and words of my Savior, Jesus Christ. In his name I pray. Amen.*

The Consequences of Choosing Evil

Then they will cry out to the LORD, but he will not answer them. At that
time he will hide his face from them because of the evil they have done.
MICAH 3:4

Micah uses some of the most extreme language in the Bible to condemn the
wicked people of Judah. He equates his countrymen with those who tear the
flesh of the poor; who eat the skin and muscle of their fellow citizens; and
who alienate God from them all. He laments that the rulers and priests, who
ought to know what justice is, have instead departed from it. Finally he cries
out, "He has shown you, O mortal, what is good. And what does the LORD
require of you? To act justly and to love mercy and to walk humbly with your
God" (Micah 6:8).

To "act justly" means to treat everybody equally under the law, to eschew
bribery, and to reject standards of punishment for the poor that differ from
the rich. Micah presented no complex or hidden messages to describe one's
relationship with God. In fact, the people had been violating a very simple
message: Walk humbly with God, exhibiting both mercy and justice.

What if they refused? Micah said they would "cry to the LORD, but he
will not answer them." To unrepentant sinfulness, God responds with silence.

What does God require of *us*? Jesus told us to love God and one another —
essentially, Micah's message. Sometimes we dislike the simplicity of the message; it's better if the message seems complicated so we can respond, "I don't
quite understand it." Then we feel no responsibility to comply.

Let us take warning from Micah: Those who turn away from what God
requires, who refuse to seek him and obey his commandments, will get no
response from God when things go bad. God will hide his face from them —
a sobering, chilling thought.

> *God, please allow me to hear with clarity and urgency the prophet's call*
> *for justice and fair treatment of all. Enable me, as a Christian, to be a*
> *person of peace, compassion, love, and service. May these simple words*
> *urge me, drive me, and compel me to take action, by the power of your*
> *Spirit, wherever you give me opportunities to serve. I pray in Jesus' name.*
> *Amen.* ❧

The Cost of Concern

The dispute became so violent that the commander was afraid Paul would
be torn to pieces by them. He ordered the troops to go down and take him
away from them by force and bring him into the barracks.
ACTS 23:10

Shared, deep experiences bring people together. And perhaps the deepest experiences of all involve suffering.

The apostle Paul, maybe the greatest Christian witness of all time, owes part of his evangelistic prowess to suffering. I don't claim he suffered willingly; I think he would have preferred to skip it. But before a fateful trip to Jerusalem, God warned him that suffering would stalk him (see Acts 9:16; 20:23). No doubt Paul could have avoided Jerusalem, received thanks and honor elsewhere, and returned safely home. But he chose the hard route.

Shortly after Paul reached Jerusalem, a mob tried to kill him. Roman soldiers quickly quelled the riot and took Paul into custody. Paul's life could have ended right there. The Romans clapped him in chains, and he remained in Caesarea for two whole years. Paul could very well have said, "You know, God, I've done my part. I've witnessed. I've sacrificed. I've not been a coward. I've gone where other people wouldn't go, and I've spoken when other people remained quiet. But enough is enough. I'm done."

Paul could have abandoned his faith, gone to Rome, and lived in peace — but in fact, his greatest witnessing continued *after* this incident, while in prison. His arrest was not the end of him, and neither was it the end of the Christian church.

What applied to Paul also applies to us. If we get proud of our status in religious and social circles and forget the mandate of Christ, then we are doomed for failure. Yes, Paul paid a severe price for his witness to Christ. But it was not the end of him. In fact, in many ways, it was just the beginning.

I thank you, dear Lord, for the joy of this day and for the blessings you
have given me from your bountiful hand. I marvel at the many evidences
of your love. And I pray that the words of admonition from your Holy
Word in this story about Paul will linger in my heart, that I might be a
faithful witness for you. In Jesus' name I pray. Amen. ❧

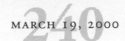

Difficult, Not Impossible

"Get behind me, Satan!" [Jesus] said. "You do not have in mind the
concerns of God, but merely human concerns."
MARK 8:33

For many years I have tried to help bring peace to the suffering people of the Sudan. When I have told others about our efforts, I have done so primarily to inform them about an important event. But the truth is, sometimes I do it to make myself look good.

Every year when Rosalynn and I take a week to build a Habitat house, we welcome publicity. We do so primarily so that people will give more money for Habitat houses and to recruit volunteers. But in fact, sometimes I speak to the media because it improves my public image.

I'm not proud of these selfish motivations. But I'm human, and we are naturally inclined to relegate the glorification of God to a secondary priority. We want to brag about our generosity and see our pictures in the paper. We certainly want our friends to know about it!

But setting our minds on the things of God is not about seeking recognition: it's about denying ourselves, taking up our cross, and following Christ. It's about assuming a duty or personal burden at some sacrifice to ourselves, for Jesus' sake—and giving him credit.

How many of us take up the burden of the cross? How many of us worry that people might ridicule us for being too close to Christ or label us as religious fanatics? How many of us are willing to risk the things we own, our wealth, perhaps social status, for the cause of Christ?

Jesus has told us to set our minds on divine things and not merely human things. If you wonder, "Can I do this?" remember that Jesus never asks us to do impossible things—but he often asks us to do difficult things.

O Lord, thank you for humbling me and for curbing my natural
tendency toward self-exaltation. Help me inventory the things in my life
that are merely human concerns, and give me the courage and strength to
go after the divine things that I have allowed to go missing. Bless me and
support me as I seek to partner in this world with my Savior, Jesus Christ.
In his name I pray. Amen. ❧

Following Christ When It Hurts

*"And if you do good to those who are good to you, what credit is that
to you? Even sinners do that."*
LUKE 6:33

After the tragic attacks on September 11, 2001, authorities arrested about 1,600 people living in America, most of them of Arab descent, who might be guilty of terrorist activities. They were imprisoned for months without being charged with any crime, without access to lawyers or even their families. Some of their loved ones made calls to human rights organizations, including the Carter Center, saying, "I don't know how to contact my husband. He was taken away and is being held incommunicado." Many others were taken into captivity in different parts of the world or locked in wire cages at Guantanamo Bay, where some of them still remain, without being tried or proven guilty. The Secretary of Defense announced that the Geneva Principles regarding treatment of prisoners did not apply to anyone suspected of terrorist activities.

When we suffer something awful at the hands of another person or ethnic group, our natural inclination is to react strongly, label them evil, and seek revenge. This is not a new thing. But it *is* an ungodly thing.

Although most people don't know it, most of the major battles during the American Revolution were fought in the South. The combatants were so filled with hatred that orders went out to grant no quarter—that is, take no prisoners. In one battle in Georgia, British soldiers were told that if they took a prisoner, they would lose their rum rations for a month. So any Revolutionary who surrendered was killed immediately with a bayonet to the stomach or a bullet to the brain. And the Americans followed suit.

When Christ tells us to do good to those who harm us, he doesn't require us to be foolish. We don't give a loaded weapon to an enemy. But Jesus also knew, and taught us, that a commitment to peace, justice, and forgiveness is a more potent weapon than hatred and revenge.

*O Lord, even though it goes against my natural tendencies and is very
difficult, help me find ways to adopt principles that will make me worthy
in your sight. As far as it is possible, help me emulate the perfect life of my
precious Savior, Jesus Christ. Amen.* ❧

Tears of Rejection

*"Jerusalem, Jerusalem, you who kill the prophets and stone those sent
to you, how often I have longed to gather your children together, as a
hen gathers her chicks under her wings, and you were not willing."*
LUKE 13:34

All of us have felt the sting of rejection. Maybe we tried to reach out to our
playmates on the ball field but discovered they didn't want us. Or maybe we
sought to become a class officer but came up many votes short. Or perhaps
we had an ambition to become a doctor but lacked the necessary abilities. Or
maybe we applied for admission to our parents' alma mater but failed to meet
the academic requirements. And, of course, I might fall in love with some
girl but discover that she feels very differently about me than I do about her.

I had my earliest sweetheart at about age thirteen. I'd get my daddy's
pickup truck (before driver's licenses were required) and take her out. Her
name was Eloise, but we called her Teenie. When a boy named Lonnie came
to Plains with his own automobile, however, she abandoned me for him. (To
save my feelings, I still say it was the automobile.)

Later I fell in love with Rosalynn. I asked her to marry me, fully expecting
her to say yes. She said no, plunging me into months of abject despair (before
she changed her mind). The point is, we all experience rejection, and it can
make us feel horrible.

Jesus suffered a lot of rejection. The Jewish religious and political leaders
never accepted him, nor did many of the citizens of Palestine. It made him
sad that people rejected him, but Jesus persevered and still loved them.

When people reject us, we must determine to follow Jesus' example. Let
us refuse to become disconsolate, bitter, or angry, but instead seek God's will,
not be deterred, and maintain a loving attitude.

*Lord, I admit that rejection is very hard for me to handle. Jesus wept
over Jerusalem's rejection but didn't allow his feelings to keep him from
completing his mission of redemption. Let me learn from his example and
determine to reject the bitterness or despair that usually accompanies my
own experience of rejection. Let me respond by seeking your guidance and
emulating your love. I pray in Jesus' name. Amen.* ❧

A Life as Surety

"Greater love has no one than this:
to lay down one's life for one's friends."
JOHN 15:13

After Joseph had risen to second-in-command of all Egypt, his brothers, who had sold him into slavery, came to Egypt to buy grain. They did not recognize Joseph, but he recognized them, and he decided to play a game.

He said he would keep their brother Simeon until they went home and returned with their youngest brother, Benjamin. But his game didn't end there. When the brothers got home, they discovered that the money they had taken to Egypt to buy grain had been returned to them. When they reported this to their father, Jacob, he expressed great concern about the money and anguish about Simeon's imprisonment. But he adamantly opposed any plan to send Benjamin to Egypt. So they left Simeon on his own until they ran out of food.

Finally a dramatic confrontation occurred between Judah and his father. Judah told Jacob that if Benjamin returned to Egypt with them to get more grain, he, Judah, would be Benjamin's surety. "If I fail to bring Benjamin back," he said, in effect, "my life is forfeit." He put up his life and his very soul as a warranty that he would not lose Benjamin.

There was no selfishness in what Judah proposed. He was totally concerned about his brother Benjamin and the health of his father, Jacob. That's why in an emotional speech he told Joseph, "I will be your slave the rest of my life in Benjamin's place, if you'll just let him go home to our father." Joseph felt so overwhelmed by Judah's selflessness that he wept on Benjamin's neck, and the brothers were reconciled.

This is the highest kind of love, a self-giving love for others above one's own self-interest. Jesus demonstrated it to an ultimate degree at Calvary, and we should get ready to follow in his steps.

Dear God, I come to you as a person who does not naturally show this kind of self-giving love. As a believer in Christ, however, I want to follow his example. So strengthen me, by the power and presence of your Spirit, and help me reflect in my words and behavior the higher call I have in Christ. I pray this in his holy name. Amen. ❧

244

To Be Exceptional

"Then the Lord said to me, 'Go; I will send you far away to the Gentiles.'" The crowd listened to Paul ... and shouted, "Rid the earth of him! He's not fit to live!"
ACTS 22:21 – 22

I had a neighbor named David Guest who raised fine Duroc Jersey hogs. A few years ago we learned that David and his wife had rented out their farm, sold their hogs, and moved to Haiti to work among some of the poorest people on earth.

Later I told David how much I admired him for it. But I soon found that, among many of our neighbors, he had lost his former social status as a sober and dedicated farmer who minded his own business. I suppose it was thought that David should have taken care of his own affairs and that he was making other Christians look bad because they weren't going to Haiti. Most of us weren't even witnessing for Christ in our own community.

Sometimes when we try to bridge a racial or social gap, our own peers condemn us. So long as we stay homogenous—let's say, white, hardworking, and members of a respected church—we enjoy mutual admiration, because everyone around us feels comfortable with each other. But if somebody does something different, like witnessing among the poor, making an extraordinary gift, or taking time off to work exclusively for Christ, we tend to become suspicious and say, "That's a religious fanatic."

The Jewish crowd patiently let Paul explain his actions, until the apostle mentioned one word: "Gentiles." This was like throwing a bomb in the audience. The mob demanded his death, and the Romans had to take him back into custody to protect him.

To be exceptional in our unselfishness, forgiveness, humility, or fervor—even in our worship of Christ—may bring condemnation. Like Paul, we must be prepared, even eager, for it.

Lord, although I like to think of myself as exceptional, I usually add, "in a generally acceptable way." Give me a clear image of the extraordinary life you want for me, perhaps full of unexpected adventures. Let me stretch my heart and love more people, making my life more full of kindness and grace. In Jesus' name I pray. Amen. ❧

245

Comfort in Distress

Praise be to the God and Father of our Lord Jesus Christ, the Father
of compassion and the God of all comfort, who comforts us in all
our troubles, so that we can comfort those in any trouble with the
comfort we ourselves receive from God.
2 CORINTHIANS 1:3 – 4

A Chinese fable tells of a woman who had only one child, a little boy. When her son died at an early age, the woman felt overwhelmed with sorrow. One day, she visited a wise man for help. The wise man said, "Yes, I have some magic that can assuage your sorrow. Go and obtain one mustard seed from a family that has not experienced sorrow."

The woman left, moving from one family to another. In that whole village, she found none that had avoided sorrow; but as her neighbors described their problems, setbacks, and losses, she listened. The experience changed her life, and she began to minister to them. Finally she saw that part of her sorrow, at least, diminished when she realized that everyone shared this common human experience. And her spirits lifted when she began to help others overcome their sorrow.

When suffering and sorrow hit us, we too can find comfort by commiserating with others who share similar experiences. But more importantly, as Christians, we can rely on the comfort that comes to us from God through Jesus Christ. He provides us with the ultimate source of solace and our greatest reservoir of strength, to help us through the losses, disappointments, and tragedies that befall us all.

For good reason, Paul calls God the "Father of compassion." As his children, we are heirs to this divine love—and God asks us to comfort others with the compassion and mercy he shows us. While this is no magic mustard seed, it is very real and much needed, and it is our Christian privilege to cherish and share it.

O Lord, sorrow is a difficult emotion to handle. Thank you for comforting
me through the power of the Holy Spirit. Let me identify with and
minister to others who have their own disappointments or losses, binding
us together for Christ's sake. Make me into a healing presence that honors
you and blesses others. In Jesus' name I pray. Amen.

246

Common Experience

*Five times I received from the Jews the forty lashes minus one. Three
times I was beaten with rods, once I was pelted with stones, three
times I was shipwrecked, I spent a night and a day in the open sea.*
2 CORINTHIANS 11:24–25

We relate better to others when something special binds us together. For
example, if I meet someone and they say, "I'm from Alabama," I often say,
"That's right next door to where I'm from!" Or if they say they're from Georgia, I ask, "What town?" and if they say, "Sandersville," I say, "I've been there
many times."

By finding these kinds of mutual experiences, we instantly gain an entrée
into another person's life. I feel this way when I meet another former submariner, farmer, or someone who shares my love for fly-fishing.

Similar troubles or challenges often yield even deeper ties. Suppose we're
both alcoholics and have struggled successfully to stop drinking. This is such
a powerful common experience that instantaneously we're almost certain to
be friends. I'm sure that veterans of the Vietnam War or those who have
served recently in Iraq or Afghanistan have very strong ties with each other.

Paul was, without doubt, the greatest Christian evangelist of all time. He
continues to witness to us today partly because we know that he, like Jesus,
suffered greatly. If any of us have been hurt by adversity or physical pain, we
know that Paul was not ignorant about such experiences. His suffering tends
to build common ground between us.

Let's take that insight as a lesson for our own witnessing for Christ. Finding common experiences can help us relate to those with whom we are trying
to share our faith. It helps to know about the prospective new Christian in
advance, or else to listen carefully during our first conversation. Any following discussion about God's love and mercy, our common human shortcomings, and the salvation that comes through faith in Jesus Christ will be much
more fruitful.

*God, when I'm going through interesting experiences, whether difficult
or pleasant, help me see your hand in them—and then show me how to
make connections with others that otherwise would go unmade. Help me,
Lord, to cooperate in your plan for my life, and shape me into a willing,
humble, and effective witness for Christ. I pray in his name. Amen.* ❧

Growing as Christians

Speaking the truth in love, we will grow to become in every respect
the mature body of him who is the head, that is, Christ.
EPHESIANS 4:15

When most students graduate from college, their heads are filled with facts and ideas, but they probably don't have much practical experience. Perhaps they have an engineering degree from Georgia Tech or MIT, but they couldn't take over a job with Georgia Power Company and begin assuming the electrical engineering responsibilities required to design, build, or operate a new power plant. Even with a college degree, most people have to work as an apprentice to get the needed practical experience.

It's the same way with our Christian faith. We can go to church, listen to sermons, sing hymns, recite a creed, and memorize the Lord's Prayer. All of that is good, but those things by themselves do not give us the experience of being a Christian or of applying the teaching of Jesus in our day-to-day experiences. We learn and mature as believers most effectively through interacting with others, especially those who are unlike us.

It's a difficult apprenticeship. It requires some experimentation, often beyond our comfort zone. And probably one of the most difficult parts of living a Christlike life is dealing with "strange" or difficult people. Think of those who seem unpleasant, unfriendly, or who might frighten us, people whom we naturally dislike or would rather avoid. Treating those sorts of people with truth and love is one of the most difficult challenges we face. It's a struggle. And yet that's the way we become more Christlike.

Imagine the people whom Paul visited, many of whom hated and abused him. Paul describes a beautiful process of Christian growth, a process that should engage us throughout our lives. Christ demands maturity of us, which requires that we learn and develop—and often struggle a bit—in the faith.

O God, spiritual growth requires a lot of me, and I need your help in the process. When I struggle, encourage me with your love; when I succeed, remind me that it is a blessing from you. If I fail, let me try again. Bless me and make me a blessing, I pray, in the name of my Savior, Jesus Christ. Amen. ❧

248

A Missionary's Questions

But Moses said to God, "Who am I that I should go to Pharaoh and
bring the Israelites out of Egypt?"
EXODUS 3:11

Who is a missionary? Is he or she someone who leaves home to work among exotic people in far-off lands like Togo or Uzbekistan? I'd define it more broadly than that. I think a missionary is someone who has received a mission to serve God.

By this definition, Moses was a missionary. While wandering around on the edge of a mountain pasture, he saw a little bush, burning without being consumed. Curious, Moses moved out of his ordinary life in order to question the extraordinary—and God sent him back to his people as a missionary.

While God uses many things to attract our attention, we may have to examine the ordinary to find the extraordinary. Unfortunately, many of us march to the grave without ever stopping to ask, "What is God's message to me? How can I accept a mission in the name of Jesus Christ, compatible with the will of God?"

Moses didn't become a missionary easily. He asked God, "Who am I, that I should go?" We all ask that question. "Who am I? In the global scope of things, who am I? I have my own fallibilities. I have my own inadequacies. I have my own sin. I'm not an eloquent speaker. I don't have much money. So who am I to be a missionary for God Almighty?"

But God can use us even if we're doubtful, even if we're not eloquent, even if we have little influence or money to give away, even if we can't travel to distant places. We can be successful missionaries, each in our own way, just by striving to follow the example of Jesus within our own circle of friends and neighbors. This is a difficult but worthy task.

O Lord, during the coming week, help me find some time to be by myself—to kneel down, be patient, and let your message come to me. Give me ears to hear. And then help me make room for your mission, that I might pursue a glorious life in the presence of my Savior, in whose name I pray. Amen.

An Entrepreneurial Spirit

All the believers were one in heart and mind. No one claimed that any of
their possessions was their own, but they shared everything they had.
ACTS 4:32

A passage like this can embarrass Americans, for it goes contrary to the spirit of free enterprise. The early church did not subscribe to a philosophy of "get all you can and keep all you can" but clearly was involved in communal sharing.

While I do not counsel church members to sell everything they have, put it into one pot at church, and share it, I do recognize that we Americans have an innovative spirit. We're entrepreneurs at heart. If we try something and it doesn't work, we try something else. This striving for success fueled the economic progress of our country. So, as Christians, why can't we devote that same degree of innovation to sharing what we have with others?

Suppose we earn fifty thousand dollars a year (about average for American families); there's no restraint against our giving ten thousand of it to worthy causes. Maybe we could devote a good portion of vacation time to charity, or those of us who are retired might devote ourselves to alleviating suffering—in Jesus' name. Any of these options would echo the spirit of the early church's communal giving.

What kind of church do we have? Are we like the early Christians, who took a chance for Christ, who let the spirit of the Holy Ghost permeate their hearts and souls, who willingly gave what they had for the care of others? It's a mistake to sit back and say, "I'll wait until everybody else does it." This is an individual thing; it comes out of our relationship with God and with other human beings. We can't all be powerful or rich, but as individual Christians we can express ourselves with a loving commitment to justice and generosity. It just takes an adventurous spirit.

God, help me learn from the example set by the early Christians to
exemplify the essence of our Christian faith. Prompt me to ask myself, "In
the remaining years of my life, how can I draw closer to Christ and better
demonstrate, in a bold and exciting way, what it means to be a Chris-
tian?" I pray this in the name of my Savior, Jesus Christ. Amen.

True Religion

Paul then stood up in the meeting of the Areopagus and said: "People of Athens! I see that in every way you are very religious."
ACTS 17:22

Paul ministered among people steeped in false religions. How would we define "true religion"? We might say, "*My* religion is true; all others are false." In America, freedom of worship means, "I can believe anything, so long as I'm sincere."

As Christians living well, we feel reluctant to criticize societal standards. So we go along with things that Christ finds offensive. The ancient Stoics said that life was like two dogs, tied behind a moving wagon. One dog resisted the movement of the wagon and was strangled. The other dog trotted along behind the wagon everywhere it went and felt at ease. The story reminds us that resistance can bring severe consequences.

As Christians we should search our hearts and explore the truths of the Bible. But faith without deeds—words without action—is hollow. Many of us tend to stop at the words. We hear the sermons, read the Bible, give a little of our money—not 10 percent, that's too extreme—perhaps attend Sunday school, and then congratulate ourselves on being good Christians.

But Paul ventured out among the people of Athens, explaining the word of Christ and debating with Jewish religious leaders in the synagogues. He courageously contended with philosophers and political leaders, saying, "I have come to propose a new way of life to you."

Like Paul, we must be willing to take chances and do things that seem out of the ordinary for us. Most of us worship the Prince of Peace but give quiet support to unnecessary wars. We know our prisons are filled mostly with the poor, minorities, and the mentally ill, but remain silent with the knowledge. We see the rich getting richer and the poor becoming poorer, but do nothing to change the system of taxation or benefits. Where is our commitment to the principles of Jesus? What sort of "true religion" do we have?

Lord, help me turn to you as my partner in the work of the gospel and look for opportunities that demonstrate in concrete, practical ways that I have given my life to you. Through my actions and my words, enable me to show the world that you are my model for life. I ask these things in Jesus' name. Amen. ❧

It's Hard to Love an Enemy

"You have heard that it was said, 'Love your neighbor and hate your enemy.' But I tell you, love your enemies and pray for those who persecute you, that you may be children of your Father in heaven."
MATTHEW 5:43 – 45

The command to "love your enemy" is both startling and unique to the Christian faith; no other religion has a parallel teaching. "Turn the other cheek," "Walk a second mile," "If someone demands your coat, give it to him"—these are just some of the things Christ commanded, and they all express a self-sacrificial love for other human beings, even for those who may never love you back or who may not seem lovable.

It is reasonable that we should love our children, our spouse, our parents, or people who love us back. But to love someone who despises us? That is very difficult. Some think the command to love our enemies makes us appear weak or as cowards and condemns us to be servile people without backbones. Others think it could hurt us socially—and it may. But Christ commanded it, and we should not respond, "Surely that doesn't *really* apply to our modern-day, competitive world. I might go broke if I forgave my competitors and treated them as friends!"

The Qur'an is the central force in most Islamic countries around the world. It has such a strong, binding power among Muslims that when an argument arises about a legal matter or the Arabic language, the disputants consult the Qur'an as the preeminent authority.

Shouldn't we Christians resolve to treat Christ's commands with as much reverence? Let us not rationalize our disobedience because we find his teachings difficult. If we should say, "Theoretically it's okay, but Jesus can't have meant for me to follow this in practice," then we're fooling ourselves. If we pray for strength, God *will* help us love our enemies.

Lord, I ask for your help as I struggle with your Word and its often difficult commands. Give me the wisdom to understand it correctly and the courage to apply it to my life in practical, meaningful ways, looking for opportunities to please you rather than for excuses to avoid the strict and difficult parts. I pray this in the holy name of Jesus, my Savior. Amen. ❧

A Transcendent Mission

"So then, King Agrippa, I was not disobedient to the vision from heaven. First to those in Damascus, then to those in Jerusalem and in all Judea, and then to the Gentiles, I preached that they should repent and turn to God and demonstrate their repentance by their deeds."

ACTS 26:19 – 20

What do you think of the word *transcendent*? Does it cause you concern? Does it prompt you to say, "I'm just a normal person. How can my life be superb?" In fact, Christ calls *every* believer to have a transcendent mission—something above and beyond expectations, even above the very good.

We tend to get bogged down in the responsibilities of daily life, struggling for good grades or a better job or a healthy home. None of these is ill advised; all are admirable. But for too many of us, that's the end of our ambition. We never reach for transcendence.

Fear often holds us back. We don't want to be *too* bold, *too* eager to stretch ourselves. But our transcendent mission doesn't have to take us to Southern Sudan or even a different state.

Paul told King Agrippa, "I have faithfully carried out my duties to tell people about repentance." His transcendent mission took him into the court of a pagan king; ours might take us to the local convenience store. Location isn't the key; our particular mission is.

Can we explain before God who we are and what we do or have done with our lives? Do we have a transcendent mission for Jesus Christ? As we analyze our lives, talents, interests, and opportunities, Christ can help us carve out our own individualized mission—a transcendent one.

All of us, at the same rate, are approaching the end of our lives, whether in a few months or a few decades. When the end comes, will people say of us, "That was a successful Christian"?

Or will they say, "Wow, what a nice tombstone"?

God, I pray that without being frightened or intimidated, I will say to myself, "I'd like to take a look at my life's mission as measured through the eyes of my Savior, Jesus Christ." And then, Lord, help me embark on that transcendent mission, knowing that sometimes I'll fail—but also knowing that, at all times, you will be with me. In Jesus' name. Amen.

Jeremiah's Promise Is Ours

"Do not be afraid of them, for I am with you and will rescue you,"
declares the LORD.
JEREMIAH 1:8

Imagine that you were quite young and also bashful — and God named you to be heaven's mouthpiece, not only to your own wicked people, but also to the nations of the world. How would you react? That was Jeremiah's dilemma.

Seemingly out of the blue, God called Jeremiah to be a prophet, just as earlier the Lord had called Abraham to move to the Promised Land, Moses to lead the Hebrews out of slavery in Egypt, and Gideon to lead the Israelites against their oppressors. A rattled Jeremiah responded, "Lord, I do not even know how to speak; I am only a boy!" And in fact, Jeremiah told the truth; he *was* only a boy. But God told him not to fear the responsibility, because God would be at his side.

Jeremiah reacted much like others through the centuries who also heard God's call. Even David, when first called, said, in essence, "No, I'm the least of Jesse's children. I'm not tall and handsome and stalwart like the incumbent king. I'm just a shepherd boy!"

Does this sound familiar? How many of us say, "I can't be significant in God's kingdom. I have no special talent!" or "I'm not influential enough to make a difference in the world"? Whenever we start thinking like this, we need to remember Jesus' promise always to remain with us, and that with God nothing is impossible. Jesus promised to send us the Comforter, the Holy Spirit, to care for me and you. You realize what that means, don't you? It means we have within us the presence of God Almighty!

God is with us, just as God was with the prophet Jeremiah. Therefore, there's no need to doubt our ability; we need only remember the presence of God.

O Lord, I admit that I am not competent to serve you as your
representative. I am not strong enough, nor do I have the wisdom, wealth,
eloquence, or godliness. And yet you have promised to be with me, and
that really is enough. I can succeed with you as my partner. Please take
my talents, great or small, and use them to enhance your kingdom. I pray
this in Jesus' name. Amen. ❧

Obedience to God's Law

*A person is not a Jew who is one only outwardly, nor is circumcision
merely outward and physical. No, a person is a Jew who is one
inwardly; and circumcision is circumcision of the heart, by the Spirit.*
ROMANS 2:28 – 29

Just calling ourselves something doesn't make it true in the eyes of God,
whether we are Jews or Christians. Jewish men of ancient times said, "I have
the mark of God's favor because I am circumcised; therefore, I must be righteous in God's sight." Christians have a similar mark: baptism. Many Christians therefore say, "Because I have been baptized, I must be righteous in
God's sight." A vast number of Christians believe that since they walked
down the aisle when they were eight years old and said, "I accept Christ as
my Savior," they are righteous in God's sight.

While there's nothing wrong with any of these ceremonies, we mistake
their significance if we say, "I can be careless about my life because no matter
what I do, I'll be forgiven. God loves me and is full of grace, and Jesus died
on the cross for my sins, so if I repent, I'll be all right. I don't have to worry
about my commitment to follow Christ and obey God's law."

This attitude is entirely mistaken. It is true that if we believe in Christ
and repent, our sins are forgiven and we are saved; but this in no way abol-
ishes God's laws. Our behavior matters! That is why Paul, the "apostle of
grace," could write, "I am not free from God's law but am under Christ's law"
(1 Corinthians 9:21). James writes, "A person is considered righteous by what
they do and not by faith alone.... As the body without the spirit is dead, so
faith without deeds is dead" (James 2:24, 26).

Genuine faith leads us to bind ourselves to Jesus in word and deed.

*Lord, sometimes the words of Scripture force me to reexamine who I am,
what I am, and what my priorities in life might be; and, if necessary, to
reorient those priorities to make them more compatible with the perfect
example set for me by my Savior. Help me have the courage and the
wisdom to seek this exciting, higher commitment in the service of my
Savior, in whose name I pray. Amen.*

A Willingness to Give

*Last year you were the first not only to give but also to have the desire
to do so. Now finish the work, so that your eager willingness to do it
may be matched by your completion of it, according to your means.*
2 CORINTHIANS 8:10–11

Paul spent a lot of time seeking contributions, and I sympathize with him. At the Carter Center, Rosalynn and I sponsor many programs around the world, with an annual budget of about $80 million. This means that we have to raise over $200,000 a day. The contributions vary, of course, but it is a constant responsibility to find individuals and organizations willing to be generous partners in our health and peace projects.

Some of our donors are quite wealthy, and there are also about 250,000 people who send us smaller contributions by mail. A few times each year, we send them a letter to describe the results of our efforts and then add: "Please keep on giving so we can continue the work."

Giving to churches or other organizations devoted to good causes is one way to help the needy. If we can't go to Africa and personally evangelize for Christ or fight the spread of diseases, then we can contribute to an organization that performs that service.

Other ways to help needy people don't involve money. Rosalynn founded a program at Georgia Southwestern State University that promotes caregiving. If we have a parent or spouse with Alzheimer's or a severely handicapped child, we are willing to devote our time caring for them. This is a great gift and a wonderful contribution.

Giving is not a matter of obligation or pressure or command; it's a way to honor God and demonstrate Christian love. We can be generous even if we have little wealth by giving what we can afford, either in time or in money. Paul says that what counts is our willingness—followed by our actual contribution.

*O God, help me see that my only limits are those that I impose on myself.
Make me into a person who gives generously out of a heart of love and
not stingily or out of compulsion, guilt, or pride. Let me become more
worthy each day to be called your son or daughter. In Jesus' name I pray.
Amen.*

When to Be Discreet

Pride brings a person low, but the lowly in spirit gain honor.
PROVERBS 29:23

Of all his sons, Jacob loved Joseph the most. To demonstrate his favoritism, Jacob gave Joseph a beautiful coat. Some translations call it a coat of many colors; others, a coat with long sleeves. Jacob gave this ornate coat to Joseph, but not to his other sons, to proclaim his love. Joseph took pride in his coat, and also felt quite proud of himself. So trouble brewed when Joseph began describing dreams that exalted himself.

In one dream, one sheaf of grain represented Joseph, while eleven other sheaves represented his brothers. The eleven sheaves bowed down to Joseph's sheaf—and the young man was foolish enough to describe the dream to his brothers. This irritated them very much, because it suggested Joseph's superiority.

In another dream, eleven stars (Joseph's brothers again) and the moon (Jacob himself) all bowed down to a single star (Joseph). Joseph also told his family about this dream, irritating even his father and mother. Joseph's brothers eventually got so fed up with his pride and arrogance that one day they decided to kill him or sell him into slavery.

This story holds a crucial lesson for us all. Just because we have knowledge of something—even something as true as Joseph's dreams turned out to be—doesn't mean we should always repeat what we know. We need to be wise about what we say, and wise about when we say it.

This is especially true in communicating the Christian message. We must be sensitive to people and their situation and not treat them as inferiors or try to show off our knowledge. We must be humble and strive to understand the special interests and needs of those with whom we wish to share our faith. This is what Jesus always did.

O Lord, as you teach me more about your ways and your world, also teach me how best to share this precious knowledge with others. Help me choose humility as a permanent way of life. Tie me as closely as possible to my Savior, Jesus Christ, that I might copy his characteristics, actions, and words. I ask these things in his name. Amen. ❧

It Makes a Difference

"For I was hungry and you gave me something to eat, I was thirsty and you gave me something to drink, I was a stranger and you invited me in."
MATTHEW 25:35

Rosalynn and I have a grandson who had some significant struggles in his young life. Fortunately, now he's doing very well as a college student. He commutes from school to home on the subway. Between his school and the subway station, he routinely passes a place where a group of homeless people hang out. Since he's been in a few scrapes himself, he has a special affinity for others who have been in trouble or are down and out. He usually stops and talks to the homeless, listening to them and buying them coffee or donuts or giving them a few dollars to tide them over.

One day, on his way from school to the subway station, our grandson spoke to his homeless acquaintances. When he continued toward the station, two men jumped out of an alley and began to mug him. His homeless friends saw the beating and ran quickly to chase off the attackers. Even writing about it makes me emotional. The reaction of the destitute people shows how much my grandson meant to them. It demonstrated the real effects of his kindness. This was an unexpected benefit.

That's the kind of bonding our own actions should produce through kindness and concern. We may not benefit ourselves, but God's kingdom will be strengthened if we act in the name of Jesus Christ.

Perhaps we could pray each morning, "Lord, as I prepare for this day, please help me respond to people as Christ has taught us." When we show kindness to others, it really does make a difference to them. It pleases God, and these special friendships will always bless us as well.

O Lord, thank you for reminding me of the power of simple acts of kindness. Help me look for ways to show kindness to others in your name. Enable me to treat them as people created in your image, not as inferiors or just as benevolent projects. May Christ live in me and be with me, whatever circumstances I face. In his name I pray. Amen. ❧

Believing the Best

Then Barnabas went to Tarsus to look for Saul, and when he found him, he brought him to Antioch. So for a whole year Barnabas and Saul met with the church and taught great numbers of people.
ACTS 11:25–26

Saul wiped out all the Christians he could find in Jerusalem. When he heard others had fled to Damascus, he obtained official permission to take his persecution there. But on the way, Jesus Christ intercepted Saul, struck him blind, and brought him to faith. Once the Lord restored Saul's sight, the repentant man wanted to proclaim his new commitment to Jesus Christ.

Other Christians didn't believe the tale. They thought Saul was just pretending in order to get inside their close-knit circle of believers, take down their names, and betray them. Barnabas, however, believed in Saul and gave him a chance. When no one else would go near Saul, Barnabas "took him and brought him to the apostles. He told them how Saul on his journey had seen the Lord and that the Lord had spoken to him, and how in Damascus he had preached fearlessly in the name of Jesus" (Acts 9:27).

Had it not been for Barnabas—a humble man with great prestige, highly respected for his burning spirit, dedication, generosity, and love—the Christian church likely would have snubbed Saul. But Barnabas risked his reputation for the man and said of him, in essence, "He's okay."

Later, in Antioch, Barnabas took on Saul as his assistant, and for a year they taught together. Barnabas was the leader, using the time to let Saul learn the details of Christ's life and what Christianity meant. Barnabas believed the best about Saul and became his willing mentor and sponsor. Without a Barnabas, there might never have been a Paul.

And that makes we wonder: Who might God have placed in *your* orbit who needs a friend, mentor, and sponsor?

O Lord, thank you for reminding me how you used Barnabas to establish the early church. Open my eyes to see the "Sauls" among us, who need a friend. Use me, Lord, as you used Barnabas, to encourage others and help them grow strong in the faith. Thank you for using me in this way. I ask these things in the name of my beloved Savior, Jesus Christ. Amen.

Who of Us Can Condemn?

*"Woman, where are they? Has no one condemned you?" "No one,
sir," she said. "Then neither do I condemn you," Jesus declared. "Go
now and leave your life of sin."*
JOHN 8:10 – 11

Rosalynn and I often go to Nigeria. Just before a recent visit, a woman there had committed adultery, which produced a baby. She'd been convicted in a Muslim court and was to be executed. The nation's president, Olusegun Obasanjo, attempted to get the sentence reversed, but without success.

Imagine what would happen if a "prophet," not officially recognized, went into that village in Nigeria and told the woman, "Your sins are forgiven." How startling! What a wave of condemnation it would provoke!

Yet that is what happened in ancient Israel. Trying to test Jesus' revolutionary ways, Jewish religious leaders brought an adulterous woman to him and asked, "What should we do with her?" Under their laws, adultery was punishable by death (at least for the women).

Christ looked down, drew in the sand, and declared, "Let him who is without sin cast the first stone." Beginning with the older men, the observers turned and left, leaving Christ alone with the adulteress. He looked up and said, "Go now and leave your life of sin."

It's easy for us to say, "Well, that's a normal thing to expect of civilized people." But then, it was a shocking deviation from the normal treatment of women. Jesus did not give women special treatment, but divine treatment. God loves mercy more than judgment—and as his followers, so should we.

*O God, give me strength and wisdom to do what I can to eliminate
discrimination, especially against the weak or the needy. Help me
remember that Christ placed them on an equal status with others. Help
me promote justice as I represent my Savior to this world. In his precious
name I pray. Amen.* ❧

A Need for Healing

He called out, "Jesus, Son of David, have mercy on me!"
LUKE 18:38

A blind man who knew very little about Christ heard Jesus was passing by and began crying out, "Son of David!" a reference to the Messiah. In effect, the man said, "Jesus, I know you're the Messiah; have mercy on me!" The healthy people in the crowd yelled at him, "Shut up! Don't bother the prophet." But he continued screaming, "Jesus, have mercy on me!" Jesus knew what the man wanted, but he asked him anyway. And the blind man replied, "I'd like to see again."

In those days, most people thought blindness indicated the victim had committed some terrible sin. So it is likely that this man considered himself desperately alienated from God; but even so, he recognized Jesus—having heard only some rumors about him—as the Messiah. And that gave him hope for his redemption.

And Christ *did* redeem him. Jesus made him whole in more ways than one. The man could see, yes, but more importantly, he also became whole in spirit. This man who a short time before was blind and had been shunted to the back of the crowd became a disciple of Jesus. He believed in the Messiah, followed Jesus all the way back to Jerusalem, and apparently devoted his life to the service of Christ.

We know much more about Jesus Christ than did the blind man. We know that he was born of a virgin, lived a perfect life, healed people, and forgave their sins. We know he raised dead people to life and that he himself was arrested, tried unjustly, crucified, and resurrected from the grave. This is more than enough to recognize who he is. But has it moved us to devote our lives to the service of Christ, as it did the blind man?

O God, I thank you that I don't have to guess about Jesus' identity or depend on rumors to make a judgment about who he is. I know far more than the blind man did, and yet often it seems I am more reluctant to follow Christ than he was. Forgive me this sin, and show me the potential blessings of dedicating my life to his service. In Jesus' name I pray. Amen. ❧

261

Invest Wisely

*"The man who had received five bags of gold went at once and put
his money to work and gained five bags more."*
MATTHEW 25:16

Peanuts have shaped my life. I began working with them when I was five years old. Every day during the growing season, except Sundays, I went into my father's fields, pulled peanuts from the ground, took them home in a little wagon, picked them off the vines, and then put them in salt water. The next morning I'd get up at four o'clock, boil about ten pounds of peanuts, and put them in twenty paper bags. Then I would walk with a full wicker basket down the railroad track about two miles into Plains and sell my peanuts for five cents a bag.

That brought me a dollar a day, a large income for those days — the same that a full-grown man would get for working almost sixteen hours a day. I saved up my money, with my father's guidance, until 1931, when cotton dropped to five cents a pound. I bought five bales and put them in my father's storehouse. A few years later, cotton reached eighteen cents a pound, and I sold mine for a nice profit.

That year the undertaker in Plains, Mr. Ross Dean, died; he left behind five houses. I bought those houses with my money, and from then until I joined the Navy, I collected a total of $18.50 in rent every month. I was fortunate to have a demanding but helpful father — and some good luck.

God gives each of us many opportunities to serve and grow in our Christian lives. Like the servant who invested his five bags of gold and gave a profit to his returning master, so we should use our talents and opportunities wisely to further the kingdom of God — following as closely as possible in the footsteps of Jesus Christ.

O Lord, thank you for reminding me that you expect me to invest what I am and own. Help me remember that while wisely investing earthly possessions is acceptable, it is far more admirable to invest my life in the work of your kingdom. Give me insight into how I may best serve you, and enable me to do so with respect and love for my fellow servants. In Jesus' name I pray. Amen. ❧

Unified in Christ

*Despite their fear of the peoples around them, they built the altar on
its foundation and sacrificed burnt offerings on it to the LORD, both
the morning and evening sacrifices.*

EZRA 3:3

Why did the returning Jews fear their neighbors? Probably these neighbors
saw thousands of Jews returning to Jerusalem, many of them skilled and confident people. They saw these newcomers taking over jobs and running civic
affairs, when for three generations the non-Jews had been in charge. They
also saw that King Cyrus, who now ruled the entire region, seemed to favor
the Jews. All of this made them angry. No wonder the newcomers felt afraid!

We have a similar situation in our country, with foreigners arriving daily.
In America, almost all our families arrived as immigrants, except for Native
Americans. Nevertheless, every generation has an aversion to new people who
arrive, which tends to engender animosity and discrimination toward them.

When I returned home from the White House, Rosalynn and I built a
little cabin in North Georgia. In doing so, we intruded on the people there,
and some of them resented it. But now we ourselves hate to see new people
arrive and build houses around our cabin. And so the old cycle continues.

It was natural for the people who had remained in and around Jerusalem to
resent the Jews returning from exile. Jealousy and animosity divided the citizens within the Holy Land. What might they have accomplished if only they
could have lived in harmony and peace with each other down through the ages!

Today, while I don't think it's particularly damaging to have Christians
who are Episcopalians, Presbyterians, Lutherans, Baptists, Methodists, and
Catholics, sometimes tension and animosity arise between us or even within
denominations. We differ over things that God deems relatively insignificant.
How much more could we accomplish if we could work together harmoniously in a common commitment to God through the new covenant?

*O Lord, all of us have been newcomers, and we all have inherited an
ancient faith. Help me focus on what you deem important and let the
other things fade away. Thank you for giving us a heritage of justice,
peace, humility, service, compassion, and love, and help me demonstrate
my faith in Jesus through my words and actions. Amen.*

263

Don't Ignore Them

"There was a rich man who was dressed in purple and fine linen and lived in luxury every day. At his gate was laid a beggar named Lazarus, covered with sores and longing to eat what fell from the rich man's table. Even the dogs came and licked his sores."

LUKE 16:19 – 21

The rich tend to ignore the poor. I consider this to be one of the most serious problems on earth.

Consider Jesus' story. Did the rich man refuse to give Lazarus food? Not really. We have no record that Lazarus ever begged for food. Did the rich man abuse Lazarus? Not really. The wealthy man worked hard, earned a lot of money, took care of himself, and ignored the beggar at his gate. That's all he did; he ignored Lazarus.

And who are the rich? I would say that rich people these days are those who have a decent home, a moderate amount of education, fairly good health care, and at least the prospect of a job. Rich people are not afraid to go out of their homes, at least in the daytime, and believe that the police and the judicial system are on their side. They generally assume that if they make a decision, it will make a difference.

Poor people, on the other hand, have few (if any) of these things. They lack adequate housing, education, health care, and job opportunities. They live in dangerous neighborhoods and have little reason to believe the police and the laws are on their side. When they make a decision, they doubt it's going to make much difference. And so they lead lives of relative hopelessness.

When you and I stand before God, we are going to have to answer for our behavior. Have we shared our wealth? Have we shared our talents? Have we shared our lives with the poor?

Or have we ignored them?

O Lord, the words of Jesus can make me feel uncomfortable, not necessarily because of what I've done, but because of things I haven't done. Enlarge my heart, make me more generous, and let me find and use opportunities to reach out to those in need, even though they may be very different from me. Help me search for innovative ways to demonstrate faith in my Savior, Jesus, in whose name I pray. Amen.

264

Fallen

*The LORD saw how great the wickedness of the human race had
become on the earth, and that every inclination of the thoughts of the
human heart was only evil all the time.*
GENESIS 6:5

In just a few days of genocide in 1994, more than 500,000 people died in
Rwanda. Rosalynn and I later visited a killing site, a small church with a few
outbuildings.

Tutsi women and children had crowded into this church while their
husbands fled into swamps and woods. The men imagined their families
would be safe in a church. But Hutus killed them all, with axes, spears, and
machetes. Today, visitors see big piles of skulls. Inside the building stand
knee-deep layers of rotting clothes, human hair, and bones. Outside is a deep
hole where several hundred bodies were dumped.

Only one woman survived. She came to the church with a baby in her
arms and one on her back. They killed her two infants, slashed her neck, and
buried her under a pile of corpses. Periodically the killers returned to examine
the bodies, checking to see if any remained alive. She lay still. I spoke with
her at length and asked if she knew who ordered the massacre. Yes, she said,
it was her neighbors who gave the orders, people she had known all her life.

Bible scholars say the human race is "fallen." In practical terms, that
means we all have a staggering capacity for evil. Biblical history reports that
things got so bad that God wiped out the whole race and started over with
Noah and his family.

Let's not deceive ourselves: evil resides within all of us, not just in maraud-
ing Hutus. Only by the grace of God and through the resurrection power of
Jesus can we partner with God to be a force for good in this world. So let us
make that choice—for peace and not war, for love and not hate.

*O God, help me remember that I am born into a human race deeply
infected with sin and that without your grace I am capable of condoning
or committing the vilest acts. May I demonstrate that in Christ all
human divisions can melt away. Make me into a peacemaker and bless
me with your love that I might share it freely. In Jesus' name I pray.
Amen.* ❧

The Worth of an Offering

Jesus said, "Truly I tell you, this poor widow has put more into the treasury than all the others. They all gave out of their wealth; but she, out of her poverty, put in everything—all she had to live on."

MARK 12:43 – 44

During her time in India in the Peace Corps, my mother worked in Vikhroli, a village near Mumbai. About twelve thousand people lived there, a place owned entirely by the Godrej family, one of the wealthiest in India.

Mama was assigned to help with family planning, but because she disagreed with policies like male sterilization, she wanted to work in the local clinic. Whenever Mr. Godrej came to the clinic, the doctor would bow down and kiss his hands or feet. But Mama went right to him and said, "I want you to let me help treat sick people who come to the clinic."

Mr. Godrej agreed on three conditions. First, Mama had to continue working with family planning. Second, she had to provide any extra medicine needed. And third, she had to get approval from the doctor.

So Mama worked two jobs but had no money to buy medicine. She told the Park-Davis pharmaceutical salesman, "I know Mr. Park and Mr. Davis very well, and if you'll give me as many of your free samples as possible, I'll write my good friends and tell them what a wonderful job you're doing here." The salesman agreed. When the Ely Lilly salesman came by, she told him, "My son Jimmy went to school with Mr. Ely Lilly's grandson, and Jimmy is a good friend of the family." She got all the medicine she needed.

That's how my mother operated. She had no money, but she gave what she had—and then some. She wrote us children that she asked God's forgiveness for lying and believed her prayer was answered.

O God, I'm grateful that you take my little and multiply it into something significant. But I also realize that my "little" is what most of the rest of the world would consider "much." So give me the generosity of spirit of the poor woman whom Jesus watched in the temple, and use me and my resources to bless others. For I pray in Christ's name. Amen. ❧

266

Are We Willing?

So Abraham called that place The LORD Will Provide. And to this
day it is said, "On the mountain of the LORD it will be provided."
GENESIS 22:14

I've wondered about the words "The Lord will provide." Many people use the phrase to excuse themselves from responsibility for taking care of those in need. This doesn't seem right.

We can say the Lord provides for the more fortunate people in Europe and America, but when I visit Liberia, where over half the people live on less than fifty cents a day, I see what it's like to live in abject poverty. It's hard to understand how the needs of *these* people are provided.

When we ride down the streets of Monrovia, Liberia's capital, we see twice as many churches as on the street of any town in the Bible Belt of America. Liberians are deeply religious people, but they have overwhelming unmet needs.

So if it is true that the Lord will provide, then how do we explain the circumstances in Liberia? We can't say those people are poor because it's part of God's plan for people to starve and to have no education or health care.

The explanation, I believe, is that the Lord provides for the world as a whole; from the earth's bounties we have plentiful food for everyone and enough resources to meet basic needs. So if the rich people are stingy and won't share with the poor, is that God's fault?

We can't sit back and rationalize that if many people in the world are sick and hungry and destitute, it's none of our concern—because God will provide. We have a responsibility as Christians to do what we can to meet the needs of these people. God wants to meet their needs through us. Are we willing to share with them?

O Lord, I'm grateful that you provide—not only for my physical needs,
but also that you give me opportunities to join with you in meeting the
needs of impoverished and suffering people around the world. Help me
emulate, as best I can, the words and actions of my Savior, and to do
so in a spirit of unity, humility, justice, and love. I pray in Jesus' name.
Amen. ❧

267

One Little Snowball

*And we all, who with unveiled faces contemplate the Lord's glory, are
being transformed into his image with ever-increasing glory, which
comes from the Lord.*
2 CORINTHIANS 3:18

What is transformation? If we freeze water into ice, that is a transformation.
If we mill a tree into boards and use them to build a house, that is a transformation.
If we form clay into a human image or into bricks and build a wall,
that is a transformation.

And if God takes sinful human beings and turns them into Christians,
that is a miraculous transformation. That's not an easy thing for us to absorb.
We can envision all kinds of mundane, routine transformations; but it's a
different proposition when we start talking about human beings. A transformation
is a total change in form. Paul says a Christian assumes the image of
our Lord!

Almost two thousand years ago, Jesus Christ brought about a transformation
of the relationship between human beings and God, and among human
beings. He died on the cross and rose from the dead so that we could become
new creatures in him. Calvary was a revolutionary, transforming event.

Now consider today's American society. Do we see things that might warrant
transformation? I can imagine a lot of things: being champions of peace;
ending homelessness; alleviating hunger; improving the criminal justice system.
But unless we citizens are willing to transform our own lives so that we
actively pursue those things, our society will see no great transformation. We
will not see the teachings of our Savior, Jesus Christ, lived out in our culture.

The beauty of a democracy is that if even one person — maybe you or
me — steps out in faith to begin such a transformation, it can have a tremendous
impact on others. Substantial reforms have a way of snowballing — but
most of them begin with a very small snowball.

Are you willing to pick up some snow?

*Lord, I tend to think of transformation only in theoretical or theological
terms. I use words such as regeneration, justification, or sanctification and
never realize how you might want me to be an agent of transformation.
Help me be the hands and feet of Jesus, and inspire me to partner with
you in transforming nonbelievers into images of Christ. I ask this in the
name of my Savior. Amen.* ❦

268

A Peaceful Export

And he will be called Wonderful Counselor, Mighty God,
Everlasting Father, Prince of Peace.
ISAIAH 9:6

Peace between nations, the absence of war—it's a dream that seems perpetually out of reach. But does that mean we should abandon its pursuit?

As followers of the Prince of Peace, we are responsible for making peace. God has given us freedom, and it is up to us how we use it. Will we use our liberty to pursue peace? I was able to do so while president, but unfortunately, the United States now seems committed to wars that often seem unnecessary.

To bring peace requires that citizens follow the example set by Jesus during his earthly ministry. Did Christ take up weapons to kill or maim? Was his heart filled with hatred toward people who disagreed with him? We know the answer is no.

Through his death and resurrection, Jesus brings peace to the hearts of those who commit their lives to him in faith. As hate and violence were not in his character, neither should they be in ours, as his spiritual children. He calls upon us, with God's help, to take the peace he has placed inside our hearts and export it to others who need it as badly as we do. That peace comes from a close, personal relationship with Jesus Christ, and it is not simply the absence of war. It brings a deep conviction that things are right between God and us and prompts feelings of joy, freedom, companionship, and fulfillment.

Isaiah had all this in mind when he called Jesus Christ the "Prince of Peace." Through faith in him, all of us have the opportunity to experience that peace in our own hearts. And also through faith, we have the privilege of exporting that peace to others.

O Lord, thank you for sending your only Son, that through his life, death,
and resurrection I might be reconciled with you. Thank you for teaching
me how to exchange my ordinary existence for one of excitement and
transcendence. I am grateful to know that with you all things are possible.
Draw me nearer to you through my Savior, Jesus Christ, in whose name I
pray. Amen. ❧

269

Wisdom from Heaven

The wisdom that comes from heaven is first of all pure; then peace-loving,
considerate, submissive, full of mercy and good fruit, impartial and sincere.
Peacemakers who sow in peace reap a harvest of righteousness.
JAMES 3:17 – 18

James describes two kinds of wisdom. One is selfish and secular and belongs to individuals with superb intelligence but who use their brains for their own self-interest. In effect, they become nothing more than shrewd criminals. James says that this leads to "disorder and every evil practice" (James 3:16).

The second form of wisdom comes from above. James says that sowing peace raises a harvest of righteousness, thus associating heavenly wisdom with peacemaking.

Christians profess to worship the Prince of Peace, but too often many are in the forefront of advocating and exalting warfare. I suffered politically during the Iranian hostage crisis by not striking Iran with our dominant military force. Much later, prominent Christians were among the strongest supporters of America's unwarranted 2003 invasion of Iraq. Too many of us have the same attitude in personal relationships.

If we want to be wise in heaven's estimation, then we should seek peaceful solutions to conflicting interests and avoid speaking harshly or falsely of others or condemning them. Instead, we must forgive our neighbors, just as God forgives us, and not allow hatred to take up residence in our hearts.

The best way to be a peacemaker is to emulate the life of Jesus Christ so our actions will exhibit his character and effectively serve God. As Christians, we have, in effect, taken an oath before God to do this very thing. So let each of us take time every day to examine our actions and priorities and continually try to reorder them so they more closely echo the perfect example of Jesus Christ. Since it is human nature to forget this, we must make an extra effort to remember it.

O God, give me courage to look within my own heart so I might measure
my performance in life against the perfect standard set for me by my
Savior. Give me the will to make whatever changes are necessary to reflect
the character and behavior of our Lord Jesus, the Prince of Peace. It is in
his name I pray. Amen. ❧

270

Peace among Abraham's Sons

*They will beat their swords into plowshares and their spears into
pruning hooks. Nation will not take up sword against nation, nor
will they train for war anymore.*
MICAH 4:3

During my presidency, three devout men met for peace talks at Camp David:
Menachem Begin, a Jew; Anwar Sadat, a Muslim; and me, a Christian. Sadat
had a brown spot in the middle of his forehead where, since childhood, he
had knelt down and put his forehead on the floor to pray. During our thirteen days of private sessions, we often worried that we would not succeed.
Sadat asked us to remember that all of us were children of Abraham, bound
together by much more than what divided us. He said this repeatedly, in
the process making Prime Minister Begin a little nervous. But his attitude
impressed me very much.

On Fridays, Saturdays, and Sundays, all three faiths used the same little
room for worship. We had to change it multiple times every week, so the
Muslims and then the Jews and then the Christians could worship. Today a
chapel has been built at Camp David for that purpose. Sadat wanted to see
a common meeting place built on Mount Sinai, and had he not been assassinated a few months after I left the White House, I think his plans would
have borne fruit. Sadat always made it plain that Muslim believers revered
Moses and Jesus Christ and that Christians and Jews were accepted in the
Muslim faith as "children of the book."

Although we have deep convictions about Christianity, we still have much
in common with those of other faiths. We should try to live peaceably with
them in a spirit of friendship, exhibiting the admirable attitude of Sadat during the peace talks at Camp David, where he made a big effort to find common ground with both Begin and me.

We Christians need to emphasize the teachings of the Prince of Peace.

*O Lord, I'm thankful for the opportunities you give us to come together in
diversity—people of different beliefs and attitudes toward life—trying
to find common purposes that encourage us to live in harmony. Teach
us to live in peace, exhibiting mutual respect and friendship and always
striving to demonstrate my commitment to Jesus Christ. I ask these things
in his name. Amen.* ❧

Humility and Peace

As they approached Jerusalem and came to Bethphage and Bethany at the
Mount of Olives, Jesus sent two of his disciples, saying to them, "Go to the
village ahead of you, and just as you enter it, you will find a colt tied there,
which no one has ever ridden. Untie it and bring it here."

MARK 11:1–2

We don't know whether finding this donkey on the outskirts of Jerusalem reflects Jesus' ability to know everything or whether he had made prior arrangements. I presume he just knew how it would all work out. In any event, the disciples followed Jesus' command, entered Bethphage, saw this colt, untied it, and brought it to him.

What is the significance of a donkey? A donkey is not, in itself, a symbol of peace. But great leaders like Charlemagne, Caesar, or Napoleon don't choose to ride a donkey into the capital city of a conquered nation. They instead mount a big white stallion, looking every inch a fierce warrior. For Jesus, a leader, to ride on a little donkey indicated humility and peace. It said, "I've come here not as a conquering hero, but as God's messenger who brings new instruction on how to live."

It probably surprised people, because they had heard about the miracles Christ performed and had been waiting for a Messiah whom they hoped would free them from their Roman overlords. They envisioned not only a religious leader, but also a secular leader and a powerful warrior, someone like King David, who would reestablish the Israelites as a powerful and dominant people.

Jesus, however, came on a donkey. And he said to the people (and to us), "Will you join my kingdom of peace?" Do we, as Christians, promote peace or war?

O God, thank you that Jesus is the promised Messiah, the Son of God,
present at the creation of the universe. I celebrate my Lord as a humble
lover of peace, whose life also epitomized justice, service, forgiveness,
compassion, and love. May these characteristics describe me as a Chris-
tian, as I serve Jesus in my daily life. I pray in Jesus' name. Amen. ❧

Make Peace

"Blessed are the peacemakers,
for they will be called children of God."
MATTHEW 5:9

During thirteen difficult days, Prime Minister Menachem Begin of Israel, President Anwar Sadat of Egypt, and I worked at Camp David to negotiate a historic peace agreement. When we returned to Washington, I was invited to address a special session of the U.S. Congress.

I had no time to develop a lengthy speech, but I decided on the way to the Capitol to quote Matthew 5:9. I wanted to say, "Blessed are the peacemakers," but I couldn't remember what came next. So I called for a Bible to be waiting for me when I got out of the limousine. Upon my arrival, a staff member slipped me a piece of paper that said, "for they will be called children of God." I repeated it as I asked Sadat and Begin to stand.

Peacemakers are very special people. They have to understand and sympathize with others who have differing points of view. Begin and Sadat's countries had been at war four times during the previous twenty-five years. They hated each other. I kept the two men apart for their last ten days at Camp David because they couldn't sit in the same room without all the old animosities coming out.

Peacemakers have to empathize with both sides, even though both sides can't be completely right. Through common trust, understanding, and flexibility, they must find a way to get both sides to come together. They must make sure that every time one side gives up something, they can expect to get something more important at the end. And finally, both sides must win. If one side loses and the other wins, the peace will not last.

Every Christian faces altercations or arguments that can degenerate into animosity or misunderstanding. But if we choose to be peacemakers — if we choose to act as children of God — then we can make a positive difference for good, as did the Prince of Peace.

Dear Lord, help me, as a Christian, realize that peacemaking is my
heritage as a child of God. Help me remember that as a follower of Christ
I must let my voice and my actions be used to strengthen your kingdom
on earth, by the power of the Holy Spirit. I ask these things in my Savior's
name. Amen.

A Precious Gift

Whoever would foster love covers over an offense.
PROVERBS 17:9

One year on August 18, I got up very early to continue writing a book. I went into my study, turned on my computer, and hit the button that displays the date. When the date came on the screen, I yelled, "Oh no!"

It was Rosalynn's birthday, and somehow I had forgotten it. I didn't have a present for her.

I quickly tried to think of what I could give her that I wouldn't have to go downtown to buy. I began to think of some things that tended to cause us trouble in our marriage, to see if I could use one of them. I realized that one thing we had argued about for thirty-five years involved my fierce commitment to punctuality. My father was a stickler for being on time, and this was further ingrained in me through my years in the Navy. Basically, if somebody is just a few minutes late, I get uptight. And if *I'm* the one who's late, I get even more uneasy. Over the years, Rosalynn and I have had a lot of arguments caused by this obsession of mine. She will claim that she has never been really late, and I have to admit that she's usually punctual.

Anyway, I wrote a note to Rosalynn that said, "I promise that I will never make another unfavorable comment about tardiness." Then I signed it and gave it to her for her birthday present. Rosalynn says that was the best birthday present I ever gave her. And so far, I've kept my promise—with difficulty.

Sometimes the most valuable gifts cost no money at all—like a commitment to promote peace, harmony, and reconciliation. The stores in Plains don't have these in stock, but they are always available through the Spirit of Christ.

O Lord, teach me how to correct my mistakes in order to love others in ways that promote peace and reconciliation. Remind me of Christ's words that the greatest among us will be the servants of all. Give me humility and bind us together in Christian love, I pray, in Jesus' name. Amen. ❧

Come Together for Joy

We proclaim to you what we have seen and heard, so that you also may
have fellowship with us. And our fellowship is with the Father and
with his Son, Jesus Christ. We write this to make our joy complete.
I JOHN 1:3 – 4

Although the Bible calls followers of Christ to come together in unity, the
Christian church today is plagued with increasing divisions, arguments, and
schisms. Within my own denomination, the Southern Baptist Convention,
we see sharp differences that often incite people to animosity, vituperation,
and a lack of grace, forgiveness, and mutual love. Even my own church, Maranatha Baptist, split off from its mother church—where I was baptized—over
the volatile issue of race relations. Fortunately, in Plains we still have a lot of
harmony, goodwill, and Christian fellowship between members of the two
Baptist churches, and also among Christians of other denominations. But
such is not always the case elsewhere.

John wrote his first epistle when the early church started to divide over
a developing heresy that, in its fuller form, was called Gnosticism. Gnostics
believed that physical existence was by nature sinful and that, consequently,
Christ could not be both human and divine at the same time. They taught,
therefore, that Christ must be purely spirit. John decided to write this letter
not only to clarify the essence of the Christian faith and refute the Gnostic
mistake, but also to emphasize the importance of unity and fellowship among
believers in Christ as Savior.

Today as then, Jesus calls Christians to come together in a spirit of unity,
forgiveness, love, and service. In so doing, we become bound more intimately
with God the Creator and his Son, Jesus Christ, and our joy can be made
complete. John reminds us that no matter what differences exist among us,
we must always strive for unity in Christian fellowship.

Lord, we are blessed that we can come together throughout the world to
praise you in harmony and unity as we study your Holy Word. I thank
you for all people who gather in your name and for the communities and
families they represent. May what we do and say bring you honor and glory.
This I ask in the name of Jesus Christ, our Lord and Savior. Amen.

PART 4
𝕸 MATURING 𝕾

More than anything else, this troubled world needs the active influence of mature Christians. This is the best possible avenue for the influence of Jesus Christ to be felt within the complex structure of our modern secular society. Those of us who worship Christ are familiar with the human and practical ways that Jesus promoted peace, justice, freedom, basic human rights, forgiveness of others, and the alleviation of suffering. This healing ministry would address the vast array of problems that afflict the world. This banner can best be raised and carried by mature Christians.

We Christians are taught to forgo personal benefit at the expense of others and to engage and understand people who differ from us, who often suffer from discrimination, abuse, isolation, and neglect. Either as public servants or as private citizens, we can accommodate the admonition of Jesus to "render unto Caesar the things that are Caesar's and unto God the things that are God's." We have to confront serious and sensitive challenges in melding private and public life, but with Christian maturity comes the ability to accommodate such conflicting pressures with wisdom and sound judgment.

Strengthened by constant consultation with God through prayer, mature Christians persevere in overcoming obstacles and take advantage of every possible opportunity to effect beneficial changes in our own lives and among those around us. God also challenges us to expand the boundaries of our personal influence. "From everyone who has been given much," Jesus said, "much will be demanded" (Luke 12:48).

In this section we'll investigate how to give God our best, to adopt high priorities, to maintain self-confidence without pride or arrogance, to magnify our influence by working with others, and to continue building a foundation of faith under the influence of the Holy Spirit.

God offers reassurance to all those who accept the responsibilities of spiritual maturity, who are "being strengthened with all power according to his glorious might so that they may have great endurance and patience" (Colossians 1:11).

Why Not the Best?

Give ear and come to me; listen, that you may live. I will make an
everlasting covenant with you, my faithful love promised to David.
ISAIAH 55:3

As a young naval officer I received an invitation from Admiral Hyman Rickover, the "father of the nuclear Navy," to be interviewed for a job. The admiral was a small Jewish man who came to America from Poland. He was, arguably, the best engineer of all time. He had a stern reputation, so I worried about the appointment.

He sat behind a desk while I sat in a straight chair in front of him. (I learned later that the front two legs had been shortened.) He asked me question after question, and I soon discovered that he knew more about any topic than I did. Every time, he would ask one more question that I couldn't answer.

Finally, at the end of the interview he asked, "How did you do in your class at Annapolis?" I breathed a sigh of relief as I described how I had done quite well. He looked at me with cold eyes and asked, "Did you do your best?" I remembered all the times when I could have studied more or learned more and instead read novels or listened to music. I started to say, "Yes, sir," but finally replied, "No, sir, I didn't always do my best." He looked at me a long time and finally asked, "Why not?" Then he turned his chair around to end the interview.

I thought I had failed, but later he chose me for the job, possibly because I told the truth. But I've never been able to forget the admiral's last question: "Why not the best?" That question has changed my life.

Christ set for us a perfect example of actions and words, and he asks us today, "Have you always done your best?" The answer is up to each of us.

Why not the best?

O Lord, I'm grateful for these ancient words from Isaiah. They remind me
of the truths of life, the decisions I make day by day. Help me tie them all
together and set for myself a standard of excellence that will be acceptable
in the eyes of my Savior, Jesus Christ, in whose name I pray. Amen. ❧

Go for It!

No one knows what is coming—
who can tell someone else what will happen after them?
ECCLESIASTES 10:14

When we profess faith in Christ, we proclaim Christ as our master and guide. We promise to serve Jesus, and most of us really mean it. And yet, so often, we hesitate. We wait for a better time to serve him, the perfect time.

"Well," we say, "I have to take care of myself a little bit right now. I need to build up my bank account so we don't have to worry about next month. After we get the kids through college and after we shore up our business, and after we pay off our house, then we can *really* serve Jesus. Someday, when we become empty nesters, or retire, or receive an expected inheritance, *then* we'll have the time to keep our promises to Christ. *Then* we'll be really good Christians. But we have to get these other things out of the way first."

Much to the contrary, the writer of Ecclesiastes tells us, "Don't wait until everything is perfect before you act. Be bold. Even before the perfect time comes, go ahead and do something. You can't keep waiting until everything gets just exactly right. You have to take a chance."

So go for it. Set big goals. Take a chance. It's better to fail striving for something that's wonderful, challenging, and adventurous than to timidly sit around and say, "I don't want to try for that, because I may not succeed. I can't risk failure."

So go ahead. Stretch your life. Stretch your heart. Stretch your mind. Take a chance. Be bold. Be adventurous. Build your life as best you can, even in the midst of life's uncertainties and unknowable facts. Serve Christ audaciously, in your own way, without trepidation. Count on God's promises—and then go for it.

God, let me start off today on the right foot by realizing that when I fully and wholeheartedly follow you and your teachings, I can enjoy a freer, more gratifying, joyful, and complete life than is possible in any other way. Forgive me my sins of foolish timidity and lack of faith in you and in myself, and bind me together with my Savior, Jesus Christ, through the Holy Spirit. In Jesus' name I pray. Amen. ❧

Our Highest Loyalty?

I gave the same message to Zedekiah king of Judah. I said, "Bow
your neck under the yoke of the king of Babylon; serve him and his
people, and you will live."
JEREMIAH 27:12

As I wrote in my novel, *The Hornet's Nest*, some colonials found it difficult to take up arms in the American Revolution. They had been British subjects all their lives and by rebelling would violate their oaths of loyalty to the king.

Likewise, during the Civil War some sincere people in the North thought only loose bonds tied the states together. They thought of each state as sovereign and believed that a central government had no right to impose unwanted laws upon them.

For a long time, I thought our top elected officials were telling the truth about the Vietnam War. Only when I became governor did I begin to see that the American people were being misled. My oldest son, Jack, considered the draft unfair because anybody who could afford college could avoid conscription. On principle, he quit school and went to serve in Vietnam. In the middle of the conflict, people had to decide where their loyalties lay.

God told Jeremiah to command Israel's leaders to accept the sovereignty of Babylon—news that few wanted to hear. For faithfully delivering God's message, Jeremiah was considered a coward, a traitor, and a false prophet by many Israelites.

That is not unlike what happened to Martin Luther King Jr. when he condemned racial segregation. He was arrested and imprisoned, and many white people in the South considered him a communist and a traitor. Yet despite overwhelming opposition, Dr. King remained true to his convictions and continued to act on his beliefs.

We must all make difficult choices—at times even between popularity within our society and loyalty to God. We must choose between peace and war, justice and prejudice, forgiveness and animosity. May we always follow Jeremiah's example. Let us choose the words of Jesus!

Lord, I know Jeremiah was the "bringer of bad news" and that the
message was yours, for the well-being of your chosen people. I also bear
a message, given to me by my Savior, Jesus Christ, so help me deliver it
faithfully. Forgive my sins and bind me together with other believers in
Christian love. I ask these things in the name of my Savior. Amen. ❦

Distractions

Therefore, since we are surrounded by such a great cloud of witnesses, let us throw off everything that hinders and the sin that so easily entangles.
HEBREWS 12:1

One of the most famous Baptists in history was Dwight L. Moody. Once when Moody was teaching on Hebrews 12:1, he came to the pulpit with a big, heavy pack on his back, maybe seventy-five pounds. The weight bent him over, and he started to preach. Everybody in the congregation soon grew concerned about the big burden on Moody's back. Finally he stopped and said, "You see, it's hard for me to preach to you while I've got this big load on my back. I'll take it off so I can devote my full time and attention to God's Word."

Then he took off the pack and opened it. Inside were not ugly, sinful things, but food and clothing and books, one of which was a Bible. And Moody said, "The point I want to make is that even the good things in your life, if you exalt them too much, can prevent your total commitment to a Christian life."

Normally when we list the kinds of things that distract us, we first think of sinful things—and that's not incorrect. The passage does tell us to put aside sinfulness. But as Moody noted, that's not the limit of what can distract us. Good things too can become impediments.

If we want to be a fine teacher or an excellent lawyer or a successful businessman or a good farmer or mechanic or nurse, that's fine. There's nothing wrong with that. But if we let our ambition for any of those things interfere with our commitment to Christ—to living out the words and actions of Jesus—then that ambition is a burden that could consume us.

Let's make sure nothing interferes with our commitment to Jesus Christ!

O God, thank you for the reminders and the promises of Scripture, especially that they still apply to me today—they are just as alive now as they were two thousand years ago! I ask you to embed in my heart and mind the lesson of Hebrews 12:1 so that I might live in accordance with the simple precepts given to me by my Savior, Jesus Christ. In his name I pray. Amen.

279

Friends and Adulterers

You adulterous people, don't you know that friendship with the
world means enmity against God?
JAMES 4:4

James wrote these scathing words to Christians, not to pagans—to church-going people, not to church-avoiding people. And yet he called these Christian, churchgoing people "adulterers." Why?

Apparently these people had decided to focus their lives on personal power, possessions, influence, and their own well-being. That made them adulterers in James's estimation because Christians are married to Jesus Christ and Jesus represents heavenly things: justice, peace, service, humility, generosity. When believers give their top allegiance to worldly things—to money or fame or power or authority or influence—they become adulterers because they have betrayed their marriage to Christ.

A Christian man can't be married and remain wishy-washy about remaining loyal to his wife. He can't say, "Well, I'll be loyal to a point; but if I meet some other woman at the office or on the street that I like as well or better, then maybe I'll align myself with her." That's obviously wrong; but many of us do just that in our relationship with Jesus. I know I have.

Each of us must make the unnatural choice to strive against our inborn tendency to pursue the world's attractions. Instead, we must work hard to become more intimately entwined with the life of Jesus Christ.

James spoke so bluntly because he wanted to get through to self-satisfied Christians. He knew that such followers of Jesus would read or hear his words, and he wanted to declare they had missed the point. If we think we're okay being mediocre or lukewarm Christians, then we haven't understood what *Christian* means. Lukewarm Christians are close friends of the world, which is why James calls them adulterers. Let us strive to avoid that kind of life!

Dear Lord, the words of James can often sound very personal and harsh,
but they also are enlightening. I know that he declared your wisdom and
that if I follow his prescription for life I will find gratifying and happy
solutions to the difficult circumstances confronting me. Give me courage
to look at myself honestly and then follow the unerring guidance of Jesus
Christ. In his name I pray. Amen. 🦎

280

No Secrets

*You have searched me, LORD, and you know me. You know when I
sit and when I rise; you perceive my thoughts from afar. You discern
my going out and my lying down; you are familiar with all my ways.*
PSALM 139:1 – 3

Have you ever done anything that still makes you feel ashamed, even though
no one else knows about it — not your husband or wife, not even your priest
or pastor? Do you have a dark or unsavory secret that you guard carefully? It
may be about some foolish thing you did, quite out of character; something
that could be called an anomaly, a deviation from the way you were raised,
an unplanned but serious mistake. Maybe you responded improperly to some
fleeting event. Maybe it's about some trouble you got into as a teenager, and
even decades later, no one else knows about it.

The psalmist reminds us that God knows all about it. No matter what
we do, no matter where we are, God knows everything about us. God knows
our innermost thoughts and the immoral actions we've seriously considered,
even if we finally decided against doing them. How sobering to realize that
nothing we do remains unknown to God!

The next time you pray, it may be helpful to say, "God, I want to confront
and confess what I did as a teenager; I'm sorry it happened, and I have turned
away from it. I repent and I ask for your forgiveness." Whatever your secret
might be, you can confront it with God, through prayer, and lingering guilt
will be erased.

God knows what you've done, why you did it, and all the circumstances
surrounding it. One of the great advantages of prayer is that you can always
be perfectly honest and frank with God. He will guide you to take any further action necessary to assuage any harm done to others. You can then be
clean and forgiven.

*O God, how foolish I am when I try to hide anything from you, for your
Word teaches me that no secret can remain hidden from you. Give me
courage to confront what I would like to remain concealed, and give me
strength to move out of darkness and come boldly and humbly into your
glorious light. I pray these things in the name of Jesus. Amen.* ❧

Showered with Heaven's Bounty

"Blessed are the poor in spirit, for theirs is the kingdom of heaven."
MATTHEW 5:3

In our world, the terms *blessed* and *poor* don't often go together, do they? And yet Christ insists that the "poor in spirit" are in fact "blessed." What does he mean?

The "poor in spirit" feel within themselves a personal inadequacy, or humility. They don't believe their own mental and physical abilities are adequate to face life and all its challenges. Since they gladly depend on God, they willingly submit their thought processes and establishment of life's priorities to the will of God, as best they understand it.

The "rich in spirit," on the other hand, more closely resemble the Pharisees, who convinced themselves they had all the answers. They were not unlike some religious leaders in our world today, who take upon themselves the role of authority in spiritual matters. They say, in essence, "This is my detailed interpretation of the Scriptures, and I expect all believers to accept it. Anyone who doesn't accept my interpretation is violating God's laws, and therefore inferior and to be condemned." We see an extreme example of this attitude among the Taliban in Afghanistan, but the tendency toward extremism occurs in our own faith as well.

The poor in spirit have no desire to assume such an arrogant attitude of superiority. They don't claim to have all the answers but instead go humbly to God and say, "Lord, I know I *don't* have all the answers. My life depends upon a proper relationship with you, and that means I am your servant, not your advisor. So lead me where you will."

The poor in spirit joyfully submit themselves to heavenly authority and through humble, persistent prayer commit themselves to doing God's will. Not being filled with pride and arrogance makes them "blessed" and inheritors of the kingdom of heaven.

Lord, give me an open heart and help me realize that these words of Jesus apply not only to his disciples two thousand years ago, but also to me today. As I relate to others, cause me to look inside my heart and soul to see what I am and what I ought to be. Give me wisdom and courage to apply this beatitude to my life. I ask these things in Jesus' name. Amen. ❧

What Really Counts?

Then some Pharisees and teachers of the law came to Jesus from
Jerusalem and asked, "Why do your disciples break the tradition of the
elders? They don't wash their hands before they eat!" Jesus replied, "And
why do you break the command of God for the sake of your tradition?"
MATTHEW 15:1 – 3

A traveling salesman visited a rural community and stopped at the country store for a drink. When he looked out the window, he saw two beautiful churches on a hill, although few people lived in that region. He said to the store owner, "Since this is Georgia, I'm sure one of them is Baptist and the other Methodist." But the man answered, "No, they're both Baptist."

"So what's the difference between them?" the salesman wondered aloud.

"There's a profound theological difference," the store owner replied. "One of them says, 'There ain't no hell,' and the other one says, 'The hell there ain't!'"

As Jesus emphasized to the Pharisees, we should never become so immersed in arguments over individual Bible verses that we start revering certain Scriptures instead of worshiping Jesus Christ. Mandatory creeds or biblical analyses, even if written by the finest scholars, can't substitute for a free and personal relationship with God Almighty. We all have a tendency to substitute creeds for relationships, and this tends to drive large wedges between Christians who have small differences of opinion.

Unfortunately, theological divisions have sapped a major portion of the church's missionary purpose. An overwhelming portion of religious news concerns the interpretation of Scripture about important issues: treatment of homosexuals, the death penalty, the authority of pastors, the priesthood of believers, and the role of women. All too often, arguments create disunity and disrupt essential ministries of the church.

We should forgo the arguments and animosity and instead work in harmony under the basic premise that "God so loved the world that he gave his one and only Son, that whoever believes in him shall not perish but have eternal life." We are all saved by the grace of God through faith in Jesus Christ—and by committing ourselves to that truth, we can avoid not only arguments about hell, but hell itself.

My gracious Lord, help me reach out to fellow Christians in a spirit of
humility and love, seeking to find the common ground on which we can
stand together in following the example and mandates of our Savior. I ask
this in his holy name. Amen. ❧

283

Obsessions

Hannah was praying in her heart, and her lips were moving but her voice was not heard.
I SAMUEL I:13

I grew up with an obsession: to attend college. My father implanted this desire in my mind from an early age. Until then, no one in Daddy's family had finished high school, let alone college. Daddy had completed the tenth grade and was well educated for his time, but he had higher aspirations for me, and I became committed to the goal. This was during the Great Depression, so financing was a major problem.

At that time, America had only two free colleges: West Point and Annapolis. I chose the latter. If anyone asked me at six years of age to name my life's goal, I would have repeated, like a parrot, "I want to go to Annapolis." In early high school I practically memorized the academy's entrance catalogs, which caused me some concern. Recruits could not have flat feet, for example, so I spent many hours examining the bottoms of my feet and rolling a Coca-Cola bottle back and forth to build up my arches. "Urine retention" was another disqualifier. I didn't know what that meant, but it worried me. I feared I would finally get to the Naval Academy, only to have the doctor say, "We're sorry, but you must return to Plains. You've retained some of your urine."

Hannah, an ancient Israelite, also had an obsession: she longed for a son. Childless for many years and in despair, she finally visited the temple, crying out to God and vowing that if she could have a son, he would be dedicated to God's service. God answered her prayers and gave her Samuel. Hannah honored her promise, leaving Samuel to live and serve at the temple with the high priest, Eli.

Obsessions can be healthy or unhealthy, but involving God in all we do ensures that our desires are proper ... and then great things can happen.

O Lord, your Word tells us that you love to give us the desires of our heart, so make my most basic desire a longing to draw near to you. Let all my obsessions be compatible with your will, and help me immerse myself as completely as possible into a constant communion with Jesus Christ, my beloved Savior. In his name I pray. Amen.

Bandar's Place

*David burned with anger against the man and said to Nathan, "As
surely as the LORD lives, the man who did this must die!" ... Then
Nathan said to David, "You are the man!"*
2 SAMUEL 12:5, 7

Have you ever encountered individuals who seemed more than willing to give
a blunt assessment of you? I have. Quite often they are my grandchildren,
who have no inclination to tell me what they think I want to hear; instead,
they tell me what they believe.

Rosalynn and I took up skiing at an advanced age. Our friend Prince
Bandar, the Saudi Arabian ambassador to Washington, let us use his ski lodge
overlooking Aspen's beautiful slopes. We took our grandchildren, and Bandar's place amazed them. It had an indoor swimming pool, many servants,
wonderful food, and a game room for the kids. One morning at breakfast,
one of my grandchildren, Jeremy—a particularly outspoken child—said in
a loud, piping voice, "Papa, are you going to die someday?"

My heart pounded with pleasure. Here was my little grandson, worried
about his papa's health! I replied, "Well, yes, sweet boy, everybody's going
to die someday. I hope it won't be anytime soon, though." A deathly silence
followed, and I couldn't wait to hear Jeremy's follow-up. Finally, he asked,
"Papa, when you die, can we still come to Bandar's place?"

Jeremy's blunt comment reminds me of the prophet Nathan when he confronted King David over his adultery and murder. Nathan first intrigued
David with a moving story, got him emotionally involved with the outcome,
and then lowered the boom. David sincerely repented, but just as easily he
could have become angry and killed Nathan. It took real courage for Nathan
to deliver God's harsh message to the king.

Likewise, we should be courageous in accepting the harsh and difficult
commands of Jesus, even if it means supporting convictions that may not be
popular in today's world.

*Dear Lord, give me a firm commitment to the sometimes difficult truths
that characterize the teachings of Jesus Christ. Help me speak the truth in
love, and grant me courage to espouse peace wherever I go. Make me into
an effective ambassador, desiring more than anything else to serve you well
as I seek to bless others in Jesus' name. I pray in his holy name. Amen.* ❧

Ignore the Scoffers

*Above all, you must understand that in the last days scoffers will
come, scoffing and following their own evil desires. They will say,
"Where is this 'coming' he promised? Ever since our ancestors died,
everything goes on as it has since the beginning of creation."*

· 2 PETER 3:3 — 4

Many people in the early church thought Christ was going to return to earth
in their lifetime. Some of them, it seemed, prayed that Jesus would come
back and be among them next month or before next Christmas—and their
prayers went unanswered. When this happened, scoffers mocked *any* belief
in Christ's return. This disturbed Peter very much.

In response, Peter wrote to believers, telling them, "Do not forget this one
thing, dear friends: With the Lord a day is like a thousand years, and a thousand years are like a day. The Lord is not slow in keeping his promise, as some
understand slowness. Instead he is patient with you, not wanting anyone to
perish, but everyone to come to repentance" (2 Peter 3:8–9). Jesus said that
no one could know the time of his return, not even him (Matthew 24:36).

In other words, it is not up to human beings to set or predict a time for
the millennium to come or for Jesus to return to earth. The reason Christ
has not returned and brought an end to this present world is because God is
patient. God wants to leave more time for people to be saved, to give everyone
a chance to know the saving grace of Jesus Christ.

Although it may seem like a long time since Jesus promised to return, to
God it's not a long time at all. We shouldn't allow scoffers who ridicule our
belief in the second coming to discourage us. Instead, let's remain strong in
our faith and trust that God knows the best time for everything.

*O God, you make it clear that maintaining hope in the return of Jesus is
a key to my spiritual growth, and so I thank you for reminding me that
Christ is coming again—even if I have to wait for his return longer than
I might like. Thank you for your patience, and use me to reach more of
those people who need to know you. In Jesus' name I pray. Amen.* 🍂

The Puzzle of Tody

"I led them with cords of human kindness, with ties of love. To them I was like one who lifts a little child to the cheek, and I bent down to feed them."
HOSEA 11:4

My sister Gloria had one child, named William; we called him Tody. He had a mental illness. From his very earliest years, my sister poured her love into him, but he had a psychological problem and never could respond to any kind of discipline, so he constantly landed in trouble.

Although Gloria spent all her available money on psychiatric care for Tody and even took on extra jobs to put her son in schools designed for troubled children, he never was able to control his actions. As a young adult, he moved around a lot and became addicted to alcohol and drugs. The last time he came to Plains, he and his girlfriend robbed a service station, then went to Gloria's house and threatened her and her husband if they revealed his crime.

After that, he moved to California, where he married a wonderful woman, got proper medication, and lived his remaining years as a good husband and father.

Tody always was very attractive and intelligent but could not control the impulses early in his life that took him away from my sister's love. As president, I stayed in touch with him with letters and by telephone every now and then, and when I visited the San Francisco area, I met with him personally. He never could reconcile with his mother during his lifetime, but he had his mother's intense love and constant forgiveness, until the very end of her life.

This case reminds me of ancient Israel of Hosea's time. God gave her every blessing: forgiveness, safety, repeated rescue from oppressors. Even so, she constantly turned away from God—the one who lavished on her his constant love.

I pray that we won't make the same mistake.

O Lord, I confess that sometimes I am unfaithful to my commitments to my neighbors and loved ones, and I forget that all my blessings come from your gracious hand. Forgive me, and give me a deeper and richer appreciation for your mercy, love, and forgiveness. I pray in the name of Jesus, the epitome of grace and charity. Amen.

A Nothing That Leads to Everything

*I consider that our present sufferings are not worth comparing with
the glory that will be revealed in us.*
ROMANS 8:18

Rosalynn has gone through childbirth four times. It is a time of anguish and pain, but after it ends and we hold a newborn in our arms, it becomes a time of glory and thanksgiving.

The apostle Paul reminds struggling Christians that, in this life, we suffer and sometimes doubt whether life has a purpose. We live in two separate but overlapping worlds, the current one and the world to come. We need not fear the future, Paul says, because through faith in Christ, we will not suffer in eternity. Christ already has taken the punishment for our sins.

Oh, we still must face many earthly challenges and problems. Not long ago, Rosalynn and I took a trip around the periphery of Africa, witnessing the terrible blight caused by AIDS. In some countries, more than a fourth of the adults had the disease. That kind of thing shocks us, and should inspire us to help alleviate their suffering.

But Paul insists that despite such real tragedies, another world overlaps this one—and already it has started for Christians. Because Christ took the punishment for our sins, through faith we have embarked upon our journey to eternal life.

Do we still sometimes have doubts? Yes. But Paul says, "You needn't have any lasting doubts. There is therefore now *no* condemnation for those who are in Christ Jesus." The fact is that nothing—not death or life, angels or rulers, things present or things to come, height or depth, or anything else in all creation—will be able to separate us from the love of God in Christ Jesus our Lord. *Nothing* can separate us from God's love. Nothing.

And that should mean everything to us.

O Lord, I admit that often I don't know how to cope with the tragedies and pain of life. I cry out, wondering whether you have forgotten me or whether my faith in Christ makes a difference. Today I acknowledge that it does make a difference, for all of eternity. Help me live as a citizen of heaven, so that I might bless those in pain on this earth. In Jesus' name I pray. Amen.

Active Patience

We count as blessed those who have persevered. You have heard of
Job's perseverance and have seen what the Lord finally brought about.
The Lord is full of compassion and mercy.
JAMES 5:11

During my boyhood years, a fine woman named Annie May Hollis worked in our house. Decades ago she moved to Albany, Georgia. About six weeks ago, in the middle of the night, her brother, who has arthritis and can hardly walk, woke Annie May up and said, "The water's coming!"

"The water's not coming," she replied. "I've been here thirty-seven years, and water's never come here." But he insisted, so she got up, found her Bible, and went out to her car. But before she could get there, the floodwaters rose to her waist and rescuers had to pick her up in a boat. She lost everything she had — the house, the car, her dog, everything.

I knew nothing about it until two women from Atlanta went down to Albany to help. There they found this seventy-seven-year-old Christian hobbling around to help her neighbors. They watched as she tried to rejuvenate everybody else's spirits. "The Lord will take care of us," she insisted. "We need not be concerned." (Later, Habitat workers built her a new home.)

When difficult times hit, let's work as hard as we can, in faith, to correct the problems. Let's not blame God, but rather look to our Creator for salvation. This is the kind of faith James describes — a faith of active patience. We must be resilient, forceful, courageous, and strong in Christ.

In my life as governor or as president, I can't say that I've ever done anything as significant with my Christian faith as Annie May did. While walking around knee deep in water, she shared her faith in Christ with others who had lost their homes. Active patience really does demonstrate the glories of Jesus Christ!

Dear Lord, help me emulate the simple but strong faith of Annie May.
As she considered her invisible faith to be far more important than a
tangible house or automobile, so let me share her conviction. May I learn
from her example and testify to the goodness of the Lord, even when
tragedy strikes. I ask these things in the name of my Savior, Jesus Christ.
Amen. ❧

289

Move Forward!

*Then the LORD said to Moses, "Why are you crying out to me? Tell
the Israelites to move on."*
EXODUS 14:15

Shortly after the Israelites escaped from Egypt, they arrived at the Red Sea.
They saw Pharaoh's army behind them and the water in front of them, and
they cried out to Moses, "It would have been better for us to serve the Egyptians than to die in the desert!" (Exodus 14:12).

While most of us have never landed in a situation as desperate as this,
we also tend to blame outside forces, including God, for the bad things that
overtake us. "Why did God let this happen to me? Why have I had such
a loss, when people not nearly so worthy as I am seem to fare better?" But
when we ask those kinds of questions, we stop moving forward. That is why,
despite our circumstances, we must continue to move forward in faith, as the
Israelites eventually did through the Red Sea.

My book *Sources of Strength* features a chapter inspired by a passage that
intrigues farmers like me: "Sow your seed in the morning, and at evening let
your hands not be idle, for you do not know which will succeed, whether this
or that, or whether both will do equally well" (Ecclesiastes 11:6). I think the
writer is counseling us to take a chance—or as God told the Israelites, "Move
forward!" We must not be so careful, so hesitant, so timid that we never act
boldly. Let us never allow self-limitations to stop us!

We all have fears, doubts, and concerns, some of them so great that we
echo the Israelites: "I would rather be a slave in Egypt than get slaughtered by
soldiers or drown in the sea." God replies, "Align yourself with me—put your
faith in me—and get moving!" God, through Christ, gives us the opportunity to strengthen our faith, overcome our problems, and move forward.

*God, as I look back on these ancient lessons, I admit that sometimes
I miss what the message can mean for me. Give me courage, Lord, to
look honestly at my life and see whether I'm hesitating because of fear or
anxiety about the future—or moving forward. Give me the grace and
the strength to move ahead for you, in you, and by your power. In Christ's
name I pray. Amen.* ❧

290

Holy Impatience

[Joseph said,] "But when all goes well with you, remember me and show
me kindness; mention me to Pharaoh and get me out of this prison."
GENESIS 40:14

Joseph landed in prison because the wife of his former master, Potiphar, had falsely accused him of attempted rape. Once there, however, the men in charge quickly made Joseph the overseer of the whole prison. After correctly interpreting the dream of the king's imprisoned cup-bearer—who promised to ask the king for Joseph's release—it looked as if Joseph might get out. But the cup-bearer forgot about Joseph, and so he languished in prison for another *two years!*

We must learn how to deal with situations that vary from what we think we deserve. I'm sure Joseph had some doubts while he sat in prison, waiting for the cup-bearer to keep his word. He might have thought, *I've been honest and sincere. I've prayed regularly and obeyed the Scriptures. I refused the advances of Potiphar's wife—yet here I am in prison, forgotten by God and even by the man whom it seemed God had provided to bring about my release.*

At times, probably all of us get disillusioned in this way. We wonder why God seems to have abandoned us, when it seems as though we were doing just what had been asked of us. Sometimes this can make us bitter toward God, and we drift away in anger and despair.

Martin Luther King Jr. probably could have identified with Joseph. But while incarcerated in the Birmingham jail, Dr. King did not become bitter; instead, he wrote about the need for "holy impatience." He meant that in times of adversity or unwarranted suffering, we shouldn't just give up. If we are fighting for a good cause and don't immediately succeed, we must be impatient in a way that God approves.

Where might you require some "holy impatience" today?

Dear Lord, help me derive from your Holy Word lessons for myself, as
did people of faith like Joseph. Give me an increasing awareness of the
presence of the Holy Spirit as I study the Scriptures and pattern my life
ever more closely after the words and actions of Jesus Christ, for it is in his
name I pray. Amen. ❧

The Darker the Night, the Brighter the Stars

*Because of the LORD's great love we are not consumed, for his
compassions never fail. They are new every morning;
great is your faithfulness.*
LAMENTATIONS 3:22 – 23

The Babylonians had conquered the southern kingdom of Judah and destroyed Jerusalem. Many had been killed, and many others taken captive. The temple lay in ruins, and all the treasures of Jerusalem had vanished. Only Jeremiah and a small remnant of God's chosen people remained in Judah. That is when the prophet wrote the book of Lamentations.

How could Jeremiah possibly talk about God's "unfailing compassion" and "great love," with everything around him devastated and many Israelites in captivity? Yet in a time of disaster and divine punishment, he turned his thoughts to God and declared, "Great is your faithfulness." Despite his despair, Jeremiah did not lose his confidence in the faithfulness of God.

Only at night can we see the stars, and the darker the night gets, the more stars we see. When I had night duty on the deck of a darkened submarine on the ocean's surface, I could see clearly and study constellations that remain invisible from most inhabited places on shore.

When my grandson was five years old, my daughter brought him from Atlanta to Plains for a visit. One night, Hugo woke up and couldn't get back to sleep. So Amy, in order not to disturb the rest of us, took him out in our front yard. Hugo was amazed; he had never *really* seen the stars before.

One of the greatest heartaches we will ever confront is death, an inevitability for all of us. When death approaches or comes to those we love, we face one of our darkest moments. In those times, we must remember the attitude of Jeremiah. Although everything had collapsed around him, he found strength and confidence in the faithfulness, goodness, and promises of God.

*God, whatever the challenges facing me, help me remember and take
refuge in your everlasting love. Let me remember that Jesus came to give
me life, not death. And as I think of the days ahead, give me courage to
reexamine my priorities and to live in closer harmony with my Savior,
Jesus Christ, in whose name I pray. Amen.* ❧

292

Believe It

The angel said to him, "I am Gabriel. I stand in the presence of God, and I have been sent to speak to you and to tell you this good news. And now you will be silent and not able to speak until the day this happens, because you did not believe my words, which will come true at their appointed time."

LUKE 1:19–20

In Zechariah's day, about 20,000 descendants of Aaron were ordained as priests. Periodically one of them was chosen by lot to go into the temple and burn incense. One day, Zechariah's turn came.

When he entered the temple, the angel Gabriel appeared and informed him that God had heard his prayer; his elderly wife, Elizabeth, would become pregnant and bear a son. The couple was to name him John, and the boy would grow up to be a special instrument of God.

Since Elizabeth was well past the age of childbearing, Zechariah didn't believe the news. In effect, he said, "I'll believe it when I see it!" For his refusal to believe, the angel struck him dumb. So when Zechariah emerged from the temple—much later than expected—many waited anxiously to hear his report. But he couldn't speak. When he made some excited gestures, people realized that something profound had occurred. Soon afterward, Elizabeth did become pregnant, just as the angel had said.

After John's birth, neighbors and family members said, "Naturally, this baby will be named after his father, Zechariah, a notable person." But Elizabeth said, "No, his name is John." Zechariah, still mute, made gestures for a writing pad and wrote down, "His name is John." At that moment, his voice returned and he praised God for all that had happened.

We can benefit from the hard lesson Zechariah learned, without going through all his pain. Here's the principle: If we pray for something compatible with God's will, then we must believe our prayer will be answered.

Dear God, thank you for blessing a fumbling old man and his elderly wife, whose lives changed forever when they became the parents of the man who blazed a trail for the Messiah. I am grateful that even in our modern, technological world, my heritage extends back to John the Baptist. Help me, like him, to point people to Jesus Christ. I ask this in the name of my Savior. Amen. ❧

A Faith That Lasts

*Teach slaves to be subject to their masters in everything, to try to
please them, not to talk back to them, and not to steal from them,
but to show that they can be fully trusted, so that in every way they
will make the teaching about God our Savior attractive.*
TITUS 2:9 – 10

Paul is not endorsing slavery here but is using an extreme example to advocate what those little modern bracelets say: "What Would Jesus Do?" In all circumstances, we should let our moral commitment to Christ prevail and not let the transient circumstances of life determine how we act.

If we are in prison for life; if we were born with a low IQ; if we are destitute or homeless—we should not let these things affect our relationship to Jesus Christ. This doesn't mean feeling satisfied with our circumstances, but rather accommodating to whatever circumstances prevail in our lives. Whether we're male or female, young or old, slave or master, we must maintain our allegiance to Christ.

Our Christian standing or acceptability before God does not depend on whether we can read and write, have high social standing, are living on the streets, or are sleeping under a bridge. As Christians, we can always act based on our inmost commitment—that is, on our allegiance to Christ—and not on transient circumstances.

What good is it if we live by our allegiance to God only when things are going well and we have every comfort we could want? And what does it mean if we put our faith on hold when things go bad or circumstances change for the worse? Is wishy-washy devotion really faith at all? True faith remains constant and goes to the core of our being, so that we live for Christ through all circumstances, no matter what life may deal us.

*O God, teach me the crucial difference between being satisfied in you
and feeling satisfied with myself. Prompt me to move forward in faith,
not so I might point to my accomplishments, but so I might point to your
all-sufficient grace. Teach me to live like Jesus did as he lived and suffered
in ancient Palestine, and give me the wisdom and strength to serve you
always. In Christ's name I pray. Amen.* ❧

Look for the Good

And we know that in all things God works for the good of those who love him, who have been called according to his purpose.
ROMANS 8:28

When bad things happen to us, how often do we ask, "What possible good could come out of this?" Frequently we do not ponder how God might use a tragedy for good.

My mother and father, so far as I could tell, were a completely loving couple. They set a good example for all their children. But no one had any doubt that Daddy was the boss in our family. When a final decision had to be made, my daddy made it—except for things relating to my two sisters and to Mama's nursing career. While Daddy lived, I doubt if my mother even knew the price of a loaf of bread or a pound of cheese. She would just order from the local store, and groceries would be delivered to our house. Later, Daddy would pay the bill.

When my father passed away at a fairly early age, Mama's life changed drastically. She had to learn how to do things on her own. She became a housemother at Auburn University for six years, and then she helped operate a nursing home in Blakely, Georgia. But she said it depressed her to be around old people; so when she saw an ad on television that proclaimed, "Join the Peace Corps! Age is no limit," that's what Mama did. At seventy, she served in India. After returning home, she made more than five hundred speeches about her time there.

After my daddy passed on, Mama lived an expanded and productive life. While I wish my father had lived longer, I saw that good can come out of tragedy. When disappointments and tragedies happen in our lives—as they will—God encourages us to look for the good that might result.

Lord, help me see all of life's experiences in the light of your goodness and grace. When bad things happen or tragedies strike, help me search for the good that you might want to bring out of them. Teach me how to get involved more productively in your world and how to use even the hard times for your glory, through Christ my Savior. In his name I pray. Amen. ❧

The Sadness of Life

Out of the depths I cry to you, LORD.
PSALM 130:1

Abraham Lincoln was possibly the greatest president we've ever had. And yet "melancholy," "sadness," or "hopelessness" stalked Lincoln throughout his life, particularly in his early years. It got so bad that Lincoln sometimes expressed a desire to commit suicide, feeling that his life was not worth living.

One factor that likely contributed to this melancholy was Lincoln's poor relationship with his father. Lincoln despised his father, and his father despised him. When Lincoln and his sister were nine and eleven years old, their mother died, and their father went off to find a new wife—leaving the two children alone for six long months. Eventually, he returned with a new wife, and Lincoln loved his stepmother; but he could never forgive his father. It got so bad that when his father lay on his deathbed, Lincoln refused his dying dad's request to see his son.

In his law practice, Lincoln told ribald jokes and laughed along with everybody else. But then he'd return to his office, sit in a chair leaning against the wall, put a hat down over his face, and sit there for several hours without moving. Nobody could disturb him. He had strange habits of sadness and despair.

After he became president, melancholy continued to dog him. Certainly, he felt on his shoulders the overwhelming burden of the Civil War and its hundreds of thousands of casualties. He didn't commit suicide, for which I'm grateful. But here was a great man who suffered with deep sadness. He needed God.

All of us go through times of doubt, sadness, or failure. Sometimes they come in rushes. But if we have faith, mixed with endurance and patience, those problems can draw us closer to God. It may be hard to believe at the time, but with God we can find a way through any trial.

O Lord, thank you for reminding me that none of us are self-sufficient and that all of us are in need. Let me remember that I have a constant source of wisdom, strength, and influence when I form a partnership with you through prayer. Help me bind myself to you through the Holy Spirit. In Jesus' name I pray. Amen. ❧

296

Staunch Hearts

"Shall we accept good from God, and not trouble?"
JOB 2:10

Job was a great, honest, and devout man. It was reported that he sacrificed every day to make intercession to God for the possible sins of his sons. Job and his wife had seven sons and three daughters, and he also owned an enormous amount of livestock and land. He was very wealthy and successful.

One day, the story goes, God assembled the angels to appear before him and Satan showed up. God said to him, "I have a wonderful man on earth named Job, who is completely loyal to me." Satan replied, "It's only because he is rich and protected! Why shouldn't he be perfect? He has no reason to steal because he has everything he wants. But if you took away his success, he'd curse you to your face." So God gave Satan permission to test Job.

As Job dined one evening, reports came in that all his livestock had been wiped out and that all his children had perished. In response, "Job got up and tore his robe and shaved his head. Then he fell to the ground in worship and said: 'Naked I came from my mother's womb, and naked I will depart. The LORD gave and the LORD has taken away; may the name of the LORD be praised'" (Job 1:20–21). Soon afterward God allowed Satan to afflict Job's body with terrible sores, and Job's wife told him to curse God and die. But Job answered, "Shall we accept good from God, and not trouble?" Throughout his suffering, Job maintained his integrity and stayed loyal to God.

Regardless of the difficulties we face, we too must retain our fidelity to God. Despite all kinds of suffering, we have the ability, in Christ, to remain strong and to persevere with the same staunchness of heart that Job demonstrated.

O Lord, I'm thankful for the example of Job and his loyalty to you, despite horrendous suffering. Help me remember that while I will have my ups and downs, it is crucial to persevere in my faith in Jesus Christ my Savior. You have promised that the blessings of faith in Jesus will be truly profound and will culminate in eternal life. In Christ's blessed name I pray. Amen.

An Unfading Inheritance

*[God] has given us new birth into a living hope through the
resurrection of Jesus Christ from the dead, and into an inheritance
that can never perish, spoil or fade.*
I PETER 1:3 – 4

Peter wrote this letter at a time when great persecution had broken out against the early church. In AD 64, for example, James, a leader of the Jerusalem church (and Jesus' half brother), was stoned to death by Jewish authorities. The same year, Paul was beheaded in Rome. By the time Peter wrote these words, it had become very dangerous to associate oneself with Jesus Christ.

Today in America we know little, if anything, about being persecuted because of our beliefs. Certainly we suffer from other things—personal losses, fears, disappointments, doubt—but in general we don't suffer because we declare our Christian faith. In fact, some people claim to be Christian just so they can profit by the association. We might be able to sell more insurance if we claim to be Christian. On our local country music station, certain businesses in Americus, Georgia, encourage people to go to church, not just to help their faith grow, but because they want to tie in the sale of hardware or groceries with a Christian image. I don't criticize them for doing so; I see nothing wrong with the practice. In fact, I'm glad that in some places it's still considered an honor to be Christian.

Regardless of whether it is persecution or suffering more generally that we face, however, Peter is telling us to make sure that we retain our knowledge of and hope in God's gracious gift. We must strive to remember that we are receiving a divine inheritance that is imperishable, unspoiled, and never going to waste. That inheritance is like a beautiful flower that never wilts, a promise that never breaks. "When you suffer," Peter says, "remember your glorious inheritance, and be strengthened."

*O God, I am grateful for Peter's words, knowing that they apply to me as
well. Help me be strong, courageous, and wise enough to open my heart
to this message so that my faith might bring me to a true and living hope.
Let my life be changed for the better, and let me demonstrate in vivid
terms what it means to be a Christian. I ask this in Jesus' name. Amen.* ❧

Jesus and Conflict

"Do not suppose that I have come to bring peace to the earth. I did
not come to bring peace, but a sword."
MATTHEW 10:34

This passage is difficult to understand, but we know that conflict marked Jesus' relationship with the world. When his disciples surrounded him—men who believed in him and who were blessed by God with inspiration and understanding of his ministry—harmony and love usually prevailed. But almost every time Jesus reached out and came in contact with the outside world—which might have been close to him but had no place in his inner circle—the word that best characterizes the result is "conflict."

The ministry of Jesus often created debate and disharmony. His words prompted misunderstanding, and his actions sometimes inspired hate. It's hard for us today to look back on the time when Christ lived on earth as a man, and understand how anyone could have hated our Savior. How could anyone have hated Jesus, whose life epitomized peace, compassion, understanding, and love? Jesus didn't respond with hatred, but he recognized that it existed. And eventually that hatred caused him to suffer to the utmost degree. Why?

Christ's life brought out such animosity, conflict, and hatred because he came into a complacent religious world, filled with men and women who prided themselves on their status as God's chosen people and on their places of worship, and suddenly tore apart their complacency. He destroyed it. He forced them to reexamine the standards they had set for themselves. They wanted to hold on to the old ways and keep their smug, self-satisfied, comfortable religion; but Christ refused to allow it. He told them they needed to repent and change, just like the rest of sinful humanity.

His message remains as true and controversial today. Whenever we bring the real message of Jesus Christ to this world, we must be prepared for conflict.

O Lord, how remarkable that the Prince of Peace could inspire such
hatred and conflict. What a dark story that tells about the depth of our
sin and the extent of our natural alienation from you! Thank you for
sending Jesus as my Savior and making it possible for me to be reconciled
to you. Help me be a person of peace and reconciliation. I pray in Jesus'
name. Amen.

Enduring Saints

*This calls for patient endurance on the part of the people of God who
keep his commands and remain faithful to Jesus.*
REVELATION 14:12

In the church's early years, most Christians looked upon Rome with approval. The Romans typically entered troubled communities—plagued with violence, corruption, and oppressive local rulers—and corrected these problems. Usually, the Romans tried not to interfere much in local affairs. They wanted to collect taxes and maintain order, so they permitted local religions to continue unopposed. In the Holy Land, for example, they let the Jews worship and provide local government in their own way.

The first Christian churches were treated the same way; but as they grew, the congregations became more of a threat to both Jewish leaders and the Romans. About AD 80, a man named Domitian became Caesar. Domitian considered himself a god and each year required everyone in the Roman Empire to offer a small sacrifice and say, "Caesar Domitian is my God and my Lord." This put devout Christians in a quandary. Those who refused were punished by death.

So the Christian church came into direct conflict with Rome, and that's one reason John wrote the book of Revelation—to encourage early Christians. He wrote it in a kind of code so that only Christians would understand its full meaning. In it, the author calls for the endurance of the saints, the people dedicated to obeying Christ. He writes, "Blessed are the dead who die in the Lord from now on" (Revelation 14:13).

In our nation, Christians are not persecuted as in earlier days. We are not subject to torture or death for our faith. But that doesn't mean that our faith does not get tested. We may suffer ridicule or discrimination for our beliefs. Revelation reminds us that we must remain courageous and resolute in following Jesus Christ.

Dear Lord, although it's tempting to skip over some of the more difficult parts of the Bible, I need to search for meaning in even its most mysterious sections. I know that you have given them for my guidance and that they can give me a greater ability to emulate the perfect life of my Savior, Jesus Christ. In his name I pray. Amen.

Christians Don't Run

So Peter was kept in prison,
but the church was earnestly praying to God for him.
ACTS 12:5

In the early days of the church, Christians numbered in the few thousands. Before James's execution, they thought they might just get by, since they were all Jewish and not causing any trouble. But after James's death and Peter's arrest, it became obvious that they were all in danger.

Still, however, they didn't try to run away. Recognizing their impotence to deal with Roman authorities, who were in bed with the Jewish religious leaders, they knew their only hope was to pray fervently to God. After Peter's imprisonment, that's what they did.

Peter had been very outspoken. The Romans must have known of his visit with Cornelius. How could the apostle have witnessed to one of their top officers without their knowing of it? So they arrested him, chained him to two guards, put him in an inner cell, and then stationed two other guards at the door. Four squads took turns guarding him. Surely they remembered the profoundly significant events that took place after Christ was executed and placed in a tomb. Despite the guards put there, Christ walked away in his resurrected body. So they wanted to make sure that nothing similar happened with his most famous disciple, Peter.

The night before Peter's scheduled execution, the apostle lay sleeping, at peace with God, not expecting to live beyond the morning. Apparently he felt that if he were executed, he had fulfilled his promises to Christ and had done his duty as a Christian.

But God rescued him.

The attitude that strengthened Peter would serve us all well today. When difficult times come, we can face adversity with equanimity, taking solace in our faith in God. Our duty to Christ is what counts—and whatever happens is the Lord's decision.

Dear God, thank you for this account of the early church and its response
to persecution. While I do not face the kind of severe trials that engulfed
them, yet Satan has ways of tempting me. Let me learn from these early
Christians and from Peter's boldness in proclaiming Jesus despite the cost.
May I do my duty as they did. In Christ's name I pray. Amen. ❧

301

Find a New Way

"But everyone who hears these words of mine and does not put them into practice is like a foolish man who built his house on sand."
MATTHEW 7:26

A bright young college student always had a clever retort for his instructors. On one test his physics professor asked, "How can you use a barometer to determine the height of a building?" The student wrote, "There are so many ways, I don't know which one you want!"

The aggravated professor called in the student and demanded, "What do you mean, there are many ways? Let's hear them!"

The student replied, "You can measure the pressure at the ground and at the top of the building, and use the difference to find your answer. Or you could measure the barometer's height and the length of its shadow, then measure the length of the building's shadow and determine the building's height. Or you could tie a string to the barometer and lower it to the ground, then measure the length of the string. Or you could drop the barometer from the top of the building and time how long it takes to hit the ground."

Just then the dean of the business school walked by, and the physics professor explained the situation. The dean told the student, "If you can suggest how to use a barometer in a business deal, then I'll suggest that you get a good grade."

"That's easy," the student replied. "I'd go to the building superintendent and say, 'If you tell me the building's height, I'll give you this nice barometer.'"

Let's learn from the student and look at how we live—how we can be doers of Jesus' words and not hearers only? In how many new ways can we change our lives for the better as we reach for the standards Christ has set for us?

Lord, help me resolve in my heart to try innovative ways to do your will, like the boy with the barometer. Enable me to look at what I am and what I have to offer, and to devise new actions and new attitudes that will bind me closer to you in a more intimate relationship. I pray this through my Savior, Jesus Christ, who gave his life that I might have eternal life. Amen.

Running from God

*The word of the LORD came to Jonah son of Amittai: "Go to the
great city of Nineveh and preach against it, because its wickedness
has come up before me." But Jonah ran away from the LORD.*

JONAH 1:1 – 3

When God commanded Jonah to go to Nineveh and announce the city's
destruction, the prophet had two options: to do what God told him or run.
He chose to run.

Obeying God would be difficult for the prophet because it went against
his personal beliefs and the prejudices of his culture. Ordinarily when God
told a prophet to condemn a nation—usually Israel—the point was to
prompt the people to repent so that they might be forgiven. So when God
told Jonah to go to Nineveh and preach against it, the object was to prompt
repentance among its citizens. But the Israelites hated the people of Nineveh;
in modern times, this would be like somebody saying, "I'm going to form an
alliance with Osama bin Laden." Jonah simply couldn't stand the thought.

Does this remind you of anyone you know? Do we ever attempt to escape
from the commandments of God? In our world, for example, sex outside of
marriage has become an accepted thing. Those who do not accept it are often
ridiculed as straitlaced or bigoted. Many Christians therefore feel tempted to
abandon God's commandments in order to fit in, to be included in society,
and to avoid ridicule.

What things prompt us to reject Scripture and run from God? Maybe we
ignore the needy, gossip, bear false witness against our neighbors, or refuse to
forgive those who have injured us. Since we all break the commandments of
God, we all are guilty of the sin Jonah committed when he tried to run from
God. As Christians, we must commit ourselves to obeying *whatever* God has
commanded, even if it opposes what society thinks—and even if it causes us
to change our own ways.

*Lord, how often I follow in Jonah's footsteps, trying to run away from you
because I think your commandments will make life less enjoyable! In doing
so, I forget that running from you always makes life more difficult in the
long run. So help me, Lord, to obey you fully, willingly, and gladly, even if
it means suffering in some way. In the name of Jesus I pray. Amen.* ❧

303

The Power of Unity

Certain people came down from Judea to Antioch and were teaching
the believers: "Unless you are circumcised, according to the custom
taught by Moses, you cannot be saved." This brought Paul and
Barnabas into sharp dispute and debate with them.

ACTS 15:1 – 2

The allies could have lost World War II. Our nation's existence hung on a very narrow balance, and things could have gone either way. Had Einstein stayed in Germany, had the battle of Midway gone differently, had we found no substitute for natural rubber, our nation and its allies could have lost the war.

The key issue that often determines the outcome of such titanic struggles is which side is the most unified, works with common purpose, and is willing to put aside petty differences and combine efforts rather than wasting its strength through internal dissension. People who embark on a mission or crusade without being united almost inevitably lose.

Such a threat arose in the early church when the "Judaizers" said no one could follow Christ without first becoming a Jew. Any Greek or Roman who wanted to become a Christian, they said, first had to become a Jew, be circumcised (if a male), and adopt the laws of Moses. The people of Antioch responded by saying, in effect, "This is wrong! I'm already saved."

This became such a divisive issue that Paul and Barnabas decided to go to Jerusalem and present it to the church's elders. They understood that this debate could strike at the heart of the evangelical movement. If the Judaizers had prevailed, the struggling Christian church might have died in its embryonic state.

Resolving division is seldom easy. But we have to make a strong effort to do so in order to avoid animosity among ourselves that sparks dissension and hurts the church's effectiveness in the world. Victory for Christ requires unity among Christians. Each of us must do our part.

O Lord, teach me to value unity, even when I must make uncomfortable
or even costly choices. Give me such a clear vision of your kingdom that
I consider it an honor, not a sacrifice, to put aside my own agenda to
achieve Christian unity of purpose. Help me serve others in love and so
fulfill the law of Christ. In Jesus' name I pray. Amen. ❧

Maintaining Unity

Make every effort to keep the unity of the Spirit
through the bond of peace.
EPHESIANS 4:3

"Unity" refers to two or more people bound together in a common way. As fellow members of the body of Christ, we are to foster such unity.

We cannot succeed as Christians or as congregations without maintaining unity. And yet, of all the historic failures of the Christian church, disunity is the most prevalent. Some two thousand years after our Savior lived, the Christian church is more fragmented than ever. It's not only Baptists versus Methodists versus Episcopalians versus Mennonites, or Protestants versus Catholics, or Orthodox versus Catholic, but divisions also multiply within denominations and within individual congregations. Clearly, this apostolic call for unity is as yet an unrealized dream, primarily because we have failed to comply with the instruction of Paul (or the words of Christ in John 17). We tend to reject the possibility of harmony because of our inability to control our divisiveness and pride.

Paul tells us that we maintain unity by remembering there is but one body, one Spirit, one hope, one Lord, one faith, one baptism, and one God of all. The only way all of it works together is by God's grace. Think of grace as God's Reward At Christ's Expense. G-R-A-C-E is a wonderful gift we don't deserve that enables us to forgive others as we ourselves have been forgiven.

Few people leave the church or reject Christianity because of a negative assessment of our beliefs. Almost invariably, people turn against Christianity after seeing other Christians who fail to personify the unity, love, and forgiveness demonstrated by Christ. The only way to overcome this natural inclination toward divisiveness is by relying, moment by moment, on God's grace. Only then can we experience true unity.

O God, give me the desire to become reconciled with others as we all
recognize that Christ is one body. Help me grasp that we Christians are
all part of that unified body and that through the grace of God we can
receive the strength to maintain the unity you desire. I ask these things in
the name of our perfect Savior. Amen. ❧

An Age-Old Enmity

When Haman saw that Mordecai would not kneel down or pay him honor,
he was enraged. Yet having learned who Mordecai's people were, he scorned
the idea of killing only Mordecai. Instead Haman looked for a way to destroy
all Mordecai's people, the Jews, throughout the whole kingdom of Xerxes.
ESTHER 3:5 – 6

During the time of Esther, the second-in-command to the Persian king was an Amalekite named Haman. When Haman rode through the streets, everyone bowed down to him—except a Jew named Mordecai. Some people think Mordecai refused to bow down because Jews worshiped God alone, but in fact, Jews had no religious law against bowing down to a public official, and throughout history they did so to their own kings and others.

But the first thirteen books of the Bible describe an ancient enmity between Jews and Amalekites, so perhaps Mordecai thought, *There's no way I'm bowing down to this despised Amalekite.* Haman reacted to Mordecai's "insult" by deciding to kill all the Jews.

This kind of escalating hatred still plagues the world today. At the Carter Center we analyze the excessive number of armed conflicts currently raging around the world. Almost all are civil wars, following the same pattern that fuels conflict between business competitors or even a husband and wife. First comes a feeling of anger because of some ancient or recent event that one side finds offensive. Communication ends, and each side builds up animosity against the other and often chooses revenge. The aggrieved side retaliates and a blood feud escalates. As things deteriorate, each side develops a sense of superiority and an aversion to compromise, because that would require elevating the other side to an equal status. Divorce, estrangement, and even combat can result.

That is not Christ's way. One of the driving forces of his ministry was seeking peaceful resolution of differences, whether among individuals or nations. Remember, we worship the Prince of *Peace*!

Dear God, I pray that a genuine sense of humility might mark my
relationships and that I might not easily take offense. I also ask that a
growing commitment to justice and peace might characterize my life so
that I can better emulate the perfect example of my Savior, Jesus Christ. I
pray these things in his name. Amen. ❧

Killing Words

"I tell you that anyone who is angry with a brother or sister will be subject to judgment.... And anyone who says, 'You fool!' will be in danger of the fire of hell."
MATTHEW 5:22

Christ uses the most terrible of crimes, murder, as an example of violating God's will. And yet we are not to think, *Since I haven't deliberately stabbed somebody in the heart, then I am okay with God. I have complied with the Ten Commandments.* Jesus says, "Hardly! If you harbor anger toward your brother or sister, it is as though you had committed murder itself."

We kill with words as well as with weapons.

Menachem Begin, former prime minister of Israel, referred to Palestinians as "terrorists" every time we spoke. *Every* Palestinian was a terrorist, no matter who they were. Each time I met with Palestinians—farmers and pharmacists, teachers and lawyers, orange growers and doctors, about 15 percent of whom were Christians—Begin labeled them "terrorists." The dehumanizing of someone by the use of a pejorative word is a sinful thing.

I once wrote a short poem titled "With Words We Learn to Hate," which said in part:

We've cursed the names of those we fought—the "Japs" instead of Japanese,
German Nazis or the "Huns," and "Wops"—when they were enemies.

Later they became our friends, but habits live in memories.
So now, when others disagree, we hate again, and with our might,
war by war, name by dirty name, prove we're right.

Christ said that if we brand someone a fool—or a terrorist—that's the same thing in heaven's eyes as killing them. Our natural tendency is to condemn our adversaries as being subhuman. Then we can rationalize our animosity and convince ourselves that we have not violated God's commandment to love even our enemies.

May the Lord forgive us.

O God, help me guard my lips so that I do not carelessly commit murder with my ill-chosen words. Help me remember how far I fall short of your glory, and give me the grace and strength to use my words to heal, not to hurt. As Jesus dwells within my heart through faith, so let my mouth speak only what honors him. In his name I pray. Amen.

A Dollar a Book

"Do not seek revenge or bear a grudge against anyone among your people, but love your neighbor as yourself. I am the LORD."
LEVITICUS 19:18

A few years ago I was invited to visit Hawaii to give an address. After I arrived, I learned that Hugh Sidey was going to moderate my panel; he writes for *Time* magazine and had made some ugly remarks about my wife. I told the organizers that I wouldn't get on the same stage with him. They replied, "But we've already invited him out here."

"Okay," I said, "then let him be on the program, and not me. I won't be on the same program with him." I presume they put him on a different panel, because I never saw him.

Since then Hugh and I have reconciled. One night we had a long flight together in a small airplane, as the only two passengers. We talked during the entire trip and learned to respect each other.

I also had to be reconciled with columnist George Will. As president, I was told that he used my stolen briefing book for my debate with Ronald Reagan, teaching him what I was going to say. This was difficult to forgive. But a couple of years ago I bought a book George had written about baseball. It was excellent, and I wrote him a nice letter. "I just bought a used copy of your book for one dollar," I wrote. "It was very good. And since I like baseball and I've learned a lot from you, I hope we can forget past differences." He sent me a polite response.

We weaken ourselves when we ignore our need to forgive those who may have wronged us. It hurts us inside and it violates God's commandment. As difficult as it is, we are not to hold grudges. If reconciliation takes buying someone's book for a dollar, then so be it.

Lord, help me take the lead when reconciliation becomes necessary. Prompt me to remember that not only am I the one who gets hurt, but too often I also hurt others. Never let me forget that you can forgive me through your grace and mercy, and give me the strength to do the same thing in my relationships with others. I ask these things in the name of my Savior. Amen. ❧

308

"We Speak for God!"

"All day long I have held out my hands to an obstinate people, who walk in ways not good, pursuing their own imaginations."
ISAIAH 65:2

Yitzhak Rabin, a former prime minister of Israel, was assassinated in 1995. He had been a friend of mine for twenty-four years. When I was elected governor, General Rabin visited Rosalynn and me in Georgia. He was the hero of the Six-Day War in 1967, in which Israel repelled attackers and occupied the Holy Land.

The year after Rabin's visit to Georgia, Rosalynn and I visited Israel as Rabin's guests, our first time there. Mr. Rabin arranged in-depth briefings for me with Israel's top generals and military leaders so I could learn about the Mideast war environment. Out of that visit I derived my intense interest in the Middle East, and later, after I became president, I worked with the Middle East's top leaders. This led to the Camp David Accords and peace between Egypt and Israel.

Some time later, Rabin and other Israeli leaders held secret talks with Palestinians, which resulted in the Oslo agreement, something almost no one in America knew about. When the Israelis publicly agreed to withdraw from certain territory—despite the convictions of some right-wing Israelis— someone decided to kill the "traitor" Rabin. The young assassin said, "God wanted me to do it."

We humans can build up within ourselves a strong element of hatred, even to the point of murder. When we feel deeply about something, it's easy to say, "I am speaking for God, and anyone who disagrees with me opposes God." This attitude can easily lead to horrible violence and conflict. So we must take care not to spiritualize our personal beliefs simply because we feel strongly about some issue.

Dear Lord, I know it must grieve you for me to fuel hatred by claiming to be in accord with your will and speaking for you. Keep such a hateful attitude far from me, and give me instead a humble heart that seeks to encourage, bless, and strengthen others in your love. Where there is hatred, Lord, let me sow peace. I pray these things in Jesus' name. Amen. ❧

An Asset or an Affliction?

For you have heard of my previous way of life in Judaism, how
intensely I persecuted the church of God and tried to destroy it.
GALATIANS 1:13

A general belief exists among historians and political scientists that our nation has become more deeply divided now than at any time in its history, with the possible exception of the War Between the States. Television maps of our country covered in red states and blue states have come to symbolize our division.

One argument that divides us is the question of morals. Most people interviewed would say, "Of course I have moral values, and I'm quite sure they are the proper ones." In particular, if we interviewed a group of deeply religious people — Muslims, Hindus, Jews, Christians, or others — most would say, "Yes, my moral values guide my life." That is legitimate and admirable. But when people become prideful and self-satisfied about their morals and values, and as a consequence become prejudiced against others with different beliefs, they have crossed the line into sinfulness. Such sin divides people. It divides the world, nations, and even the Christian community.

Ponder this question: Is Christianity necessary for establishing democracy? Sometimes we Christians think so, and we start equating the two. This is a mistake.

The three largest democracies have different religions. India is the largest, where the primary religion is Hinduism. America comes next, and then Indonesia, an overwhelmingly Muslim country. Religion and democracy are not necessarily correlated, but people tend to believe their own brand of government or religion makes them superior to others. So we start treating other nations and their people as inferior.

Saul was convinced that his Judaism made him superior, and so he treated Christians as animals. When our moral values become a source of pride and prejudice against others, then they become an affliction instead of an asset.

O God, as you build within me certain moral convictions, help me
maintain a concern for all people, regardless of their values. Remind me
that my righteousness comes from you, through faith in Christ, and that
I have no right to be filled with personal pride and arrogance. Help me
emulate the example of my Lord, who epitomized peace and love, but
always with humility. In his name I pray. Amen. ❧

310

Special Meals

Jesus took bread, and when he had given thanks, he broke it and
gave it to his disciples, saying, "Take and eat; this is my body."
MATTHEW 26:26

When I was growing up, family meals provided very important opportunities to contemplate our life together. We normally ate in what we called the breakfast room, a tiny space between the kitchen and the dining room. On Sundays, however, we ate in the dining room. Sunday meals were special times.

When Rosalynn and I had children, our mealtimes continued to be sharing times. Our oldest son liked to argue, so he brought up controversial subjects to spark debate. These were lively times.

Even at the White House, we had most meals together. They gave me a chance to get away from being president of the United States and to be the father and husband of my own family.

The very special meal of Passover celebrates the release from Egyptian slavery of the ancient Hebrews. When I was in office, I received several invitations to share Passover meals, a sobering and wonderful ceremony. These meals start with a prayer of thanksgiving and feature bitter herbs and other symbolic foods. The father explains the meaning of Passover, families sing from the Psalms, and then they eat a meal of lamb and unleavened bread and drink wine.

Jesus' last meal with his disciples celebrated the Passover. But during this meal, Jesus unexpectedly equated the bread with his body and the wine with his blood. You can imagine the disciples' bewilderment! Today, we understand his meaning. We Christians celebrate the "Lord's Supper" with reverence and gratitude and with renewed dedication. As we eat the bread that represents his broken body and drink the wine that represents his spilled blood, we remember Christ's supreme sacrifice. Christ intended for this meal to bring us together in unity and common purpose. The meal is symbolic — and therefore much more than a meal.

O Lord, I'm grateful to ponder this timeworn but never dull subject,
which I've studied since childhood — when Christ met in a loving way
with his disciples, just to have a supper of thanksgiving with them. Help
me contemplate in a probing, incisive, and profoundly personal way the
deepest meaning of my relationship with Jesus Christ, my Savior. In his
name I pray. Amen. ❧

A Worthy Call

Be kind and compassionate to one another, forgiving each other,
just as in Christ God forgave you.
EPHESIANS 4:32

My favorite theologian is Reinhold Niebuhr. When I first became involved in politics, I read a book of his titled *Moral Man and Immoral Society: A Study of Ethics and Politics*. It describes how to conduct one's self in public affairs. How do you apply Christian principles when engaging in a competitive campaign, when confronting political adversaries, or when working in some legislative body?

The purpose of politics, Niebuhr says, is to establish justice in a sinful world. Justice means guaranteeing human rights and treating everybody fairly. According to Niebuhr, this is the highest possible goal for a political leader.

Yet Niebuhr insists that this high goal is not nearly so exalted as the Christian's central calling: to love one another, especially with *agape* love. This is self-sacrificial love for someone who may not deserve to be loved, who refuses to love you back, love that brings no recognition for your efforts. It is the kind of love that Christ personified.

Kindness and gentleness, crucial expressions of love, are required of all Christians. When Paul says, "Be kind and compassionate to one another, forgiving each other, just as in Christ God forgave you," he's going at least as far as the Golden Rule. This was Reinhold Niebuhr's favorite verse. It's a high standard, and one that none of us can meet on a consistent basis. But it's one to which we should aspire as a worthy goal.

As we become embroiled in inevitable disagreements—in politics, within families, with coworkers or neighbors or church acquaintances—our natural inclination is to derogate those who disagree with us. We may aim to paint our opponents in a bad light and so exalt ourselves by damaging the reputation of our adversaries.

Paul says, "Don't do it." And when we fail to obey this counsel, we dishonor the God who sent his Son to die for our sins.

God, I ask that you give me the strength and courage to face my own
shortcomings and to reach out to others whom I might have aggrieved,
perhaps in my own family or church or community. I cannot do this
without your Spirit empowering me, Lord, so I ask for help. In Jesus'
name I pray. Amen. ❧

An (Almost) Perfect Trap

*Then he said to them, "So give back to Caesar what is Caesar's,
and to God what is God's."*
MATTHEW 22:21

The Jews of Jesus' day despised men like Matthew, fellow countrymen who collected taxes for the hated Romans. They considered any Jew who served Rome to be a traitor.

One day, Jesus' opponents tried to trick him. "Is it lawful to pay taxes to the emperor?" they asked. Since Jesus had preached that only God should be worshiped and obeyed, they figured that however he answered the question, he'd be in trouble.

But Jesus asked to see the coin used for paying the tax. "Whose image is this?" he asked. They answered, quite obviously, "The emperor's." And then Jesus surprised them with his reply. They grew silent and slunk away.

Jesus brilliantly solved the religious-political dilemma put to him; but today we often struggle with similar questions.

Some of the most vivid experiences of my life occurred during the Civil Rights era. Ordinarily we are to obey the decisions made by our elected leaders and the laws they pass. For almost a hundred years after the War Between the States, U.S. laws endorsed "separate but equal" schools, job assignments, and other privileges for whites and blacks.

In 1948 I was a submarine officer, and my commander-in-chief, Harry Truman, ordained that segregation end in all armed forces. Later, growing numbers of citizens said, "Racial prejudice is not right," and demanded that everyone be treated as equals. Men like my friend Ambassador Andy Young and the Reverend Martin Luther King Jr. were willing to be jailed for their convictions. Thousands joined them. Eventually the Supreme Court made a ruling and our nation's laws changed because increasing numbers of people finally said, "This is right."

We may not have the keen insight of Jesus, but as Christians and citizens of various nations, we have an obligation to ask, "What is the command of Christ?"

Dear God, in this world I often find it difficult to know whether our laws and political decisions harmonize with your moral standards. I want to follow you, but many times I feel unsure what is right and what is wrong. Help me know how to be a good citizen, while realizing that my true citizenship is in heaven. Let me live more like Jesus, in whose name I pray. Amen. ❧

313

Use the Law to Change the Law

Peter and the other apostles replied:
"We must obey God rather than human beings!"
ACTS 5:29

As Christians, how should we react to our government when we think it's wrong? Are there times when we should challenge the laws of our nation?

Years ago, many of us didn't think the Vietnam War was necessary or that separate but equal treatment of our black neighbors was right. And so thousands of people came from all over the country, white and black together, to demonstrate against the nation's laws. Many of these courageous people landed in jail. One of the youngest, one of my best friends, was put in jail in Albany, along with Martin Luther King Jr. More and more Americans watched this happen and began to say, "Our laws are not fair."

Paul, who insisted that Christians respect their government, wrote, "Let everyone be subject to the governing authorities, for there is no authority except that which God has established" (Romans 13:1). At the same time, Paul reserved the right to abide by the ultimate laws of God. He used his Roman citizenship to great advantage but eventually chose state execution rather than agreeing to confess Caesar as Lord.

And how about Peter, when he and the other apostles were ordered to stop preaching? Peter and his friends answered, "We must obey God rather than any human authority." Does this mean that Paul and Peter disagreed? No. The problem is not between Paul and Peter, but between interpreters who take various parts of Scripture out of context.

Respect the government. Change it, if you can, according to the law. If the laws directly violate God's Word, then exert your influence, even if it might mean getting punished for a while. And do the same thing in your relationships, maybe with your neighbors. Don't be too afraid of being different!

O Father, many times I read the Holy Scriptures in a selective way, finding one verse that suits me and excluding others that don't. In so doing I tend to overlook the clear message of Christ. Help me act boldly, as a Christian, in espousing the principles of my Savior, Jesus Christ; and wisely, as a citizen, in deciding how best to shape public policy. In his name I pray. Amen. ❧

When Is War Justified?

"But I tell you, do not resist an evil person. If anyone slaps you on the right cheek, turn to them the other cheek also."
MATTHEW 5:39

Ever since the time of Christ, Christians have struggled with the question, "What is a just war?" When is it permissible to initiate a deadly conflict to further the goals of a nation?

Saint Thomas Aquinas, who lived in the thirteenth century, spent a lot of effort attempting to answer this question. Aquinas struggled with the verse about turning the other cheek. The definition of a "just war" that he developed, which has greatly influenced Christians ever since, insists that war should be a last resort—after all peaceful alternatives have been exhausted.

I faced this issue as president on several occasions. One example was when Iranian militants captured and held American hostages. I prayed more during that year than at any other time. We could have destroyed Iran with our powerful military, but in the process many innocent Iranians would have been killed. And there is little doubt that our hostages would have been assassinated by their captors in retaliation against our attacks. So I decided, contrary to most of the advice I received, to try to resolve the issue peacefully. We used economic pressure and persistent negotiations.

I never went to bed during the last three days of my presidency, working nonstop for the release of the hostages. At 10:00 a.m. on my last day in office, they were released to board an airplane; but Ayatollah Khomeini wouldn't let the plane depart until after I was no longer president. Five minutes after noon, the plane took off, and all the hostages came home safe—and to freedom.

Lord, I pray that our nation might be a land of peace and that it might find a way to resolve its international differences based on the simple message of our Savior, whom we worship as the Prince of Peace. Strengthen me to become an ambassador of peace in whatever arenas of life I find myself. In Jesus' name I pray. Amen. ❧

Stewards of the Earth

God blessed them and said to them "... Rule over the fish in the sea and the birds in the sky and over every living creature that moves on the ground."
GENESIS 1:28

A debate rages between Christians concerned about global warming and other Christians who say global warming, even if it exists, is not our responsibility. Who's right?

The last time Rosalynn and I visited Alaska, headlines proclaimed that polar bears were likely to vanish within twenty-five years. Melting polar ice is causing sea levels to rise. Eskimo coastal villages in existence since the Ice Age already are being abandoned, and soon Glacier National Park will have no glaciers.

It's foolish to deny that global warming is occurring. For centuries we have been spewing out enormous quantities of carbon and sulfuric oxides and similar substances, and these atmospheric gasses have made our environment into a kind of hothouse. Scientists first made these discoveries during my presidency. My scientific advisor, a geologist named Frank Press, came to me early in 1979 and said, "Mr. President, scientists at Woods Hole Research Center have detected extraordinary increases in the earth's temperature, and we don't know if their data are accurate."

I told him to assemble a panel of world scientists and see if they could substantiate the report. He returned about fifteen months later and said they had decided it was, indeed, a worrisome trend and that a major part of global warming was likely caused by human beings cutting down trees, destroying forests, and polluting the air.

What do you think? No doubt you have guessed my opinion. While we may disagree on the causes or rate of global warming, shouldn't we all agree that we have a responsibility to take care of the earth? God made us its stewards, and we are to use its resources wisely. The Bible says that God's wrath will come upon those "who destroy the earth" (Revelation 11:18). Shouldn't such a warning at least grab our attention?

O Lord, teach me the important difference between being a steward of your creation and being a selfish abuser of what I own or control. I know that with great privilege comes great responsibility and that this applies to stewardship of the earth. Let my actions be guided by wisdom, generosity, and concern for others, even those yet to be born. In Jesus' name I pray. Amen. ❧

What Would Happen?

A person may think their own ways are right,
but the LORD weighs the heart.
PROVERBS 21:2

My second day in the White House, we held a reception for key military officers and enlisted men. Rosalynn and I stood in the receiving line and shook hands with about two thousand people. It surprised us how many top military people, whether master sergeants or generals, referred to their faith in God. They would say, "God give our country peace," or "God be with you." More than any other group we encountered, the members of the military made it clear that they wanted my decisions as president to be guided by God. And they wanted me to have God's blessing.

Quite often we tend to categorize people as good or bad, based on our limited perspectives. "The military" might be our last guess as to who would most likely express faith in God. We might expect them to say, "I want better pay and retirement benefits," or "Let's be ready to defeat all our enemies." All human beings have this tendency either to stigmatize somebody based on flimsy evidence or to exalt someone on equally flimsy evidence (particularly if they agree with us).

As president and in later years I've had many opportunities to travel and learn the unique perspectives of people around the world. As a result, I've begun to see that Americans are legitimately subject to tough criticism, because quite often we're far better at preaching Christian principles than we are at putting them into practice.

Our nation's attitude toward foreign aid is a case in point. While foreign aid often is the best investment we can make as a peaceful way to meet the challenges of alien philosophies and antagonistic policies, members of Congress are inclined to vote against it, seeing it as unpopular with voters. But what would happen, I wonder, if our political actions better matched our religious rhetoric? How might things change around the world if we let our worship of the loving and generous Prince of Peace influence our international policy decisions?

O Lord, help me confront and overcome my natural tendency to
stigmatize or despise other people, and help me give others the benefit
of the doubt. May I represent my Savior well and follow his example in
every sphere of my personal life, and so influence our national life. I am
grateful for your blessings! Amen. ❧

A Call for Repentance

"Those eighteen who died when the tower in Siloam fell on them—do you think they were more guilty than all the others living in Jerusalem? I tell you, no! But unless you repent, you too will all perish."
LUKE 13:4 – 5

Exactly one year ago, in 1994, a church group in Alabama assembled to prepare for an Easter pageant. Twenty people died when a tornado hit and the church building collapsed on them. Four of the victims were small children, who had been happy about their first Easter show; one was the four-year-old child of the pastor. Many in the Christian community wondered why these innocent children, gathered in a church building, died just a few days before the Christian world celebrated the resurrection of Jesus Christ.

When I first came home from the Navy, a young woman in my Bible class and I often jogged together. She had a five-year-old son who had died, and she could never understand why her innocent child had been taken from her. I know of no question that feels more troubling to human beings than this one.

Jesus wept over the death of loved ones and he expects us to grieve their loss. But in Luke 13 he tells us not to obsess over how *long* we live on earth, but how *well* we live. He urges us to repent whenever we fail to fulfill the reason for our creation. Jesus is telling us, "Take a look at yourself and strive for the highest quality of life possible, no matter how many years you may have." He himself did not have a long life, but he accomplished everything God sent him to do.

No change we must make to have a full relationship with Christ is a sacrifice. Rather, such changes open the door to more peaceful, joyful, adventurous, and gratifying lives.

God, again I'm challenged by the incisive nature of the Holy Scriptures. Give me a receptive heart and an open mind, and plant within me a seed of guidance, based on simple truths that never change. Help me be adventurous and courageous in seeking a more intimate relationship with my Savior, Jesus Christ, in whose name I pray. Amen. ❧

318

A Flawed but Useful Life

But the thing David had done displeased the LORD.
2 SAMUEL 11:27

In Israel's King David we see a life filled with glory and disgrace, joy and sorrow, thanksgiving and repentance. David may be the most diverse and conflicted character in the entire Bible.

How do you assess his life? If you had to summarize David's life or write an epitaph on his tombstone, what would you say? Certainly he was a very human character. Like all of us, David did things contrary to the basic mandates of God. The Bible says all of us have sinned and fallen short of the glory of God, and that the wages of sin is death (Romans 3:23; 6:23). This combination of verses summarizes the trouble we have in our relationship with God. David epitomized that trouble—and yet one characteristic remained constant in his life: he loved God and put his faith in God. When David committed terrible deeds—we might even call them atrocities—he acknowledged them with courage, repented of his sins, and asked God for forgiveness.

But why *did* God forgive him? Some might say, "David's murder and adultery were so terrible, I can't understand why God would forgive him. And I don't see why the Bible considers David such a hero." We must remember that God forgave David not because of who David was, but because of who God is. God loved him, and God's love for us is as great as his love for David.

David was a fallible, fault-filled human being, and yet God used him in great ways. Jesus Christ himself was descended from David, and he often pointed out his prized family heritage. That means that, despite our own weaknesses and faults, God also can use *us* in the most exalted, exemplary, challenging, and gratifying ways.

Dear God, sometimes I feel shocked by the Bible's frank description of people I consider both heroes and villains. Help me remember that in each of us there lives both villain and hero. When I fall short of the perfection of my Savior, Jesus Christ, I ask that I might quickly repent and turn away from my sin, and instead become a champion of justice and peace and fairness and forgiveness. In Jesus' name I pray. Amen. 🕊

Obstacles to God

*Jesus answered, "If you want to be perfect, go, sell your possessions and give
to the poor, and you will have treasure in heaven. Then come, follow me."*
MATTHEW 19:21

A rich young man once asked Jesus what he must do to gain eternal life.
When Jesus told him to keep the commandments, the man responded,
"Which ones?" Apparently he wanted to have a better relationship with God
as cheaply as possible. Jesus named several commandments: "You shall not
murder, commit adultery, steal," and so on. The man replied that he had kept
them all! Still he felt a void. What should he do?

As he often did, Jesus answered the question indirectly. He told the young
man to sell his possessions, give the money to the poor, and follow him. Jesus
looked into this man's heart and saw what stood between him and a full relationship with God — in this case, an infatuation with wealth and possessions.

Like the young man, we need to remove any obstacle that comes between
God and us. In my own case, I have to be careful about an excessive desire
to have enough money to meet all my family's needs and desires — and to
ensure a comfortable retirement. Such an obsession can become an obstacle
in my relationship with God. I confess that I have enough wealth to meet all
my requirements and to be generous to others who are in need. This is just
one of the worldly desires against which we must guard as potential obstacles
to a full Christian commitment.

Christ wants us to look into our hearts and say, "What separates me from
a total commitment to my Savior, Jesus Christ?" We must get rid of the mind-
set that says, "How cheaply can I do this? How much can I hold on to and
still have an adequate relationship with God?" We must be willing to give up
anything that stands between God and us.

*Dear God, help me identify and abandon the ambitions or priorities that
interfere with my willingness to follow Christ. Help me see myself clearly,
and give me the courage, through prayer and self-analysis, to correct
defects in my life and be drawn nearer to you, that I might follow Christ
with a more dedicated and liberated spirit. I ask this in Jesus' name.
Amen.* ❧

Recognizing the Son of God

And when the centurion, who stood there in front of Jesus, saw how
he died, he said, "Surely this man was the Son of God!"
MARK 15:39

The Roman governor, Pilate, recognized Christ as innocent. He knew that the Jewish leaders had contrived false evidence against him and so he announced, "I find nothing against this man." But because he feared for his position and wanted to avoid a riot in Jerusalem, he sentenced Jesus to be scourged, beaten, and finally crucified.

Perhaps trying to assuage his conscience, Pilate ordered a sign nailed to the cross: "Jesus, King of the Jews." Jewish leaders objected: "Say only that he *claimed* to be king of the Jews." Pilate replied, "What I have written, I have written." It is interesting that in the relatively insignificant matter of a sign on the cross, Pilate remained honest. But in the profoundly important matter of executing an innocent man, the governor yielded to self-interest and political pressure.

At the cross, Roman soldiers rolled dice to see who would get Jesus' clothes. One got his sandals, another received his outer cloak, and so forth. Although these men played key roles in the most profound event in history, they remained ignorant of it. Instead, they struggled over winning a peasant's tunic.

Are we guilty of similar attitudes? In our everyday lives, do we ignore the magnificent gift of God and instead focus on insignificant, worldly things? Or like Pilate, do we cave in on important things and remain strong on trivial ones?

One soldier, a centurion, finally looked up at Jesus—apparently noting his remarkable words, astonishing demeanor, and the eerie darkness before his death—and declared, "Surely this man was the son of God!" May we all look up from our everyday concerns to recognize the true identity of Jesus Christ, and then allow this knowledge to transform profoundly the way we live.

> *Lord, I often wander through life from one day to another, never*
> *experiencing the full joy and peace of the transcendent life you offer me.*
> *Help me grasp the simple answer of trying to be successful in your eyes*
> *by emphasizing the things that I can't see, like peace, justice, humility,*
> *forgiveness, and love. In the name of my Savior, Jesus Christ, I pray.*
> *Amen.* ❧

321

The Truth of Consequences

"This is what the LORD *says: 'Out of your own household I am going to bring calamity on you. Before your very eyes I will take your wives and give them to one who is close to you, and he will sleep with your wives in broad daylight. You did it in secret, but I will do this thing in broad daylight before all Israel.'"*

2 SAMUEL 12:11 – 12

David repented of his adultery with Bathsheba and his murder of Uriah. God forgave him for both — and yet the remorseful king still had to face the dire consequences of his sin.

The first blow fell when the innocent baby born as a result of David's illicit union with Uriah's wife became ill and died. From then on, David's family suffered under a divine curse. His sons fought over his throne, conspired against one another, and even murdered each other.

When we commit some sin — even though we repent, appeal to God for forgiveness, and receive it — we may still have to face serious consequences. Maybe we lie or gossip, and afterward truly repent and say, "Lord, I have lied about that person. I know that her reputation has been hurt because of what I said, and I ask you to forgive me." God will certainly forgive us and give us another chance; but that other person still has been hurt by our sinful actions. As a result, we may well suffer the consequences of our immoral behavior.

We must not forget that sin, although it can be forgiven, always has devastating effects on those it touches; that is why we should strive to avoid it. Let us take advantage of every opportunity we have to heal the wounds we have opened. God calls us to compensate and try to repair the damage we have caused. Let us determine, by the Holy Spirit, to spread blessing instead of suffering.

Holy God, help me avoid the tragedy David created. I know that I can repent and turn to Christ and know that my sins will be forgiven. But let me not forget that in Christ, I have the spiritual resources necessary to reject sin. And, Lord, give me the will to repair any damage that I inflict on others. I ask these things in Jesus' name. Amen. ❧

322

Church Discipline

*"If your brother or sister sins, go and point out their fault, just between
the two of you. If they listen to you, you have won them over. But if they
will not listen, take one or two others along, so that 'every matter may be
established by the testimony of two or three witnesses.' If they still refuse to
listen, tell it to the church; and if they refuse to listen even to the church,
treat them as you would a pagan or a tax collector."*
MATTHEW 18:15 – 17

Do you belong to a church that handles congregational problems in the fashion Jesus describes in this passage? Quakers used to sit in total silence until one member started moving in some specific way and began to speak a concern about another member or confess something he had done himself. A prayerful exchange of ideas would ensue, and corrective action would follow.

Among some Puritans, if a woman were known to be gossiping, for example, she would be admonished; if she repeated the offense, she either was put in stocks or dunked in a nearby stream for at least sixty seconds. I'm guessing that usually stopped the habit! Thieves would be put in stocks, whipped, or even executed. The church, not the government, enforced a very strict criminal code.

While I'm not suggesting we return to those practices, we should obey Christ when he tells the church to administer discipline. How much better off we would be if the church carried out these instructions! This happened more often in the past. My uncle Jack was expelled from a Methodist church when, contrary to the rules, they caught him dancing. They urged him to stop, but he refused; so they kicked him out. That may be one reason I'm a Baptist!

The point is, back in those days, the church strictly enforced the standards it had adopted. Deviation from those standards brought either repentance or consequences—and Christ is the one who authorized the practice.

*Lord, once again I'm confronted by a disturbing Bible passage, but one
that also offers me help in complying with your will. Although I look
upon Jesus as the utmost in gentleness, in this case his words sound
harsh—but the harshness is eased by the knowledge of God's eternal and
unlimited grace and love. I thank you for this, in Jesus' name. Amen.* ❧

323

The Dash

What do people gain from all their labors
at which they toil under the sun?
ECCLESIASTES 1:3

At the funeral service for the mother of Martin Luther King Jr., a preacher from Cleveland, Ohio, gave one of the shortest and most memorable sermons I've ever heard. On her grave, he said, would be a marker noting her name, her birth date, and the date of her death. Between these dates would be a little dash — and he wanted to discuss only the interval represented by the dash.

Since someday all of us will have a tiny dash on our headstone, we too should ponder what will fill it. Too often we imagine it filled with notable and publicized accomplishments; but in the long run, will those things matter most?

Let's think back on the most memorable, pleasant times of our lives. Were they times of striving for success, or were they moments when we *really* connected with God or with other people?

One time three of my young grandchildren spent a weekend with Rosalynn and me. They had an opportunity to go see *The Lion King* movie, but earlier I had mentioned that I needed to tear down an old pier in our pond. When I urged the children to see the movie, they insisted instead on helping me tear down the pier. So that afternoon we waded in mud about knee deep and struggled to tear down the boards and frame. I'll never forget it, although we achieved very little. In fact, the following morning I had a backhoe pick up the whole pile of debris and put it in a truck. It could have removed the pier in a few minutes, but we had enjoyed our afternoon together.

Our lives have two parts. One involves busyness and a striving for achievement. We sometimes ignore the other times when we focus on intimate relationships with God and other people — that dash in between, when we nurture the fullness of life.

God, thank you for the good life you've given me. Help me think deeply about what I'm doing in the time of the dash, in the years you give me. Enable me to make them count for you, and so to bless those whom you love and for whom Jesus died. In Christ's name I pray. Amen. ❧

The Blessings of Old Age

Gray hair is a crown of splendor;
it is attained in the way of righteousness.
PROVERBS 16:31

Retirement is a turning point in life — either a downhill slope into inactivity and resentment, or a time filled with new enjoyment, learning, and adventure. After we retire, we can try the things we once wanted to do but couldn't because of daily responsibilities and lack of money — the good things that captured our attention when we were young and filled with idealism, hope, and a wide range of interests. I once wrote a book about this called *Virtues of Aging.*

I served in the military for eleven years. As a new officer, freshly graduated from Annapolis, I made three hundred dollars a month. Out of this I had to pay ninety-two dollars for rent and fifty-four dollars for expenses on the ship. After buying uniforms, food, and other necessities, Rosalynn, I, and our growing family had little money left. But we felt happy and secure. We lived in a government housing project after retiring from the Navy, and I began pursuing some things that had interested me in earlier years.

When we left the White House, my staff and cabinet officers took up a collection to buy me a present. My secretary told me secretly it was a jeep, which I didn't want. I enjoyed woodworking and wanted to make furniture, so they took the gift money and bought tools to furnish a woodworking shop. I've enjoyed that gift as much as anything I've ever received, and since then have made over a hundred pieces of furniture. I also took up painting, writing books, fly-fishing, and bird-watching, and Rosalynn and I have had much more time for involvement in our church and community affairs. None of these commitments are expensive.

Advancing age needn't become a time of despair, trepidation, fear, or hopelessness. It can instead be a time of blessing, a time to enjoy our family and the good life God has given us.

O Lord, as I become older, I pray that you help me see this time as a special gift from you, to be mined for the treasures you've placed there. Open my eyes to the new opportunities available. In fact, help me use wisely every day you've given me, for the sake of your Son, Jesus Christ. I pray this in my Savior's name. Amen. ❧

Marriage Advice from a Former President

But those who marry will face many troubles in this life,
and I want to spare you this.
I CORINTHIANS 7:28

When Rosalynn and I celebrated our fiftieth anniversary, the news media wanted to interview us. Rosalynn usually speaks first when we get relationship questions, and she said, "We try to give each other plenty of space. We've learned not to try to dominate one another, but to let each other enjoy independent lives as much as possible."

That's true, but at the same time we also share as many things as possible. For years, we have tried to convince each other to join in favorite hobbies, to see if we both might like them. As a result, we do a lot of things together. For example, we ski together; I started skiing when I was sixty-two years old, and Rosalynn joined me. We enjoy bird-watching and fly-fishing together, and we play tennis against each other. Obviously, we share family and business responsibilities. We do as many things as we can as partners, which gives us many opportunities to enjoy each other.

We are determined to end each day in a spirit of harmony, even though we have some difficult times. We try to resolve our differences before we go to sleep. Each night we alternate reading the Bible aloud, usually in Spanish. When we're apart, we read the same Scripture. For us, it works as a kind of healing process, and we've been doing it for more than thirty-five years.

It is up to each couple to decide what they can do to enjoy a healthy marriage. It's important to find common ground, not dominate each other, and find ways to communicate and reconcile when one person hurts the other. These habits have helped us through a lot of years, and perhaps they can do the same for you.

O God, what a tremendous gift you gave us with marriage! Help us explore how to enjoy its glories and minimize its difficulties. Enable us to find areas of common ground, and teach us effective means of reconciliation when things go a little sour between us. Use my marriage to help me understand the true meaning of love. I pray in Jesus' name. Amen. ❧

A Willing Subordination

*Wives, in the same way submit yourselves to your own husbands so
that, if any of them do not believe the word, they may be won over
without words by the behavior of their wives, when they see the
purity and reverence of your lives.*

I PETER 3:1 – 2

How do we deal with the concepts of subordination and submission? In a time
of women's liberation, such a concept can cause trouble. The extreme policy
of the Southern Baptist Convention to deny equal status to women became
enough of a problem in our own family that Amy, our daughter, withdrew
from the church. This Scripture was mistakenly interpreted to mean that
women are inferior to men, a faulty notion that rightly troubles many of us.

In fact, biblical submission does not require women to yield to domination or mean they are inferior in any way. Consider one definition of submission: "the willing acceptance of a prevailing societal order, as we accept
common laws, so as to achieve some meaningful and beneficial outcome."

In the days of Peter, Paul, and Christ, a married woman was considered
the property of her husband, with almost no rights but a multitude of responsibilities. Even in such a culture, the biblical writers did not call women to
subordinate themselves to their husbands as chattel; rather, they called Christian wives to submit to the socially approved authority of their husbands,
who, with love, must willingly submit to the divine authority of Christ. This
arrangement of mutual submission represented a sharing of responsibility and
authority. Far from enslaving women, it liberated them. Paul wrote, "There
is neither ... male [nor] female, for you are all one in Christ Jesus" (Galatians
3:28).

Benefits accrue when both parties subordinate themselves and their ambitions to the authority of Jesus Christ. When that occurs, this text prescribes
a divine route to true liberation.

*O Lord, I am grateful for messages in the Bible that cause me to ponder
deeply and search my own heart. I give you thanks for this biblical
explanation of the proper relationship among Christians—whether we're
black, white, poor, rich, male, or female—and for the reminder that we
are all equal under you and the same in your eyes. For this I am truly
thankful. In Jesus' name I pray. Amen.* ❧

Erotic Love Was God's Idea

Let him kiss me with the kisses of his mouth —
for your love is more delightful than wine.
SONG OF SOLOMON 1:2

I fell in love with Rosalynn during my time at the Naval Academy as a midshipman. She was a close friend of my younger sister, but it took me a long time before I really noticed her. One Sunday night I picked her up outside the Methodist church and after a movie I dropped her off and drove home. The next morning my mother asked, "Jimmy, what did you do last night?"

"I went to a movie," I replied.

"Did you go with anybody?" she asked.

"Yes, ma'am, I went with Rosalynn Smith."

"What did you think of her?"

"She's the one I'm going to marry," I declared.

Rosalynn, however, had promised her father she wouldn't marry until she finished college, and so when I asked her to marry me, she said no. Eventually, I managed to change her mind (after she'd tried all the other boys in Sumter County who weren't in the military). The Song of Solomon is like the story of Rosalynn and me; it's about a young couple in love.

Because the book frankly celebrates physical love between a man and a woman, the few pastors who preach from it are very likely to say something like, "This book *really* describes how much God loved the Israelites, or how much Christ loved the church." While I won't dispute such interpretations, if you just read the book, you won't see such a focus anywhere in the text. I think it intends to show that all aspects of love are blessed by God and are to be cherished. Although sometimes we feel embarrassed by discussion of sexual love, even within marriage, the Song of Solomon leaves no doubt that God also cherishes *passionate* love.

Dear Lord, I'm thankful that you created sensual and erotic love to be shared freely between husbands and wives. I know this can be no more intense than your boundless love toward us in Christ. May our own marriages grow in this area, and may others get a flavor of your love for them by watching love blossom between sweethearts and spouses. In Jesus' name I pray. Amen. ❧

A Challenge for Modern Parents

Start children off on the way they should go,
and even when they are old they will not turn from it.
PROVERBS 22:6

I grew up in an isolated community about three miles west of Plains. The center of my life was my home, my mama, my daddy, and our black neighbors. These sources provided almost all the counsel, advice, and instruction that shaped my early life.

We had no electricity on the farm. We had a radio that ran on batteries, though, and on occasion we'd turn it on to hear a favorite program and then turn it off again so the batteries wouldn't run down. We listened to programs like *Fibber McGee and Molly* and *Little Orphan Annie*. Our lives were quite encapsulated. All we got from the outside world came in a local newspaper and the few times we listened to the radio. Few other voices shaped our pattern of living or molded our hearts.

Today, however, even in the earliest years of life, children begin to hear and consider all sorts of conflicting voices. A current debate rages about television talk shows. Some people want to censor them; others want to prevent any censorship. I don't watch these shows, but I've been told the hosts describe bizarre human adventures and discuss themes of adultery and violence and laugh about them as though they were common and acceptable aspects of life. Children are much more mobile and independent than they used to be, and so they often come into contact with these strident voices.

All these changes make it easy for children to stray from the beneficial Christian influence of their families. That's why we parents must make every effort to communicate proper values to our children, telling them about the God who created them and describing the perfect life of Jesus as our example. Parents' voices now must compete with many others, so we have no choice but to try extra hard to be heard.

Dear God, I realize that we face fierce competition to gain our children's attention. Many of the voices clamoring to be heard have no commitment to you or to the values of your Word. So help me, Lord, to speak clearly and boldly, and help me live out the convictions I proclaim. I pray in Jesus' name. Amen.

Teaching the Next Generation

*He decreed statutes for Jacob and established the law in Israel, which he
commanded our ancestors to teach their children, so the next generation
would know them, even the children yet to be born, and they in turn would
tell their children. Then they would put their trust in God and would not
forget his deeds but would keep his commands.*
PSALM 78:5 – 7

In 1981 I was asked to make a speech at a small Methodist college in Southern Japan. I had been out of the White House only a few months, and they
felt overawed that a former president would even visit their school. Everyone
looked nervous—the professors, the administrators, the students, and their
parents. So I decided to begin my speech with a joke.

It takes a long time to translate English into Japanese, and the Japanese
sense of humor differs markedly from ours, so instead of my funniest joke, I
chose my shortest one. I told it, the interpreter translated it—and the whole
audience collapsed into laughter. I had never had a better response to a joke,
and I couldn't wait to finish my speech so I could ask the interpreter how he
translated it.

When I later inquired, however, the man ducked his head, looked the
other way, and changed the subject. When I persisted, he finally said, "Mr.
President, I told the audience, 'President Carter told a funny story. Everyone
must laugh.'"

As the psalmist knew, teaching has its difficulties; but even so, we have
an obligation to pass on our faith to our children and to their peers. It is
sobering to realize that Christianity always is just one generation away from
extinction. If our generation doesn't teach younger people about Christ, then
what will the next generation have to pass along? Every Christian should be
able and eager to tell others the truth about Jesus Christ and how to be saved
through his sacrifice.

*O Lord, help me be willing to teach others about Jesus, in my own
way, appropriate to my abilities and opportunities. May I accept the
responsibility of sharing what I know about Jesus Christ and your love for
us all. Allow me to point others to the light that can give them a life of joy
and peace. I ask these things in the name of my Savior. Amen.*

Growing Up in the Faith

We will not hide them from their descendants; we will tell the next generation the praiseworthy deeds of the LORD, his power, and the wonders he has done.

PSALM 78:4

I started out in life almost preordained to be a Christian. My parents were Christians, everybody in Plains was a Christian, and my father was a Baptist deacon and Sunday school teacher. From the time I was three years old, I memorized Bible verses that taught me the rudiments of our faith. Back then, a visiting preacher came in each year for a weeklong revival, with morning and evening services every day. I accepted Christ as Savior at one of those meetings when I was eleven years old.

I taught Sunday school classes at Annapolis, and when I was stationed on a ship, I tried to attend services. Even at sea in a submarine, on special occasions, I would hold religious services in cramped spaces between torpedoes. When we came into port, I would go to whichever church in Norfolk had the earliest service. That often meant attending Catholic services before going home to Rosalynn and my children.

When I returned home from the Navy in 1953, both Rosalynn and I assumed the role my father had taken: we taught Bible lessons. When I was governor and then president, we joined the Baptist church nearest to where we lived. When we returned home to Plains, we joined Maranatha Baptist Church, where I've been teaching Sunday school lessons for many years.

The point is that my lifelong commitment to Christ began as a child. My parents and my community fulfilled their responsibility to pass on the Christian faith to me. Each of us must do that for our own descendants. Think what a tragedy it would be if any generation failed in this responsibility! We have a divine charge to pass along our knowledge of the saving sacrifice of Jesus Christ.

Lord, let me never forget that I am a partner with you and, therefore, never need to face trials, tribulations, sorrows, or fears alone. Thank you for the people in my life who have helped me to know you better, and give me the strength and wisdom to become a reliable guide for others who need to know you. I ask this in the name of my Savior, Jesus Christ. Amen.

From Errant Children to Accurate Arrows

*Like arrows in the hands of a warrior
are children born in one's youth.*
PSALM 127:4

Saint Francis of Assisi was the son of a rich merchant. During the first nineteen years of his life, Francis wasted his father's money, got drunk, and acted very selfishly. He joined the army and served there until enemy forces took him prisoner. After his release, his life changed—to some degree. He visited Rome, encountered a beggar, and decided to try begging. He gave away all his material possessions and lived among the beggars for a year. Finally, he returned home, still searching for a proper role in life. There he also started giving away his possessions.

When his father learned of his actions, he accused Francis of going insane and beat him. Francis replied that he was only trying to follow the Scriptures. Although his father didn't understand or approve, nine people soon decided to follow Francis in his commitment to own nothing and to work among and for the poor.

One day Francis visited a little, dilapidated church. While praying, he received a message from God to repair the church. Francis thought this meant "repair this particular building." So he took part of the money he had received from begging, and he and his friends repaired the little church building. When they finished, it occurred to Francis that God might be calling him to something larger.

Shortly thereafter, Francis and his friends visited Rome and got an audience with the pope; in 1209 Pope Innocent III unofficially endorsed Francis's simple "rule" for serving the poor, and in 1223, Pope Honorius III officially declared the Order of Saint Francis.

God intends that our "arrows," our children, fly where the Lord directs them to go. As parents, are we willing to let them soar?

O God, it's not always easy for me to recognize the difference between legitimate parental guidance and illegitimate interference with your divine direction. I love my children—but I know that you love them even more. May I therefore always want the best for my children, remembering that "the best" always means your will for them, wherever that may lead. In Christ's name I pray. Amen. ❧

Divorce Court

To the married I give this command (not I, but the Lord): A wife must not separate from her husband. But if she does, she must remain unmarried or else be reconciled to her husband. And a husband must not divorce his wife.
1 CORINTHIANS 7:10–11

When I was a child, nobody got a divorce. It just wasn't done. I never knew of any divorcees in Plains; we thought it happened only in New York or Hollywood. We did know of some married people who lived with somebody other than their spouse. In fact, my godmother, a nurse, lived with a senior doctor while still married to another man. The two never got divorced, and I guess the community somehow accepted adultery more readily than divorce. Since then, of course, people's views on the issue have changed.

Rosalynn and I have been married and loyal to each other for sixty-five years, but some of our children have had unhappy marriages that ended in divorce. Now remarried, they have harmonious and successful second marriages. How should we feel about that?

Although I agree with Paul's concern about divorce, I don't condemn my children for what they've done, even though it was a grievous thing for us when their attempts at reconciliation ended in failure. We loved their first spouses like our own children, and when they decided they couldn't get along with each other, it really hurt. But I can't condemn them.

God clearly desires peace between husbands and wives, and Christians should make every effort to salvage a troubled marriage. A husband and wife who share a deep Christian faith, who worship together as families, are certainly better able to resolve problems and incompatibilities between them, and other Christians can be of help. That's the overwhelming message Paul gives us. But that doesn't mean we should ostracize or condemn those who wind up in divorce court.

O Lord, I'm grateful for a chance to ponder one of the most difficult and controversial portions of your Holy Word. Help me do all I can to encourage others in their marriages, even as I work to make my own marriage both strong and successful. Help us resolve even our most difficult problems with mutual respect, forgiveness, and love. I pray in Jesus' name. Amen.

333

Advice to Widows

*Now to the unmarried and the widows I say: It is good for them to
stay unmarried, as I do. But if they cannot control themselves, they
should marry, for it is better to marry than to burn with passion.*
I CORINTHIANS 7:8 – 9

Once when Rosalynn and I visited the northern part of Ethiopia, we saw some tiny caves, no bigger than a bed, carved into solid rock. The parents of the men who lived inside those caves had placed them there when they were small boys. People brought them food and revered them as holy men. People thought these men had never sinned because they sat in their caves for an entire lifetime. They assumed the cave-dwellers had developed extreme self-control.

Paul had very different advice for unmarried women and widows. He told them if they lacked self-control appropriate for single Christians — if they hungered for a sexual relationship within marriage — then they should not live a sequestered life alone, but rather choose marriage.

It is interesting that Paul writes only about women and doesn't even mention widowers. That may be because widows nearly always outnumber widowers. When I served as president of the Lions Club in Plains, we had a Christmas party for our spouses. One trivia question asked, "How many widows do you think live in Plains, and how many widowers?" I remember the answer very distinctly: fifty-one widows and just one widower (Rosalynn's grandfather). Even in more recent days, we normally expect wives to outlive their husbands.

If a husband dies and leaves behind a widow, then that widow is free to remarry if she does not wish to live alone. If she desires to be part of an intimate relationship again, she should go ahead and remarry. She's entitled to do so, and no one should condemn her.

*O Lord, help me see this text not only as instruction for widows who
desire to get remarried, but far more as the sort of godly outlook that you
want all of us to have, one that endorses freedom and compassion rather
than harsh rules. Let me realize that I have an obligation to deal with
others in love, regardless of their situation. I pray these things in Jesus'
name. Amen.* ❧

334

A Proven Love

And this is his command: to believe in the name of his Son, Jesus
Christ, and to love one another as he commanded us.
1 JOHN 3:23

When John tells us to "love one another," what does he mean? The English language muddies the water for us, since it has only one word for "love." We may say that we "love" our children, or that we "love" cats, or that we "love" to watch baseball or build furniture; but clearly we don't "love" all these things in the same way. So what does John mean?

At the time I was running for president, two Baptist missionaries from my home church, Jerome and Joanne Etheridge, set out to serve in Togo, West Africa. Jerome noticed that the villages in that area had no clean water to drink. So he went to every village within eighty miles of their Togo home and, using well-drilling equipment mounted on the back of a two-ton truck donated by some North Carolina Baptists, drilled a well for every village. In all, he drilled more than 130 bore holes, 120 of which struck water. If he dug a dry well, he simply tried again until he succeeded.

Jerome and Joanne also founded eighty churches in those villages, and five thousand individuals accepted Christ through their dedicated work. They illustrate for me the ultimate form of love, the kind John is talking about here—namely, *agape* love.

Agape love is unconditional. It loves someone who may not be attractive or will not repay us or even acknowledge our affection. *Agape* is sacrificial love that encompasses humility, service, compassion, and forgiveness. God loved us so much that he gave his only Son—the ultimate act of *agape* love.

As we analyze our lives and shape our personal habits, let us remember John's injunction. Let us truly love one another. And in so doing, we will prove to the world that we belong to Jesus.

O God, help me resolve in my heart to live closer to my Savior, Jesus
Christ, and to share freely with others the blessings you have given
me. Show me how to become a living illustration of the words that
best describe Christ: peace, love, justice, humility, service, forgiveness,
compassion, and, most importantly, love. I ask these things in his name,
who loves us. Amen. ❧

Is Love God?

Whoever does not love does not know God, because God is love.
1 JOHN 4:8

The statement "God is love" seems very simple. For many of us, it was the first Bible phrase we memorized. But we must recognize an unfortunate tendency to misinterpret it.

Some people reverse the statement to mean that any love is godly, or "love is God." Such an approach can be misleading and even dangerous. With this interpretation, we exalt physical love too much, particularly if we obsess over some human affiliation in our life. We may say, "The love I feel right now for that pretty woman is transcendent; it's the most important thing in my life, superseding everything else." In doing this, we let passion and misplaced adoration dominate us.

Even when love does not involve sex or passion, we can exaggerate its importance. Perhaps the purest form of human love is of a child for its parents or of parents for a beloved child. On occasion, even this can become a form of illicit worship.

Jesus, the greatest proponent of love, recognized the seriousness of this temptation and said, "Anyone who loves their father or mother more than me is not worthy of me; anyone who loves their son or daughter more than me is not worthy of me" (Matthew 10:37).

This is a difficult concept to understand or accept, but we must contemplate its meaning. The kind of universal love advocated by Christ tempers and stretches our hearts and minds to encompass a truly transcendent form of love. It embodies the finest aspects of the forms of love mentioned above but is permanent and encompasses those who may not be lovable, who may not love us back, and from whom we can derive no personal advantage. This enhances even the mutual human affections in our lives without derogating or subjugating our love for Jesus.

Dear Lord, help me understand the great difference between "God is love" and "love is God." Help me remember that all good things, including love, flow from you and have their ultimate source and expression in you. Allow me, Lord, to be a conduit of your love to those around me, for your glory and their blessing. I pray these things in the name of Jesus Christ. Amen. ❧

Prisoner of Jesus Christ

I, Paul, the prisoner of Christ Jesus for the sake of you Gentiles ...
EPHESIANS 3:1

Why would Paul call himself a "prisoner of Christ Jesus"? He himself gives us the answer: "for the sake of you Gentiles." While Paul might have been in Roman custody, God had the apostle in the right place to do what he had been called to do (see Acts 9:15–16).

Paul had become a prisoner of the Romans on behalf of Christ—as his servant, under his domination. Even as a prisoner of the Romans, Paul was guarded, constrained, controlled, and inhibited from certain actions by Christ.

In a similar way, each of us is a prisoner of *something*. What do we serve? What constrains us, controls us, captures our minds? As we look back over our past week, what things concerned us most? Most of them, probably, related to human ambitions: achieving a certain goal or worrying about some mistakes we've made. Those kinds of things tend to imprison us and often rise to the top of our consciousness.

We should not condemn *all* those things. They are natural to us, after all (see Matthew 6:32). What Paul tells us, on the other hand, is very *un*natural, although very good. As a prisoner of Christ, he intended to obey the word of Jesus in order to realize his life's ambitions.

In the last letter Paul wrote—while awaiting his execution in a Roman prison—the apostle wrote, "The Lord stood at my side and gave me strength, so that through me the message might be proclaimed fully and all the Gentiles might hear it" (2 Timothy 4:17). Jesus accompanied Paul into the prison, where he strengthened him to do his final work.

Do we recognize we are equally protected?

O Lord, I know that Paul went to Jerusalem knowing the danger. There he was arrested and spent the rest of his life as a prisoner until his execution. He was willing, Lord, to go where you sent him and to do what you asked him to do. May you grant me the strength to do the same. In Jesus' name I pray. Amen. ❧

The Narrow Gate

*"Enter through the narrow gate. For wide is the gate and broad is
the road that leads to destruction, and many enter through it."*
MATTHEW 7:13

Plains, Georgia, has a population of 635 and boasts eleven churches in the community; so the vast majority of us profess to be Christians, to have accepted Christ into our lives. Two billion others on the planet profess the same thing. And yet Jesus calls the gate "narrow" and says few will find the way to eternal life. What does he mean?

Most of us define Christianity in a broad, accommodating, and comfortable way. We don't want to feel constrained by some narrow definition of Christ's teachings. We prefer to forget about the uncomfortable parts of the Sermon on the Mount and say, "I'm okay. I'm no worse than anyone around me. I'm a satisfactory Christian."

We rationalize, "Hey, I have my own responsibilities—to myself, my spouse, my children, my grandchildren. I'll take care of them first, and then I'll consider living self-sacrificially. I have my own legitimate responsibilities to fulfill now and for a few more years, but after I retire I'll have more time for my Christian duties."

Before long, such procrastination becomes our mode of existence. We come to feel that our inaction is okay. We reason, "If God didn't agree with the way I live, then why would I enjoy the blessing of living in this wonderful, free nation? Why would God let me have nice clothes, plenty of food, a decent home, and nourishing fellowship with other believers? If I weren't worthy as a Christian, then why would God give me all these blessings?"

It is *exactly* to individuals who reason in this way, who rationalize their thoughtless and self-centered lifestyles, to whom Jesus says (some would say, harshly), "Narrow is the gate that leads to eternal life."

*O Father, I'm thankful for Jesus' guidelines for achieving a simple but
glorious life, a transcendent life, a worthy life, a full life, an enjoyable
and gratifying life. Help me define the Christian faith in a way that helps
me to live more compatibly with the example Christ set for me. Forgive
me my sins and shortcomings, and grant me a spirit of peace and love. In
Jesus' name I pray. Amen.* ❧

Living beyond Reproach

Now the overseer is to be above reproach, faithful to his wife,
temperate, self-controlled, respectable, hospitable, able to teach ...
not quarrelsome, not a lover of money.
I TIMOTHY 3:2 – 3

"Overseer" means leader of a congregation. Young Christians going to seminary to prepare themselves for ministry might read these words and say, "I give up! There's no way I can meet all those requirements." And there is no denying the rigorous nature of Paul's prerequisites for church leadership. They are not easy to fulfill, and sometimes are difficult even to understand.

For instance, Paul says a pastor must be faithful to his wife. Does this mean that a pastor must be a man? That a pastor must be married? That the pastor cannot be a polygamist? That the pastor must not cheat on a spouse? Or that a divorced person cannot be a pastor?

What about the requirement that a pastor be temperate? Does that mean he or she cannot overindulge in food or drink — or pleasure?

Does the requirement that a pastor not love money mean that the size of a salary cannot be important?

What about the requirement that a pastor manage his or her own family well? We can't always control children! I have four children and twelve grandchildren, and I would hate for my own character to be determined exclusively by how *they* behave. So far, all of our children and grandchildren have escaped prison — but I can't say they haven't violated certain laws (and I can't say that I haven't, either).

Paul issues these requirements for pastors (and then deacons) as a guide to choosing church leaders; but he does not intend to exclude the rest of us. All of us should be temperate in our personal habits, avoid greed, stay faithful to our loved ones, and honor our commitments. As Christians, we represent Christ to others. Therefore, all of us should seek happiness by striving to live beyond reproach, always seeking to do the will of God.

God, please teach me, through your Word and through life, what it means
to live a holy life. Help me avoid asking, "How close to the line can I get
without being condemned?" Instead, prompt me to ask, "How can I best
represent Jesus in every situation, and how can I be a blessing to others?"
In Jesus' name I pray. Amen.

Free to Worship

In the first year of Cyrus king of Persia, in order to fulfill the word of the
LORD spoken by Jeremiah, the LORD moved the heart of Cyrus king of Persia
to make a proclamation throughout his realm and also to put it in writing.
EZRA 1:1

My uncle Tom Gordy was captured in 1941 by Japanese troops and served four years as a prisoner of war. He was tortured and weighed less than a hundred pounds when finally released. The same thing happened to servicemen during the Vietnam War, including James Stockdale, a classmate of mine at the Naval Academy. He was chained and tortured for seven years, but remained strong and resolute. Later, he said, "You must never confuse faith that you will prevail in the end—which you can never afford to lose—with the discipline to confront the most brutal facts of your current reality."

These accounts echo the deep pain suffered by the Jews captive in Babylon. They longed to return home and worship as they had in the past. And then one day, seventy years after their captivity began, along came King Cyrus, the ruler of what we know today as Iran. This powerful Persian king fulfilled the prophecy of Isaiah by conquering the Babylonians. He became the world's dominant leader, a clever military commander, and a shrewd politician. He adopted a policy toward local religions that foreshadowed the Romans' later practice. He knew he would stir up firestorms by trying to change a people's basic religious beliefs, so he didn't try. In 539 BC he issued an edict from the throne that permitted Jewish people to return to Jerusalem and build an altar. At last they could worship as their Scriptures prescribed.

How do we feel about the freedom of worship? Most of us take it for granted. But James Stockdale didn't take it for granted, nor did the Jews who returned from exile. Freedom of worship is a precious thing—a painful discovery when we lose it.

O Lord, I am grateful for the freedom we have in America to worship as
we choose. I'm thankful to live in a society that lets us exercise our basic
rights, and I pray that I might use these opportunities for your glory and
for the service of others. I pray in Jesus' name. Amen. ❧

Speak the Truth!

The LORD hates ... a lying tongue.
PROVERBS 6:16 – 17

I remember the first time I became aware of a president misleading the nation. It involved a man I respected and admired: Dwight Eisenhower. When Soviets accused Ike of flying spy planes over Russia, the president responded publicly that the United States was not, had not, and never would fly a spy plane over Russia. Later, when a U.S. spy plane was shot down over the Soviet Union, our president got caught telling a lie.

Many more lies were told about the Vietnam War. One of the reasons I was elected president was because people were looking for a leader to tell the truth. While campaigning, I said that if I ever made a misleading statement, the people shouldn't vote for me. From that day on, news reporters determined to catch me speaking falsely.

One day my press secretary, Jody Powell, said to my mother, "A very important reporter from the *Washington Post* wants to interview you; she's going to write a very good article, Ms. Lillian, and I hope you'll give her the interview." My mother did not like talking with reporters, and especially women, but finally she agreed. The reporter came in, sat down, and began asking some not-so-friendly questions; very quickly she came around to my claim that I was always truthful. Mama said, "That's right, even when Jimmy was a small boy." The reporter asked, "You mean he has *never* lied?" Mama replied, "No, except maybe a little white lie now and then."

"Aha!" the reporter exclaimed. "A white lie. What do you mean by *that*?"

Mama replied, "Remember when you came to the door awhile ago, and I said you looked very nice and was glad to see you?"

Let's make every effort to tell the truth, since God hates a lying tongue.

God, I thank you that your Word never changes. Thank you for showing me that, a thousand years after Solomon, Jesus Christ demonstrated that your mandates are permanent. Help me turn away from my sinful ways of gossip, selfishness, and twisting of the truth, and give me the strength to renew my commitment to demonstrating what it means to be a Christian. I ask these things in the name of my Savior. Amen. ❧

341

Remember the Truth

We must pay the most careful attention, therefore, to what we have heard, so that we do not drift away.
HEBREWS 2:1

I suppose every Christian has endured times of deep confusion and disillusionment, times when she began drifting away from God. Certainly I have gone through such times.

Often these times occur when we lose a loved one, maybe at a premature age. It can also happen when we lose contact with Christian friends, or we fail to reach some important life goal. Rosalynn became particularly distressed when I failed to get reelected as president in 1980. I had to reassure her that we could still have a bright future and a good life.

At such times, we may feel that God is unfair, that he has abandoned us, or that we have misplaced our faith. That's when we may start drifting away from God—not actively, but steadily. Gradually we start losing our Christian fervor.

The author of Hebrews reminds us that we know the gospel message. We understand the true story of Jesus Christ. We know what he did during three years of public ministry. We know he was crucified, buried, and resurrected. We've read about his miracles; maybe we've even experienced some for ourselves. We know that through his sacrifice we can be totally forgiven and reconciled with God and inherit eternal life. We have all this information available to us—and the writer warns us never to forget it, especially when more worldly priorities bark for our attention.

I doubt that many of us intentionally turn away from Christ. Instead, we turn away from him, or at least from a strong commitment to him, by slowly forgetting the truth. We begin to pay more attention to our selfishness, comfort, and security, and so we start drifting. We must avoid this at all costs by clinging to what we know to be true.

Dear Lord, I pray that you would use these wise and cautionary words from the book of Hebrews to give me strength and courage and a renewed commitment to Jesus, my Lord. Help me be bold, assertive, ambitious, and even aggressive in my commitment to emulate my humble and gracious Savior. Let these things come true in my life. I ask this in Jesus' holy name. Amen. ❧

342

The Indispensable Book

When the king heard the words of the Law, he tore his robes.
2 CHRONICLES 34:19

On my first trip to Great Britain as president, I visited London and requested a tour of Westminster Abbey. Guides led me to a room where forty-seven men had worked on the first English translation of the Holy Bible. They began their work in 1604 and in 1611 finished what we know as the King James Bible.

Rosalynn and I stood there with a large group of reporters from the White House press corps, fascinated by how these scholars studied the ancient texts and translated them as accurately as possible into the language of their day. They knew they were working on the most important book in the history of humankind.

As a little boy in school, I was taught never to treat the Bible with disrespect, to keep it in a prominent place, and never to put another book on top of it. Even now, when I lay down the Bible and start to put a novel or something on it, I remember my early habit and place the Bible on top instead.

In a day when many appear to take the Holy Scriptures for granted, it seems strange that anyone might not have access to them. But that is exactly what happened in Judah after the Assyrian destruction of Jerusalem. The people forgot about the one true God and the holy book and instead worshiped heathen deities. When Josiah took the throne, the young king began removing pagan worship from Judah. As his servants cleaned out the temple, a priest found part of the Scriptures and later read them to the king. Josiah tore his clothes when he realized that his people had forsaken the Law, incurring God's wrath.

God gives us his Word for our instruction and blessing. It truly is the one indispensable book.

God, I am grateful that you give me the opportunity to take advantage of this clear guide to a life that's acceptable in your sight. Grant me wisdom to delve into the Scriptures more deeply and more completely and to obey the divine instruction I find there, based on the perfect life of my Savior, Jesus Christ. In his name I pray. Amen. ❧

Every Believer a Priest

But you are a chosen people, a royal priesthood, a holy nation, God's
special possession, that you may declare the praises of him who called
you out of darkness into his wonderful light.
I PETER 2:9

I have always believed in the priesthood of all believers: each of us having direct access to God and not requiring any intermediary to relate to the Lord. With the help of the Holy Spirit, we can study and comprehend the Scriptures, pray to God, and seek divine guidance. But these days, the church's views on this subject have started to change.

In some Baptist churches, it has gotten to the point where a few people will say, in essence, "You must emphasize these Scriptures, to the detriment of others; and if you don't agree, then you're not a good Christian." Instead of pastors being servants of their congregations, some have become powerful demagogues, dominating the congregation and imposing their personal views and interpretations on everyone.

For thirty years I've been a professor at Emory University, which has a fine religion and theology school. The university has been careful to assure that professors who teach in the theology school are not all cut from the same cloth. No one has to sign a creed that says, "I will teach this way and no other." In the past, our seminaries customarily let pastors express their own ideas, so long as they believed in the fundamentals of the Christian faith. That's becoming less prevalent today. One major Baptist seminary recently fired every professor who believed that women might be pastors, deacons, or even teachers.

I believe these kinds of changes conflict with the idea of the priesthood of all believers. Each of us has the sobering responsibility to study the Scriptures and to come to our own conclusions, through prayer and meditation, about God's mandates. This is religious freedom.

O God, what a privilege I have to be able to come directly to you and to your Word, without a dominant intermediary. Help me take seriously this privilege and conduct myself with the kind of gravity that Jesus personified during his earthly ministry. When I disagree with others, help us to continue caring for each other and so show the world your infinite love. In Christ's name I pray. Amen. ❧

344

The Intimacy of a Few

*That day when evening came, he said to his disciples, "Let us go over
to the other side." Leaving the crowd behind, they took him along,
just as he was, in the boat.*

MARK 4:35 – 36

Jesus sometimes preached from daybreak until dark, thronged by audiences
that came from Jerusalem and beyond to hear his words. Clearly, Jesus could
draw a crowd.

But Jesus also knew when to *leave* a multitude to teach a more intimate
group. To the crowd, he said nothing "without using a parable. But when he
was alone with his own disciples, he explained everything" (Mark 4:34). In
other words, Christ's teaching changed depending on whether he addressed
many people or his close group of followers.

We can learn from Jesus' example. In a small group of trustworthy companions, we can go into greater depth. We can share our own experiences
and reveal the innermost thoughts of our mind and the secrets of our heart.
We can more easily reveal our own shortcomings, fears, or concerns. We can
admit a failure that has been concealed or maybe sinfulness that has become
a habit. If we wish to witness to others about our faith, quite often we can do
so much more effectively in a small group or even one-on-one.

Christ chose to leave the crowd in order to teach a few people, on whom
he would depend to establish his church. He knew he had to share more
openly with his disciples than with the multitude, with whom he used simple
parables. So he and his closest supporters got into a boat and cast off from
shore.

We can let the general public know through our words and actions about
our basic beliefs, but we may be able to witness more effectively in smaller,
more personal groups, where we can reveal more of ourselves or teach more
in depth about what it means to have a personal relationship with Christ.

*Lord, grant me the wisdom to know how to minister most effectively
to others, whether they are members of a crowd, in a small intimate
group, or individuals. I thank you for blessing me in so many ways with
opportunities to serve you. In the name of your Son, Jesus, I pray. Amen.* ❧

Does Science Disprove Miracles?

"Lord," they answered, "we want our sight." Jesus had compassion
on them and touched their eyes. Immediately they received their sight
and followed him.
MATTHEW 20:33 – 34

Many people, even Christians, feel uncomfortable with the miraculous. Do we *really* believe that Christ changed water to wine and calmed the wind and the waves on the Sea of Galilee? Do we *really* believe that he gave sight to the blind and healed lepers?

Some doubt the miraculous because of their narrow commitment to scientific theories. Through science we can do and discover things that, even a few years ago, seemed impossible; now we take them for granted. We can cure fearsome diseases such as leprosy and "cast out demons" by effectively treating mental illnesses. In many cases we can restore sight to the blind. Shouldn't this incredible progress we've made in medical science be considered a miracle and a gift from God?

I concentrated my studies on science and have never seen any genuine conflict between science and religion. When I consider all the discoveries we've made, my own faith is strengthened, not weakened. The detection of subatomic particles, the ever-deeper exploration into the ancient and expanding universe, the unearthing of an intriguing fossil, and the discovery in neuroscience that more neurons exist in one human brain than all the known objects in space—God created it all!

God's flair for the miraculous is something we Christians must accept because the miracle of the resurrection is essential to our faith. Therefore, let's not look at scientific discoveries as hostile to Christianity, but rather as further confirmation of the power and majesty of God. Every time human intelligence is permitted to make new scientific discoveries, it should reconfirm our sense of awe and faith in almighty God. Science does not eliminate miracles. It simply lets us see how miraculous is God's creation.

Most gracious and loving God, I thank you for the beauty of your world
and the love that binds us to you and those around us. I thank you for the
miracle of the resurrection and for showing me through it how much you
care for us. Help me depend on you as you shape the events of my everyday
life. In Jesus' name I pray. Amen. ❧

A Crucial Match

*Consider what a great forest is set on fire by a small spark. The
tongue also is a fire, a world of evil among the parts of the body.*
JAMES 3:5 – 6

Some years ago, a woman who worked for the forest service in Colorado
received an unpleasant love letter from her boyfriend. In anger she burned
the note and drove away; but the flaming envelope blew into the trees and
began a fire that destroyed 120,000 acres of forest and hundreds of homes.

A tiny flame can cause enormous destruction.

In a similar way, the human tongue can do terrible damage. A boss might
sarcastically demean an employee and not think much of it, but the nasty
comments could devastate the employee and ruin his self-image. Such is the
power of the tongue.

James says, "With the tongue we praise our Lord and Father, and with it
we curse human beings, who have been made in God's likeness. Out of the
same mouth come praise and cursing. My brothers and sisters, this should
not be" (3:9 – 10). James is right, of course; and yet, who among us has not
belittled a fellow human being? None of us probably goes very long without
at least *thinking* about insulting someone, perhaps the jerk who cuts us off
in traffic or the ingrate who forgets to say thank you for some nice thing we
did. James marvels that we deliver such insults using the same instrument we
use to praise God—like employing the same baseball bat to hit a ball and to
bludgeon a victim.

Let's not allow the words of our mouth and the meditations of our heart
to contradict one another. Let's remember our commitment to Jesus Christ
so that we can resist the demonic urge (whenever we feel tempted) to say
something spiteful or misleading, knowing that our words and our Christian
ideals should match.

*O Lord, help me recognize that James's words are not harsh and
condemnatory, but rather intended to inspire me toward godlier behavior
and urge me to live a transcendent life, full of joy and peace in your name.
Use the image of the fire to help me rein in my tongue, and use my words
both to glorify you and to bless others. In Jesus' name I pray. Amen.* ❧

How Jealous Are You?

*Saul had a spear in his hand and he hurled it, saying to himself, "I'll
pin David to the wall." But David eluded him twice.*
1 SAMUEL 18:10−11

After killing Goliath, David served King Saul in Israel's army and in the palace. He had no ambition to replace Saul. In fact, throughout his life David
stayed loyal to Saul, the anointed one of God.

But when David returned from defeating the enemy, the women of Israel
sang, "Saul has slain his thousands, and David his tens of thousands" (1 Samuel 18:7). This saying made Saul insanely jealous and he lost control of himself. Jealousy made him mentally unstable, and on several occasions he tried
to kill David.

What in your life causes jealousy? How subject are you to becoming jealous? Maybe a classmate you knew in college or high school has become very
successful. Or maybe you are an attorney and a former colleague starts getting a lot of publicity, collecting big fees, and becoming very wealthy. Or
maybe other people in your hometown seem to do quite well socially and
often get their photographs in the newspaper. Or maybe some obnoxious
person moves into your neighborhood and builds a home next to yours, much
nicer, with two expensive cars always in the driveway. Or maybe your friends'
kids do better in school than your own. Or maybe you're a college student
who struggles in your studies, and you see other students who seem to excel
at almost everything they do, almost without trying. Things like these can
prompt us to become jealous.

We're all subject to jealousy. I know I am. But we have to resist it, not only
because it is sinful, but because it can cause us to fight against God—just as
Saul did when he tried to kill David, the young man God had anointed to
become the next king of Israel.

> *O God, when others seem to be doing better than I am, or when they
> succeed while I struggle, help me fend off the monster of jealousy. I am not
> strong enough to do this on my own, and I submit myself completely to
> your guidance, direction, and partnership. Fill me with the wonderful,
> exhilarating grace and love of my Savior, Jesus Christ, in whose name I
> pray. Amen.* ❧

348

MARCH 7, 2004

Betrayers All?

*"The Son of Man will go just as it is written about him. But woe to
that man who betrays the Son of Man! It would be better for him if
he had not been born."*
MATTHEW 26:24

It's very easy for us to separate ourselves from Judas Iscariot—and in most ways, we are right to do so. His betrayal was probably the most dramatic duplicity in human history, horrible not only because of who Christ was, but because it involved a breaking of the most intimate trust. We can't betray somebody who doesn't trust us.

Christ loved Judas, just as he did the other disciples. He placed great responsibility on them all to be his chosen twelve, to aid him in nurturing the people, taking care of their needs, and witnessing to them. He shared with that small, intimate group the truths and principles and historical events that led to the founding of the church in which we worship today. Jesus placed a major trust in his disciples.

And Judas turned his back on it all.

I doubt that we'll ever *really* know why Judas betrayed Christ. Some think it was for money alone; others suppose he felt let down that Jesus did not take decisive steps to become the secular king of Israel. Whatever his reason, we tend to disassociate ourselves completely from him.

Even as Christians, however, we may be closer to Judas than we'd like to think. It may shock us to realize that our own sinfulness put Christ on the cross. We believers are just as responsible for the crucifixion as the Romans or the Jewish religious leaders or Judas Iscariot. In a way, all of us have betrayed him because each of us has sinned.

Such an unpleasant thought should cause us to repent, turn from our sins, and stand in awe of God's incredible mercy and forgiveness through the sacrifice of Jesus Christ, the Son of God.

*Dear God, I admit I have sinned against you and trust you will give
me a firm awareness of my sin, not to condemn me, but to drive me to
the cross where I will find forgiveness and life. And, Lord, enable me to
follow as best I can the perfect example of my Savior, in whose name I
pray. Amen.* ❧

Honest Inquiry

"How can someone be born when they are old?" Nicodemus asked. "Surely they cannot enter a second time into their mother's womb to be born!"
JOHN 3:4

Nicodemus was a learned scholar and teacher and a member of the ruling religious council of Israel. As a Pharisee, he knew the law of Moses, so it took courage to question a basic teaching of those Scriptures.

Nicodemus came to Jesus by night and began the conversation with flattery. Jesus answered him, "Very truly, I tell you, no one can see the kingdom of God unless they are born again." Apparently Nicodemus thought a person needed only to keep the law. Jesus disagreed. Instead, the Savior insisted that no one could enter the kingdom of God without being "born from above." Nicodemus couldn't comprehend Jesus' statement. His previous life experiences restricted his comprehension.

We're not so different from him, are we? Often we don't comprehend life's truths because we limit the words we're willing to accept. How much better to follow Nicodemus's example and keep our minds open and be willing to change! If we have a question, let's explore it. We're not going to change God by asking a question! God Almighty is even more awe-inspiring and worthy of worship and exploration than I thought as a child.

Eventually Jesus gave Nicodemus a one-verse summary of the entire Bible: "For God so loved the world that he gave his one and only Son ..." Christ's words picture an expanding throng of individuals to be cherished. He prompts us to share what we have and to look beyond our own family to a broader, more inclusive one.

The answer to Nicodemus's questions changed his life. While it's true that he came to Jesus deeply troubled by something, at least he had the courage to ask his questions. May his bravery inspire our own.

O Lord, I ask you to give me the inclination and courage to ask questions that bother me. Stretch my life, stretch my heart, stretch my mind, stretch my environment, stretch my definition of things in a way that pleases you and blesses others. I ask these things through my Savior, Jesus Christ. Amen. ❧

A False Premise

*"Who, being innocent, has ever perished? Where were the upright
ever destroyed? As I have observed, those who plow evil and those
who sow trouble reap it."*
JOB 4:7 – 8

Had God made a mistake with Job? Did some horrible error in heaven bring down God's wrath on a guiltless man? How else to explain the calamities that had overtaken him and crushed him into the dust? That is, unless he had done something evil to deserve such disaster.

Job's friends gave him no comfort. One friend, Eliphaz, told him that only a terrible sinner would be so punished. "Why don't you just admit it?" he demanded. Bildad, another friend, told Job that his seven sons and three daughters must have sinned, otherwise they would not have suffered such tragic deaths. And *all* of Job's friends told him he should admit his secret evil actions and repent of them. Then, they said, he would be forgiven and the punishment would stop.

Although few of us have suffered as Job did, many of us labor under the same warped theology that plagued his friends. Just as they thought Job must have sinned terribly to deserve such punishment, so today many of us believe in the other half of that mistaken equation: namely, we think our many blessings come as rewards for our goodness. We believe we *deserve* wealth and security. Both halves of that kind of thinking are just plain wrong.

Our quality of life does not necessarily have anything to do with how badly or justly we have behaved. Therefore, we shouldn't look at people who are poor or suffering and think, *They must have done something to deserve that.* Neither should we look with pride at our own blessings and think, *I must be a good person to deserve all this.* God sends rain on the just and the unjust.

O Lord, when I ponder Job's life, a rich and righteous man who lost everything but never turned against you, I am both instructed and humbled. When I face misfortune, help me remain equally loyal. Also help me, with humility, to wipe away animosity and scorn for those who seem less blessed than I am. I pray in the name of my Savior, Jesus Christ. Amen. ❧

Do Not Judge

Judge nothing before the appointed time; wait until the Lord comes.
He will bring to light what is hidden in darkness and will expose the
motives of the heart.

1 CORINTHIANS 4:5

Since the time of my baptism, I've had nine pastors. All have differed from one another. One was an eloquent preacher who could deliver a whole sermon and quote Scripture without once looking at his notes. He served as my pastor while I was president and attended First Baptist Church in Washington, D.C. Another pastor was a great builder. Whenever he took over a church, everyone expected him to add to the physical size of the facilities. He liked to design and raise money for expansions. During my time as governor, he led in adding a large sanctuary to Atlanta's Northside Drive Baptist Church. A few of my pastors were outstanding counselors, although they might not have excelled in the pulpit. But anyone in the congregation with a problem could go to them and know they would receive gentle, wise care.

Pastors, however, often come in for stinging criticism. So did early apostles. That's one reason Paul wrote to the Corinthians, who had been quite critical of him. He told the leaders of the church—who should have understood the teachings of Jesus—not to judge one another. Jesus said, "Do not judge, or you too will be judged" (Matthew 7:1). Paul also left judgment to God.

Paul's instruction applies just as much to us as to the ancient Corinthians. To turn against one another and condemn each other is a serious sin. Both pastors and fellow parishioners inevitably have their differences and it is not our place to judge them. We should not ignore church problems or overlook those who fall into sin, but we must refrain from exalting ourselves above them, since we all are sinners in need of God's forgiveness.

O God, help me learn to apply Paul's teaching and leave all judgment in your holy hands. I confess that too often I accuse others of wrongdoing. So give me grace and humility to focus on my own deficiencies rather than on those of others. In Jesus' name I pray. Amen. ❧

Doubting Teresa

Be merciful to those who doubt.
JUDE 1:22

Mother Teresa was a compassionate and loving person, whom we might all wish to emulate. But after her death, articles written about her caused a great deal of controversy. The *New York Times* and other news media gave her death a lot of attention; many of the stories concerned her private letters, published upon her death.

Those letters revealed that at times Mother Teresa felt she had lost her faith. She had said, "I don't know if I believe in God or not; I don't know if I have any faith or not." She later stipulated that after her death these letters should never be revealed. But their publication (against her wishes) caused a sensation in the media and a great deal of consternation and speculation among the general public.

I think we must understand that most people, almost without exception—regardless of how devout they might seem—have times when they feel as though they've lost their faith. We need to spend time searching our hearts for reassurance that our beliefs are well grounded. We feel compelled to discover whether there really exists a God of mercy and peace who cares about us and who will ultimately set things right. Even the disciples, after Jesus' crucifixion, plunged into a crisis of faith. They huddled together and clearly doubted whether Jesus really was who he said he was.

We don't have to fear or fall into despair if we sometimes have doubts about our faith. We all have to face rough things in life, and sometimes they shake us. But that's a normal part of a life of faith. Maybe that's why Jude tells us to "be merciful to those who doubt." Certainly, we have no cause to condemn Mother Teresa. In any event, she now has passed from doubt to certainty—as will we.

O God, I'm grateful for this word about showing mercy to those who doubt—because sometimes I'm the doubter. I sometimes wonder if you exist, if you care, if you see my troubles, and if you will help me. Thank you for your patience, grace, and faithfulness. Strengthen me, help me show mercy to doubters, and make me into a reason for them to believe in you. In Jesus' name I pray. Amen. ❦

Head *and* Heart

If anyone builds on this foundation using gold, silver, costly stones,
wood, hay or straw, their work will be shown for what it is, because
the Day will bring it to light. It will be revealed with fire, and the
fire will test the quality of each person's work.
I CORINTHIANS 3:12 – 13

These days there seems to be a prevailing sentiment that the best way to measure the success of a church congregation is to count how many new members it can add each year. Growth in numbers becomes an end in itself.

But how do many churches gain more members? Some of them, of course, are located in fast-growing suburban communities where newcomers actively look for a religious home. A dynamic church program and outstanding preaching also prompt rapid growth. Others grow by preaching a relaxed message that requires nothing of anyone: "Join us for pleasure and profit. We have a tennis court and a swimming pool. We're air-conditioned, and our building is beautiful and constantly expanding. Many of our members are very influential. Come and be blessed."

Another kind of Christian theology eliminates church altogether. It says, "We don't need worship services. Let's just work with poor people by taking them food and supplies, or by building Habitat houses. That's the totality of our faith."

Someone has said there are five kinds of Christian ministry. One is Christian living, based on constant communication with God through prayer. Another is holiness, a life set apart for God. A third is being Spirit-filled. A fourth is showing compassion. And the final one is evangelism, telling people about Christ.

Do you see anything wrong with any of them? I don't. The truth is, we need *all* of them. To choose only one or two, to the exclusion of the others, is like saying, "I want my heart but don't need my brain."

I don't recommend you try that one.

O God, may I strive for superlative Christian fellowship and not accept
the lowest common denominator in my church congregation. Inspire
me with your Holy Spirit and strengthen me with my faith in the risen
Jesus. Bind us together in Christian love and let us all follow the perfect
example of our Lord, Jesus Christ. In his name I pray. Amen.

354

Who Needs Healing?

"I am the LORD, who heals you."
EXODUS 15:26

When did you last admit your need for healing?

Most often we have no problem making it public when we need healing from a physical ailment or sorrow. If someone in the family is ill or we lose someone close to us, we want others to know about our grief and our need for prayer and support.

At other times, however, we conceal our need for healing. When we or loved ones have a mental illness, make a ridiculous mistake or embarrass ourselves, or perhaps commit some serious offense, it is natural to conceal these things; but likely they will become public knowledge despite our best efforts.

At still other times we have needs that may be concealed more easily. If we have an awkward weakness, fail in some important pursuit, feel lonely or destitute, have temptations we can't resist, or feel some personal inadequacy to face an unavoidable problem, then we try to keep it to ourselves—even hide it from trusted friends or loved ones. Why this reluctance?

Most likely we do this to avoid proof of our vulnerability, of being too weak to deal by ourselves with the challenges of life. We prefer to perpetuate the illusion that we can take care of things on our own, that we can heal ourselves. We want people to believe that we are good Christians, able to avoid temptations.

But the truth is otherwise, isn't it? We know that *all* have sinned and come short of the glory of God. Jesus taught repeatedly that we need to confess our weaknesses, failures, and needs and repent of wrongdoing, and that with God's help we can overcome difficulties and be forgiven of our sins.

Who needs God's healing? We *all* do. So let's find the courage to admit our needs.

O God, I am grateful that although you know all about me—that I am a weak, inadequate, sinful, hurting person in need of a healing touch— you love me anyway and want to have an intimate relationship with me through faith in Christ. Help me admit my needs, Lord, not only to you, but also to others whom I can trust. In Jesus' name I pray. Amen.

355

Someday We Will All Be Dead

Then people go to their eternal home.... Remember [your Creator]—
before the silver cord is severed, and the golden bowl is broken.
ECCLESIASTES 12:5 – 6

Some people let the past consume them. They dwell on what happened years or even decades ago, either favorably or unfavorably. Some look on the "days of yore" as a halcyon era: "Everything was just right then; *now* look at the shape of things!" Others see nothing in the past but a series of disasters. They believe past misfortune has brought them to their present state of failure, and they spend their time dwelling on it and hating it: "If only I had been born wealthy! If only I had gotten a good education! If only I had more opportunities!" Every dismal circumstance in the present they blame on the past.

Still others spend their time dwelling on the future. They honestly think, *Someday I'm going to be a good Christian. Someday I'll be really unselfish. Someday I'll be nice and helpful to other people, even the unpleasant and unattractive ones. Someday I'm going to take a large part of my wealth and share it with others in need. Someday I'll become an example for others to follow.* The problem is, these people never actually get around to changing their lives and doing any of these wonderful things. The "right time" simply never arrives ... and then it's too late.

Ecclesiastes counsels us to focus on the present. What are we doing with *today?* It's so easy to postpone the thought of unpleasant or troubling circumstances. And too easily we daydream about a blissful future. But Ecclesiastes counsels us to remember God *now*, before it's too late. Remember, and seek to live in accordance with God's commandments—because someday we will all be dead.

Dear God, I'm grateful for a chance to read these profound words from Ecclesiastes and pray that I might carry with me the lesson they teach. Help me seize today and use it to spread your influence throughout the world, beginning within my own small circle of influence. Enable me to follow the perfect example that Jesus Christ set for all human beings. I ask these things in his precious name. Amen. ❦

356

A Long-Term Perspective

This is what the LORD says: "When seventy years are completed for Babylon, I will come to you and fulfill my good promise to bring you back to this place."

JEREMIAH 29:10

Jim Stockdale, my classmate at the Naval Academy, spent seven years as a POW in Vietnam. His captors tortured him more than twenty separate times. Although many of his fellow prisoners died, somehow Jim survived. He won the Congressional Medal of Honor, one of only two in my class.

To explain why he survived, Jim described what he called "transient optimists." These men would build up expectations for a prompt release—before Christmas or before Easter or before some other date—and every time those days came and went without bringing freedom, they despaired. The dreary cycle made them increasingly despondent until finally they gave up and died.

Jim considered his imprisonment to be long-term and yet retained undeviating confidence in himself, his nation, and his faith. He avoided repeated heartbreak.

Jeremiah saw his countrymen taken into captivity by the Babylonians—God's judgment on a sinful and unrepentant nation. A false prophet named Hananiah soon predicted that within two years the Jews would return home, bringing the temple treasures with them. But Hananiah did not speak for God, and the Lord gave Jeremiah a true divine message: the captivity would last seventy years. In other words, the return to Judah would not take place within their lifetimes. The prophet had depressing news, but it ended in hope. The Judeans would have to remain patient and not lose faith in God's promise to redeem them.

We also have to remain patient and realize that we're going to have ups and downs. We're going to feel frustrated. At times the world may seem like a very bad place. Even so, we must maintain a long-term trust that the Lord ultimately will set things right.

Dear Lord, how easily I give up hope when my world seems to grow dark, or to place my trust in unreliable schemes and expectations. Help me put my confidence in you and in the promises you make in your Word. When I suffer setbacks or unexpected sorrows, draw me to your Son and deepen my confidence in his unchanging love, expressed most fully at the cross. In Jesus' holy name I pray. Amen. ⹂

357

All in God's Plan

She got a papyrus basket for him and coated it with tar and pitch.
Then she placed the child in it and put it among the reeds along the
bank of the Nile.
EXODUS 2:3

Moses was born to Hebrew slaves. Because Pharaoh had ordered the death of all Hebrew baby boys, Moses' mother put her infant son in a waterproof basket and hid it in the reeds along the river. Pharaoh's daughter happened to be walking nearby, and when she saw the basket, she retrieved it, found the baby, and adopted him. And so Moses grew up as the son of Pharaoh's daughter.

As an adult, Moses secretly killed and buried an Egyptian whom he had seen abusing a Hebrew slave. The next day, when Moses rebuked two Hebrews for arguing, they responded, "Who do you think you are? We saw you kill the Egyptian yesterday!"

Instantly Moses fled from Egypt to Midian, where he saw some Egyptians abusing a group of shepherd girls. Moses helped the girls, and as a result he met their father and eventually married one of his daughters. Moses spent the next forty years tending sheep in the desert.

Moses therefore spent four decades learning about Egyptian culture (and about the plight of the Hebrew slaves) and then another forty years learning about the desert and how to survive in it. These things probably didn't seem especially significant to him at the time; but later he would use his skills and knowledge in serving God and God's chosen people. His time in both Egypt and Midian was part of a divine plan to prepare Moses for a special assignment later in life.

Even though our lives sometimes seem strange and trying, we should remain open to the possibility that God is preparing us through difficult times for a specific task in the years ahead.

O Lord, I am grateful that you included the story of Moses in your Word
and especially how you prepared him through trying circumstances to
become one of the Bible's greatest heroes. Help me learn from Moses
and realize that I can have a life of fulfillment, joy, peace, adventure,
challenge, excitement, and success as measured by the standards of my
Savior, Jesus Christ, in whose name I pray. Amen. ❧

358

Darkness to Light

The people walking in darkness have seen a great light; on those
living in the land of deep darkness a light has dawned.
ISAIAH 9:2

What comes to mind when you think of darkness? What's the darkest place you've ever been? Rosalynn and I have visited many caves. We've been inside the Carlsbad Caverns and the cave in Hannibal, Missouri, where Tom Sawyer and Huck Finn supposedly had an adventure. We've even been in Spanish and French caves, home to beautiful cave paintings. Almost invariably when we entered one of those caves, a guide relished turning off all the lights. Instantly everything went pitch black. We could see absolutely nothing.

About 730 years before the birth of Christ, Assyria reached the peak of its power. Eventually it took Israel into captivity—a time of great sorrow, despair, and hopelessness among the Israelites. And that's when Isaiah made this prophecy.

The Israelites felt trapped in utter darkness. Their gloomy present made it impossible for them to imagine anything but a dismal future. They felt betrayed by inept kings who had led them astray, and in despair because of the political and military changes overtaking their society. But also they felt abandoned by God, who had promised their ancestor, Abraham, that they would succeed. They wondered how God could let pagan leaders and their armies subjugate the Holy Land.

So when Isaiah made his prophesy about a great light, it seemed incomprehensible to them. As prisoners, how could they rejoice? As captives, what plunder could they divide? In exile, what harvest could they produce? Finally they realized Isaiah was talking about the future, a time when God would save them from their oppressors and from their own disloyalty.

Today we realize that Isaiah was also predicting the coming of Jesus Christ, the Messiah. Because he is the Light of the World, no darkness is a match for him. It wasn't then, it isn't now, and it never will be.

O God, as a follower of the Light of the World, let me shine your light
into the darkest corners of my world. Remind me that I can do this
through acts of benevolence, compassion, and love. Help me be an agent
of peace as I follow the instructions given to me by the Prince of Peace. In
the name of Jesus Christ I pray. Amen. ❧

Rejoice!

While they were there, the time came for the baby to be born, and she gave birth to her firstborn, a son. She wrapped him in cloths and placed him in a manger, because there was no guest room available for them.

LUKE 2:6 – 7

Shortly before Mary gave birth to Jesus, the Roman emperor ordered that a census be taken in all occupied territories. He wanted to make sure he was getting all the taxes due him. So this young couple headed to Bethlehem, Joseph's ancestral home, to be counted. When they arrived, they had to stay in a stable because all the guest rooms were occupied. There, among the sleepy animals, our Savior came into the world.

What an extraordinary event! Christmas is always an exciting time, because it commemorates the birth of God's Son, our Savior. Christmas should be filled with joy and praise and thanksgiving, not merely an opportunity for further historical analysis. Sometimes we revisit the old stories so much that we stop paying attention to how significant they really are. The birth of Christ was, in fact, the greatest thing ever to happen in the history of the world. God Almighty, Creator of the universe, came to us in human form!

The event had been foretold many generations before. Prophets spoke of the Messiah's coming: "But you, Bethlehem Ephrathah, though you are small among the clans of Judah, out of you will come for me one who will be ruler over Israel, whose origins are from of old, from ancient times" (Micah 5:2), and "His greatness will reach to the ends of the earth" (Micah 5:4). A few centuries later, it all came true.

Each Christmas, and all throughout the year, we can be grateful for this amazing prophetic fulfillment. The Messiah, destined to save all believers from their sins, was born in a Bethlehem stable. What a juxtaposition of the divine and the human! Let's remember that and rejoice in it.

O Lord, turn my heart toward Jesus as I remember his long, love-filled journey from heaven to earth. Fill my heart with joyful praise as I celebrate the coming of God to earth. Let me be inspired to bring this joyful Christmas news to others who might know little of the miracle of the birth and life of your Son, Jesus Christ. In his holy name I pray. Amen.

God Finds a Way

Joseph also went up from the town of Nazareth in Galilee to Judea, to Bethlehem the town of David, because he belonged to the house and line of David. He went there to register with Mary, who was pledged to be married to him and was expecting a child.

LUKE 2:4 – 5

Why did Mary accompany Joseph to Bethlehem? Why didn't she just stay behind in Nazareth? It was a long and tedious journey, even for an able-bodied person. On a donkey, the trip would have taken at least three days. Besides, robbers hid along the way, and winter had arrived.

If I were a woman on the verge of having a baby, I probably would have chosen to stay behind with my mother, father, and friends. Even in those days, Mary probably had access to a midwife. Who do we think delivered the baby in Bethlehem? That task fell to Joseph, and in those days, men usually did not stick around for a child's birth.

I never saw the birth of any of our four children. Three of them were born while I served in the Navy, and the last thing Navy doctors wanted was a husband hanging around. They always lied to me. They would say, "The baby can't possibly come within the next eight hours or more; you might as well get some rest." So I'd go to a movie or back home to wait. And when I returned, there was the baby, already born. Years later, though, I saw the birth of two of my grandsons, the children of my daughter, Amy.

I'm guessing that Joseph was trying to protect Mary. She might have run into trouble if she had given birth in Nazareth before their wedding. Whatever the reason, their trip south fulfilled Isaiah's prophecy that Christ would be born in Bethlehem.

God finds a way, always. God always makes good on his promises — even if it takes a donkey, a long trip, and a fumbling husband-to-be. God always comes through.

O Lord, as Christmas approaches, I thank you for the opportunity to look back at this story and to remember the impact it has had on our world. Let me be filled with joy and peace during this wonderful celebration. I ask this in the name of my Savior, Jesus Christ. Amen. ❧

361

Flesh and Blood Will Fail

I declare to you, brothers and sisters, that flesh and blood cannot inherit the
kingdom of God, nor does the perishable inherit the imperishable.
1 CORINTHIANS 15:50

Is there a resurrection? And if so, what is it? This was the major issue between the Pharisees and Sadducees, and Paul used this controversy to spark a debate between them, distracting them from their accusations against the apostle. The resulting confusion probably saved his life and resulted in his transfer to Rome.

Perhaps you have your own doubts about the resurrection. How can there be a transformation after death from one existence into something completely different?

In our text, Paul claims that Christ was crucified, buried, and three days later rose from the dead. He accepts these facts: "For if the dead are not raised, then Christ has not been raised either. And if Christ has not been raised, your faith is futile; you are still in your sins" (1 Corinthians 15:16–17). Without the resurrection, Paul says, all Christian preaching about Christ and his divinity is both useless and a lie.

When wheat sprouts, does it look like the grain of wheat earlier planted? No; its character has undergone a total transformation. The resurrection is something like that. While no one can precisely describe the character of our resurrected bodies, a clear relationship exists, like that of a seed and a full-grown plant. If you still have trouble "getting it," Paul might say to you, "Please consider the power of our Creator." The fact that we don't understand something doesn't mean that it's incomprehensible to God or that it can't be real.

Since Christ died and rose again, we have vivid and eternal proof that believers will be resurrected. And if it's impossible for God Almighty to resurrect us human beings, then it was also impossible for our Savior to be resurrected. The resurrection of Christ provides proof that there will be a resurrection in which all his followers will participate.

O Lord, thank you for sending your Son into the world to die for my sins
and then to exercise your almighty power to raise him from the grave.
Thank you for making me acceptable in your kingdom through faith in
the risen and reigning Jesus Christ, my Lord. This I pray in his name.
Amen. ❧

From Darkness to Light

"See, darkness covers the earth and thick darkness is over the peoples,
but the LORD rises upon you and his glory appears over you. Nations
will come to your light."
ISAIAH 60:2 – 3

As a young man I trained as a submariner. To qualify, I had to ascend from the bottom of a hundred-foot-deep water tank. In the dark, our bodies were subjected to extreme pressure. It scared all of us.

We had only a half-inch rope line anchored to the bottom of the tank, with a buoy attached at the top, to lead us to the surface. Each of us had to emerge from a high-pressure container and rise a hundred feet, clamping the little line between our feet to control how fast we rose. Ascending, we had to exhale constantly and watch the bubbles in front of us so we would rise at the same rate. If we went too slowly and got below the bubbles, we could sink to the bottom and risk drowning. If we went up too fast, we could get "the bends." I went from feeling fear and trepidation in the dark and oppressive environment, to emerging into brilliant light, freedom, and normal breathing.

Isaiah dealt with something similar. The people of Judah would face seventy years of captivity in Babylon, under strong pressure to assimilate into the pagan culture. Eventually they could return home to Jerusalem — but what would await them there? The temple would lie in ruins, and Jerusalem would be full of foreigners worshiping strange gods. And yet Isaiah promised a bright future for the Israelites at a time of abject weakness, when the nation had lost the political preeminence.

God wants to do for us what was done for Israel. Even in times of darkness and ruin, God wants us to glimpse the glory to come by bringing us into a bright, even brilliant, future — to use light to conquer darkness!

Lord, as I read the ancient words of Isaiah, let me realize that the
darkness that sometimes comes over me is temporary and that through
faith in you I can always transcend the dark side of life into the light of
love you have for me. Let this promise reassure me in dark times, I ask in
the name of Jesus. Amen. ❧

Courageous Humility

Daniel replied, "No wise man, enchanter, magician or diviner can
explain to the king the mystery he has asked about, but there is a
God in heaven who reveals mysteries."
DANIEL 2:27 – 28

Nebuchadnezzar was a powerful, brutal, and intelligent king who one night had a disturbing dream. He woke up worried about what this dream could mean for himself and for his people, so he summoned his advisors and said, "Interpret my dream for me." These charlatans thought, *Let's just make up something. How will he know the difference?* So they asked the king to describe his dream.

But King Nebuchadnezzar knew his men. "Before you tell me what my dream *meant*," he demanded, "you must tell me what my dream *was*." The advisors objected, "Nobody can do that, not even the gods!" Their rash response angered King Nebuchadnezzar and he replied, "If you can't tell me my dream and what it meant, then I'll have you all executed." So the king issued a blanket order to decapitate his advisors and bury their corpses in dung heaps.

As advisors-in-training, Daniel and his three friends were included in this murderous order. So when Daniel heard about it, he asked for a little time. He and his friends prayed earnestly, and that night God implanted in Daniel's mind the dream of Nebuchadnezzar. The next day, Daniel appeared before the king. When the king asked if Daniel could describe his dream and interpret it, Daniel humbly replied that no mere mortal could do so; however, he knew a God in heaven who "reveals mysteries." Then Daniel told the king what he wanted to hear, thus saving the lives of all the king's advisors.

Daniel refused to take credit for what only God could do. The king got his answer, but only through what we might call courageous humility—confidence based on submission to God—something we could all use.

O Lord, thank you for showing me, in the life of Daniel, what can
happen when courage meets humility. I know from Daniel's story that you
used him in great ways for many years, for he never lost either his courage
or his humility. May that be true of me too as I seek to emulate the perfect
example of Jesus Christ. I pray these things in his name. Amen.

364

Depend on God

"Where can I get meat for all these people? They keep wailing to me, 'Give us meat to eat!' I cannot carry all these people by myself; the burden is too heavy."
NUMBERS 11:13 – 14

At some point in their wilderness wanderings, the Israelites grew tired of manna, their "bread from heaven." They wanted meat and demanded that Moses give it to them. Angry and frustrated, Moses cried out, "Lord, I can't do this by myself!" Notice that he *didn't* say, "I can't do this." Rather, he said he couldn't bear his burden without God's help.

When we feel overwhelmed with anguish or bereft of confidence and hope, we should remember Moses' cry. We would do well to follow his example and cry out, "God, I can't do this by myself. I need you!" In times of acute need, let's reaffirm our ties of dependence upon God Almighty.

Troubling experiences often bring this truth to our consciousness. In dark times, we learn that we cannot depend on ourselves alone. We go through a period of anxiety and fear, and then, finally, we put our faith in God—not easily, not quickly, not as a matter of certainty, but because we search our hearts and souls and say, "I'm not able on my own to face these circumstances. I must turn to God Almighty."

We all have troubles in life. Maybe we set a goal for ourselves that lies beyond our ability. We may lose someone we love or suffer serious illness or face a temptation we cannot overcome. At such times, we often feel reluctant to admit our inadequacy and instead blame our troubles on other factors. And so long as we refuse to rely on God, we continue to suffer.

Let's not do that. The next time we feel inadequate or overwhelmed, let's seek a divine partner in prayer and depend on God's incredible wisdom and strength.

Lord, when I feel overwhelmed by life and imagine that my burdens are too heavy, help me remember that you are the answer to my difficulties. You promise to help me through my Savior, Jesus Christ, who died to wipe away my sins. Use my troubles to lead me to a greater life, a successful life as measured by your holy standards. I ask these things in the name of Jesus. Amen. ❧

For Those Who Wander

"For the Lamb at the center of the throne will be their shepherd; 'he will lead them to springs of living water.' 'And God will wipe away every tear from their eyes.'"
REVELATION 7:17

Sheep win no awards for intelligence. Since most have no mind of their own, they tend to follow whoever's in front. That's why shepherds have to watch their flocks *all the time*. If they don't, some their sheep almost certainly will wander off.

Sheep may seem big at first sight, but once you shear them, they shrink. Once on a visit to Australia, we stopped at a farm during sheep shearing time; and when they discovered I used to shear sheep on our farm as a boy, they trained a TV camera on me and made me shear one of those poor animals. Somehow I got through the process, and by the time I finished, that sheep looked very small (I won't tell you what else it looked like). A sheep shorn of its wool shows its utter vulnerability—not a pretty sight.

The Bible compares us to sheep because we reflect many of the animal's unflattering characteristics. We don't always adhere to our beliefs and convictions; too easily we get led off into sin and error. So the prophet Zechariah noted, "The people wander like sheep oppressed for lack of a shepherd" (Zechariah 10:2). In fact, the Bible often uses the phrase "like sheep without a shepherd" to describe us (see Numbers 27:17; 1 Kings 22:17; Matthew 9:36). Without a shepherd, we have little hope.

But thank God we *do* have a Shepherd, Jesus Christ, whom Peter calls "the Shepherd and Overseer of your souls" (1 Peter 2:25). Jesus is the Good Shepherd (John 10:14), the Great Shepherd (Hebrews 13:20), and the Chief Shepherd (1 Peter 5:4). And as our Shepherd, he will lead us to springs of living water, where God will wipe away every tear from our eyes (Revelation 7:17).

It's really not so bad being a sheep—so long as Jesus is your Shepherd.

O God, thank you for revealing yourself not only as the Shepherd of Israel, but also as my Shepherd. Too often I wander off and make myself prey for all sorts of wolves. But you are always there, watching over me, directing me, and protecting me. Thank you for bringing me into your flock—and as you have blessed me, so make me a blessing to others. In Jesus' precious name I pray. Amen. ❧

Endless Possibilities

Suddenly a sound like the blowing of a violent wind came from heaven and filled the whole house where they were sitting. They saw what seemed to be tongues of fire that separated and came to rest on each of them. All of them were filled with the Holy Spirit and began to speak in other tongues as the Spirit enabled them.

ACTS 2:2 – 4

At Pentecost, a loud rushing sound made God's presence known. As soon as the disciples had received the Holy Spirit, they started speaking in languages they had never learned, and those hearing them could understand them in their own dialects.

Glossolalia is the Greek term for speaking in tongues. The New Testament uses it in other places as well, never derogating or condemning it. But these latter instances appear very different from what happened at Pentecost. In these cases, while the Holy Spirit moved people to speak in tongues, nobody could understand them. Just the opposite happened at Pentecost. The disciples spoke in tongues and *everybody* could understand them, no matter what language they spoke.

The main thing is not that the disciples spoke in tongues, but that for the first time in history there came an international awareness of the Holy Spirit's presence, which led to better comprehension of who and what God is. God's power became obvious to everybody as the Holy Spirit imbued the disciples with enormous, unanticipated capabilities and authority. From that day forward, they were transformed from a group of timid, fumbling peasants, who didn't know what to do and who often made mistakes, into (we might say) religious supermen. They could do anything they wanted, provided they followed God's will. They learned that if they submitted themselves to God's will, their accomplishments would know no limits.

The same is true for us. If we submit to the will of God and accept the guidance of the Holy Spirit, we can accomplish anything.

O Lord, I am grateful to review once again the story of Pentecost, a transforming experience that's interesting but also applicable to my own life. Help me recognize that if I truly search for wisdom and submit to your will, I can succeed in life—in every way that counts—through your grace and my faith in Jesus Christ. I pray in the name of my Savior. Amen. ❧

TIMELINE

September 27, 1923	Marriage of James Earl Carter and Bessie Lillian Gordy in Plains, Georgia
October 1, 1924	Birth of James Earl "Jimmy" Carter Jr. in Plains
1928	The Carter family moves from a house in Plains to a farm in Archery, a couple of miles away
1941	Graduates from Plains High School
1941–42	Attends Georgia Southwestern College in Americus
1942–43	Attends the Georgia Institute of Technology in Atlanta
1943	Enters the U.S. Naval Academy, Annapolis, Maryland
June 1946	Earns BS degree from the U.S. Naval Academy, 59th in class of 820; commissioned Ensign
July 7, 1946	Marries Rosalynn Smith in Plains
August 1946	Assigned to the USS *Wyoming* out of Norfolk, Virginia
July 3, 1947	John William "Jack" Carter born in Portsmouth, Virginia
June–December 1948	Officer's course, U.S. Naval Submarine School
June 5, 1949	Promoted to Lieutenant (junior grade)
April 12, 1950	James Earl "Chip" Carter III born in Honolulu, Hawaii
November 10, 1951	Assigned to duty aboard the USS *K–1*
June 1, 1952	Promoted to Lieutenant
June 1952	Accepted into the Navy's nuclear submarine program

August 18, 1952	Donnel Jeffrey "Jeff" Carter born in New London, Connecticut
October 16, 1952	Begins duty with U.S. Atomic Energy Commission
July 22, 1953	Death of James Earl Carter Sr.
October 9, 1953	Resigns commission in Navy to return to Plains to run Carter Farms; also runs Carter's Warehouse, a general-purpose seed and farm supply company
October 16, 1962	Loses primary for the Georgia State Senate in the 14th District by 139 votes; irregularities prompt a recount and a new election
November 6, 1962	Wins new election by 831 votes
January 14, 1963	First term of office begins as Georgia State senator
1964	Wins reelection to the Georgia State Senate
1965	Second term of office begins as Georgia State senator
Spring 1966	Lillian Carter announces she will join the Peace Corps; she is sixty-eight years old when she begins her service in India
September 1966	Denied Democratic nomination for governor
October 19, 1967	Amy Lynn Carter born in Plains
May 1968	Drives with some Christian friends to Lock Haven, Pennsylvania, to witness for Christ
November 1970	Wins election for Georgia governor
January 12, 1971	Becomes Georgia's 76th governor
March 5, 1973	Appointed congressional and gubernatorial campaign chairman for the Democratic National Committee
May 1973	First trip to Israel
December 12, 1974	Announces candidacy for president of the United States
July 1976	Wins Democratic Party's nomination for president on first ballot

November 2, 1976	Elected president of the United States
January 20, 1977	Inaugurated as 39th president of the United States
August 4, 1977	Department of Energy established
September 7, 1977	Signing of Panama Canal Treaties
October 5, 1977	Signing of international covenants on human rights
September 5, 1978	Camp David Middle East Peace Talks begin with Israel, Egypt, and the United States
September 17, 1978	Signing of Camp David Accords
December 15, 1978	Announcement of normalization of relations with the People's Republic of China
January 29–31, 1979	Chinese leader Deng Xiaoping visits Washington
March 26, 1979	Signing of Egyptian-Israeli Peace Treaty
June 18, 1979	Signing of SALT II Treaty in Vienna with Soviet Premier Leonid Brezhnev
October 17, 1979	Department of Education established
November 4, 1979	Hostages taken at U.S. Embassy in Teheran, Iran
December 27, 1979	Soviet Union invades Afghanistan
April 24, 1980	Mission to rescue Iran hostages fails
May 18, 1980	Mount Saint Helens erupts
August 13, 1980	Nominated by Democratic National Convention for second term
November 4, 1980	Ronald Reagan wins presidential election
December 2, 1980	Signing of Alaska Lands legislation
December 11, 1980	Signing of Superfund Act to clean up toxic wastes
January 16, 1981	Final terms negotiated for release of American hostages in Iran
January 20, 1981	Ronald Reagan inaugurated at noon as 40th president of the United States

January 20, 1981	12:20 p.m. EST, American hostages released in Teheran
January 21, 1981	Meets with former hostages in Wiesbaden, Germany
October 6, 1981	Assassination of Egyptian president Anwar Sadat by Muslim extremists
April 21, 1982	Appointment announced as University Distinguished Professor at Emory University in Atlanta
1982	Founds the Carter Center, a nonprofit nongovernmental organization that addresses national and international issues of public policy
September 26, 1983	Death of Ruth Carter Stapleton (sister)
October 30, 1983	Death of Lillian Carter
October 2, 1984	Groundbreaking for the Carter Center in Atlanta
October 1, 1986	Dedication of the Carter Center
1986	The Carter Center begins a campaign to wipe out Guinea worm disease, which afflicts an estimated 3.5 million people in twenty countries in Africa and Asia
September 25, 1988	Death of Billy Carter (brother)
March 5, 1990	Death of Gloria Carter Spann (sister)
November 4, 1995	Assassination of Israeli prime minister Yitzhak Rabin by a Jewish extremist
December 10, 2002	Awarded the Nobel Peace Prize for "decades of untiring effort to find peaceful solutions to international conflicts, to advance democracy and human rights, and to promote economic and social development"
2010	Guinea worm disease reduced to fewer than 1,800 cases in four African nations

NIV Lessons from Life Bible

Personal Reflections with Jimmy Carter

Jimmy Carter, General Editor

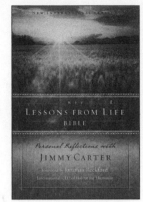

The *NIV Lessons from Life Bible* takes President Jimmy Carter's years of teaching Sunday school lessons at Maranatha Baptist Church in Plains, GA, and meshes them with the text of the NIV Bible. Through "In Focus" articles, "Bible in Life" notes, in-depth studies, and insightful observations and reflections, President Carter's teachings in this Bible provide fresh insights for you to study and contemplate.

Features:

- The full text of the clear, accessible NIV translation
- Foreword by Jonathan Reckford, International CEO of Habitat for Humanity
- "Bible in Life" notes: short, application-oriented notes on particular verses
- "In Focus" articles: longer articles on particular topics
- Short prayers of application on select passages
- Reflections: brief one-sentence sayings and quotations by Jimmy Carter
- Presentation page

Available in stores and online!

ZONDERVAN®
.com

NOTES

NOTES